NEW ASIAN MARXISMS

■ a *positions* book

# NEW ASIAN

# MARXISMS

Duke University Press ■ Durham and London ■ 2002

*Edited by* TANI E. BARLOW

© 2002 Duke University Press
All rights reserved
Printed in the United States of
America on acid-free paper ⊗
Designed by Amy Ruth Buchanan
Typeset in Scala by Tseng
Information Systems, Inc.
Library of Congress Cataloging-
in-Publication Data and original
publication information appear on
the last printed page of this book.

CONTENTS

TANI E. BARLOW

## Preface: Everything Diverges

In the contemporary epoch . . . nothing resembles anything else, nothing joins up with anything else, everything diverges.

—Alain Badiou, *Deleuze: The Clamor of Being*

■ Why publish this anthology now? There are a host of overlapping reasons to consolidate these essays into a volume. One motive is to showcase the body of Marxist work unfolding under the general auspices of the *positions* project. Another is to alert Marxist scholars in other domains about work going on in this one. A third is to put a breathing point or comma at this moment to an ongoing work in progress. The distance of a pause offers interested readers a chance to gauge the objectives of contemporary Marxist criticism in or about "Asia," and to measure their achievements against these scholars' analytic or critical goals. Laid out together here it is easier to discern the outline of general projects engaging Marxist scholarship in this relatively obscure domain of so-called Asian studies.

The question of what is valuable about these essays and William Pietz's thoughtful introduction to them is related to the reasons for this book's publication. Pietz's critique, coming as it does from a different (primarily activist) domain, is exemplary precisely because it is written at a moment common to us all—the present. Pietz, like the other scholars who contributed papers to this collection, lives in the turbulence of late capitalist modernity. Their work—and here I respectfully disagree with Pietz—is not so much a series of essays about disillusionment or hope as an attempt to confront desacralization on a profound scale and in light of absolutely specific historical catastrophes. Thus a highly invested, even pedantic concern with the places where everything has diverged does not counsel disillusionment. On the contrary it confirms to me a willingness to excavate the here-and-now.

What the papers and the comment say to me is that Asianist or not, the common project is not post-Marxist, but a postorthodox Marxism.[1] In this regard, Pietz is exactly suited to the task of critic, for he also is not pining for a "new proletariat." He is looking at local struggles and particularly at the theoretical commonalities that may bind them together.

Orthodox Marxism has two preoccupations: the dream of universal history, and the problem of the subject or agent of that teleology, the proletariat. Largely eschewing the presumption of either, what appears in this volume are a series of studies that probably would not have been considered "Marxist" at all a generation ago. As the late Bill Brugger noted, the essays coexist uneasily even now.[2] They are not *meant* to coexist. Each study presses its claim to the Marxist tradition for disparate reasons that are important to spell out. Some draw on abandoned or underused resources in cultural and theoretical Marxism. Howland, Dai, Johnson, and Liu affiliate in eccentric and useful ways with the academic Frankfurt school, augmenting and deforming that Anglo-European theoretical archive in the process. Other critics mobilize Maoist and post-Maoist Marxisms. Shin, Seth, Sugiyama, and Dutton particularly seek ways of visualizing and exploiting analyses inspired at a specific conjunctures or in immediate, often violent actions. But each of these unique and perhaps oddly juxtaposed papers nonetheless appears to reach for the "universality through singularity" that Pozzana particularly showcases in her exploration of early Marxist Li Dazhao.

Each of these scholars looks at historical moments with the presentist eyes of the Marxist tradition of historical scholarship. This imparts a seriousness to historical projects that is sometimes lacking in other forms of history writing. For Claudia Pozzana and Alessandro Russo, for instance, as for Sylvain Lazarus and Alain Badiou, the French philosophers whose works infuse theirs, the need to historically describe the epoch is paramount. Equivocations aside, this is a continuation of Marxist concerns in a postorthodox vein—which is to say that the labor expended in the patient and detailed, sometimes dismaying scholarship anthologized here has immediate goals.

First, similar to the Subaltern Studies publications, which opened new archives and theoretical resources as a means of detecting non-elite and often only obliquely representable subjects who had histori-cally eluded, evaded, or resisted elite dominion, the work here at-tempts to enter worlds outside the prevailing historiography of area studies. (I will have more to say about historiography below.) Second, these essays evoke the shock of recognition that marks an encounter with the historical moment on its own terms, and they are only sec-ondarily concerned with reinforcing orthodox teleology. This objective is perfectly in line with the defining cultural Marxist commitment to human liberation. It differs only to the degree of its preoccupation with the question of singularity in historical experience. As Pietz re-minds us, because "singularity equals the time of possibility, [it] is an eternally recurring reality in our concrete experience." Of course, to exploit the possible as the eternal is one aspect of recognizing the Marxist tradition's attention to the potential available in all human situations. But scholarship abstracts this insight; historical studies are valuable to the degree that they provide some recognition that another person, perhaps a person like me, sought out a time of possibility and realized it.

Third, and in spite of recognition that consciousness and the shock of immediacy are problems in historical representation, historical naming—periodizing—moors us, the contemporaries, to an accreted global past. The job of critical historians in the generous and capa-cious historical tradition of Marxism should be to locate instants of typicality in what is otherwise a heterogeneous flux of simple social experience and intellection. Why should historians bother to focus on policing and enforcing orthodox teleology and orthodox concepts of agency? Certainly our skills and capacities are better served in locating and describing diverse historical subjects, appreciating the immedi-ate historical stakes that these subjects confronted, gauging our own relationship to the past in light of their experience, and consequently wagering our own energy on the possibilities of a better future.

By and large the papers collected here are contributions to a broadly construed Marxist project of historical studies. The authors seek to de-lineate moments of human experience that require special attention from critical historians in the present who are compelled to find the best ways of understanding our epoch in relation to those pasts. If we do not know when our epoch began, how do we know what signs of distinctiveness we should be looking for when we read the heteroge-neous historical archive? The questions taken up and debated must always include cognizance of the nature of our own era. This involves understanding fully, for instance, the significance of the Cold War and its relationship to the colonial era or the relationship of colonialism and capital accumulation and other markers of modernity. Otherwise, we would have trouble saying why the thought of a Li Dazhao strikes such a chord in us a century later and a world apart, or why his thinking contributes to our own. Nor would we be able to seek out other figures of Li Dazhao's stature that we might put to our own uses.

So although Pietz has a provisional point when he reads these essays both as disillusioned and disillusioning, another way to interpret them is as forays into postorthodoxy. Here the object is different. Even in light of the manifest disasters of the twentieth century, these scholars' work suggests that the task remains of wrenching out of the flow of so-called progressive history those timeless moments that Badiou calls generic. In the prosaic language of historians these would be the "significant" moments, appearing singular at first because they are new. Later their subject forms or their institutional logics may be extracted or universalized, for example, the French Revolution, colonial modernity, the advent of women, late capitalism.[3] These are events that compel the critic's attention because they are the mooring points, the means through which contemporaries judge where we are located. Naming them is nothing less than the act of distinguishing what an era is and what demarcates it as such.

According to Donald M. Lowe, late capitalism is historically unique. What makes late capital singular is that now, in the epoch of its dominance, exchange value has destabilized all use value. Use values are social and cultural and consequently are historically conditioned. Formerly, use values were not integral to the dynamic of capitalist production though they supported and were slowly transformed by the social relations of production. In late capital, on the contrary, production has incorporated all social relations of consumption and reproduction into one single, dynamic circuit of production, consumption, and social reproduction. This event formed the structural foundation for the destabilization of all use values and our experience of ubiquitous commodification. Now a commodity is a bundle of characteristics—designed, packaged, produced, and advertised not because we need it but because we *must* consume it to keep in motion the ever-accelerating, late-capitalist production circuit. The consumer absorbs exchange value almost exclusively now, and does so in the form of commodities designed to embody enviable, sexualized qualities of lifestyle infused with a fabricated sense of nostalgia.[4]

Lowe's is a recognizably Marxist characterization of what makes the common era unique. But it does not presume either historical teleology or a specific agent or preeminent historical subject. Assuming for the moment that Lowe's argument is correct—that late capital is actually an epoch characterized by the destabilization of all use values by exchange value—a further point cannot be ignored. Is our way of thinking about the present through its filiations with the past sufficiently learned? Is it sufficiently critical to sustain us in the struggle that Pozzana calls, echoing Li Dazhao, "mutual aid" or collaboration across lines? Is it sufficiently flexible to enable the project that Pietz envisions—Marxist theorists carefully reading the situational cultural politics of myriad communities? Is the Marxist scholar merely an academic disciplinarian, or can this scholarship actually intervene and resolve on the basis of useful insight into the great afflictions of this age? What and how should Marxist scholars think about a general project?

Here Badiou's speculation about the task of philosophy is valuable in thinking about what critical historians could do in light of the impasses of Marxist tradition. Badiou, whose claims are relatively modest, argues that the sole task of philosophy is to play the handmaiden and to ensure a place where naming practices can unfold and be critically considered. Naming practices themselves and the names they propose arise out of manifold historical conditions: " 'situation,' a state of things, any presented multiple whatsoever,"[5] or "heterogeneity" in the parallel language of Badiou's longtime friend and collaborator, Sylvan Lazarus.[6] The valuable point here for critical historians is a further insight of Badiou's. Once thought "accedes to *its* times," he argues, and is created by contemporaries of the times, then what coalesces is what he calls an "event," a thinking that both characterizes its moment and is the epoch's literal supplement. It is not that only contemporaries or persons of some specific locale can grasp or use the event and the thinking it engenders. To the contrary, such truths are quite portable. But, their reiteration is both distinct from the conditions that gave rise to them and "suspended to an event" that is irreducible to all established knowledge coming before or after it.[7] When, out of a general situation, scholars and historians or philosophers extract a specific event, what is usually just heterogeneous time may suddenly crystallize into genre or typicality.

The historicity of the conditions that gave rise to the event also predicates singular subjects. There is no reason to limit the preoccupation with subjectivity to the catachresis of the "proletariat." Nor is it necessary to subordinate all the desires and objects of the various historical subjects to the project of one universal emancipatory struggle. Properly speaking, historical subjects are singular. They are not singular because they are necessarily classes or because they are individuals. Rather, they are singular because they are inextricable from the event that has conditioned them and because they offer—to those of us who would recapture their importance—exemplary subjectivities rooted at once in the immediate and the infinite, as are we ourselves.[8]

Given that late capital is itself our "situation," is it not possible that within the myriad experimental possibilities that the new Marxist scholarship is providing are keys to understanding our time and its connection to the larger, more singular and abstracted "event" of global capitalism? This is what links Brugger's insight that this volume's essays are juxtaposed eccentrically and Pietz's view that the volume represents a general disillusionment with critical scholarship at the end of existing socialism. Yet, neither eccentricity nor disillusionment lies at the true center of this project; rather, these essays are part of a growing movement toward new Marxist historical scholarship. This scholarship is empirical in that it is archivally grounded, and theoretical in that it constantly seeks new strategies for understanding the past through the present.

The most pressing tasks of this resurgence no longer involve simply reiterating or confirming the situation; to go on endlessly about the priorities of late capitalism is redundant now. As Lowe and others have demonstrated, the expanding circuit of production-consumption-reproduction is so all-consuming that commodification is normative. Late capitalism has become inextricable to experience and consequently so familiar as to be merely situational. The stakes become far more complex once we ask the question of how situation is becoming event: How, that is, do we characterize and describe the contours of this moment? Is it truly the case that this sequence of events has changed human history forever? When no one may doubt that the situation is late capitalism and the question of what constitutes the event arises (to work in Badiou's terminology), it is not at all surprising that critical scholarship is preoccupied with questions of periodization and temporality. When is late capital? When is postcolonial? When is colonial modernity? When is "globalization"? It is no coincidence that this refrain—what time is this?—preoccupies us now. Besides its polemical value, orthodoxy serves no other purpose in this context than to discipline experimentation and to defend the ranks of the enlightened against contamination from the new social movements that are not now particularly new and often struggle in the absence of mass movement.

The question of when is our time is linked to the question of who we are.

As social movement theorists have argued for decades, the most pressing scholarly tasks lie with the recasting of what the subject of emancipation looks like. The making of the English working class; the making of Indian women; the institutionalization of gendered national subjects; recasting the subjectivity of abjected sexual groups in relation to heteronormativity; reclamation of racialized, stratified, gendered, minoritized subjects—each scholarly project has commanded attention, and each has absorbed the energy of an outstanding scholar—E. P. Thompson, Dipesh Chakrabarty, Mrinilini Sinha, Vicky Ruiz, and Lata Mani to name a few. It is not such a stretch from this body of scholarship to argue that critical feminist studies is yet another site where the investigation into the subjects of women's liberation has transpired over time. This project—reclaiming out of the flux of the heterogeneous archive an exact representation of what "women" constitute historically—preoccupies many scholars, myself included. One may seek, as Meng Yue, Dai Jinhua, Zhang Jingyuan, and their students do, to call this theory project a historical form of *écriture feminine (nüxing xiezuo)*. Or, it is possible to focus on the historical excision of subject positions for women, as Lata Mani has. What is critical feminist history except the place for investigating subjects for women's liberation? Howland's question of where the subject of the "Chinaman" appears in a specific social text is a micrology. The macrology of the patient, sometimes brutally wrong-headed attempt to liberate the other into subjectivity is written and rewritten and rewritten. This is perhaps what Gayatri Spivak means when she says that feminism is about subjectivity.

There must be a dolorous accounting of the desacralization (see, for instance, Dai Jinhua and Marshall Johnson) of social or communitarian bonds and their use values. But equally there is, in this body of scholarship, anticipation about the possibility that in our time scholars are being called on to relocate provisional subjects in events and to clarify their historical projects, for better and for worse. These provisional subjects may include the defeated, the resentful, the compromised, the imperfect. What this accounting may produce, in the best outcome, is the chance to reperiodize the past and to recommit scholarship to the painful project of learning to be free of the political tragedies of our time while never forgetting their looming actuality. The search in scholarship for subjects historically is a way of engaging the past in the critical demands of the present.

In 1991 when the *positions* project began publication, it began with a manifesto.

Mindful of the dissolution of the discursive binary East and West, *positions* advocates placing cultural critique at the center of historical and theoretical practice. The global forces that are reconfiguring our world continue to sustain formulations of nation, gender, class, and ethnicity. We propose to call into question those still-pressing, yet unstable categories by crossing academic boundaries and rethinking the terms of our analysis. These efforts, we hope, will contribute toward informed discussion both in and outside the academy.

*Positions*' central premise is that criticism must always be self-critical. Critique of another social order must be as self-aware as commentary on our own. Likewise, we seek critical practices that reflect on the politics of knowing and that connect our scholarship to the struggles of those whom we study. All these endeavors require that we account for positions as places, contexts, power relations, and links between knowledge and knowers as actors in existing social institutions. In seeking to explore how theoretical practices are linked across national and ethnic divides, we hope to construct other positions from which to imagine political affinities across the many dimensions of our differences. *positions* is an independent refereed journal. Its direction is taken at the initiative of its editorial collective as well as through encouragement from its readers and writers.

In this dedication of scholarship to self-reflexivity and the patient, often tiresome work of redrawing the relation of critic and community, a temporal sense is implied but not explicitly developed. Ten years later, in this collection of published papers the promise of historicity and our project's connection to the projects of other scholars and subjects in other times bear fruit. The papers here attempt to give proper names to situations. Even more, there is in them yearning to know whether our time is singular. If so, how did it begin, and what does it consist of beyond the normal flux of heterogeneous social life? If not, where in relation to the singularities of the past—imperialism, colonialism, industrial capital, globalization, fascism, socialism, mass violence, and the exuberant energy of modernity—can our time be said to belong? In recognizing this possibility of renaming our intellectual terrain, perhaps there is also a chance to redeclare what Marxist scholarship can mean in the future.

## NOTES

I appreciate Nikhil Pal Singh's kind comments and evaluation of this essay. Donald M. Lowe, whose readings and invaluable responses enriched the writing has, as usual, my warmest gratitude. He even did the index.

1 See Lisa Rofel, "Modernities and Their Discontents," *positions* 9, no. 3 (2001) for a description of postorthodox Marxism.

2 Bill Brugger, "Marxism, Asia, and the 1990s," in "Marxist Scholarship," special issue of *positions* 3, no. 2 (1995): 630–641.

3 For a philosophically naive and practical position on this matter, see "History and Heterogeneity," special double issue of *positions* 6, nos. 1 and 2 (1998).

4 Donald M. Lowe, *The Body in Late-Capitalist USA* (Durham, N.C.: Duke University Press, 1995).

5 Alain Badiou, *Manifesto for Philosophy*. Trans. by Norman Madarasz. (New York: SUNY Press, 1999), 37.

6 See Natacha Michel, "The Time of Thought: On Sylvain Lazarus's *Anthropology of the Name*" (unpublished review, trans. by Donald M. Lowe, Claudia Pozzana, and Alessandro Russo), 3 August 1999.

7 Badiou, *Manifesto*, 81.

8 This point is made elegantly by Claudia Pozzana, in "Spring, Temporality, and History in Li Dazhao" (this volume). Here, the usefulness of Badiou's insight lies in the question of how a critical history can be written, and I am deforming his philosophic project in ways of which he may not fully approve.

## Introduction: Decency and Debasement

The first gods measured out memory with a *jicara* in order to share it out, and all the men and women came by to receive their measure of memory. But some of the men and women were larger than the others and then the measure of memory was not seen equally in all. It shone clearly in the smallest and in the largest it was made opaque. Because of that they say that memory is greatest and strongest in the smallest and it is harder to find in the powerful. That is why they also say that men and women become smaller and smaller when they grow old. They say it is so memory will shine more brightly. They say it is the work of the oldest of the old: to make memory great.

And they also say that dignity is no more than memory which lives. They say.
— Subcomandante Insurgente Marcos, e-mail communiqué of 25 August 1998 (translator unknown)

■ A *jicara* is a small bowl made from a gourd. I had to look it up in a Spanish dictionary, and that's what it said. The term may have all sorts of meaningful cultural resonances, but I have no idea what they might be. But you don't have to know what a jicara is to get Marcos's point about the asymmetrical relation of memory to the powerful. For history's winners, prevailing social arrangements are themselves a daily testimony to their special self-worth, while the bloodier truths of how they arrived at their privileged position exist as a threat to the good conscience their sense of decency desires. There are so many things that the powerful need to forget. But for those who exist in a world rigged to debase them, the subjective value of dignity needs the objective affirmation of a "memory which lives." The act of remembering is itself a valorization process, and a living memory is a current of spiritual power whose source is beyond the reach of the powers that be. But even memory needs its materialities, if only a small bowl and a site where the living can gather to announce that the dead are also present—ancestors, friends, whomever we care about enough to identify their struggles with ours—our dead. The dead still live as long as there are jicara bowls, little pots to pass out their memory as our dignity, our life as their life. Religious traditions, at their best, are very good at fashioning such tools of solidarity. Marxism has been less successful at this form of production. This seems to me less the result of inherent theoretical shortcomings than of historical circumstances. The cult of the great leader and memorials to martyrs of the revolution—this has always been the religious apparatus of the new princes. It is harder to invent new forms of communal solidarity. In his autobiography, Nelson Mandela recalls a gesture of secular communion made by Nat Bregman, his "first white friend":

> One day, at lunchtime, we were sitting in the office [where both worked] and Nat took out a packet of sandwiches. He removed one sandwich and said, "Nelson, take hold of the other side of the sandwich." I was not sure why he asked me to do this, but as I was hungry, I decided to oblige. "Now pull," he said. I did so and the sandwich split roughly in two. "Now, eat," he said. As I was chewing, Nat said, "Nelson, what we have just done symbolizes the philosophy of the Communist Party; to share everything we have." He told me he was a member of the party and explained the rudiments of what the party stood for. . . . I heard him out, asked questions, but did not join. I was not inclined to join any political organization, and the advice of [his white employer] Mr. Sidelsky [against emulating the radical politics of a fellow African employee, Gaur Radebe] was still ringing in my ears. I was also quite religious, and the party's antipathy to religion put me off. But I appreciated half that sandwich.[1]

The real point of the anecdote, and of Mandela's decision not to join the Communist Party, has to do with leadership. That his friend Gaur Radebe had opted against getting a college degree and in favor of joining the Communist Party taught Mandela "that a degree was not in itself a guarantee of leadership and that it meant nothing unless one went out into the community to prove oneself."[2] But Mandela decides that Bregman's communist revaluation of the sacramental breaking of bread is not powerful enough to justify abandoning the religious traditions that are so meaningful to him and so integral to the community he seeks to lead. The attempt at a communist transubstantiation fails: It's just a sandwich. Cultural revolutions are not so easily accomplished.

A lesson is here for those of us seeking to realize a vision—democracy or, to give its materialist name, communism—that would be truer and more profound than religion. We might recall that this is not a new problem, nor is the turn of thought that arises when one is forced to confront its full difficulty. At a time when no educated intellectual could believe in religious superstitions about the continuing life of the dead, when, indeed, the emerging episteme seemed to demand "the annihilation of all past traditional references" (as Claudia Pozzana says of the 1916 China confronted by Li Dazhao, though here I am referring to Rome around 45 B.C.E.), Cicero found his thought forced into a new kind of reflection on cultural materialities. "I have learnt more about the proper way of worshipping the gods," he writes in *De Natura Deorum*, "from the poor little pots [*capedunculae*, small bowls used in sacrifices, according to my Latin dictionary] bequeathed to us by Numa . . . than from all the theories of the Stoics [the great modernists of his day]."[3] As a materialist of the Marxist variety, I want not only to learn from the little pots that cultures make to share out the living memory of a common struggle, I want to learn how to make new ones. New bowls strong enough not to shatter under the barbarism and violence of what the hegemonic discourse, despite the best efforts of Bruno Latour, still calls modernity.[4]

All this is to explain that I come to this collection not as an expert on Asia nor as an academic (I am neither), but as someone obsessed with very particular local struggles (as it happens, in Los Angeles) and specific theoretical issues. I read to learn what struggles and theories concern the authors and to look for clues to a discourse that would highlight the commonality among these diverse struggles. I read to discover a language of common struggle or even just a theory for linking separate local struggles (as "archipelagos of meaning," to use Marshall Johnson's concluding phrase) in relations of mutual aid. This is the problem I think about when Claudia Pozzana speaks of a "radical crisis of Marxism." From, let us say, the founding of the Second International in Paris in 1889 to the collapse of the Soviet Union in 1989, Marxism provided the name for a common struggle, the struggle of those committed to fighting the exploitation of the oppressed. Not everyone thought Marxism was the right way to do this, but everyone understood that what Marxism, as a name, as a political identity, meant. At the end of the Cold War, even leftists who so hated the bloody betrayals of "actually existing socialism" that they would never have imagined calling themselves Marxists or communists felt great despair when the Soviet Union dissolved. Its brand of state socialism may have been the most obscene betrayal of our own best hopes, but these were our hopes, our illusions. It is strange how much the October Revolution seems to have meant now that it is over. Even for those who did not believe in it, the second world, as it was called, represented a world-historical force whose very existence challenged the power of first world capitalism. It stood for the possibility of a global alternative even as most knew it was not itself that alternative. It is not the loss of the reality but rather the loss of possibility that made the first half of the 1990s (when some of these essays were written) such a time of disillusionment for the left.

It seems to me that this collection might have been called *Twelve Essays in Disillusionment and a Poem of Hope.* Although the essay by Pozzana strikes the keynote for this volume by thematizating a contemporary crisis of Marxism, not all the disillusionment recorded in these essays derives from the failings of Marxism. Most do, if only because half the essays concern the People's Republic of China. Sanjay Seth's examination of the Naxalite movement in India is certainly about Marxism's shortcomings, as is Sugiyama Mitsunobu's study of Japanese schools of Marxist economics. But, the essays by Youme Park and Gi-Wook Shin on South Korea discuss disillusionment with the commitment to democracy of Marxism's great nemesis, the United States. The corrosive analysis by Marshall Johnson of nationalist historical preservation practices for constructing "China" in Taiwan has nothing to do with lost Marxist illusions. And D. R. Howland's reconstruction of Luo Sen concerns an encounter that occurred decades before Marxism meant anything in Asia. It is less the subject matter of the essays than the time of their composition, along with the methodologies they employ, that makes it possible to say that this collection as a whole is about Marxism.

The thoughts provoked during my own reading of this volume returned time and again to the problem of subjectivity and its Marxist theorization. This may simply be a result of the particular interests I bring to this collection. The Marxist theory of subjectivity is the primary topic for only three of these essays—those by Jing Wang, Dai Jinhua, and Liu Kang—and even these focus on the diverse issues of voluntarism, consumerism, and aesthetics. But insofar as I have a coherent response to offer, it must take the form of a discussion of this problem, tracking a materialist theory of subjectivity through certain conceptions of historical singularity, social identity, and economic modernity that appear in these texts.

Singularity is, of course, the fundamental category for any critical historical consciousness. Any historian insists that each event and situation must be understood in its uniqueness. Moreover, to focus on historical singularities is to foreground the category of subjectivity: to understand "what happened" means understanding what it meant to those to whom it happened at the time. Because the interpretation of a past event such as the Cultural Revolution is itself a significant factor in the politics of the present, the historian must overcome the "virus of the present," as Alessandro Russo puts it, by reflecting "on each political situation as singular and endowed with its own proper mode of political thinking." There is nothing in this historical conception of singularity peculiar to a materialist theory of subjectivity. Surely what distinguishes a historical materialist approach to subjectivity is an emphasis on the formative influence of those material objects and class antagonisms that are decisive in a particular mode of production. The question has always been how to develop such an approach without letting its analysis of economic structures and the social identities they construct erase the complex singularity of concrete events (their contingency) and the autonomous subjectivity of historical actors ("voluntarism"). Among the texts in this collection, this theoretical problem is most directly addressed by Howland and Pozzana.

In his essay, Howland seeks to reconstruct the subjectivity (or "absent biography") of "Perry's Chinaman," Luo Sen, whose position in the Japanese-American negotiations of 1853–54 had been occluded in the authoritative American (and, presumably, Japanese) accounts of the event. He characterizes his method for doing this by citing Adorno's precept to "abide insistently in the particulars" and Benjamin's idea of "construction from particulars." Such a method seeks to break through Benjamin's "reified continuity" imposed on history by "the ideology of progress" (or, as other authors in this volume might prefer to put it, the ideology of modernization). When Howland states that "the steamship defined the epoch," he is making a familiar sort of historical materialist assertion. What is distinctive is his conception of how this defining process occurs. As the most publicly visible power object functioning within a technologically integrated developmental bloc consisting of coal- and iron-produced machinery, the steamship (along with the locomotive) was certainly the great icon of industrial modernity from the 1830s to the 1910s (when petroleum energy and new engines offered up the automobile and electrification). Howland adopts Benjamin's notion of the "dialectical image" to examine how such objects of economic production become objects of cultural production as well. When new technology becomes established as the infrastructure of a given social world, the authority inherent in its functional importance is expressed in the material presence of its most characteristic objects. A new realism forms in recognition that these particular objects (and the larger system they represent) must be the instruments by which our dreams and desires may be fulfilled. An entire social imaginary congeals within the passive materiality of these inert things. Their very particularity is experienced as the material index of the invisible historical dynamism driving a society as a whole toward a destined future. (As Heidegger put it in his essays on the history of ontology, their presence stands as the revelation of a new "destining.")

This dynamism may be articulated back into the language of traditional culture. Samuel Wells Williams, the American missionary Howland discusses, was typical of nineteenth-century Protestant Americans who viewed the modern industry that made the nation a rising economic and military power in the world as the earthly instrument of "God's plan." This was the accepted formulation for Christian Americans wishing to reconcile the realism of their reason with the vision of their faith. Such an ideological formation can be (and often has been) studied according to the methods of intellectual history: One can discover the key figures who forged the new discourse, trace the routes of its dissemination, and appreciate its functional significance for the society of its time. The materialist cultural criticism developed in "Western Marxism," whether Benjamin's approach to cultural artifacts as dialectical images or Merleau-Ponty's existential phenomenology, differs from such intellectual history. It views ideologies as specific forms of rationality and imagination that have been generalized out of particular historical experiences; its primary concern is to analyze the concrete linkages mediating such totalizing reconciliations of rational argument and collective fantasy by a method of theorization from things in their particularity. Such a materialist analysis entails a kind of self-reflexive interrogation that violates modern academic standards for achieving objectivity and therefore truth. In my view, the real offense consists not in any refusal to be held accountable to the truths that historical scholarship can establish (any discipline capable of proving that the Donation of Constantine was a forgery is well worth adhering to). In his essay, Howland clearly holds his argument accountable to what few truths conventional history can establish about Luo Sen. It is rather the added dimension that Liu Kang in his essay calls "the inscription of self-reflexivity" that is the real offense: The unrepressed subjectivity of the self-reflexive historian supposedly pollutes the analysis, transforming history into a literary fiction that is incapable of objective truth.

What is really at stake is the taboo that keeps official history separate from living memory, because the latter is politically dangerous. Yet to comprehend the nineteenth-century ideology of progress — to see how its vision of modernization as a manifest destiny functioned as a secular religion — one must discern its embeddedness in lived particularities by means of what modern historians would dismiss as literary imagination. To experience the trembling iron of a steamship or a locomotive as it mastered time and space with unprecedented power, to experience a Maxim gun or a Krupp cannon firing its burst of sovereignty over human life, was to feel the incarnate force of historical destiny at work in one's hands, even if only fascist poets like Marinetti ever dared celebrate it in words. Given the very different materialities embodying the distinctive economic logic and military culture of Tokugawa Japan, how could such a sensibility not appear to represent barbarism rather than civilization?

By examining the American-Japanese negotiations that culminated in the Treaty of Kanagawa, Howland focuses on a moment of cross-cultural encounter between societies with incommensurable modes for valuing material objects as embodiments of divine power ("divine" in the sense of divination, future determining). Such encounters are particularly revealing for materialist cultural studies. When the Americans make gifts to the emperor of such things as miniature railways, a telegraph, a telescope, and guns, while the Japanese give such items as "a gold lacquered writing table," Howland is surely right that these are not just displays of national commodities that might become exports in international exchange. They are assertions of cultural identity by means of particular material objects embodying the values informing either culture. For Howland, the incommensurability of Japanese and American modes of valuation finds no resolution; the treaty is simply a recognition of the superior military power of the Americans. Nor is he interested in what would interest me: the functional importance of the American objection to the debasing treatment of visiting American sailors as the basis for establishing alien rights in Japan. Rather, he finds a sort of alternative resolution for the whole episode in the gift-giving practice of the forgotten mediator, Luo Sen: his signing of hundreds of fans for his Japanese hosts, a calligraphic gesture that drew on a common tradition of literary spirituality to mark the unrepeatable singularity of each moment of personal encounter, leaving a material trace of a spiritual truth that cannot be "objectified" and is not transferable through any extended system of exchange.

The lesson Howland derives from the reconstructed biography of Luo Sen is that the truth of subjectivity is realized only through an aesthetic apprehension of universality through singularity. As Howland puts it, "Through the course of his successive obsessions with particular, beautiful objects, the individual subject comes to understand the universality of beauty." This is, to be sure, a kind of materialism, but it is one that finds its truth outside of (or in alienation from) the historical. History—the American steamship, or the aircraft carrier that is its successor—remains. The historical importance of the war system remains. As Pozzana reminds us in her essay on Li Dazhao, Marxism was founded in Asia after World War I in part because, at the time, the October Revolution seemed to represent "the only event running counter to the logic of war." Although twentieth-century state socialism proved unable to escape the logic of war, the appeal of Marxism to people around the world has been as a revolutionary project that would end not only class exploitation but also the war system that has always been the barbarism of "civilized" states. Given the insistence of You-me Park and Sanjay Seth in this volume that we think about violence, I do not think that a Marxist theorization of singularity in terms of an aesthetics of beauty is what we're after.

It is interesting to turn from Howland's Western Marxist reconstruction of Luo Sen's aesthetic of singularity to the idea of singularity presented in Pozzana's translation and discussion of Li Dazhao's "Spring." If I read him correctly, Li Dazhao does not conceive singularity as the way universal beauty transcends history but rather as the way a particular moment of earthly beauty may be retained as an image of eternity, a living memory that frees one to reenter history as a contemporary. Written at a time of radical disillusionment, according to Pozzana, "Spring" is a poem of breakthrough, of resolution. It accepts all the rising forces of the crisis to achieve a new vision and thereby divine a new path of hope to the future. Li Dazhao's vision of the eternal renewal of spring thinks history as "the whole of singularity" and in doing so establishes us (or the students whom he addresses) in a universal time that might be called contemporaneity (or, as Johannes Fabian would say, "coevalness"[5]). This is what most struck me about "Spring": in it there are only contemporaries. Jin Shengtan theorizes about *Zhou* and *Yi* in the same space-time as Thomson and Tait theorize cosmological physics. Emperor Han Wudi tames barbarians in the same world where Teddy Roosevelt hunts polar bears. Confucius and Byron speak to us on equal terms. All the history that was and all the history that will be is here in a liberating moment of poetic reflection limited only by Li Dazhao's repertoire of knowledge and imagination. By regarding all of history as itself a singularity, the poem achieves a materialist conception of historical time as itself eternity: eternity as the contemporaneity shared by the living and the dead.

Such a historical consciousness is no less true than those that divide history into discrete periods. There are good reasons to discriminate among societies according to the different economic and cultural logics that organize them. Historical materialism is certainly right to notice the epoch-making importance of new technologies of production, such as the steamship. But grand periodizations of world history, whether according to modes of production or stages of civilization, tend to absolutize the divide between the living and their predecessors of the "premodern" past. Such universal periodizations are consistently used to absolve modernity's own genocides by conceiving modernization as an objective fate and by mapping periodized history as a developmental hierarchy onto the peoples and societies of the present world. Whole peoples may be regarded "primitives" ("our living ancestors") or "feudal remnants," "survivals" whom history itself has judged to belong already among the dead, thereby absolving the "moderns" who proceed to make them dead. While the discourse of modernity condemns genocide as a willful act performed by those who refuse its imperatives and thereby fall back into "ancient ethnic hatreds," it forgives the objectively inevitable genocide of cultures that would refuse the modern destiny. The project of modernization is thus premised on a sort of reverse sacrificial logic where it is the dead (including the "living relics" of resistant cultures) who must sacrifice their existence for the living. Certainly the implicit premise of contemporary neoliberalism is that the vast majority of people in the past and of the generation alive today must be regarded as waste, as necessary sacrifices if nations are to climb up the ladder of per capita GDP to the point where there bursts forth the flower of a sizable middle class, whose innate (and apparently unique) sense of decency will lead them to demand things like democracy, human rights, and an end to civilization's appetite for annihilation. The Pinochets of the world, the Somozas, the Mobutus, the Reza Pahlevis, the Saddam Husseins (until he lost his way), and for that the matter the Stalins and Li Pengs of modernization's "socialist alternative," must be regarded, sadly, as indispensable tools for building the material conditions for a just future society. It's a sad fact that, if the modernization lifeboat is to reach the promised land (call it freedom, democracy, communism), most of the people on board have to be chucked over the side. Periodized historical narratives that divide moderns from nonmoderns are spiritual constructions, mirrors hung on the doorway leading into the House of Modernity, to protect the inhabitants from being haunted by the angry ghosts of the nonancestral dead. But periodizations, whether or not they are used to justify the genocidal logic of modernization, are not more true than the historical consciousness that refuses all periodization. When does one moment end and another begin? It is just as true to regard the whole of human history as occurring in a single moment, and therefore to regard everyone, living and dead, as contemporaries.

Li Dazhao makes this historical consciousness real in his poem. It does what Johnson, at the end of his essay, calls on cultural critics to do: "to transpose undoing the dualities of objective and subjective, of space and time, into a solidarity with those who are . . . contemporary but distant in space and those who are distant in time." The poem represents one of those new jicaras that Marxism must learn to fashion. Li Dazhao offers us a materialist eternity. To touch the earth, as Gautama did, is to touch the sacred relic connecting us to the whole of it and to each other. In "Spring" we find Benjamin's Angel of History leaning against the railing of a tower overlooking a springtime garden in a foreign land. The season of spring, the age of youth, is the thing we desire both in the reality of its present existence and in the potency of its possible future. This is not a utopian vision: the time of possibility is an eternally recurring reality in our concrete experience. In his poem, Li Dazhao offers us a singularly real moment from his life as a universal image of our changing earthly existence as itself eternity: the eternal endurance of possibility, of hope, that is one aspect of the temporality of the material world. For him, this is a revelation powerful enough to be the equal of religion: "As for myself, I think that one should believe in the endless Spring of humanity, in the same way that religious people believe in God."

Indeed, the next words of the poem, at least in Pozzana's translation (on which I am wholly dependent), are "more so." The claim that our belief in what the poet calls "the endless Spring of humanity" should be stronger than the belief of theistic faiths is made in reference to the modern science of biology. Although the "biologists' warnings" to which Li Dazhao refers are perhaps biological theories of racial degeneration that, one hopes, no longer speak to us, it is still the intellectual revolution of modern biology, specifically the Darwinian retelling of human history, that has disempowered traditional theistic expressions of divinity. I could not disagree more strongly than with the views that Pozzana quotes from Alain Badiou, who apparently prefers "the self-asserting rights of the Immortal" to "human rights" and who locates "Sovereignty" in assertions of "opposition to the will-of-being-an-animal." Surely Li Dazhao is locating eternity in our experience of the earth and our capacity to retain a living memory of spring, not in the willful denial of the truth that we are mortal animals. If the first gods were invented in rituals that proclaimed an absolute difference between humans and other animals, as some hypothesize,[6] then modern biology's subversion of the human-animal distinction is perhaps the true cause of the historical death of the gods of religion. It is still possible to tell the story of human history, and our part in it, in religious language ("God's plan" or whatever), but people know this is merely an overcoding of the stories modern science tells on the authority of secular materialism. History has changed the ground of belief, as Li Dazhao recognized. Although my Christian friends tell me that the core of their belief consists in the act of praising God, I cannot help thinking that the power of religion has come from their ability to express the truth that the dead live. Perhaps it is just my own peculiar obsession, but I do not believe a Marxist culture can be established until atheists can learn ways of saying how it is literally true that the dead—all of them—still live with us. It is this that I find in Li Dazhao's vision of history as eternity itself, an ongoing singularity within which, when regarded as a whole, all the living and all the dead live together as contemporaries.

Much as this reading (more likely, misreading) of Li Dazhao's "Spring" speaks to me, I do not think I could guess from the poem itself that the author would go "out into the community to prove himself," as Mandela says, by organizing rickshaw drivers and helping found the Chinese Communist Party. Certainly there is a radical vision here whose universal contemporaneity entails a spiritual leveling that implicitly challenges the power of any established hierarchy of differently valued social identities. But one can find as much in any enduring religious tradition that has not been wholly subsumed into a state ideology. "Nothing is easier," we read in the *Communist Manifesto*, "than to give Christian asceticism a Socialist tinge."[7] (One is tempted to add that nothing has been easier than to give Marxist socialism an ascetic tinge.) What is specifically Marxist about this vision? What has it to do with the historical materialist theorization of subjectivity in terms of class exploitation? The answer, it seems to me, may be found in the linkage that Marxism discerns between the objective category of exploitation and the subjective category of debasement. As Marx put it in his most famous paragraph on religion (the one with the endlessly misconstrued "opium of the people" line), to be a communist means to accept what Marx ironically calls "the categorical imperative" not only to end economic exploitation but "to overthrow all conditions in which man is a debased, enslaved, neglected, contemptible being."[8] The novelty of Marxist materialism is its insistence that debasing structures of domination must be traced through their political and legal institutions to economies of exploitation in which they have a functional significance. This means interpreting the social identities proper to particular hierarchies of rank, status, and political rights in terms of the economic category of class. To say that Marxist materialism interprets history in terms of class struggle means (or should mean) that it analyzes the interdependence (if one prefers, the dialectic) of particular forms of objective exploitation and particular forms of subjective debasement. It develops this interpretation to discover how to establish a just system of objective economic valuation that would affirm the subjective value—the dignity—of the debased. Isn't that the point?

In any event, it is this materialist problematization of subjectivity that I think of when I read Liu Kang's call for a "reinscription of 'self-reflexivity' as a proper Marxist problematic." Self-reflexivity for historical materialists is not the self-reflexivity of Descartes or Kant or, for that matter, Nagarjuna—the self-reflexivity of a disembodied consciousness. Hegelianism and the Vajrayana surely come closer to the mark, though not close enough. Ours is the self-consciousness of "a corporeal, living, real, sensuous, objective being," as Marx once put it, piling on as many materialist qualifiers as he could, whose reality is expressed in and reflected from other "real, sensuous objects."[9] Because ours is a materialist consciousness, as Michael Taussig has compellingly argued, otherness, alterity (indeed, "alienation") is inscribed in human self-reflexivity, imparting to it an inescapably mimetic logic.[10] Our mimetic desire makes us want the value of seeing ourselves reflected back from whatever we are not. Because difference is the medium of our identity, we intensify the alienness of others to reveal our dignity in their strangeness, be they animal gods, our ancestral dead, or foreigners. So-called primitive religions do this primarily along a temporal axis; their masks and rituals are mimetic technologies that realize the value of the living through the ongoing judgment of those dead who form the substance of one's own identity. Lacking such traditions, moderns use those among the living with whom they do not identify to display their own ethical value to themselves, at the expense of their Others' lives, which is only proper because they are performing the genealogical function of "living ancestors." Civilized states have always tried to subsume the genealogical temporality of kinship "blood relations" by mimetic technologies whose logic of unification may be characterized as fractal analogy. The cosmological architecture of temple states and the sacred regalia of royal monarchies display in material form a proper order that is supposed to be replicated throughout the society. A comparable unification by fractal reflection is achieved in the form of literary culture in the master Confucian analogy of the five social relations. Hegel offered a modern version of this system of representational analogy when he argued that the concept of freedom (the destiny of universal history) is actualized for all citizens in its universal form in the sovereign power of free decision exercised by the head of the state (in his case, the Prussian state). Because Marxism was developed as a democratic critique of all such politics of reflective representation, its political materialism has been a persistent embarrassment for the vanguard party ideology of Leninist states.

Particularly for those of us more familiar with the political aesthetics developed in Western Marxism, Liu Kang's essay clarifies the very different significance that aesthetic theory and the concept of subjectivity has had in socialist states. Specifically, he illuminates the way Maoism conceptualized the representational authority of the Communist Party as "objectivity" and therefore devalued criticism of its policies as mere "subjectivity." The difficulty of criticizing the Leninist model even in post-Mao China was brought home to me in Jing Wang's essay when she expressed doubt that Wang Ruoshui and Hu Qiaomu "were ever aware that the Party question and the subjectivity question make up two sides of the same coin." Given my own inability to grasp the discursive parameters of the debates about socialist alienation and Marxist humanism in 1980s China, what most interested me about the essays by Jing Wang and Liu Kang was their mention of the way these debates were quashed as "spiritual pollution" by linking the ideas of "the early Marx" to a campaign against pornography. This reinforces my belief that Marxist cultural studies needs to examine historical forms of human degradation not only to understand the ways in which the debased organize their own dignity against the powers that rule them but to learn how cultural discourses about degradation are used as a form of social power. It would be valuable for cultural critics to examine the "concrete particulars" that allowed a highly theoretical argument about socialist alienation to be cut off by equating humanism to pornography as the theory and practice of a debased spirituality that threatened socialist decency.

*Decency*, "conduct conforming to propriety," is perhaps the most Confucian word in the English language. Michael Dutton begins his essay by citing the Confucian assertion of a subjective standard of propriety that remains constant throughout the objective history of changing political regimes. The idea of decency is a powerful social fact, however much its particular conception of proper social relations varies from culture to culture. There is nothing more natural for radical cultural politics to debunk than the "decency"—the pretense to moral respectability—of the powerful. But, cultural standards of decency are a political resource available to anyone in a society, not just the powerful. This truth first struck me while reading about the "Mothers of the Plaza" during the dirty war in Argentina: They alone could act publicly during the period of state terror because they were immune to being "disappeared" as a result of the very sexism that, from a larger political perspective, progressives would wish to abolish.[11] It seems to me that this example raises a more complex issue than that of having to choose between ideological purity and effective politics. The reasons why many feminists may be more comfortable adopting the mantle of Emma Goldman than of Mother Jones are doubtless complex. I suspect that one of these reasons may be an unreflective condemnation of all traditional forms of decency by those who assume that radical politics must be countercultural. To dismiss the social power of the maternal persona deployed by the Mothers of the Plaza as nothing but a component of oppressive patriachal systems, rather than as a resource for oppositional politics, might be a sacrifice as unnecessary as it is disempowering.

A similar error is made by those who refuse to acknowledge the progressive potential of religious traditions simply because they are the institutionalized forms of decency of an unjust society. One of the local campaigns that I was recently involved in was an effort by a service workers labor union to organize in a Catholic hospital system. Because Catholic social teaching has articulated the value of a just workplace and, indeed, of labor unions, it was crucial to gain support from a group of Catholic priests and other local clergy who support the campaign as a matter of religious conscience. Indeed, the most effective political movement in Los Angeles in recent years has been the Living Wage Coalition, a movement of labor unions, religious groups, and community organizations that has succeeded in passing pro-labor laws by appealing to various communities' general sense of decency that traditionally have no love for labor unions, nor for denunciations of exploitation, but that also know the money cost of a decent life and hold religious beliefs about the right of all to such. Indeed, some organizing campaigns at particular businesses have succeeded only by gaining support among people with whom targeted business owners share common religious values and with whom they socialize as equals. Though having their decency impugned by an employee or a labor union would mean nothing to them, it turns out that the good opinion of their social equals matters a great deal. Living wage campaigns may seem like an insufficiently radical program to would-be revolutionaries, but they articulate a radical truth: Under capitalism money replaces land as the ground of social existence; it is the thing without which people cannot live, decently or otherwise.

Like the democratization movement in South Korea, the living wage movement would change in response to the state's recourse to violence and police repression (which is, in fact, the situation for some communities in other parts of Los Angeles). But to think that there can be no radical politics outside a context of violence would be to fall into the trap of what You-me Park calls "the police interpretation" ("to focus solely on the barbarity of the state and the bloody sign of terror deliberately constructed by the military state," to think of revolutions solely in terms of "graphic bloodshed and scattered glorious moments"). Because states at times crush democratic movements seeking to transform the legal system by means of massacres and campaigns of state terror, this does not mean that laws cannot sometimes be radically changed by nonviolent methods asserting the moral authority of an established social ethic.

My point is that the revolutionary project of instituting a material economy that would revalue social identities so that no one's dignity depends on another's debasement should not blind one to the power represented by existing cultural systems of decency. They are often premised on the very values and sense of justice that Marxism is trying to make real. Nor should Marxist scholars ignore the systemic function of organized debasement outside the workplace and, indeed, outside what capitalism misrepresents as the economy proper. Few academic writers study how societies systematically organize debasement to construct the belief of the powerful in their own decency. Yet the routine moral condemnation and indeed the criminalization of groups that are integral functional parts of the economic system— "illegal" migrant workers, for instance—is a political necessity for regimes to claim legitimacy. Fortunately, some cultural historians have begun to study the social and economic function of debasement.[12] There are both legitimized police powers and disavowed personal pleasures that the decent derive from the debased. Class analysis must learn to examine these systems if it is to understand the mode of subjective valuation that endows the political regime of a given social formation with its ethical power. Surely there are enough ethnographic and sociological studies of diverse cultures to make the assertion that any society has a certain infrastructure of debasement (witchcraft institutions, a criminal underworld). Both the moral economy and the institutionalized power of the privileged depends on such an infrastructure. Routine forms of debasement are essential components in political economies. Their vital importance may be gauged by the intensity of reaction against movements that threaten to remove their stigmatization. Attributing dignity to homosexuals, regarding prostitution as "sex work," suggesting that drugs be regulated rather than criminalized—such proposals can threaten the stability of an entire social economy.

If there is a subjective component to class analysis, it must consist of examining the social function of systems of decency and debasement that form the moral economy required for a given structure of economic exploitation to operate. This is one way to approach the problem of social policing that Dutton discusses. Indeed, I think that such an approach can use the traditional Marxist history of modes of production, as long as one remembers that the social relations of earlier modes are not abandoned but rather subsumed into the new social formation and thus transformed, not as "relics" but as integral functional components. One may posit an original sexual division of social labor, but the patriarchal ideology that values the work of "economic" production over the work of biological reproduction is still very much with us, as are generalized metaphors of heterosexual union as the moral ground of social unity. If the social division of town and country first ideologized the moral superiority of "intellectual work" over manual labor, this too is still with us as a resource for ideologues of the computer revolution and a global economy based on intellectual property rights. History, as Dutton says, is very much a matter of "repetitions with difference."

A class analysis of historical social identities must also learn to avoid distorting people's real subjectivity—their actual ideals and concrete desires. Marxism's adherence to the ideology of modernity has been a prime cause of such misrepresentations. This is the point that I take from Seth's extraordinary essay on the "revolutionary excess" of the Naxalite movement as "an instance of 'unforgetting' . . . where Marxist categories came to be penetrated and shaped by the categories informing peasant insurgency." Beginning as a Marxist-led peasant revolt, the movement developed into a series of violent gestures for "turning the world upside down." Its spectacular killings staged a radical revaluation of the traditional hierarchy of landlord and peasant. In doing so, Seth argues, it posed a fundamental question for Marxism and in particular Maoism, whose "schema of revolution in an agrarian society entailed the 'forgetting' or misreading of aspects of peasant experience and consciousness." Because Marxism, just as much as liberal capitalism, has viewed modernization as the path of its own destiny, Maoist revolutionaries had to "forget" the subjectivity of the peasants themselves. As Seth puts it, "a subjectivity or consciousness has been attributed to the peasant that is not, and could not be his own." In misrepresenting "the peasantry as a class which dreams of a transparent, secular society rendered subject to human control," Marxists blinded themselves to the indigenous categories of peasant mobilization: localism, territoriality, religiosity.

Moreover, the peasantry is the class that has endured exploitation throughout world history. All "premodern" civilizations were built on extraction of the agrarian surplus they produced. This is also how Marxist states such as the Soviet Union and the People's Republic of China have modernized themselves, since the Cold War cut off foreign finance capital as a source of investment. Peasants do not mobilize by suddenly achieving a consciousness that they are the victims of "man-made exploitation," the radical consciousness that can mobilize an urban proletariat. They know perfectly well they are and have always been exploited by the class whose power rests less on property ownership than on organized violence. Peasants do not mobilize against exploitation. They mobilize against annihilation. Seth notes the radicalizing effect of Indira Gandhi's forced sterilization campaign in 1975. In Mexico, the Zapatista revolt arose in response to President

Salinas's abolition of the *ejido* land system in favor a free market in land ownership in 1992; established under the Agrarian Law of 1915, ejidos were communally owned lands granted to villages as reparations for past injustices.[13] The abolition of the ejido system, enacted in anticipation of the North American Free Trade Agreement (NAFTA) with the United States and Canada, broke Mexico's fundamental social contract with the peasantry. This was an assault on the material base of the Chiapan peasants' very existence.[14] Certainly annihilation can mobilize anyone: the radicalization of South Korean politics discussed by You-me Park and Gi-Wook Shin was forged in the living memory of the Kwangju massacre. But peasants have different resources: possession of land on which they can subsist autonomously and, if lucky, mountains or swamps to which they can escape. What is most often called the struggle of indigenous peoples are the struggles of those for whom freedom—autonomy—takes the form of land. If urban radicals are to achieve solidarity with those engaged in indigenous struggles, the difference in both subjectivity and material goals must be theorized and respected. This difference has nowhere been more emphatically expressed than in the decision of the Lakota Nation in South Dakota a few years ago to reject a huge monetary settlement they had won from the U.S. Supreme Court as compensation for the theft of the Black Hills. It was the land they wanted, not its money value.[15]

Unlike those for whom agrarian autonomy is a viable option and those whose spiritual culture takes a territorial form, exploited groups that cannot survive outside the wage and money system must seek to reshape the system of monetized obligations and legal rights of the state under whose rule they live. It is true that discrete ethnic minorities within a capitalist society have the option of identifying themselves as a people unto themselves with an inherent right to national self-determination as a territorial state. But economic globalization, as well as the history of apartheid in South Africa and of Indian nations in the United States, indicates how problematic are most contemporary movements for territorial autonomy. Indeed, it is part of the vitality of the Zapatista movement that it understands that its demands for the local agrarian autonomy of Mayan peoples can only be won by using its struggle to support a more broad-based effort to transform the Mexican state—a strategy that may have been vindicated with the 2000 election of President Vicente Fox and his signing of the San Andreas Accords recognizing the legitimate land claims of indigenous peoples in Mexico.

For most proletarianized groups, a territorial independence movement is not an option. The only alternative is to form civil and political movements that seek to remedy the violence and exploitation they suffer by restructuring power relations within the existing state. If the history of the twentieth century has taught Marxists nothing else, it has demonstrated that the Leninist model for doing this—the direct seizure of the state by a revolutionary party purporting to exercise the dictatorship of the proletariat—is a failed experiment. If we accept Russo's analysis of the Cultural Revolution, Maoist China was no more immune than any other state to the political dialectic that gives history the character of struggle. A crisis of authority within the central state leaves local spaces outside its control; there, a multiplicity of autonomous groups organize themselves into diverse factions that ultimately coalesce into two antagonist alliances contesting for state power. The model of the one-party state has proved no more able to escape this dynamic than has the model of a state with no parties (the model on which the United States was founded). Russo argues that the ultimate confrontation between "Scarlet guards" and Red Guards during the Cultural Revolution expressed "a subjective breakdown internal to the working class" that could only happen in a Leninist state in which the political authority of public officials was legitimized in terms of the social identity "working class." However, in Russo's view, this was merely the second world form of a global "crisis of the category *political party*" that has culminated in a post–Cold War politics of movements in "civil society" that refuse the traditional political aspiration of becoming the ruling party of a state.

Personally, I do not agree with the claim that political parties no longer matter. But even were this so, does the rejection of the idea of a unified party of the working class mean that class analysis is irrelevant in "the new politics" of civil society, local movements, and nongovernmental organizations? Has history moved us beyond "the political category of class" in the sense that we should abandon the effort of class analysis to understand subjective identities by locating their social ground in economic systems and their historical dynamism in the structural antagonism created by systemic exploitation? Obviously, I myself do not think so. Rather, I think there is need for a better class analysis, one that more truly takes into account the contribution of cultural studies by grasping the particular interrelations among institutional forms of objectified value and subjective experiences of personal value—of dignity and debasement—as these are lived and remembered within historical structures of power that, more often than not, have been established through successful crimes against humanity.

NOTES

1  Nelson Mandela, *Long Walk to Freedom: The Autobiography of Nelson Mandela* (Boston: Little, Brown, 1994), 74.
2  Ibid.
3  Cicero, *De Natura Deorum*, trans. H. Rackham (Cambridge: Harvard University Press, 1979), 327.
4  Bruno Latour, *We Have Never Been Modern*, trans. Catherine Porter (Cambridge: Harvard University Press, 1991), 2nd *Petite réflexion sur le culte moderne des dieux faitiches* (Le Plessis-Robinson: Synthélabo Groupe, 1996).
5  Johannes Fabian, *Time and the Other: How Anthropology Makes Its Object* (New York: Columbia University Press, 1983).
6  Chris Knight, *Blood Relations: Menstruation and the Origins of Culture* (New Haven, Conn.: Yale University Press, 1991).
7  Karl Marx and Frederick Engels, *The Communist Manifesto* (New York: International, 1948), 33.
8  Karl Marx, *Critique of Hegel's "Philosophy of Right"*, trans. Annette Jolin and Joseph O'Malley (Cambridge: Cambridge University Press, 1977), 137.
9  Karl Marx, *Economic and Philosophic Manuscripts*, trans. Rodney Livingstone and Gregor Benton, in *Karl Marx: Early Writings*, ed. Quintin Hoare (New York: Random House, 1975), 390.
10  Michael Taussig, *Mimesis and Alterity: A Particular History of the Senses* (New York: Routledge, 1993).
11  John Simpson and Jana Bennett, *The Disappeared and the Mothers of the Plaza: The Story of the 11,000 Argentinians Who Vanished* (New York: St. Martin's, 1985).
12  See, for example, Gail Hershatter's multilayered analysis of the social uses of publications in China that decry the scandal of prostitution in *Dangerous Pleasures: Prostitution and Modernity in Twentieth-Century Shanghai* (Berkeley: University of California Press, 1997), 393.
13  Enrique Krauze, *Mexico: Biography of Power*, trans. Hank Heifetz (New York: HarperCollins, 1997), 352.
14  George A. Collier, *Basta! Land and the Zapatista Rebellion in Chiapas* (Oakland, Calif.: Institute for Food and Development Policy, 1994).
15  Edward Lazarus, *Black Hills, White Justice: The Sioux Nation versus the United States, 1775 to the Present* (New York: HarperCollins, 1991).

Dreaming of Better Times: "Repetition with a Difference"

and Community Policing in China

Zi Zhang asks: "Can one know what the future will hold in ten dynasties' time?"
Confucius responds: "The Yin dynasty inherited the notion of propriety from
the Xia. Therefore we can know what has been *added* and *subtracted*. The Zhou
dynasty inherited their notion of propriety from the Yin, and from this we can
know what has been added and what has been subtracted. Others may continue
to use this notion of propriety as inherited from the Zhou. Therefore, even in
one hundred dynasties' time, we can still know."
—Confucius, *Analects* (emphasis added)

■ Can one be so certain of the past, let alone of the future, as the great
sage? On this, I think, more recent events in China have their own
story to tell. . . .
The time is 1994; the city, Beijing.
As one rides through the streets of this city as it commemorates
the centennial of the birth of the "Great Helmsman," one is struck by
the number of vehicles that display a double-sided portrait of his face.
On the one side, there is the young, fresh-faced revolutionary Mao, on
the other, a more benevolent and aging father figure. There is nothing
added to nor subtracted from these double-sided portraits save for the
compulsory beautifications made possible by the airbrush. The power
of such a portrait, however, lies not in its physical beauty and accuracy
but in the symbolic renewal it connotes. It is in the "additions" or "subtractions" in memory formation that the picture of Mao becomes less

a form of remembrance than a potent and very contemporary political symbol. The recognition of this point leads us to a very different set of propositions to those advanced by the great sage, Confucius.

How are we to account for the popularity of this double-sided portrait? Is it Party propaganda, superstition, or a faded remembrance of more stable times that leads to this double-sided portrait being purchased and displayed? Which side of this "Maoist coin" is favored in the act of display, or is the very "double-sidedness" itself a tactic, designed deliberately to capture the widest possible constituency? On the one side, there is a young rebel Mao for the "Cui Jian" generation,[1] while on the other there is an aging statesman for those who crave more stable times. There is, it appears, a Mao for all. Yet this multiplication of Mao images to the extent that there is indeed a "Mao for all" leads to irony. It undermines the unity of what He stands for and replaces it with a multiplicity of possible meanings. This, in turn, shifts the spotlight from the (real) Mao to the uses of Mao or, more accurately, to the uses and politics of memory and its redeployment.

It is the way in which memory is played on through this double-sided portrayal of Mao that takes us beyond the face and the figure. This "double-sided form of remembrance" focuses attention on the ambiguity and multiplicity of things remembered. It puts a focus and a face on the politics of the act of remembering. Moreover, it offers a form of remembrance which, though ambivalent in meaning, is nevertheless visible, focused, conscious, and celebrated. If this reedification of Mao offers something of the venerated and visible side of remembering Mao, a more unconscious side is captured, not in the photographic image but in the actions of the Chinese public security forces. Here one finds the "double-sidedness" of Mao remembered in another way.

In contemporary policing, one discovers many of the tactics and technologies of Maoism "remembered" and redeployed as mechanisms through which public order can be maintained in times of economic and social reform. Remembrance for the public security forces differs in kind from the double-sided Mao portraits. There is little that is conscious about their process of remembrance. Hence, the "remembered technologies" of contemporary policing are not celebrated as Maoist procedures but reappear almost unnoticed and largely unannounced as mundane practices of everyday policing. Nevertheless, by silently reinforcing a continuity with the past they also fortify the idea of these procedures as natural. Furthermore, by redeploy-

ing Maoist tactics in new domains and for new ends they also operate to bring forth change. The Janus-faced nature of these redeployed
Maoist tactics and technologies has been made possible only because
such devices have successfully secreted themselves in everyday life.
It is through this process of secretion that they derive their symbolic
power, while their utilitarian strength is derived from the fact that
they are not repetitions of the "same" but "repetitions with a difference." The symbolic strength of "repetition" combined with the flexibility offered through often hidden "additions" and "subtractions" to
"remembrance" constitutes the very basis on which "repetition with
a difference" operates, and it is this notion which is at the theoretical
heart of this essay.[2]

There is therefore a dual theoretical object in opening with this
notion of "repetition with a difference." First, it enables the theoretical
benefits derived from this notion in terms of ongoing debates within
Western social theory circles about the past and power to be highlighted. The work of Michel Foucault is central to this discussion. Second, it allows a critique of the burgeoning Chinese literature that con-
signs the past to "relic status." "Repetition with a difference" makes
it possible to think about recalling the past in a more dynamic fashion. By relying on, and extending, the work of Marx and Benjamin in
this area, this essay suggests that "the relic" plays a far more constitutive role in the formation of contemporary discourse and government
strategy than these theoretical approaches would allow. This paper exemplifies this through a detailed examination of strategies of contemporary social policing in China. It is with regard to the technologies
and strategies deployed in the area of social control that it is suggested
that the Chinese police are indeed "dreaming of better times." Such
technological "remembrances" in policing, then, are neither fortu-
itous nor necessarily conscious. They are a combination of pragmatic
management decisions about contemporary policing needs built on
often unconscious desires to return to more stable times. Moreover,
they indicate an attempt to think through such a return—again, sometimes consciously but at other times not—in the language of the past.
It is in focusing on the strength and power derived from these less
visible and therefore sometimes incalculable technological and strategic "additions" and "subtractions" that this paper is propelled away
from the logic and concerns of Confucius. At the same time, it is in recognizing the possibility of "technologies of power" as heterogeneous
combinations of different forms (be that sovereign, semiotechnical,
disciplinary, or possibly some other form) that this essay also has cause

to depart from the work of more recent "philosopher-sages" of power in Western social theory.

## "REPETITION WITH A DIFFERENCE" AND WESTERN AND CHINESE SOCIAL THEORY

The concept of "repetition with a difference" offers a means by which certain forms of Marxist argument can be redeployed to redirect debate around Foucault's work on power. Generally, debate in this area has been dominated by what could only be described as the "commodity argument." That is to say, an argument that has centered on a critique of Foucault's so-called inability to answer the question of who holds power.[3] However, criticism structured in this way offers little room for fruitful engagement as it dismisses Foucault's insistence that it has been the "how" and not the "whom" of power that has been central to his endeavours in this area.[4] Through the deployment and discussion of the notion of "repetition with a difference," Foucault's notion of power can be taken seriously. That is to say, power can be examined not in terms of "who controls" but rather in terms of *how* it is constituted. At the same time though, it can be critiqued as historically too segmented. Thus, this notion of "repetition with a difference" depends on an emphatic restatement of the postmodern insistence that there can be no formal transhistorical unity to power. This, in turn, opens onto the ground on which a critique of the discursive unity of "disciplinary" in Foucault and post-Foucauldian works is made possible. Hence, one can no longer speak of purely disciplinary forms of power not because we recognize them only as "disciplinary blockades" (Foucault) but because their very constitution and theoretical strength may well derive from forms of remembrance that are anything but disciplinary.[5] Moreover, when these forms are "reenacted" they do not automatically lead to disciplinary ends, and it is at this point that the politics of repetition translates into the difference of reenactments. This difference also disturbs those simplistic accounts of Foucault that interpret his work on power to mean a trajectory from premodern to modern, disciplinary forms. The question here is, if disciplinary power just supercedes sovereign and ideological power, then how are slippages "backward" within the modern period, into sovereign and ideological forms, possible? Here, but in a somewhat different setting, the concerns of this paper brush against those of certain contemporary Chinese social theorists who attempt to deal with contemporary Chinese problems by blaming the powers of the "relic."

And while there is cause to doubt the appropriateness of this approach theoretically, there is no denying its political strength.

Nowhere is the political strength and popularity of relic arguments more obvious than in the documentary television series *Yellow River Elegy*. First screened to audiences in June 1988, it broke all viewing records,[6] despite the fact that it stood in stark contrast to recent valuations of Chinese tradition prevailing in the newly industrializing economies of Taiwan, Singapore, and Hong Kong. This documentary series forwarded an orthodox Weberian view that traditional, Confucian-dominated Chinese dynastic values fettered development. In this, and many other mainland Chinese accounts, tradition becomes a signifier of decay, a shackle, and something overcome only by the process of "opening up." Here, the documentary reiterated a theme already central to political discourse in China, namely, the issue of "feudal remnants." Discourse on "feudal remnants" has a long history in China but reemerged in its current form in 1986 in the work of one of China's foremost scholars, Su Shaozhi.[7] Su critiqued the existence of feudal remnants within contemporary China, for he claimed they acted as fetters on the Chinese socialist modernization program. The point to be noted, however, is that relic arguments have gone well beyond intellectual debate and have even emerged in the realm of government. Like the double-sided face of Mao, however, the policing of those unhealthy "remnant forms" is subject to a wide variety of interpretations.

## POLICING THE REMNANTS

In 1988, Zhao Xiaogang and Guo Zheng, in an article in the internal Chinese police magazine *Police Research,* outlined the relationship between crime, backwardness, and development. They pointed out that:

> Development is part of a natural tendency toward social advancement and a revolution against the barbarous and the backward. If there is a lack of reasonable strategies and development planning, however, then no precautionary measures are available to halt the erosion of cultural and spiritual values. If this occurs then there will be few restraints upon the spread of criminal activity. . . . But crime should not be used as an excuse to halt or slow down the open-door policy or economic reform. On the contrary, it demonstrates the need for all levels of society to become involved in the fight against crime.[8]

Here we are offered a series of explanations and strategies for crime prevention which deem policing to be part of the wider fight against barbarousness and backwardness. The "problem of tradition" (namely, the problems caused by the process of overcoming the barbarous and backward) appear alongside the means of resolution (i.e., "the need for all levels of society to become involved in the fight against crime"). This method of resolution, elsewhere labeled the "mass line in policing,"[9] has the privileged role of protecting the socialist spiritual values against erosion or degradation during the process of development. So far, Zhao Xiaogang and Guo Zheng's argument shares the same grounds as those offered in the "feudal remnants debate" and in the script of the *Yellow River Elegy* insofar as they all present "reemergences" as "relic forms" and thereby inherently ascribe to them a passive, negative role. None of these works can account for either the dynamism of "relic forms" or their ambivalence. For instance, the postrevolutionary regime in China has in certain key respects reinvested in traditional dynastic mechanisms of social control to police socialism. Such a revalorization of dynastic forms of social control are not mere repetitions but "repetitions with a difference." Under this banner, "reappearances" can be discussed as something other than "returnings to," and it is at this point that one begins to ask questions about the politics of remembrance.

In Zhao Xiaogang and Guo Zhen's account, the politics of remembrance take the form of bifurcation, with tradition becoming little other than the sum total of negatives that are perceived to be hindering the economic reform program. The modern/traditional dichotomy operates as a means by which to relabel those elements identified as useful, as modern, and those perceived to be dangerous as traditional. In this way, the "mass line" becomes unambiguously modern because it helps solve problems allegedly raised by tradition. What this does, in effect, is to disallow attempts to understand technologies like the mass line as historically ambiguous (i.e., as complex and unstable combinations of both modern and traditional technologies of social control). Yet, when one looks at technologies such as the mass line in policing, it is precisely in the ambiguity of its signification process that its strength lies.

Neighborhood and village committees in every village, town, and street in socialist China are the heart of the mass line in policing, and as such, have impeccable Maoist credentials.[10] Yet Maoist techniques of mass mobilization have a lineage that radically predates Maoism and can even be traced back to the village pacts of the Ming and Qing dynasties.[11] Certainly, the moral homilies about filial piety, propriety, and so forth, outlined on the banners of the dynastic village pact meeting halls, have given way to the street blackboards and banners proclaiming socialist spiritual civilization. Nevertheless, at a purely technical level, one finds that their mode of operation and organizational form are not at all dissimilar. Similar sorts of arguments can be mounted about the household registration system through which every household in the country is a registered unit, and family members wishing to move from one jurisdictional area to another must alter their household register and get permission from the authorities. In the contemporary period, this system has been inextricably linked to the demographic demands of the central plan and still constitutes the basis for all of China's census work. Planners consider it a key technology of socialist economic organization and, as such, it is regarded as absolutely different from registration systems that operated in the dynastic period.[12] Nevertheless, there are some significant areas of overlap with the dynastic systems of registration. First, it is worth recalling that early dynastic systems of registration aimed to keep the peasants on the land or to free them only for the soldiery. Maoism was little different in this respect, and it is significant that in the Maoist period demographic policing was such that the only real alternative employment for the peasant was the army. Indeed, even in contemporary China the social implications of this system are such that at least one contemporary mainland Chinese critic has insisted that this system operates as a means by which a caste-like system of distinctions has been enacted between city and rural dwellers.[13] Nor is it simply a form of class differentiation based on location that is reinforced by this system; gender discrimination is another side effect.

In both the dynastic system and the current system of registration, the family-household unit operates as the principal unit of calculation, and it is invariably the patriarch who is responsible for the register. The maintenance of the household as the unit of calculation leads to an empowerment of the household head who registers the family and ensures that household records are accurate. It is the location of the male that continues to be the location of the family. Hence, despite the very real alterations to the system of registration in the postrevolutionary period, in some crucial respects, the legacy of the past is all too apparent. What this historical ambiguity suggests is that even the labeling of a remembrance as a particular manifestation of (a past form of) power that is "returned to" is problematic. Indeed, it suggests that it is in this very ambiguity that much of its symbolic strength as a technology lies. Thus forms that may have traditionally operated as technologies of sovereign power are often multifaceted. They can, at any one moment, within a new constellation, display a disciplinary side while, in another moment, or for another constituency, display or "return to" a sovereign form. They are, in other words, not exhausted by the singularity of their original use or role but are of value (either consciously or unconsciously) precisely because of their dynamism, ambiguity, and "instability."[14] Yet it is a dynamism, ambiguity, and "instability" that must remain hidden if such techniques are to maintain their symbolic strength. Here then lies the (Foucauldian) "positivity" and productivity of this form of ambiguity. It is this ambiguity that ensures that such technologies function as mechanisms enabling a transition from the old to the new, and that they do this by *appearing* to reinforce the same. It is therefore impossible to treat revolutionary claims as simply mythical. To read the post-1949 communist regime as just another dynasty on this basis would be erroneous, for it would fail to note the very different concerns and constituencies of these reenacted (old/new?) technologies. Contrary to both the new-dynasty thesis and the "feudal remnants" thesis, the ambiguity of such reenacted technologies is a sign of their productive capacities.

## A QUESTION OF TRADITION

Marx's *Capital* helps us explore the reasons for such ambiguity.[15] In this work, Marx discusses the structural preconditions for the emergence of the capitalist mode of production but notes that these are insufficient to bring about social transformation. Marx states:

> It is not enough that the conditions of labour are concentrated at one pole of society in the shape of capital, while at the other pole are grouped masses of men who have nothing to sell but their labour-power. Nor is it enough that they are compelled to sell themselves voluntarily. The advance of capitalist production develops a working class which by education, tradition and habit looks upon the requirements of that mode of production as self-evident natural laws. The silent compulsion of economic relations sets the seal on the domination of the capitalist over the worker. Direct extra-economic force is still of course used, but only in exceptional cases. In the ordinary run of things, the worker can be left to the "natural laws of production."[16]

In other words, Marx notes the way social change is orchestrated under the sign of nature. He explains how, to be successful, the process of transition needs to be regarded as little other than an extension of some organic or natural law. It is only in this way that capital can ensure workers' voluntary compliance and acceptance of the system. So, too, in China, the collectivism of socialism built on and constituted itself as the natural heir to the collectivism of the pastoral dynastic state. It is for this reason that one can identify a range of similarities between postrevolutionary organizations and techniques and those of the dynastic period. Many of the Maoist forms of social organization, from the mass trial through to the work unit, can be seen in this way. One should be in no doubt, however, that there have been fundamental shifts in the regimes that such technologies police and the way these operate. While one side effect of this has been to reinforce certain elements of tradition, a less well-advertised consequence has been to make possible a whole series of changes that would otherwise be inconceivable.

Neither Maoism nor China are exotic or unique in this regard. Western societies have also employed past forms and archaic techniques in a similar fashion. Walter Benjamin, in his unfinished "arcades project," found precisely these sorts of continuities in form used to introduce radically new technology into early capitalism. Benjamin noted that the new technologies of early capitalism "imitated precisely the old forms they were destined to overcome."[17] It was in this way, he suggested, that early photography mimicked realist painting, that the first railcars mimicked the stagecoach, and that the first electric lightbulbs were initially constructed in the shape of old gas lanterns. For Benjamin, the most telling mimicry of all was to be found in the form adopted in the early shopping arcades. Here, he noted that despite the new uses made of iron and glass, the architectural structure of the arcades mimicked that of the Christian cathedral and, in so doing, seemed to mock the god of heaven by installing the god of consumption.

To explain these paradoxical forms, Benjamin, too, returned to Marx, but his reference point was not *Capital* but the "Eighteenth Brumaire of Louis Bonaparte." In this essay, Marx discusses the way revolutions, "in the creation of something which does not yet exist . . . borrow their names, slogans, and costumes so as to stage the new world-historical scene in this venerable disguise and borrowed language."[18] For Benjamin, as much as for Marx, such historical restagings were not by chance but because the "revolutionary new" was unimaginable at that time, and therefore cultural memory was evoked in order to set the stage for revolution. As Marx put it succinctly, "the dead served to exalt the new struggles, rather than to parody the old."[19] Hence, new technologies would return to old forms to situate revolutionary change. Benjamin, however, goes further than Marx and suggests that this desire to be clad in the uniform of the past also emanated from a deeper psychological desire to " 'return' to a mythic dreamlike time when human beings were reconciled with the natural world."[20] These traditional dreamlike forms thereby constituted "telltale signs" of a deeper psychological desire for a return to a lost social utopia when the world was as one. In the case of Benjamin, however, this exploration of psychological desire did not lead him to attempt to uncover the unconscious, but followed "more on the track of things rather than the soul."[21] Benjamin saw his task as translating psychological desire onto the wider social and materialist map, not back to the unconscious.

At this point, the inappropriateness of Benjamin's argument may seem all too apparent. To argue that either the Maoists or the contemporary police wish to return to a mythical time of peace and harmony in the dynastic period would, of course, border on the absurd. Indeed, it is one of the hallmarks of socialism generally (the Chinese variant included) that it can (to use Marx's words) "only create its poetry from the future, not from the past."[22] Yet it would be premature and foolish to dismiss Benjamin's arguments in their entirety, for there is, as the double-sided portraits of Mao hint at, another side to this coin. There is a past that both the contemporary public security authorities and many other Chinese people do wish to revive and return to, and that is the period prior to the erosion of socialism's cultural and spiritual values.[23] At this point, it is important to recognize that the contemporary use of the mass line in policing is itself a form of mimicry. The memory evoked by reinventing mass line–style technologies in the contemporary period is not that of the dynastic past but that of the pre–Cultural Revolutionary Maoist past. Hence, the social utopia of this dream is not dynastic China but the Maoist China of the 1950s. At the same time, the mass line approach benefits by its unconscious, never stated, and possibly never known connection with the dynastic past, for it is through this that the "revolutionary" appears "natural," "normal," and obvious.

"Each period," Benjamin once exclaimed, has a "side it turns toward the dream, its infant side," and in contemporary China, that infant side is the embryonic Chinese socialist state with its widespread and enthusiastic commitment to socialism and its low crime rate.²⁴ For the Communist Party, this era forms the dream-image of a Chinese social utopia. Yet the desire to return to the 1950s is not simply nostalgia. There are policy implications associated with this kind of dreaming. In particular, the central authorities have demanded that the public security forces improve social order so that it more accurately approximates the level of social harmony allegedly enjoyed then.²⁵ The return, however, is proving highly problematic for reasons outlined in the internal police document quoted below:

> How is it possible to compare the situation today—when modernization is in full swing and when the scale, speed, and scope of change in society, politics, economics, and cultural systems is so great—with that of yesteryear? Given that the situation with regard to law and order is the result of objective environmental factors, it seems hard to imagine the likelihood of a return to the 1950s. Under the influence of such evaluation criteria, public security organs undoubtedly neglected the actual conditions and were eager to achieve success by resorting to any short-term measures, even those which ran contrary to their own interests.²⁶

As the social harmony of the pre–Cultural Revolution became the mythical goal to be aspired to, the Chinese police themselves reinvested in a hybrid form of Maoism in their attempts to return to this harmonious China of the past. Both the success of law enforcement in this early period and the partial failure and long lead-time associated with the current drive to professionalize the force have smoothed the path for this revival of the Maoist legacy. As noted above, it is more than nostalgia or superficial mimicry that has marked the return of Mao. Earlier, it was pointed out that Marx explained historical mimicry in terms of the cultural memory it evoked. In China, the memory evoked in the resurrection of mass line–style policing is one that recounts a culturally specific form of collective community will and a regime of self-policing that is disciplinary.²⁷ It is this cultural memory that still has a certain currency even in the China of economic reform. These same factors enable us to trace cultural memory back beyond the 1950s to the dynastic period. It is this collective cultural memory that is unconsciously "recalled" when mass-line mechanisms are operationalized in contemporary China. Hence, while the Party may politically "recall" such mechanisms and institutions as socialist, their real strength derives from their ability to tap into a much deeper historicocultural memory. Thus, although the socialist period and the dynastic period are radically different, the cultural referents they address and the ways they constitute the social subject, share common ground. This point is no less true of contemporary forms of mass line policing.

The current "Maoism" of the Chinese police is a very different creature from that which existed prior to economic reform; a strategic and specific form of Maoism is now in play. "Repetition with a difference" has produced a form of Maoism with a difference. It is a strategic rather than principled form; it is one largely confined to the field of social order and born of failure rather than founded on revolutionary success. The failure I am referring to is, of course, the inability of the public security forces in the period of economic reform to come to terms with crime in the ways they once could, and it is this failure that must be investigated before the specificity of the mass line renewal can be satisfactorily appreciated.

### THE DECLINING ABILITY TO CONTROL CRIME

One of the most significant side effects of economic reform has been the rapid rise in crime. Indeed, it has reached the point at which the police now define the current period as a criminal "high tide" and by far the most serious in China's postrevolutionary history.[28] In all previous "high tides," there were never more than fifty thousand serious criminal cases registered in any one year. In the current period, however, more than 100,000 serious criminal cases have been reported. Figures used in internal Public Security Ministry documents also indicate the general rise in numbers of such cases.[29] Throughout the early 1980s, on average, about sixty thousand serious cases were reported annually with few fluctuations. After 1985, the figure increased sharply, with eighty-four thousand serious cases registered that year and ninety-eight thousand cases the following year. In 1987, there was another sharp increase, bringing the total to 122,000 cases. In the first nine months of 1988, the figures for serious crime had reached 128,000 cases, thus surpassing the total number of cases registered in the previous year and doubling the number of cases registered in 1984.[30] Recent figures indicate that the upward trend is continuing. Between January and May 1990 the total number of serious criminal cases registered stood at 171,000—that was a 23.2 percent increase over the figures for 1989[31]—while the figures for 1992 show a further increase, with 1.58 million cases being registered, 450,000 of which were serious crimes.[32]

There has also been a significant demographic shift in the incidence of crime. Economic reform has resulted in a significant growth of urban sites and population. Between 1978 and 1987, the number of cities in China grew from 192 to 381, and all existing cities became much larger.[33] Between 1978 and 1988 the average annual growth rate of city populations was 16.1 percent.[34] A massive sample survey on migration patterns in the 1980s discovered that 60 to 70 percent of migrants came from rural areas. The overwhelming characteristic of this migration was the transfer of rural populations into the densely populated eastern coastal regions and the transfer of rural populations into the cities. It is estimated that between 1983 and 1988, approximately 13.5 million people moved permanently from rural regions into the cities.[35]

Further compounding the problems caused by this massive rise in the cities' permanent populations are massive increases in the numbers of temporary urban residents seeking work. All over China, this transient population has become a serious problem. By 1989 it was officially reported that the floating population had reached sixty million people, most of whom were unemployed rural laborers heading to the city in search of work.[36] This rise in the urban population more or less mirrored the rise in serious crime in urban areas.[37] In the period since 1984, the number of serious criminal cases registered in cities increased from less than one-third to just under one-half of the total number of serious criminal offenses committed, while those in rural areas dropped from 70.2 percent in 1984 to 56.9 percent in 1988. In 1984, 29.8 percent of registered serious criminal cases (amounting to twenty thousand cases) took place in the cities. Since 1985, however, the number of cases perpetrated in the cities has risen dramatically. By 1987, there were fifty thousand serious crimes committed in urban areas, and this amounted to 41.4 percent of the total. From January to September 1988, 43.1 percent of all serious cases were committed in the cities, and it was estimated that there would be more than sixty thousand serious cases in the cities that year.[38] Nor is it simply the massive increase and demographic shift in crime that is of concern to Chinese public security forces. This increase in crime comes at a time when the police are plagued by a shortage of human and material resources and by the obsolescence of their previously successful policing methods. In the short term, this crisis in policing has, if anything, reinforced the moves back to the mass line.

One of the consequences of the long-term commitment to a mass line–style in policing has been a very low ratio of police to popula-

Table 1  The Number and Nature of Public Security Personnel in 1987 and 1990

| Nature of police work | Number of personnel in 1987 | Number of personnel in 1990 | Change in number of personnel |
|---|---|---|---|
| Total number of police personnel | 1,200,000 | 1,380,000 | 180,000 (+15%) |
| Professional police officers | 600,000 | 769,000 | 169,000 (+28.2%) |
| *including:* | | | |
| Public security administration personnel | 320,000 | 307,000* | −13,000 (−4.0%) |
| Police dealing with criminal matters | 150,000 | 79,000 | −71,000 (−47.3%) |
| Other | 130,000 | 383,000 | 253,000 (+194.6%) |
| People's armed police | 600,000 | 611,000** | 11,000 (+1.8%) |

*Sources:* 1987 figures: Wang Zhongfang, 481; 1990 figures: *Law Yearbook of China—1991* [*Zhong guo falü nianjian*] (Beijing: Law Yearbook of China, 1991), 947.
*The 1990 figures are a compilation of the following two categories introduced from 1988 onward: Police involved in public order work, 150,000; Household registration police, 157,000.
**The 1990 figures for the people's armed police include the following: Fire brigade, 93,000; Border patrol, 83,000.

tion. Indeed, in terms of police to population ratios, China has one of the smallest police forces in the world, but it is a force massively augmented by volunteer labor from the mass line neighborhood committee structures.[39] While resources have gone into the ministry to increase the size of the force and the quality of the officers, the overall profile of the force and the consequent need to maintain the mass line–style of policing has changed little over recent years. Indeed, in the current climate of a rising rate of urban crime, there is every indication that the increased resources given to the police have strengthened rather than weakened this mass line approach (see table 1).

Between 1987 and 1990 there has been a 15 percent rise in the number of police in China, but these police have not been allocated evenly.[40] By far the biggest increase in personnel was registered in the miscellaneous category that covers such areas as traffic control. Here a 194 percent increase was noted and indicates an attempt to keep pace with emerging social trends. Obviously, the need for traffic police is the effect of phenomenal growth in the number of motor vehicle registrations in the period of economic reform.[41] Other areas of policing, however, have not faired quite so well, and this leads one to speculate that the police are indeed hard-pressed to cover all areas. Despite the significant growth in serious crime in recent years, there has been a substantial drop in the number of personnel allocated to the specialized departments dealing with criminal investigation (over 41 percent).[42] In light of this, it is interesting that the number of professional community police has not dropped significantly but has remained more or less static,[43] indicating their continued importance to overall policing strategies. The fact that personnel numbers have not risen, however, means that the community police are even more dependent on the mass line organizations to effect their strategies than they were previously. Thus, mass line organizations remain the bedrock on which a stable social order is maintained. Preventative policing through mass line methods to control "key areas" is still very much the basis of the system. As the police theorist Lu Zhiqing points out:

> Over a long period of time, public security organs have emphasized prevention of crimes through the control of key areas. The concept of controlling key areas means, in practice, the prevention and control of illegal and criminal activities through the control of people (people known to be harmful to society), sites (places known to be frequented by people engaged in illegal and criminal activities), and targets (targets known to be vulnerable to harm by illegal activities).[44]

Lu goes on to argue that while the control of people, sites, and targets continues to be the basis of Chinese policing, it has been seriously eroded by the massive influx of population into the cities and the erosion of traditional institutions. Nevertheless, despite limited resources, the police have continued to rely on this method. What one discovers, then, is that the police have opted for "reform" and have adopted "special measures" to deal with their new-found problems rather than radically reconstituting the regime of policing.[45] They deploy the mass line in a much more selective way than in the past and for very definite ends and with a very specific community in mind. One finds, for example, greater effort invested in revamping the mass line organizations in the cities rather than those in the countryside, and, similarly, one finds certain groups and crimes targeted for more mass line attention than others.

Revamping the mass line in the urban areas required legislatively strengthening the role and power of the neighborhood committees, the local security committees, and the small groups.[46] Additionally, effort has been directed into keeping the urban security committees active.[47] Hence, while nationwide figures indicate that both the number of functioning committees and the participation rates within these committees have remained more or less static over the past few years, this masks a significant increase in committee numbers and participation rates in urban areas and their corresponding decline in rural areas (see tables 2 and 3). In this respect, the targeting of "key sites" has led to an emphasis on urban mass line policing.

If targeting key sites can be said to have led to a concentration of police resources in urban areas, targeting key people has led to "special measures" for groups that figure prominently in the crime figures. Three groups targeted by "special measures" are juveniles, the "special population," and transient criminals. Each "special measure" is, in its own way, an extension of the philosophy of mass line policing, and all bear the "birthmarks" of Maoism. Special measures were long used by Mao to deal with political opponents. In the period of economic reform, however, they have drifted into their current, less overtly political role. Nevertheless, as will be clear from below, they are still very much concerned with crimes of the mind and with transformation.

Possibly the most obvious mass line–based, "Maoist" new measure is the one which is neither an administrative nor a criminal sanction but a program of political and ideological education for those "in need" of such (re)training.[48] This program, instituted to deal with youths who are in some sort of "moral danger" or who have committed very minor crimes, is termed "social help and education," and it is deemed to be "a new form of and new invention in mass line participation."[49] Mass line organizations are advised to liaise with other units so that an all-round program of social help and education can be instituted to reform such youths in their own communities. While social help and education takes no single form, it invariably turns on notions of reintegrative shaming and constant surveillance and, as such, it has proven to be a useful model by which to police groups other than juveniles. A new and more draconian form of social help and education has, for example, been devised to reintegrate paroled prisoners from the reeducation through labor institutions.[50] Most significant of all,

Table 2  Figures on the Public Security Committees in 1986 and 1989

|  | Total number | Internal* | City and town | Village |
|---|---|---|---|---|
| *Committees* | | | | |
| 1986 | 1,174,456 | 291,548 | 154,084 | 728,824 |
| 1989 | 1,175,510 | 309,366 | 170,525 | 695,619 |
| gain or loss over time | +1,054 | +17,818 | +16,414 | −33,205 |
| percent change | +0.9 | +5.9 | +10.6 | −4.5 |
| *Personnel* | | | | |
| 1986 | 5,305,447 | 1,580,426 | 858,943 | 2,866,078 |
| 1989 | 5,182,573 | 1,574,887 | 951,519 | 2,656,167 |
| gain or loss over time | −122,874 | −5,539 | +92,576 | −209,911 |
| percent change | −2.3 | −3.5 | +10.8 | −7.3 |
| *Number of retired cadres involved in this work* | | | | |
| 1986 | 328,002 | 44,298 | 248,967 | 34,737 |
| As percent of all participants | 6 | 2.8 | 29 | 1.2 |
| 1989 | 416,438 | 69,112 | 301,109 | 46,136 |
| As percent of all participants | 8 | 4.4 | 31.7 | 1.7 |

*Sources:* Wang Zhongfang, 485; *Law Yearbook of China—1991*, 947.
*Internal, in this case, means internal to the enterprise or work unit.

however, have been the draconian adaptations of certain elements of this program in dealing with what are described by the police as the "special population."

In March 1985 the Ministry of Public Security issued internal *Regulations on Management Work for the Special Population*.[51] These regulations highlighted six categories of "suspects" who were to be carefully policed by local-level public security units and by all local mass line organizations.[52] A variety of measures could be used to police this suspect community and, though the measures recommended included help and education and "legally based surveillance," they also included "secret forms of surveillance." Irrespective of any other measures taken, all those categorized as part of the special population had

Table 3  Figures on the Public Security Small Groups in 1986 and 1989

| | Total number | Internal* | City and town | Village |
|---|---|---|---|---|
| *Committees* | | | | |
| 1986 | 3,049,759 | 407,763 | 394,300 | 2,247,696 |
| 1989 | 2,486,914 | 394,199 | 474,849 | 1,617,866 |
| gain or loss over time | −562,845 | −13,564 | +80,549 | −629,830 |
| percent change | −18.4 | −3.3 | +20.4 | −28 |
| *Personnel* | | | | |
| 1986 | 6,743,436 | 1,312,576 | 1,083,385 | 4,347,475 |
| 1989 | 6,586,563 | 1,344,700 | 1,291,364 | 3,950,499 |
| gain or loss over time | −156,873 | +32,124 | +207,979 | −396,976 |
| percent change | −2.3 | +2.4 | +19.1 | −9.1 |
| *Number of retired cadres involved in this work* | | | | |
| 1986 | 444,979 | 45,195 | 359,985 | 39,799 |
| As percent of all participants | 6.6 | 3.4 | 33.2 | 0.9 |
| 1989 | 592,309 | 82,152 | 450,922 | 59,235 |
| As percent of all participants | 9 | 6.1 | 34.9 | 1.5 |

*Sources:* Wang Zhongfang, 485; *Law Yearbook of China—1991,* 947.
*Internal, in this case, means internal to the enterprise or work unit.

their right of movement withdrawn and special files opened on them to enable the monitoring of their activities.[53] While social help and education utilized the mass organizations and categorization of persons to establish a regime of reintegrative shaming, the management of the special population used the same organizations and similar regimes of classification to survey and control. Here, then, are the two sides of the same mass line Maoist coin, one reintegrative, the other highly coercive. Here is where a wedding of disciplinary power to more overtly coercive forms occurs and where, because such power is "unstable"— one form mutating into others—police are able to respond "flexibly." This ensures that offenders are instilled with a fear that worse can come if they do not mend their ways.

Although the above two cases constitute some of the "special measures" adopted in relation to the stable population, other more ad hoc measures have been instituted to deal with suspects deemed less stable. Special methods now allow police to detain for investigation suspects who are transients and people deemed likely to flee. To expedite cases involving transients who may hide their identities and residences, "special measures" are now available. The 1961 administrative regulations dealing with detention and investigation were revived and augmented by new measures passed in 1980 and 1985.[54] Similar to the measures adopted for the "special population," particular types of suspects have been targeted for this special treatment.[55] The targeting of this group however, has not been accompanied by disciplinary or even semiotechnical methods of retraining. Rather, very different forms of power are now in evidence. Financial limitations, loose controls over detention periods, and a reliance on local authorities have all colluded to produce an institution that has, in recent years, been characterized by a certain largesse in the way power is deployed.[56]

Indeed, in some ways, the largesse of this special form of detention works in conjunction with the general crackdowns and campaigns against certain types of crime. As one recent assessment concludes:

> Currently, the public security situation is grim. Various kinds of sudden emergencies and serious disturbances are contributing to instability. Thus, those to be detained for investigation should not be confined to suspected transient criminals. . . . It will be self-defeating and restricting the role public security organs can play in the struggle against crimes if the criteria of detention are too strict and few people can be detained for investigation.[57]

### MAOISM WITH A DIFFERENCE: THE CAMPAIGNS

If the targeting of people and places has brought back Maoist mass line measures that have, in turn, reinforced a style of arbitrary policing and detention, it is in the area of the targeting of particular types of crime that one discovers the most obvious reemergence and mimicry of the political forms of Maoism. Nowhere is this revitalized "Maoism with a difference" more in evidence than in relation to what one group of Chinese police scholars has described as the "campaign theory" (*yundong lun*) of policing.[58] This style of policing mimics the campaign style of politics that was the hallmark of Maoism.[59] Contemporary police campaigns in China utilize a sort of rhythm method similar to those that became the political hallmark of Maoism. Whereas Mao saw certain types of political deviation as warranting a campaign to purge these elements from the ranks of the people, the police campaign against certain types of criminal activities. The best example of this type of policing in recent years has been the 1983 "serious strike" anticrime campaign. This targeted street crime and led to sentences on the target crimes being massively increased and the rights of defense and appeal being significantly limited. This policing technology yielded results that were as mixed as those of the Maoist era. The types of crimes targeted were reduced significantly for a while, but once the pressure was off, they quickly reemerged and soon rose back to their old levels.

While there are many commonalities between these two forms of campaigning, one must be wary of drawing too close an analogy. Unlike the Maoist campaigns of old, current police campaigns against crime are far more punitive than transformational. The Maoist campaigns of the 1960s and 1970s were all disciplinary (in a postmodern sense) insofar as they were predicated on the idea that they would, like the Cultural Revolution, "touch the people to their very souls" and transform them into new socialist persons. The Maoist campaigns of old offered a methodology of social transformation. By comparison, even the most extensive of the policing campaigns launched in the post-1979 economic reform period have been overtly punitive and semiotechnical. In the current period campaigns have been launched not to revolutionize and mobilize the populace but to teach them that "crime does not pay." The idea is not to transform but to frighten. Nowhere is this better exemplified than in the handbooks of the judicial workers, where we are told that the use of mass trials in such campaigns is designed to "frighten the criminal, encourage healthy trends, give publicity to the legal system, and educate the masses."[60] There is little by way of transformation offered here. Indeed, the transformation of the offender is now stated to be the specialized task of others.[61]

What was once a principled technology of Maoism is now a strategically deployed device of policing. A technology that once made somewhat grandiose claims about reinforcing the mass line in legal work now constitutes little other than a formal shell through which the masses are "educated" and frightened. As we have seen, this "formal shell" still has effects on the way places, people, and target crimes are policed, but it would be quite wrong to see such methods as simply a return to Mao. What can be said, though, is that all of the measures that have been adopted to police certain people, places, and crimes have radically altered the basis of the mass line, yet have all done so under the sign of Mao. Here, one can see the way in which "the new" cannot be conceptualized and how even innovations are thought of only in terms of old Maoist ways. At this point it is useful to recall Marx's words from the "eighteenth Brumaire," where he notes that the reliance on great historical events of the past to represent revolutionary events of the day is not the conscious act of a clever and confident new ruling class, but an expression of their lack of imagination and their inability to conceptualize the new in anything other than historical terms. This whole process, Marx claims, can be equated with learning a new language:

> The beginner who has learned a new language always retranslates it into his mother tongue: he can only be said to have appropriated the spirit of the new language and to be able to express himself in it freely when he can manipulate it without reference to the old, and when he forgets his original language while using the new one.[62]

The contemporary Chinese police, no matter how hard they try to learn the new language of reform, are forever forced back to their mother tongue of Maoism by their own lack of imagination and by the pragmatic necessity to "make ends meet." While this new pressure may lead them to look for innovative redeployments of old technologies, the redeployment of campaign-style policing and the mass line cannot be seen as purely pragmatic. If one were to examine the new "problem crimes" policed by the campaigns, for example, one would quickly discover that they have generally proven to be anything but a clear-cut success.[63] It is also obvious that many of the other "special measures" have been no less problematic. The return to Mao is not purely pragmatic but also inextricably linked to the inability of the police to think outside of Mao. In this respect there is a strange parallel that can be drawn between the lack of imagination of the Chinese police and the obsessions of the Chinese dissident. Both, in their own ways, are burdened by the memory of their mother tongue.

Zhang Hongtu, an avant-garde Chinese artist (formally of the Central Art Academy in Beijing and now a resident of New York) has become famous for his redrawings of Mao portraits and posters. Through Zhang's work, Mao has been metamorphosed at one time into Jesus and his disciples at the last supper, at another, into a Chinese Joseph Stalin. The one constant in all Zhang's paintings is the figure of Chairman Mao. When asked why he constantly redraws the Great Helmsman, Zhang's answer was supremely simple:

> The Mao image has a charisma of its own. It's still so powerful that the first time I cut up an official portrait of Mao for a collage I felt a pang of guilt, something gnawing away inside me. Other people, in particular other Chinese, may well feel the same. As long as this "power to intimidate" exists, I will continue to do Mao.[64]

The Chinese police, in a sense, will continue to "do Mao" because for them, there is also something of the charisma, something of the power, and something "gnawing away inside." The difference between Zhang and the Chinese police, however, is that it is the police, and not Zhang, who now hold the power to intimidate.

This paper ends as it began, with the image(s) of Mao and the power of the portrait. It began with the Mao of the taxi drivers and ended with the Mao of the dissident. Those two images offer physical and highly visible reminders of the power of Mao. The clues to the continued and embedded influence of Mao in China, however, lie in less visible evidence and indeed require much more detective work if a case is to be mounted. It has been a central concern of this paper to furnish such evidence. The paper has pointed to the continued use of Mao-inspired notions of mass line policing, of administrative sanction, and of campaign-style police work. At the same time, it has been suggested that such technologies and organs have been significantly modified so that they fulfill the demands of policing in the China of economic reform. Such borrowing and modification has been labeled "repetition with a difference" and this offered the appearance of naturalness to a process of change. Maoism drew from, and drew away from, dynastically produced mechanisms and technologies just as the current regime reenacts, with modification, the political technologies of Mao. In this respect, technologies of power are not exhausted by the singularity of their use or by their original use-form. The vibrancy of these technologies lies in their flexibility. It is at this point that the arguments of Chinese scholars, who suggest such "presences" constitute the problem of feudal remnants, is critiqued. Such mechanisms are not archaic insofar as they play and continue to play a dynamic role in society. Nevertheless, they impose historically and culturally specific limitations on the imagination. The deployment of these technologies in contemporary China offers a means for examining the multilayered way power is exercised. While acknowledging the Foucauldian point that power is relational, this paper also suggests that these relations of power, as evidenced through such technologies of power as the campaign, the mass line in policing, and so forth, are often a complex mix of various forms of power that are flexible—and again—not exhausted by any original singularity of use. The disciplinary campaigns of Mao that are currently operationalized as coercive mechanisms offer a good example of what is meant here. The flexibility of these technologies came from the fact that such a capacity to transform themselves was always inscribed within them. Such technologies were never purely disciplinary, for such purity offers little other than a disciplinary "blockade." In this respect, at least, the positivity of power lies in its ability to operate in a plurality of registers for different times, different constituencies, and different operations. Moreover, it is in relation to which of these many faces of power will come to dominate that the space for a reinscription of the notion of struggle into the lexicon of power becomes possible. But to pursue this would lead on to another, very different story.

NOTES

I would like to thank Deborah Kessler, Kaz Ross, Elaine Jeffreys, and Rob McQueen for advice and help on earlier draft, and also the anonymous reviewers whose recommendations provided the basis for the final revision of this article. I would also like to thank the Australian Research Council for their generous assistance. Last, I would like to express my appreciation to Peter Williams, who helped me coin the term I use to explain the various ways in which "history" resurfaced to inform contemporary discourse.

1 Cui Jian is undoubtedly the most significant "rock" star to have emerged in China but is also a politically sensitive figure for the socialist regime. With songs such as the "New Long March Rock and Roll," and album covers featuring Cui Jian wearing a red blindfold, it is hard to see how the Party could not regard him with some concern. Although his songs often lyrically praise the Party and its history, such praise is undercut by the fact that they also suggest less than flattering comparisons with the present Party line. His performances, album covers, and songs, then, are often designed rather deliberately to taunt the Party, for there is quite a lot of commercial benefit to be gained from being the bad boy of Chinese rock and roll. For the young of Beijing, at least, Cui Jian has become something of a cultural icon.

2 In raising this idea of repetition with a difference I am extrapolating on one of the main themes of my book, which plots the transition from dynastic patriarchal power in China to a China that alleges to be "of the people"

(see Michael R. Dutton, *Policing and Punishment in China: From Patriarchy to "the People"* [Cambridge: Cambridge University Press, 1992]). In many respects, this paper is an attempt to tease out and extend certain implications of this more substantial work, and, as a result, the focus of attention has shifted. Thus, though the book engages with the work of Foucault and power, it does so to question the centrality of individuation in the formation of disciplinary power. This paper again engages with Foucauldian notions of power but, as one will very shortly discover, to very different ends.

3 Said's reading of Foucault and power offers a good example of this (see Edward W. Said, "Foucault and the Imagination of Power," in *Foucault: A Critical Reader,* ed. David Couzens Hoy [Oxford: Basil Blackwell, 1986], 151).

4 Michel Foucault, "Questions of Method: An Interview with Michel Foucault," *I and C: Power and Desire* 8 (spring 1981): 5.

5 A discussion of the idea of the "disciplinary blockade" is given in Michel Foucault, *Discipline and Punish: The Birth of the Prison* (London: Peregrine Books, 1986), 195–210.

6 *Yellow River Elegy* was first screened on 14 June 1988 to an estimated viewing audience of 70 million people. It was rescreened a month later, allegedly at the behest of Zhao Ziyang. According to China Central Television statistics, over 200 million people saw the series altogether. After the 4 June 1989 massacre, the series was roundly condemned by the Communist Party leadership. For excerpts from the *Yellow River Elegy* in English and later critiques, see *New Ghosts and Old Dreams: Chinese Rebel Voices,* ed. Geremie Barmé and Linda Jaivine (New York: Times Books, 1992), 138–164.

7 For a more detailed elaboration of Su Shaozhi's work, see Dutton, *Policing and Punishment,* chap. 1.

8 Zhao Xiaogang and Guo Zheng, "Chengshi fazhan yu fanzui" [The development of the city and crime], *Gong'an yanjiu* [Police research] 4 (1988): 31–37.

9 For further details on the mass line in policing, see *Gong'anxue gailun* [An outline of police studies] (China People's Public Security University Press, 1985), 85–98.

10 For an argument that offers "confirmation" of these Maoist revolutionary credentials, see James Brady, *Justice and Politics in People's China* (London: Academic, 1982).

11 The security sections of these contemporary local committees often utilize the concept of the pact as a technique by which to maintain law and order. The term *pact* was precisely the designation given to them in traditional times. See Sun Bingzhu, "Jumin weiyuanhui, cunmin weiyuanhui de xingzhi, dewei he zuoyong" [The role, status, and character of residents' committees and village committees] *Zhongguo zhengfa daxue* [The journal of the Chinese University of Political Science and Law] 2 (1983): 84.

12 For an orthodox rendition of this position see Zhang Qingwu, "Basic Facts on the Household Registration System," *Chinese Economic Studies* 22, no. 1 (fall 1988); rpt., New York: M. E. Sharpe (ed. and trans. Michael Dutton).

13 It is argued by at least one contemporary Chinese scholar that this has meant that the system has become a castelike system in the current period, with peasants forced to stay in poor conditions on the land while city dwellers enjoy the benefits of modern life. See Gong Xikui, "Zhongguo xian xing huji zhidu xiushi" [One perspective on the current household registration system in China], *Shehui kexue* [Social science] (1989): 32–36.

14 Here I am drawing on an idea outlined by John Macarthur in a very different context in his work on postmodernism and architecture (see John Macarthur, "Foucault, Tafuri, Utopia," [master's thesis, University of Queensland, 1983]).

15 I have explored this in more detail elsewhere (see Dutton, *Policing and Punishment,* 228–229).

16 Karl Marx, *Capital,* vol. 1 (London: Penguin Books, 1976 ), 899.

17 Susan Buck-Morss, *The Dialectics of Seeing: Walter Benjamin and the Arcades Project,* (Cambridge: MIT Press, 1991), 111.

18 Karl Marx, "The Eighteenth Brumaire of Louis Bonaparte," in *Surveys from Exile: Political Writings Volume 2,* ed. and trans. David Furnbach (Middlesex, England: Penguin, 1973), 147.

19 Ibid., 148.

20 Buck-Morss, *Dialectics of Seeing,* 114.

21 Walter Benjamin quoted in Winifried Menninghaus, "Walter Benjamin's Theory of Myth," in *On Walter Benjamin: Critical Essays and Recollections,* ed. Gary Smith (Cambridge: MIT Press, 1991) 302.

22 Marx, "Eighteenth Brumaire", 149.

23 As one researcher from the Chinese People's Public Security University recently noted, the memory of the 1950s is cherished because it is thought of as a time when "doors could be left unlocked at night and even valuables on the ground would not be taken." See Wang Yong, *Zhongguo jingli wenti yanjiu* [Research on police force in China], paper presented at the Beijing International Police Science Research Conference, Beijing, 7–11 November 1993.

24 Walter Benjamin, quoted in Rolf Tiedemann, "Dialectics at a Standstill," in Smith, *On Walter Benjamin,* 269.

25 Huang Jingping, Li Tianfu, and Wang Zhimin, "Gong'an guanli xiankuang" [The situation with regard public security management], *Gong'an yanjiu* [Police research] 4 (1988): 6–7.

26 Ibid., 6.

27 Some may object to the ascription of this as "disciplinary" (in the Foucauldian sense) insofar as it is far from individuating. As noted earlier, however, I have suggested elsewhere that collectivity does not rule out certain forms of social specification and observation. Indeed, in certain instances,

it can even enhance it. For further details see Dutton, *Policing and Punishment*, esp. 291–324. See also Michael Dutton, "Disciplinary Projects and Carceral Spread: Foucauldian Theory and Chinese Practice," *Economy and Society* 21, no. 3 (August 1992): 276–294.

28 There have been four "high tides" since 1949. The initial postrevolutionary period (1949), the "period of temporary difficulty" after the Great Leap Forward (1958–1962), the Cultural Revolution period (1966–1976), and the current period. See "Dangdai woguo xingshi fanzui de jiben tedian" [The basic character of crime in contemporary China], in *Zhongguo xianjieduan fanzui wenti yanjiu, di vi ji* [Research into crime in the current period in China, vol. 1] (Beijing: Chinese People's Public Security University Press, 1989), 40. This is an internal report prepared by the Ministry of Public Security Research Unit Number Five.

29 The importance of internal statistics in relation to this article does not derive from any claims that they are somehow closer to "truth." The argument presented here does not require a belief in the veracity of statistics offered but in an allied point which is that they are believed in and/or used by strategists within the Public Security Bureau. Hence the importance of the "internal" tag.

30 Ibid., 40–41.

31 See Wang Fang, "Guanyu dangqian gong'an gongzuo he shehui zhi'an qingkuang" [Concerning current public security work and the law and order situation (A report to the Fourteenth Session of the Seventh Standing Committee of the People's Congress, 25 June 1990]), in *Zhongguo falü nianjian—1991 nian* [The Chinese law yearbook—1991] (Beijing: Chinese Law Yearbook Publishing House, 1991), 742. Elsewhere in the volume, it notes that four types of crime account for 446,775 of these most serious cases. The four types of crime are murder, armed robbery, rape, and serious theft (ibid., 942.)

32 Zhang Weihang, "An Overview of Criminal Offences in Present-day China," paper presented at the Beijing International Police Science Research Conference, Beijing, 7–11 November 1993.

33 Cities are defined as those places with a high-density residential population of one hundred thousand people or more (see Zhang Qingwu, "Basic Facts on the Household Registration System," 75). This growth was also accompanied by a growth in the cities themselves. The number of cities that boasted a population of over one million grew from 13 in 1978 to 25 in 1987, those with populations of between half a million and one million grew from 27 to 30 in the same period, and those with populations which were more than two hundred thousand but less than half a million grew from 60 to 103. All figures are drawn from *Zhongguo chengshi tongji nianjian* [Chinese cities statistical yearbook], quoted in Zhao and Guo, "Chengshi fazhan yu fanzui," 31–32.

34 The proportion of urban residents in China has increased from 14.4 per-

cent in 1982 to 19 percent in 1987, according to "The Basic Character of Crime in Contemporary China," 42.

35 The survey from which this information was drawn covered 1 percent of China's total population and was quoted in Zhao and Guo "Chengshi fazhan yu fanzui," 33.

36 Dutton, *Policing and Punishment,* 333. For a more detailed account of the rise of the "floating population" see ibid., 325–340.

37 The correlation between crime and immigrant populations in China has been noted by a number of scholars and a number of studies. In Beijing, for example, each passing year has seen an increased percentage of crime committed by immigrants. By 1987, 32 percent of all those incarcerated for a crime by Beijing authorities were nonlocals and 18.6 percent of all new arrests were transients. By 1988, this latter figure had risen to 24.6 percent. See Yang Wenzhong and Wang Gongfan, "Liudong renkou dui shehuizhe'an de yingxiang" [The influence of the floating population upon social order], *Gong'an yanjiu* [Police research] 2 (1989): 52–53.

38 "The Basic Character of Crime in Contemporary China," 43.

39 In 1985, China had 6.03 police for every ten thousand people (Wang Zhongfang) and, though this has risen to 6.5 per ten thousand more recently (Zhang Zhaoduan), it is still very low by world standards. It is a low figure irrespective of whether we compare it with advanced capitalist countries (some comparisons are Japan [21.2], the United States [21.7], France [34], and Austria [40] ), other developing states (India [16.6], Pakistan [10.9]), or even former and existing socialist states (North Korea [14.8], the former Soviet Union in 1986 [12], the former D.D.R. in 1984 [33.6]). See Wang Zhongfang, *Zhongguo shehui zhi'an zonghe zhili de lilun yu shixian* [Theory and practice of comprehensive management of public order in China] (Masses Press, 1989), 486–877; For more recent figures see Zhang Zhaoduan, *Lun woguo jingcha xiandaihua fazhan zhanlue* [The development strategy for the modernization of China's police], paper presented at the Beijing International Police Science Research Conference, Beijing, 7–11 November 1993.

40 Despite the slight increase in the police to people ratio noted above, it is worth mentioning that the ratio of police to people in the city is actually slightly worse than the national average. In the city there are only six police per ten thousand people. See Wu Heping, *Zhongdeng chengshi gong'an zhihui zhongxin de jianshe yu zuoyong* [The construction and function of public security command centres in medium-sized cities], paper presented at the Beijing International Police Science Research Conference, Beijing, 7–11 November, 1993.

41 To use Beijing as an example, private vehicle ownership has risen from just 545 vehicles in 1984 to 25,151 in 1989. Moreover, the rate of purchase is also increasing dramatically with over eleven thousand of these cars being

bought between 1988 and 1989. For a full breakdown and analysis of these figures see Ren Yuxing, "Shilun siren qiche de fazhan ji duice" [Outlining the development of private vehicle ownership and some countermeasures] *Gong'an yanjiu* [Police research] 3 (1990): 15–17.

42 In the city of Kaifeng, for example, police caseloads have increased tenfold in the ten-year period from 1982 through to 1992 and the ratio of police to cases has increased sevenfold: From 0.8 to 1 in 1982, to 5.6 to 1 in 1992 (Wu, "The Construction and Function of Public Security Command Centers in Medium-Sized Cities").

43 A 4 percent drop in the number of community police was indicated in Table 1, but this drop may be more the result of changes in methods of categorization than actual decreases in personnel. Unlike the category "police dealing with criminal matters," which has remained constant throughout this period, the category for "administrative personnel" has been further divided in recent years. Since 1989, the yearbooks have abandoned this category and divided the remaining police into "police involved in public order work" and "household registration police." An amalgam of these two categories has been used in this paper to estimate police numbers in the administrative field. For further details see the two yearbooks in question. For the 1987 undifferentiated figures see *Zhongguo falü nianjian—1988 nian* [Law yearbook of China—1988] (Beijing: Law Publishing House, 1989), 824. For the new methods of categorization see *Zhonguo falü nianjian—1989 nian* [Law yearbook of China—1989] (Beijing: Law Publishing House, 1990), 1091.

44 Lu Zhiqiang, "Shehuikongzhi yu jianli xunjing zhidu" [Social control and the establishment of a system of police patrols], *Gong'an yanjiu* [Police research] 1 (1989) 55.

45 Ibid., 56.

46 Measures specifically designed to strengthen the role of the urban neighborhood committees in public security work and in educating the young were brought in on 29 August 1989 by the Standing Committee of the Seventh National People's Congress. See "NPC Standing Committee Brings New Measures," *Beijing Review* 32 (11–17 September 1989): 4–5.

47 It is probably important here to note the radical shifts in discourse that have been effected under the banner of reforming the mass line. In community policing the political metaphors of the Maoist past have tended to give way to the economic ones of Deng Xiaoping. The mass-line organs in the cities have been strengthened through the importation of the reform ideas first explored in the agricultural sector and then later in industry. Thus, as with any other enterprise, local level police units and neighborhood security committees are to be reformed so that they maximize efficiency through a material-reward system. All such organs are currently experimenting with various forms of "contract" and all operate under an economically driven

"responsibility system." It is beyond the scope of this article to detail the problems associated with this form of "economism," but it goes without saying that such importations have not been unproblematic. For a detailed outline of the various methods attempted and details of these reforms see Xu Hanmin, *Renmin zhi'an 40 nian* [Forty years of people's public security] (Beijing: Police Officer Educational Publishing House, 1992), 148ff.

48 There are eight categories of youth said to be in need of social help and education. These are: (a) those who have committed petty thefts; (b) those who have committed minor sexual offenses; (c) those who have committed weapons offenses; (d) those who have been involved in minor property crimes; (e) those who committed minor legal offenses at work; (f) those who take notice of reactionary propaganda; (g) those who have "relapsed" since they were released from some form of detention; (h) those who have committed other minor offenses. For further details see Shao Dao-sheng, *Zhongguo qingshaonian fanzui de shehuixue sikao* [Considerations on the sociology of youth crime in China] (Beijing: Social Science Literature, 1987), 196–197.

49 "Social help and education" is defined as the mobilization of "sectors of society to educate youth who have committed minor offenses in order to help them correct their mistakes and to encourage them to embark on a path of healthy development" (ibid., 196).

50 For further details on the selection of candidates for this program and how it is instituted in this case see ibid, 199–206.

51 For further details, see Deng Zhaoren, Yang Weixin, and Zhao Fengcan, *Chengxiang gong'an paichusuo yewu zhishi wenda* [Questions and answers on the professional knowledge relating to police stations in city and country areas] (Beijing: Masses, 1987), 26.

52 Yu Lei, "Zhongdian renkou zhi'an guanli" [The management of security of the special population], in *Zhi'an xingzheng guanli* [The study of public security management] (Beijing: Chinese People's Public Security University Press, 1987), 90.

53 Deng et al., *Questions and Answers,* 30.

54 The additional documents stipulating what kinds of people are to be detained for investigative detention are document 80, number 56, of the State Council and document 85, number 50, of the Public Security Ministry, both of which are quoted in Li Kangrui, Xu Deyong, Zhou Jingnan, and Mao Tongkun, "Shilun shourong shencha lifa de jige wenti" [Legislative problems of detaining suspects for investigation], *Gong'an yanjiu* [Police research] 2 (1989): 61–64.

55 There are five categories of people designated as warranting this special type of investigative detention. These are: (a) those who are suspected of committing crimes in many places, or who have committed crimes and conceal their true names and addresses and their background; (b) leading

members of vicious criminal gangs who need to be brought to justice or sentenced to reeducation through labor, but whose cases are so complex that not all the facts are known and insufficient evidence has been gathered against them; (c) suspected ring-leaders of mob violence, rioting, and serious incidents of assault, vandalism, and looting; (d) those who demand an audience with higher authorities to air their grievances in times of important activities of the state; (e) unreformed elements released from reform through labor and reeducation through labor who are likely to commit crimes again. For further details on each of these categories, see ibid., 64.

56 The study quoted above notes that in some places a "cavalier" attitude has developed in relation to the detention of people under these regulations. In some places, over twenty categories of suspects have been liable for detention, not five. In other cases detention has lasted for years rather than months. An investigation undertaken in Hunan Province into investigative detention revealed that only 30 percent of detainees deserved to be held. Moreover, there are cases of people simply being detained and not "investigated." The study found that in some cases, the suspects had been locked up for up to five years (see ibid., 61; 64).

57 Ibid., 62.

58 That is, the utilization of short, sharp campaigns against particular forms of crimes defined as "problem crimes." Huang Jioping, Li Tianfu, and Wang Zhimin, 6.

59 This campaign style of politics is close to the flux and reflux view of history central to traditional Chinese doctrine. This apparent similarity has led to accusations that Mao's worldview was closer to the Buddhist and Taoist one than it was to one inspired and informed by Marxist dialectics. See *Mao Tse-tung Unrehearsed; Talks and Letters: 1956–71*, ed. Stuart Schram (Middlesex, England: Penguin Books, 1974) 26.

60 *Jiancha yewu wenti* [Questions and answers on the professional work of the procuraturate] (Beijing: Law Publishing House, 1986), 28.

61 I am referring here, of course, to the judicial organs of reform through labor and reeducation through labor.

62 Marx, "Eighteenth Brumaire," 147.

63 Studies undertaken suggest that although campaigns affect target crimes for a short while, the crimes soon reemerge once the campaign is over. Moreover, the amount of resources needed to target a crime means that less glamorous but nonetheless necessary forms of policing are neglected (see Huang, Li, and Wang, "The Situation with Regard to Public Security Management"). For figures indicating the possibility of a long-term failure in the campaign-style policing strategy, see "The Basic Character of Crime in Contemporary China," 40–55. In suggesting failure on the basis of these figures, though, some caution should be exercised. Even if one were to assume that such figures were accurate, it should be pointed out that they do

not tell the whole story, for campaigns utilize administrative sanctions at least as much as the criminal code. The figures in this area are extremely unreliable and are also all classified. Without a thorough investigation of these latter figures, then, any suggestion of failure or success has to be treated with caution.

64 Quoted in Barmé and Jaivine, *New Ghosts and Old Dreams*, xxvi.

# Constructing Perry's "Chinaman" in

# the Context of Adorno and Benjamin

The historical materialist must sacrifice the epic dimension of history. The past for him becomes the subject of a construction whose locus is not empty time, but the particular epoch, the particular life, the particular work. He breaks the epoch away from its reified *historical continuity*, and the life from the epoch, and the work from the life's work. But the result of his construction is that *in* the work the life's work, *in* the life's work the epoch, and *in* the epoch the course of history are suspended and preserved.

—Walter Benjamin, "Eduard Fuchs, Collector and Historian"

Knowledge can only widen horizons by abiding so insistently in the particular that its isolation is dispelled. This admittedly presupposes a relation to the general, though not one of subsumption, but rather almost the reverse. Dialectical mediation is not a recourse to the more abstract, but a process of resolution of the concrete in itself.

—Theodor Adorno, *Minima Moralia*

■ On the second of the two voyages that marked Commodore Matthew C. Perry's expedition to Japan (1853–54), official interpreter Samuel Wells Williams was accompanied by, in the words of the U.S. government congressional report, "a very intelligent and educated Chinaman."[1] An English translation of the journal kept by this "Chinese native" during the visit to Japan was appended to the official report, as "a specimen of the intelligence . . . and . . . the views of an

Oriental, uninfluenced by the prevalent opinions of our countrymen around him."[2] Like the other geological and botanical specimens collected on the voyage,[3] the Chinaman's account was an object of scientific inquiry, and was offered with an orientalist enthusiasm for local color as a footnote to the successful expansion of U.S. naval power, scientific knowledge, and commercial interests.

Further references to this Chinese individual, including a surname, "Lo," have long been available in two accounts of the expedition: the personal diary of Williams;[4] and the later reconstruction by Oliver Statler, whose references to Lo are all based on Williams's diary.[5] Only in 1983 did scholars obtain the name Luo Sen,[6] when Beijing University historian Wang Xiaoqiu reprinted Luo's Chinese diary of the expedition, the one on which the English "translation" was based.[7] Aside from Luo Sen's emergence into the historical record during the year 1854, no other traces of him have been found.[8] Wang guesses that he was an English-speaking Cantonese member of the foreign missionary community in Hong Kong,[9] but Perry admits to being unable to "interchange thought" with the Chinaman because of differences of language.[10] The English version of Luo's diary includes a statement referring to his patriotic "devotion and efforts" in "the [Opium] war with the English," in spite of which he was "neglected" by Chinese officials, but this has not yet been verified, and it is not included in the Chinese version.[11]

Historians wanting to reconstruct Luo Sen's participation in the voyage, to tell "how it happened," would be hard pressed to arrive at a biographical identity for him—as the work of Wang Xiaoqiu demonstrates. There is simply not enough information, and consequently, the historiographical desire for *resolution* of the particulars of Luo's participation cannot be satisfied. For example, we are told in the few available accounts of Luo that he served as Williams's "teacher,"[12] or as his "clerk";[13] yet Luo describes himself as Williams's "friend."[14] Wang overlooks these inconsistent descriptions of Luo altogether, admitting only that Luo accompanied the mission. By contrast, Oliver Statler's dispersed references to Luo in *Shimoda Story* produce a composite portrait of Williams's comrade as loyal translator, poet, and Chinese man of letters: precisely the kind of illusion and resolution that a reconstruction undertakes, made more easily in Statler's text, because his purpose is not at all to provide some comprehensive biography of Luo.[15]

My point, to be sure, is not that a historical reconstruction like a biography is incapable of dealing with complexity: the issue at hand is not the resolution of complex details. Instead, the issue I raise is that all extant reconstructions of the Perry expedition have failed to adequately account for Luo Sen's participation. He has either been utterly ignored—as in all the contemporary accounts by other participants in the voyage, save Williams—or he has been appended as a curiosity and afterthought, as with Hawks's official *Narrative*.[16] Or, as in Wang Xiaoqiu's work, Luo has been named as a first example in a history of Chinese travel to Japan in the modern age.[17] In all these cases, his historical participation in the Perry expedition has been neither directly addressed nor resolved.

A solution does not lie in writing another narrative or in finding something else to replace the absent biography. Rather than attempt to reconstruct Luo's participation in the Perry expedition so as to consolidate his course of action with that of the expedition, I have embraced the repeatedly conflicting mix of personal, cultural, and political motives that both constituted the expedition generally and determined Luo Sen's representations particularly. The result, this essay, can only be described as an *unresolved juxtaposition* of some of Luo's moments during the expedition, and it necessarily confounds a reader's conventional expectations. Because I have wanted to preserve both Luo's history and that of the expedition—to coordinate his particularity and that of the expedition as a general event—I have discarded the synthetic logic underlying historical reconstruction. There is no general point here derived from particular evidence through the use of induction and deduction. My effort is instead analogical, using structural replications to forge a measure of coherence. And because I have wanted to describe the form of my undertaking, I have represented a "method" imagined by Walter Benjamin and Theodor Adorno in the 1920s and 1930s—the practice of *construction,* intended as both (1) a specific interpretation of material elements of the past, and (2) an alternative form of historical knowledge.[18] Rather than reconstruct Luo Sen's history, this essay attempts to "construct" his role in the Perry expedition. What follows most resembles a description and demonstration.

## CONSTRUCTION AS HISTORICAL MATERIALISM

In describing their efforts as acts of construction, both Adorno and Benjamin were deliberately calling into question the historicist practice of "reconstruction"—that aspiration to reconstruct the past "as it really happened." According to Benjamin's diagnosis, this historicist "verism" followed from nineteenth-century historians' pretensions of scientific investigation. When historians inappropriately employed inductive reasoning, arriving at general principles from the particulars of the past, they misconstrued sources and essentialized their multiplicity to arrive at a false appearance of unity.[19] To Adorno (and Max Horkheimer), this was the problem of "the false identity of the general and the particular."[20] Rather than collapse the variety of past phenomena into a few simple categories according to principles of abstract similitude, Benjamin and Adorno emphasized difference and the particularity of phenomena. Construction demanded sustained attention to the integrity of elements of the past.

The attack on historicist reconstruction followed two lines of thought. In the first place, Benjamin and Adorno argued that reconstruction was necessarily complicit with idealism—what Benjamin called the "epic" in history. Historians who reconstruct the past impose on the particular elements of the past some *reified continuity*, introducing an idealist framework in the interests of temporal continuity. The most common epic in the nineteenth and twentieth centuries has been the ideology of progress. According to Benjamin,

> It was inevitable that the concept of progress should run up against the critical theory of history the moment that progress was no longer presented as a measure of specific historical changes, but rather as a measure of the span separating a legendary beginning from a legendary end of history. In other words: as soon as it becomes the signature for the course of history *in its totality*, the concept of progress is associated with an uncritical hypostatization rather than with a critical placing into question.[21]

The uncritical hypostatization of historical continuity was grounded in the (false) security of the present. Convinced that one's present vantage point corresponds to both the most advanced state of humankind and the most advanced state of historical knowledge, the historian who reconstructs the past reads the past as inevitably leading to the present. To Adorno and Benjamin, such a history was instead a "march of regression,"[22] "integration" with the bourgeois and totalitarian state,[23] and the "triumph of domination."[24] If, in our age, the concept of historical continuity (or "progression") invariably inscribes an order of progress on the details of the historical past,[25] construction, by contrast, begins by placing the present in a critical position.[26] It cancels the idea of progress in itself.[27]

Accordingly, and in the second place, construction was to proceed by "actualization," by making "specific," "graphic," or "concrete" the elements of the past,[28] or, in Adorno's words above, by "abiding . . . in the particular." This was a double motion. On the one hand, construction necessitated granting historical objects their integrity and autonomy, allowing an object to "constitute itself," so to speak.[29] Rather than reduce an object to a mere example of some general principle, one who engaged in construction began by attempting the work of a poet—to express the particular without direct reference to the general.[30] But on the other hand, construction demanded an intervention in the temporal continuity of history. Benjamin's famous and violent metaphor was the explosion: the historical object is "blasted out of the continuum of the historical process," and consequently, "construction presupposes destruction."[31] In other words, construction was to exhibit the *discontinuity* of objects in the past.[32] In a striking comparison, Benjamin equated this "rescue" of phenomena from their transmission as "heritage" to the historian's practice of quotation: "To write history . . . means to *quote* history. But the concept of quotation implies that any given historical object must be ripped out of its context."[33] The product of historical construction, then, would be a new juxtaposition of historical objects freed from their received, abstracted continuities.[34]

Clearly, it would be difficult to identify this description of historiographical practice with Marx's visionary laws of historical development (only posthumously designated "historical materialism" by Engels in 1892). Indeed, the systematic description of modes of production, stages of development, base and superstructure, and the certain direction of class struggle has many features of the nineteenth-century epic of progress.[35] As Benjamin enigmatically put it in his "Historico-Philosophical Theses," Marxism too was guilty of a "theological" illusion, the reification of historical continuity.[36] But even though he castigated this "illusion of vulgar Marxism,"[37] he nonetheless continued to describe his practice of construction as "historical materialism." Implicit in the work of both Adorno and Benjamin are two justifications for this usage.[38] One primary requisite for historical materialism was a persistently critical position vis-à-vis the ruling classes, the victors of history.[39] As is commonly known, the collective work of Adorno, Benjamin, and the Frankfurt School generally—often described as "critical theory"—was motivated by a shared opposition to capitalist society and its bureaucratic structures. A second requisite was the demand for concreteness described above. Construction begins with material objects and elucidates the discontinuities and tensions among such concrete remains of the past. That is, rather than "muster a mass of data to fill the homogenous, empty time" of universal history, the historical materialist constructs a set of objects to describe the specificity of historical processes at work.[40] To call Benjamin and Adorno's practice of construction "historical materialism," then, is to affirm their relation to Marxism but to acknowledge their shift of emphasis from "historical" to "materialist." To forestall the epic in history, one begins with the material of the past and exhibits its historical significance.

This procedure, it must be admitted, is necessarily a "second-order" process. For its sense of historical significance, construction depends on the earlier historiographical work of reconstruction. That is to say, it begs the question of the epistemological problems presented by reconstruction in the first place; but this, after all, is the nature of critical practice, which is always dependent on some prior "other." The point of Benjamin's metaphor of "explosion," I believe, was that although historical significance and continuity remain inherent in fragments of history when they are blasted free, the critical procedure was to examine those fragments in deliberate opposition not simply to received idealist reconstructions but to any desire for historical continuity. As one commentator has noted, Benjamin was rejecting the "totalizing structure" that informed historical reconstructions.[41]

## THE INTERPRETATION OF THE IMAGE

A procedural consequence of Adorno and Benjamin's desire to abandon the received contexts of abstract continuities was a heightened concern with *form*. Indeed, Adorno and Benjamin can be described as "formalists" insofar as they underscored the form of their interpretations, the form of knowledge they were constructing, and the form of truth they were offering.[42] In their attempt to revise critical thought so as to both cancel dominant idealisms and forge a new connection between the particular and the general, their practice of construction was guided by Benjamin's early and idiosyncratic work, *The Origins of German Tragic Drama*, in which he introduced the analogies that repeatedly described both the form of the elements of the past that were to be the objects of construction and the form of the construction as a whole. The object was to the constructed whole as a piece of glass to a mosaic, as a fragment to archaeological excavation, as star to constellation. There was nothing *given* about the unity of the whole; rather, it was a configuration (or "objective, virtual arrangement") of particular elements.[43] The construction as a whole was an *idea*, an interpretation of phenomena that the historical materialist objectified as *concepts*. Concepts, in other words, mediated the movement from particular and objective phenomena to the general idea represented in the whole.[44] In contrast to the work of the poet, who expresses the particular without reference to the general, the historical materialist objectifies such particulars conceptually, to represent them collectively in an interpretation. In contrast to the epic historian, who inductively reduces a host of particulars to an abstract and general thesis (too often given in advance, as with "progress," "culture," or a biographical "individual"), the historical materialist "abides in the particular." Rather than engage in deduction or induction, he *describes* objectified particulars and constructs an interpretation of their historical context.[45]

To indicate the particular phenomenon as conceptualized object, Adorno and Benjamin most often used the term "image." But "image" was more than the particular; it was also the point of mediation from the particular to its larger sociohistorical context. In Adorno's thought, the "historical image" was a material manifestation of both the conceptualized object and its historical specificity.[46] A striking example of this is his discussion of the image of the *intérieur* in the work of Kierkegaard; Adorno found a point of mediation for nineteenth-century bourgeois society in the intérieur, both the space of rented lodgings and the "subjectivity" of the individual thinker at work.[47] By conceptualizing the material conditions of Kierkegaard's writing as intérieur, Adorno managed to generate a description of the historical particularity—the specific limits—of "inwardness" in Kierkegaard's thought. Drawing on Adorno's work on Kierkegaard, Benjamin developed the idea of "dialectical image" to theorize the "historical index" available in the image. Given that Benjamin's images claimed to rupture all historical and temporal continuity, he conceived "dialectical images" as mediating the Then and the Now that admit the possibility of all historical thought.[48] The "dialectical image," in other words, emphasized both the discontinuity between past and present, and the contradictions or tensions among the elements in the past.[49] In the preliminary work on his "Arcades Project," Benjamin described his method of juxtaposing images as "literary montage"—an exhibition without commentary—in which he intentionally avoided the form of "subjective" but more clearly theoretical and mediated interpretation that Adorno practiced.[50] Such a "montage" of dialectical images promised to produce jarring temporal effects from the alienated "thing-ness" of historical objects, but it did so at the risk of appearing arbitrary or merely ironic.[51] Adorno's method, by contrast, was informed by a "sociological" understanding, and, as we have seen above in the Kierkegaard example, he proposed that interpretation pursue two lines of discussion: the analytical moment of dividing (past) experience into objects and concepts; and the representational moment of reassembling objects with insights from their sociohistorical contexts.[52]

As such an object of a construction, the image mediated the "unreconciled objects of immediate reality" and the subjective experience that gave rise to the interpretive act of construction. Above all, it was this *formal* nature of the image—as the form of an object presented in art—that allowed its "absorption" by a perceiving subject.[53] (Adorno would call this point of indifferentiation between subject and object the moment of "truth," a point to which I will return.) In the interpretive act of construction, these juxtaposed, fragmentary, and mutually interruptive images worked constructively to produce the "idea" of the interpretation—quite unlike links in a chain of deduction or induction. Like a work of art, the construction was based *not* on a propositional logic of subject and predicate but on a logic of "inner harmony." Only when understood as a unity—as a synthesis of elements—did a construction contribute to knowledge.[54]

## AN ALTERNATIVE FORM OF KNOWLEDGE

It is clear from the content of most of the work of Adorno and Benjamin that their choice of terminology, "image," was informed by a dominant concern with artistic and literary criticism. Indeed, "image" is most at home in discussions of aesthetic objects, perceptions, and experiences. Far from wanting to engage in art criticism as it had hitherto been defined, Adorno and Benjamin understood that the interpretive power of the image emerged from its ability to mediate not only reality and the interpretive faculties but also the two dominant forms of knowledge: art and science. Insofar as art was a form of knowledge antithetical to science, art provided a model for constructing a form of knowledge different from these current epistemologies. In a passage from *The Origin of German Tragic Drama*, which possibly provided Adorno with his two-part method described above, Benjamin wrote:

> If it is the task of the philosopher to practise the kind of description of the world of ideas which automatically includes and absorbs

the empirical world, then he occupies an elevated position between that of the scientist and the artist. The latter sketches a restricted image of the world of ideas. . . . The scientist arranges the world with a view to its dispersal in the realm of ideas, by dividing it from within into concepts. He shares the philosopher's interest in the elimination of the merely empirical; while the artist shares with the philosopher the task of representation.[55]

According to Adorno, science abstracts and reifies the empirical into signs that are read as positive facts, while art transforms the empirical into images.[56] The act of construction, then, was meant to bridge the practices of art and science by interpreting objects as images.

Both Adorno and Benjamin intended that the practice of construction lead to the collapse of individual disciplines in favor of some larger history of humanity. Benjamin in particular imagined this general philosophical-critical project as "cultural history," and an appropriate field for historical materialism. The danger in such an enterprise was that it risked a return to positivism. On the one hand, the notion of "culture" since the nineteenth century had been abstracted and reified into a continuous entity. On the other hand, with the domination of the capitalist economy, culture had been "fetishized," reduced to commodities, and its history had become a mere "piling up of treasure."[57] Adorno's criticism in the "debates" was that Benjamin had indeed fetishized his images because, by omitting a theoretical moment of mediation, his method was indistinguishable from positivism.[58] Benjamin responded that a possible solution lay in moving beyond simply presenting the facts surrounding the object to some rigorous placing of the object in an historical perspective—precisely what Adorno had imagined.[59] From its materialist beginnings, interpretation was to account for the sociohistorical context.

## THE EPIC IN HISTORY

As a major expansion of the United States into the Pacific, the Perry expedition basked in the idealism of the nineteenth century. Samuel Wells Williams described the mission as "spreading civilization to Japan," introducing not simply advanced technology like the daguerrotype, the telegraph, and the railroad, but more importantly, the rule of international law, the extension of liberty, and the word of God.[60] This beneficent work necessarily depended on and was in fact an expression of U.S. state power. Government officials indicated that a primary motivation for the expedition was a desire to compel Japanese authorities to atone for the "outrageous treatment of shipwrecked American sailors" who had been "detained in loathsome Japanese prisons" on multiple occasions during the 1840s.[61] Satisfaction of this problem demanded the creation of a commercial treaty or convention that would allow for the opening of Japanese ports to American ships, consuls, and commercial agents, and would specify U.S. rights in Japan to trade, whale, establish coaling stations, and appoint a minister to "the Japanese court at Yedo."[62] Williams, who had been sent by the American Board of Missions to serve as missionary and printer in Canton, had provided U.S. officials with maps and intelligence of Japan, gathered in the course of otherwise fruitless trips there (like that of the *Morrison* in 1837), and, in missionary work with shipwrecked Japanese sailors, had also begun to learn to speak Japanese.[63] Hence he was Perry's first choice as official interpreter for the expedition, and his multiple allegiances reflect the inseparable efforts of missionary and official on behalf of God and U.S. government in the hinterlands of the barbarian Orient.

If the spread of civilization animated the epic of progress for Americans like Perry and Williams, a far more considerable epic informed the ideals of missionaries like Williams: God's plan. Williams declared early in his *Journal* that "the Japanese policy of seclusion is not according to God's plan of bringing the nations of the earth to a knowledge of his truth,"[64] and accordingly, he understood the success of the expedition as an "extension of God's kingdom to Japan."[65] The inscrutable logic of God's plan, however, confounded Williams at times—when, for example, he considered the hypocrisy of Perry and his officers in dealing with the Japanese, "calling them savages, liars, a pack of fools, poor devils; cursing them and then denying practically all of it by supposing them worth making a treaty with." Williams reflected, "Truly, what sort of instruments does God work with!"[66] Even if he could not comprehend that God would employ such petty agents, his stray remarks disclose a very human logic at work. For Williams, the world of the nineteenth century was divided between the pagan or barbarian nations and the Christian or civilized nations. Yes, civilized nations had their share of duplicitous and immoral specimens of humanity— the evil at work in the world—but the merest exposure to Christianity was at least an improvement over the benighted and polluted state in which Williams found heathens like the Japanese.[67] Access to the gospel was a first step in bringing civilization to Japan, for God's word would begin to free the Japanese from the tyrannical rulers who kept them in their pagan state, opening the way for advanced technology and domestic liberty, if not international law.[68] Prim Williams did not question the appropriateness of U.S. naval power to also serve as God's instrument.

A similarly transcendent idealism is evident in Luo Sen's diary, where he refers to *tiandao,* or "Heaven's Way." Modeled on the seasonal patterns and occasional fluctuations of earth and sky, Heaven's Way was somewhat indifferent to both the moral imperatives of God's plan and the gradual betterment of the spread of civilization. When Luo invoked Heaven's Way, he understood a process of unceasing change underway in the cosmos, change perhaps motivated in favor of one or another development but not necessarily commendatory of any in particular.[69] But because the sage-kings of antiquity had modeled human institutions on Heaven's Way, correspondences between nature and society had been established.[70] To Luo, Heaven's Way in the mid–nineteenth century seemed to be bringing the nations and peoples of the earth closer together, and the Perry expedition was another testimony to that process.[71]

As cases of reified historical continuity, all three of these idealisms share a dependence on abstracted *signs.* Luo Sen, for example, stood on deck the first morning of the voyage, and where another might have seen only clouds, he noted:

> To the south, the clouds resembled a winged lion soaring to the vault of Heaven; to the north, the atmosphere was low and broken, like a man gasping for breath. Only a few small clouds clustered toward the lion, and the steam from the lion's muzzle bore down upon them. Gradually, the broken clouds in the north dissipated, and the figure of the lion strengthened. . . . These portents of Heaven's Way pertain to our undertaking: initial difficulties are not promising, but eventual success is certain.[72]

The ability to read signs like this requires an awareness of the idealist narrative in advance of looking for signs. One must know to associate particular details like clouds with a predetermined conceptual framework like Heaven's Way, and to associate the north with Japan and the south with the U.S. navy. At the same time, one must know that signs may take only certain forms. Williams, for example, found evidence of "God's hand and blessing" in countless "preservations" during the voyage. Such evidence included not only the mild weather but also the capable person of Perry, the fitness of the ships, the good health of the crew, the reliability of provisions, and so on.[73]

But Williams was no reader of portents like Luo, and he did not notice the remarkable symmetry of events beginning and closing his diary of the voyage—a pair of unpleasant incidents involving the deaths of drunken American sailors.[74] In his understanding of God's plan, signs were only favorable; consequently, the two incidents were random and offered no meaning to a larger ideal. Clearly, the abstract correspondences that relate such a sign and its referent are conventional and necessarily misuse deduction and induction. Where deduction guides the search for particular signs, induction serves to reconfirm the predetermined generality.[75] The alternative, as Adorno and Benjamin proposed, was to begin with the concrete.

## THE EPOCH IN HISTORY: STEAMSHIPS

The history of the Perry expedition was determined mostly by the steamship, that technological breakthrough that freed mechanical and military power from winds and currents in the nineteenth century. The steamship defined the epoch, as Americans learned to sail the Pacific at will, crossing the distant western water boundaries of the continental republic. On the one hand, the enterprise was a search for commercial partners—ships raised expectations of shipping. On the other hand, the enterprise was a voyage of discovery—ships promised passage to different lands and peoples. The steamship, in other words, was a pretext for the expedition, giving material ground and form to its possibilities.

Williams, Luo, and other participants in the expedition consistently mention two specific items associated with steamships: coal and trade.[76] Coal was obviously needed to fuel the steam engines that powered the ships, but the inability to transport sufficient quantities of coal meant that overseas sources of supply had to be found. Hence Americans were interested in the possibility of Japanese coal. Need, however, was indistinguishable from entitlement. As an editor for the *Edinburgh Review* wrote, praising the Perry expedition, "The Japanese undoubtedly have an exclusive right to the possession of their territory, but they must not abuse that right to the extent of debarring all other nations from participation in its riches."[77] To ensure that the needed coal was secured from Japan, the promise of trade was invoked lest anyone confuse the taking of coal with piracy or mistake the American principle of "friendly and commercial intercourse" for imperial habits of colonization.[78]

Nonetheless, trade is predicated on an exchange, and in return for

Japanese coal and provisions, Americans had to give something. Luo Sen noted at one point that a delivery of Japanese supplies was followed by American offers of hard drink—likely whiskey.[79] The Japanese declined. Because the Japanese apparently refused all payment for supplying Perry's squadron at the start of the stay in Japan, Perry took the measure of refusing further supplies unless some form of payment were accepted.[80] With his sailors clamoring to go ashore and buy local goods, Perry asked both sides' "finance committees" to negotiate exchange rates between American silver and gold coins and Japanese copper cash. American money would be used as a medium of exchange.

This settlement alerted Luo and Williams to the extraordinary gold-to-silver ratio in Japan, about 4.7 to 1, which in the short run satisfied the more general problem of trade and exchange. In the decade between 1858 and 1867, when the ratio was 15 to 1 outside Japan, U.S. and British traders flooded Japan with foreign silver in exchange for gold, tea, and silk, causing unprecedented inflation of basic commodity prices in Japan.[81] At the time of the expedition, however, neither Luo nor Williams considered local products in terms of future trade; Williams was unenthusiastic, and Luo found them inferior to Chinese goods.[82] Although sailors and officers scrambled to buy mementos when an occasional bazaar was arranged for them, the inflated prices and lottery system—by naval rank—left buyers dissatisfied.[83]

Accordingly, "open trade" did not figure in the Treaty of Kanagawa that Perry signed on 31 March 1854. Aside from the immediate purchasing of provisions and mementos and the giving of gifts, a general practice of trade was deferred until some future time, with the result that trade turned out to be a more ideological matter than coal. Although Williams had imagined that Japanese coal and provisions might lead to the United States sending advanced technology to Japan, this practice did not materialize and was consequently reified as an ideal element of multiple ongoing histories: U.S.–Japan friendship, the spread of civilization, and the expansion of God's kingdom. Trade, in other words, joined the elements of current historiographical epics.[84]

Even as ideology, American claims regarding trade were questioned by some Japanese negotiators. Hirayama Kenjirō, one of the officials assigned to the Perry case, pointed out in a written statement to Luo Sen that conflict was sure to arise because trade was predicated on a desire for profit—the root of immorality, according to the teachings of Confucius and Mencius. He wrote:

Profit is something all mankind desires, and is the womb of all evils. Confucius spoke rarely of profit, hoping to block its source. My ancestors prohibited intercourse with foreign states, because desire for profit misled the ignorant and study of the principles of curious arts deceived the foolish. When the stupid strive among themselves over profit and curiosity, they forget morality in their haste—loyalty, filial piety and modesty—to the point of denying their fathers and rulers.[85]

Hirayama reminded Luo of the moral alternative:

Heaven's Way is all-pervasive, its subtle principle nourishes all things. Even those who dwell in the night-realm of icy seas, in lands of obscurity—is not everyone a child of Heaven and Earth? Who does not love and befriend his fellow man? The sage-kings of antiquity embraced all mankind with a common benevolence, without distinguishing between one and another. If throughout all the earth, the principles for mutual intercourse were one—propriety, complaisance, trust, and rightness—then a Great Harmony would prevail and we would see the heart of Heaven and Earth manifested. But if commerce is conducted through competition for profit, then quarrels and litigations arise. I would rather we desist than have cause for regret![86]

Hirayama's objection to trade with the United States points out a series of contradictions between these different views of human intercourse. On one hand, Hirayama claims to prefer the moral society established by ancestral example, in which fathers and rulers maintained order through the cultivation of specific virtues. In such a setting, commerce was a necessary evil to be strictly controlled; intercourse with foreign lands too was best restricted. For his part, Williams remained unmoved by Hirayama's precaution.[87] He was unsure of the sincerity of the message, because he had found evidence on many occasions of a contrary morality—evidence such as the Japanese reception of shipwrecked Americans, the way Japanese rulers demeaned common people, the contempt of Japanese men to Japanese women.[88] But on the other hand, Williams and his compatriots were searching for trading partners, that categorically open fraternity safeguarded by rational self-interest and compromised only by heathen customs. (In large measure, expedition reports of local customs served to confirm the status of the Japanese as barbarian or heathen.[89]) Converting the heathen would presumably assist the expansion of trade, but as Hirayama well knew, this conversion to open trade was being forced on Japan by military might, and he had cause for suspicion.[90]

It is noteworthy, then, that Hirayama's message was given to Luo Sen in the literary Chinese language that they shared. As categorically "Chinese," Luo was potentially the individual most sympathetic to Hirayama's appeal to Confucius and the other Chinese sage-kings of antiquity. But Luo's reaction was guarded. The Chinese version of his diary mentions nothing, while the English version contains the following written response to Hirayama expressing gratitude for his acknowledgment of a common humanity:

> We have come together like leaves . . . floating on the water, and on me has fallen the light of your instructions. When you say that all in the world are the children of heaven and earth, and that they should treat each other according to the principles of propriety, complaisance, good faith, and righteousness, your words are great and correct, and are sufficient to show the generous spirit of universal and equal benevolence which belongs to the school of our sages. For every word in your letter I shall ever be grateful. I shall wear it at my girdle and always keep it in remembrance.[91]

If Luo's gratitude seems obsequious, his praise is self-assertive. Hirayama's words are great because they honor "our sages." It is a formal and balanced response that successfully ignores the issues at hand—trade and profit—even as it seems to confirm Hirayama's common ground. The question lies in Luo's "our," either a reference to something shared by individuals or groups, Chinese and Japanese, or an assertion of the precedent of Chinese culture.

## THE LITERARY CHINESE LANGUAGE

Like the steamship that forged crossings between different lands, the literary Chinese language, too, enabled passages among peoples speaking different vernaculars. Literary Chinese is thus a second material ground for the Perry expedition, and the one that specifically determined Luo Sen's inclusion. To Perry, this "Chinese of the mandarins" was analogous to Latin in medieval Europe, a universal language of communication in Eastern Asia.[92] Perry thus depended on Williams and Luo to communicate with the people of Japan in literary Chinese. Although Dutch and English interpreters were occasionally available, Williams was not confident about speaking Japanese, so he and Luo repeatedly had to make use of literary Chinese.[93]

Direct communication with Japanese officials and scholars in literary Chinese was written and took two forms. One was a calligraphic practice called "brushtalking" (*bitan* or *hitsudan*), in which Luo (accompanied by Williams) and his interlocutors sat with brush, ink, and paper and wrote to each other in Chinese characters. This was a form of language particular to educated Chinese and Japanese; that some Japanese in the nineteenth century were quite proficient in literary Chinese is due to a pedagogical movement of the early eighteenth century, but in addition, this *kanbun*—what Japanese call "Chinese writing"—had long been an official style of writing in Japan.[94] The Japanese version of the draft treaty negotiated between Perry and the shogun's official, for example, was written in literary Chinese or *kanbun,* and it was this that Williams and Luo translated into English.[95] Brushtalking, in other words, was an extension of the ability to read and write literary Chinese.

A second significant usage of literary Chinese for communication was the practice of occasional poetry, a highly specific form of conversation that typically overlapped with situations of brushtalking. Many of Luo's brushtalking interactions with Japanese scholars, monks, and officials included such exchanges of poetry, which were valued as demonstrations of ability and appreciation, and which, for the Japanese, produced treasured mementos of extraordinary encounters with a Chinese scholar.[96] The ability to respond in verse, to reproduce allusions to seasonal and historical themes, demonstrated not only one's erudition but also the existence of a cultured community linguistically linked to Chinese history.[97] Brushtalking and occasional poetry, in other words, promised to dispel certain abstracted distinctions between "Chinese" and "Japanese" based on ethnic, geographic, or cultural determinants. Literary Chinese was a language available to members of otherwise different communities, and hence offered concrete evidence of that common humanity to which Hirayama Kenjirō alluded.

But clearly, this version of a common humanity privileged the Chinese past and language. What is remarkable about the use of literary Chinese during the Perry expedition is that *Japanese officials* enlisted Chinese tradition as a point of resistance to Perry. Luo Sen was their conduit, for he communicated to Williams who in turn communicated to Perry. As we have already seen, Hirayama appealed to a Chinese moral tradition in an attempt to win Luo's sympathy against his American companions' desire for profit. In another situation, a Japanese official known simply as "Meitoku"[98] criticized Luo for seemingly abandoning "his" Chinese tradition by allying himself with the Americans. He wrote in brushtalk: "Since you are a Chinese scholar, how is it that you attend upon these shrike-tongued barbarians? Is this not what the *Mencius* calls 'falling from the tall tree of clarity into the valley of darkness'?" Luo responded with a poem:

> Roaming Japan at pleasure, reminiscing old connections;
> To not connect in speech: doubly wounds the spirit.
> The carved inscription not understood—the wind amidst the
>     clouds?
> The chisel's tooth unknowable—the unicorn in the world?

> Jade that links city walls must return to its master;
> Jewel named "Chariot reflector": bound to depend on one man.
> Eastern outsiders study the rites, finally without companions,
> Southern domains with wealth of talent, spontaneous and
>     original.

> From antiquity, heroic men continue to wear their swords,
> In the present age, the champions bury each other in turns.
> To ride the wind and sail the waves; an entire life of caution,
> A myriad miles and distances far, yet like the closest neighbors.[99]

Through the relentless series of parallel contrasts, Luo emphasizes the confounding of habitual perceptions. Where the first stanza reiterates the long history of Chinese and Japanese contacts, linked through a common writing, and employs obscure allusions to question whether anyone understands the results to which present signs point, the second stanza more significantly questions Meitoku's cultural claims. In the same way that the ancient king of Zhao's rare jade could not be purloined through treachery, nor the king of Wei's magic jewel be made to work for another, did Luo's "belonging to" China mean that he was therefore bound to certain Chinese traditions? He suggests not. Japan's isolation was no fair exchange for forces sailing up from the south. He, Luo Sen, was acting in a way contrary to common expectations and, according to the third stanza, proving through his act that claims of division and desires for isolation paled in the face of real human encounters. It is a daring motion, to give up the claims of one's cultural identity—the old practices of shared languages and poetry—and to cast one's lot with the uncertain new, in the form of a wealth of Western talents that could diminish the distances among peoples.

But in denying that a common humanity is necessarily grounded in the Chinese past, Luo contradicted the earlier experience—his appreciation of Hirayama's statement of a common humanity in Chinese moral terms. His Chinese identity was in jeopardy, and this is because his anomalous presence among U.S. navy personnel was doubly problematic to Japanese officials: he was allied with both American aggression and a Chinese cultural vision, both of which could be turned against him. That seems to have happened during the interval between those two experiences. Although Luo's diary did not mention it, Williams referred to an unpleasant incident during the expedition's stay in Hakodate, the northern port opened to U.S. ships. In the course of brushtalk negotiations over American rights to travel in the countryside about Hakodate, Luo and Williams were accused of having deliberately misinterpreted Perry's position and having made unauthorized threats. Where Perry had wanted access to an area seven *ri* outside of Hakodate, Luo and Williams had written ten, and so on.[100] Official Japanese displeasure seems to have been a deliberate attempt to discredit Luo and Williams, because the outcome of the "problem" was that Dutch interpreters would thereafter replace the use of literary Chinese in official communications,[101] and this change was officially written into the "Additional Regulations" that supplemented the Treaty of Kanagawa and were signed on 17 June 1854.[102] Thus the practices of brushtalking and occasional poetry revealed their ideological moment: literary Chinese may have facilitated international communication among individuals, but in the difference between hostile state governments, its claim to commonality was overruled.

GIFTS AND RESOLUTION

The material objects that remained in the wake of the Perry expedition describe a final material level of the passage of ships and men. The history available in these many things congeals in the image of the gift—in opposition to the other material determinants of the expedition. Where coal and provisions were purchased only to be used up, and general trade deferred to some future time, gifts were specific transfers from giver to receiver. They were finite acts intended to crystallize the moment of interaction, to please, and to indebt. To use the words of American members of the expedition, gifts were one kind of "memento" or "memorial," a thing imbued with reified memory.

If only because they figure in so many accounts, the most celebrated reminders of the Perry expedition were the official gifts. The United States initiated the giving on 13 March 1854 to mark the finalization of the draft treaty that in turn marked Japan's submission to U.S. demands. For the emperor of Japan were a miniature railway, a telegraph with three miles of wire, a pair of boats, a telescope, a set of agricultural implements, a large quantity of books, cloth, liquors, tea, perfumes, guns, and much more. Smaller numbers of gifts were given to the empress and to the many officials involved in the negotiations. They were carefully graded for quantity and quality according to bureaucratic rank.[103] Japanese officials responded on 24 March, which marked the finalization of revisions to the draft treaty that had previously marked the U.S. gifts to the Japanese emperor. From the Japanese government and the officials in charge of negotiations, the U.S. government received a variety of items: a gold lacquered writing table, writing boxes, paper, bookcases, censers, trays, shell goblets, porcelain and lacquered cups, bolts of silk, umbrellas, brooms, and more. Similar gifts in correspondingly smaller quantities were given to Perry and his chief officers.[104]

In offering gifts, strategy is paramount.[105] Not only are the given objects carefully considered, but the timing and style of their transfer as well. While the assortment of items given to Japan reflected the latest in American technology and manufactures—commodity items amenable to trade—their presentation largely baffled the Japanese, most of whom were unfamiliar with the majority of items. They were unloaded from the American ships, many still in brown paper and packing crates, and in the course of the next ten days, U.S. personnel set the machines to working, so that they could be viewed in operation at the same time that the Japanese gifts were presented.[106] Only on 31 March, after the signing of the Treaty of Kanagawa, did Perry turn over the list of American presents to Hayashi Noboru, the commissioner in charge of negotiations.[107] In addition to the general thrust of their utility, the assortment of items expressed a desire to *inform* the Japanese emperor about conditions in the United States. The many books included histories of the United States and the State of New York, the Annals of Congress, farming and engineering manuals, and catalogs of libraries and post offices. That the emperor might not read English was not a concern. And Perry overlooked the shogun entirely, focused as he was on relations with the Japanese empire.

For its part, the Japanese presentation was designed to dazzle the Americans. Williams noted that although the overall quantity was smaller than the American gifts to Japan, the colorful presentation was a stunning spectacle for the eyes.[108] As luxury crafts and more mundane manufactures, they corresponded to the American gifts, but by comparison, their usefulness was more readily apparent. These expressed the finest Japanese artistry and craftsmanship, intended for domestic enjoyment. Accompanying the display of Japanese gifts, however, was an additional display of spectacles calculated to emphasize the symbolic might of Japan. As Perry left the exhibition hall, he was shown 200 bales of rice—each weighing 135 pounds, for a rough total of 27,000 pounds—ready to be loaded on board his ships. This was a personal gift from the emperor. Thereupon a group of sumo wrestlers came forth and demonstrated their strength by shouldering the bales two at a time, some offering further demonstration as one man lifted a bale with his teeth, and another performed somersaults while holding a bale. In due course, a sumo match was held for the Americans' entertainment, which proved to be an exciting and violent show.[109] A final exchange on that day was personal, as Commissioner Hayashi gave Perry a pair of swords, three guns, and two sets of coins—manly gifts presumably intended to show his personal appreciation for the manner in which Perry had conducted negotiations, for Perry had given Hayashi precious time to work out the details of opening the northern port of Hakodate to American ships.[110]

Hayashi's personal gift revealed the illusion of an exchange of official gifts, for the true gift is personal. Perry's swords, guns, and coins became his own property—mementos of Japan, Hayashi, and the negotiations to take home on his return voyage. The official Japanese gifts, by contrast, were to be crated and shipped home to the U.S. government in Washington, where some official would decide whether to give them to the individuals for whom they were intended, to deposit them in the State Department, or to sell them at auction for the benefit of the U.S. Treasury.[111] These official Japanese gifts were thus fetishized—alienated from their producers, givers, and receivers, and transformed into both material evidence of the opening of Japan and booty to dispose of for profit. What is striking is that the difference between the two forms of gifts caused Perry to reflect on his role as an official of the U.S. government. To what extent should he invest privately in the expedition? As commodore, he was expected to conform to Japanese customs of giving gifts, but he knew that his expenses would not be reimbursed by the government on his return.[112] Up to the point of receiving Hayashi's gift, Perry had considered the official presents "trifles"; then he became aware of their potential as personal mementos, a possibility denied by U.S. government policy. True mementos, however, demanded a personal commitment, a private investment that would not be reimbursed. Hayashi's gift, in other words, *confounded* Perry. Perry had already given in his official capacity; should he do more? His decision was to propose that the U.S. government adopt more reasonable policies for future expeditions; like European states, the United States should maintain proper economy through a combination of fixed allowances and extraordinary expenses.[113] Always the official representative, he does not appear to have found the wherewithal to respond privately to what seems to have been Hayashi's personal generosity.

Luo Sen, by comparison, was little interested in the official gifts and the sumo match; he noted only the miniature train, the telegraph, and the other curious machines.[114] He was instead busy giving away gifts of his own—poems and other examples of his calligraphy, most of which he wrote on paper folding-fans. He estimated that during the first month in Japan alone, he had inscribed over five hundred fans, an extraordinary number that he attributed to a Japanese love of Chinese characters and poems, and to Japan's long isolation from foreigners. In every trip to a government office, it seemed that everyone brought forth a fan with a request for him to inscribe it.[115] That fans proved to be numerically the most important memento dispersed by the Perry expedition is due undoubtedly to the compatible significance of the folding-fan for Luo Sen and the many Japanese who requested his calligraphy. Symbolic of rank, goodness, unfolding prosperity, and separation, folding-fans served better than literary Chinese to mediate Luo Sen and his Japanese acquaintances. He was honored in the request for his calligraphy, which allowed him to demonstrate his skill, and then he returned his gift with the original loan. An inscribed fan was a most appropriate gift, for it signified the giver's imminent separation, while containing his hand. In other words, its ideological import was symmetric with its simple utility as art object or breeze-maker.

The history of the Perry expedition thus finds a resolution in Luo Sen's folding-fans, a resolution unavailable in its stated goal of a treaty. For the treaty (or treaties, written in multiple languages) was an abstract exchange much like the official gifts. It was a document that claimed to unite nation and nation, people and people; that promised perpetual peace and amity, as well as future courses of action; and that bound all citizens and subjects to its articles.[116] However, even as the treaty was signed, arguments continued over access to the Bay of Yedo; within ten weeks, U.S. sailors were jailed for stealing from a sake shop and beating up the shop owner.[117] The treaty, in other words, invoked an ideal narrative of future U.S.–Japan interaction and established a precedent on which future repetitions of the visit could proceed. At best—and the point was well taken—the treaty confirmed the superi-ority of U.S. military power. In the same way that Luo Sen's fans dem-onstrate the untruth of official gifts and the idealism of trade, so the treaty demonstrates the untruth of future peace and amity.

## TRUTH

As a deliberate negation of current idealisms and notions of histori-cal continuity, the validity of a construction would seem to rest on its own idiosyncratic merits.[118] Some commentators have pointed out that Adorno and Benjamin's theory of knowledge is exceptionally indi-vidualistic,[119] and indeed, such a characterization is in keeping with their understanding of truth as reflected in their works. Because the question of truth is inextricably bound to the problem of received idealisms like "progress," their criticism of historicism was at the same time a negation of the theory of truth underlying historicist re-construction: truth as rational, objective, unitary, and universal—not unlike a theory of progress. Such a version of truth serves to guarantee the validity of knowledge; in tautological fashion, one might say that a reconstruction is true because it reproduces idealisms accepted as true.[120] Construction, by contrast, was intended as a different form of knowledge and was necessarily grounded in some other understand-ing of truth. To Adorno and Benjamin, truth was experiential, frag-mentary, and momentary, and served not so much as guarantor of the validity of knowledge as a mark of "authentic" or "genuine" experi-ence.[121] This individual moment of truth, however, was best under-stood in terms of an aesthetic experience of beauty. That is, aesthetic truth served as a model for this other truth imagined on behalf of ma-terialist constructions, but typically, Adorno and Benjamin described the latter only analogically. They concentrated their efforts instead on explicating the nature of aesthetic truth.

An early step in producing this alternative version of truth was Benjamin's attempt to problematize the relationship between truth and objects of knowledge. Where knowledge is constructed from ideas and relies on some method to attain its object, truth is not such an object, but is instead a particular essence that accrues to representa-tions (in turn, objects of knowledge) in a manner outside of rational consciousness. As Benjamin put it, truth "is not open to question."[122] Furthermore, the relevance of truth differs from that of an object of knowledge. Benjamin maintained that we continue to study some sys-tems of thought—Plato's theory of ideas, Hegel's dialectic—because, even though the knowledge they offer has been superseded and they have lost their claim to scientific truth, they possess a meaningful integrity as *images of reality*.[123] It is this status as image that enables an element of the past to have access to *aesthetic* truth, because, as Benjamin explained (drawing on Plato's *Symposium*), truth is the content of beauty. The beautiful image is the site of truth, although not in perpetuity, for truth "is not so much beautiful in itself, as for whomsoever seeks it."[124] In other words, the beautiful image is true only as a particular object for a particular subject in a particular encounter.

Although Benjamin admitted that such a formulation was open to charges of "relativism," his and Adorno's foremost goal was to interrupt the unmediated link between the absolute subject of idealism and its corresponding prop of transcendent truth. The subject was one point of interruption, for insofar as truth was not an object of knowledge, it was also "intentionless." Rather than search out the truth, an individual more or less happened upon it.[125] Hence for Benjamin, truth was not subjective, but objective: truth provoked the absorption of the subject by the object.[126] A second point of interruption, as I have related above, was provided by the image itself. From its location in the image, aesthetic truth arrests time; it interferes with temporal succession when objects are broken loose from their "given-ness" in historical continuity and presented afresh to a viewer as image. Hence the images in a construction are more pertinent to the concreteness of lived experience than to the received knowledge possessed by the subject.[127] The "historical index" of an image was in fact a dimension of historical and aesthetic truth, and by virtue of its mediating role between subjects and objects, an image managed to "redeem" fragments of the past from oblivion, making them available for experiences of truth.[128] These experiences were not so much "relative," then, as determined by a constellation of particulars in a manner impervious to the "critical" scope of idealism.

Adorno, whose theory of aesthetics developed beyond that of Benjamin, first outlined his understanding of this paradoxical moment of aesthetic truth in *Minima Moralia*, which is, incidentally, perhaps the best example of a construction available to us.[129] Beauty, according to Adorno, "as single, true, and liberated from appearance and individuation, manifests itself not in the synthesis of all works, in the unity of the arts and of art, but only as a physical reality: in the downfall of art itself. This downfall is the goal of every work of art, in that it seeks to bring death to all others."[130] Adorno alludes to two of beauty's most important traits here. First, it is for Adorno the most certain occasion of concreteness (and in view of his materialist orientation, this explains why he refers this understanding of truth to aesthetics). Second, beauty has a doubly "negative" essence. A beautiful object exerts a negative force on its competitors—other beautiful particulars—and at the same time, Adorno says elsewhere, beauty also acts negatively on the subject.[131] That is, the beautiful object confronts a subject in a relationship of negativity (described as "infatuation") and provides the occasion for mind to intervene and reassert the subject vis-à-vis the beautiful object. In this process, called "contemplation"(*Betrachtung*), a new relationship of existence is established between the beautiful object and the subject, wherein the subject negates his own infatuation and thereby comes to accept the real and distinct beauty of a unique and external object.[132] This is the "downfall" of art. At the same time, this act of contemplation is both "a residue of fetishistic worship" and "a state in overcoming such worship." Adorno calls it "the moment of enlightenment, the dispelling of illusion by the mind's self-enlightenment"—in fact, the "genesis of beauty."[133]

In elaborating this negative dialectic of beauty, Adorno writes,

> The universality of beauty can communicate itself to the subject in no other way than in obsession with the particular. No gaze attains beauty that is not accompanied by indifference, indeed almost by contempt, for all that lies outside the object contemplated. And it is only infatuation, the unjust disregard for the claims of every existing thing, that does justice to what exists. In so far as the existent is accepted, in its one-sidedness, for what it is, its one-sidedness is comprehended as its being, and reconciled. . . . But if one-sidedness is cancelled by the introduction from outside of awareness of universality, if the particular is startled from its rapture, interchanged and weighed up, the just overall view makes its own the universal injustice that lies in exchangeability and substitution. . . . Doubtless, no thought is dispensed from such associations; none may be permanently blinkered. But everything depends on the manner of transition.[134]

Here we see two possible outcomes for an encounter with beauty. The first, favorable to Adorno, is this: through the course of his successive obsessions with particular, beautiful objects, the individual subject comes to understand the universality of beauty. But this universality, Adorno goes on to say, has content in impenetrability alone. It can never be recovered or objectified as truth. At the same time, the truth of beauty is realized only through each particular gaze of infatuation, a gaze within which each particular beauty provokes and commands its subject to linger. "Aesthetic truth," then, is the subject's reconciling himself to this fact of the one-sidedness of beauty (beautiful particulars), an understanding achieved through "contemplation."

But as Adorno writes, "everything depends on the manner of transition." If the subject should move to cancel beauty's one-sidedness and impose on the beautiful particular some idealistic criterion for "beauty," a process arrived at through abstraction—exchanging and substituting beautiful particulars—and proclaimed as universal, then concrete beauty is destroyed along with its actual truth. This supplement of an idealistic notion of beauty is to Adorno the error of the "short cut"—seeking "abstracted correspondences between different things." He criticizes this style of thinking on two accounts: first, for recklessly subsuming the particular within some predetermined universal; and second, for deceptively applying such received "universal truths" to invalidate unwelcome particulars.[135]

By contrast, "the bliss of contemplation consists in disenchanted charm." In the one process, the subject seeks to place a beautiful particular in a preestablished and pseudo-universal hierarchy of beauty based on some abstracted criteria; in the other, he is content to linger with the beautiful particular, satisfied by the hope that another beauty is possible. Adorno means to assert the particularity of truth, which is never truth-in-general. And in the passage quoted above, he ventures from aesthetic truth to hazard an explanation for a more "philosophical" mode of truth:

> One might almost say that truth itself depends on the tempo, the patience and perseverance of lingering with the particular: what passes beyond it without having first entirely lost itself, what proceeds to judge without having first been guilty of the injustice of contemplation, loses itself at last in emptiness.[136]

The two criteria on which truth depends, as explained here, correspond to Adorno's explanation for aesthetic truth as it is generated by the dialectic of beauty: (1) "without having first lost itself"—this is the spell of infatuation, the gaze in which the "universality" of beauty is experienced; and (2) "without having first been guilty of the injustice of contemplation (*Anschauung*)"—this is the phase of the dialectic in which the subject perceives beauty's one-sidedness, and which Adorno analyzes as favorably leading to "contemplation" (*Betrachtung*), the subject's acceptance of beauty's one-sidedness and his perception of aesthetic truth.

Adorno insists that these two moments are prerequisite for all processes of "truth"; thus truth for Adorno must first of all be a confirmation of particularity. Without this, an individual's claims to both knowledge and powers of judgment are but the groundless platitudes of idealism. In the same way that an individual's realization of aesthetic truth is the outcome of his experience with analogous concrete particulars and is a realization known only as it is experienced, so too all truth known by humankind must arise from dialectical interactions with particulars, and is at most a form of knowledge more akin to Christian "faith" than the rational version of "truth" modeled on geometric proof. Truth is individual; it is always self-conditioned by its success at explaining particular sets of facts. In other words, truth is "known" only in experience with particulars.[137]

## SIGNIFICANCE

One might rightly wonder why Adorno offers this painstaking description of aesthetic experience. Aside from quite ironic statements of motive—that "the teaching of the good life" is the "true field of philosophy"—he is certainly not constructing a general ethics.[138] That is, he does not offer reflections on his personal practice by way of an example on which readers are to generally model themselves. Rather, Adorno's reflections in *Minima Moralia* are a particular individual's contribution to the *knowledge* of human life, the "damaged life" we lead in the estranged present. Adorno is careful to construct his text in such a way as to mediate his authorial intention and a reader's comprehension. This mediation, he designates "significance" (*Deutlichkeit*).

Significance, Adorno writes, refers ambiguously "to the organization of the subject matter as such and to its communication to the audience." In other words, "significance designates the point of equilibrium between reason and communication."[139] Rather than being trapped by the inertia of meaning, Adorno's text proceeds with an eye to representation and an eye to reception. Certainly there is no guarantee that a reader will understand Adorno precisely "as he is written." Nor does Adorno intend this. That which is significant is so because its form demands interpretation, and the act of interpretation is both criticism and composition, a "writing about" and a "writing to."[140] Hence the linguistic material of the text, in a final analysis, ensures the availability of communication that is built into the form of construction as both practice and knowledge.[141]

Significance is thus an open-ended concept, which lends to a construction an available point of mediation to some other reader or time. Adorno wrote confidently in 1969:

> Open thinking points beyond itself. For its part, such thinking takes a position as a figuration of praxis which is more closely related to a praxis truly involved in change than is a position of mere obedience for the sake of praxis. . . . This emphatic concept of thinking is by no means secure; no security is granted it by existing conditions nor by the ends yet to be attained nor by any type of organized force. Whatever was once thought, however, can be suppressed; it can be forgotten and can even vanish. But it cannot be denied that something of it survives. For thinking has the momentum of the general. What has been cogently thought must be thought in some other place and by other people. This confidence accompanies even the loneliest and most impotent thought.[142]

Adorno's program was always to convict others of untruth, while maintaining a scrupulous honesty in making no personal claims to truth. In "speaking" of truth, one falls silent.

The significance of a construction of Luo Sen's participation in the Perry expedition, then, lies not in providing a fuller, emended history of the expedition, as is the point of so many revisions of history, but in suspending all versions of historical continuity in an attempt to resolve the reverberating cluster of anonymous reversals surrounding Perry's "Chinaman," reversals ponderously symbolized in Luo Sen's hundreds of folding-fans: rank, goodness, prosperity, and separation.

## NOTES

I am especially grateful to Tani E. Barlow and Jim Hevia for their encouragement, and to Linn Freiwald and Howard Kaplan for their wise suggestions. The research and writing of this essay were generously funded by a grant from the Joint Committee for Japanese Studies of the Social Science Research Council and the American Council of Learned Societies with funds provided by the Ford Foundation and the National Endowment for the Humanities.

1 Francis L. Hawks, *Narrative of the Expedition of an American Squadron to the China Seas and Japan, performed in the years 1852, 1853, and 1854, under the command of Commodore M. C. Perry, United States* (Washington, D.C.: Nicholson, by order of the Government of the United States, 1856), 2:395.

2  Ibid.

3  In addition to Hawks, see James Morrow, *A Scientist with Perry in Japan: The Journal of Dr. James Morrow*, ed. Allan B. Cole (Chapel Hill: University of North Carolina Press, 1947).

4  Samuel Wells Williams, *A Journal of the Perry Expedition to Japan (1853–1854)*, printed as *Transactions of the Asiatic Society of Japan* 37, no. 2 (1910); rpt., Wilmington, Del.: Scholarly Resources, 1973.

5  Oliver Statler, *Shimoda Story* (Rutland, Vt.: Tuttle, 1971). I note that Statler's primary focus is the Harris expedition of 1856–58.

6  The transliterations of "Lo" and "Luo" refer to the same Chinese surname. The former is the old Wade-Giles romanization; the latter is the newer *pinyin* system.

7  Luo Sen, *Riben riji* [Japan diary], in *Zaoqi Riben youji wuzhong* [Five early diaries of travel to Japan], ed. Wang Xiaoqiu (Changsha: Hunan renmin chubanshe, 1983), 27–44. Luo's diary first appeared in Chinese in the monthly *Xia'er guanzhen* (English title: "Chinese Serial") (November 1854; December 1854; January 1855). According to Hawks, the English translation appeared in the Hong Kong newspaper *Overland Register and Price Current*, 11 September 1854. Williams's son, Frederick Wells Williams, states that his father translated Luo's diary for the "Hong Kong Register," but I find no such newspaper and believe that Frederick meant the *Overland Register*. In any event, the English text differs in so many ways from the Chinese diary that it might be more appropriate to call it not a "translation" but an alternative version. See Frederick Wells Williams, *The Life and Letters of Samuel Wells Williams, LL.D.: Missionary, Diplomatist, Sinologue* (New York: G. P. Putnam's Sons; Knickerbocker, 1889), 218.

8  The very recent historical reconstruction by Peter Booth Wiley adds no new knowledge of Luo; like Statler, Wiley relies on Williams's diary for information about Luo. See Peter Booth Wiley, with Korogi Ichiro, *Yankees in the Land of the Gods: Commodore Perry and the Opening of Japan* (New York: Viking, 1990). Incidentally, Wiley uses the preferred pronunciation of nineteenth-century lexicographers for Luo's personal name, "Shen"; hence his unusual usage "Luo Shen."

9  Wang Xiaoqiu, "Shi chuan zhongwu kan dongbu: *Zaoqi Riben youji wuzhong* xu" [First ventures through heavy mist to view the East: an introduction to *Five Early Diaries of Travel to Japan*], in *Zaoqi Riben youji wuzhong*, 10. Wang reiterated his comments regarding Luo Sen in *Jindai Zhongguo qishi lu* (Beijing: Beijing chubanshe, 1987), 211–214.

10  Hawks, *Narrative*, 2:395.

11  Ibid., 2:400.

12  Williams, *Journal*, 83.

13  Hawks, *Narrative*, 1:395; and Williams, *Life and Letters*, 212.

14  Luo, *Riben riji*, 28.

15  Statler, *Shimoda Story*, 40, 103, 128, 346.

16  The travel records from the Perry expedition are exhaustively surveyed in John Ashmead, *The Idea of Japan, 1853–1895: Japan as Described by American and Other Travellers from the West* (New York: Garland, 1987), 50–65. I am grateful to David Tucker for drawing my attention to this work.

17  Wang, *Jindai Zhongguo qishi lu*, 211.

18  My willingness to imagine a common program for Adorno and Benjamin is very much due to Susan Buck-Morss, *The Origin of Negative Dialectics: Theodor W. Adorno, Walter Benjamin, and the Frankfurt Institute* (New York: Free Press, 1979).

19  Walter Benjamin, *The Origin of German Tragic Drama*, trans. John Osborne (London: NLB, 1977), 38–44 (hereafter *OGTD*). Cf. Adorno's discussion of "historicity" in *Kierkegaard: Construction of the Aesthetic*, trans. Robert Hullot-Kentor (Minneapolis: University of Minnesota Press, 1989), 33.

20  Max Horkheimer and Theodor W. Adorno, *Dialectic of Enlightenment*, trans. John Cumming (New York: Continuum, 1972), 121 (hereafter *DOE*).

21  Walter Benjamin, "N [Re the Theory of Knowledge, Theory of Progress]," in *Benjamin: Philosophy, Aesthetics, History*, ed. Gary Smith (Chicago: University of Chicago Press, 1989), 70.

22  Theodor W. Adorno, *Minima Moralia: Reflections from Damaged Life*, trans. E. F. N. Jephcott (London: NLB, 1974), 219 (hereafter *MM*).

23  Walter Benjamin, "Theses on the Philosophy of History," *Illuminations*, trans. Harry Zohn (New York: Schocken, 1969), 258.

24  *DOE*, 3–42 passim.

25  Benjamin, "Theses," 260–261.

26  Benjamin, "N," 60.

27  Ibid., 47. There is a second way in which construction places the present in a critical position. Insofar as historical reconstruction reifies the "presence" of a historian's interpretation (work is described favorably as "timely" or "up to date," unfavorably as "dated"), historical construction instead interferes with that presence of action, at the risk of confusing the present and the past (defined as a series of past "Now-times"). Preliminary forays into this issue of the temporality of construction have been published in *Walter Benjamin's Philosophy: Destruction and Experience*, ed. Andrew Benjamin and Peter Osborne (London: Routledge, 1994); see especially the respective contributions by the two editors.

28  Benjamin, "N," 47ff.

29  Ibid., 66.

30  *OGTD*, 161.

31  Benjamin, "N," 60, 66.

32  For an insightful meditation on this aspect of Benjamin, see H. Harootunian, "The Benjamin Effect: Repetition and the Possibility of Different Cultural Histories," unpublished ms.

33 Benjamin, "N," 63, 66.

34 Cf. the Russian Formalist notion of "defamiliarization," in Tony Bennett, *Formalism and Marxism* (London: Methuen, 1979), 20ff., 50ff.

35 See Etienne Balibar, "On the Basic Concepts of Historical Materialism," in *Reading Capital*, ed. Louis Althusser and Etienne Balibar, trans. Ben Brewster (London: NLB, 1970), 201–308.

36 Benjamin, "Theses," 253ff. See the sympathetic discussion of these issues by Rolf Tiedemann, "Historical Materialism or Political Messianism? An Interpretation of the Theses 'On the Concept of History,'" in Smith, *Benjamin: Philosophy, History, Aesthetics*, 174–209.

37 Walter Benjamin, "The Paris of the Second Empire in Baudelaire," in *Charles Baudelaire: A Lyric Poet in the Era of High Capitalism*, trans. Harry Zohn (London: NLB, 1973), 104.

38 In the "Adorno-Benjamin debates," Adorno objected not so much to Benjamin's invocation of "historical materialism" as to Benjamin's omission of a theoretical position that would allow for mediation of the elements in his Baudelaire construction. See Theodor W. Adorno, "Letters to Walter Benjamin," in *Aesthetics and Politics*, ed. Ronald Taylor (London: NLB, 1977), 129.

39 Benjamin, "Theses," 256.

40 Ibid., 262f. In his discussion of "Thesis XVII," Rolf Tiedemann points out the origin of "construction" in Marx's afterword to the second edition of *Capital*. See "Historical Materialism," 185.

41 Harootunian, "Benjamin Effect," 14. Note that this was also a motive of the German romantics earlier in the century; see Kathleen M. Wheeler, introduction to *German Aesthetic and Literary Criticism: The Romantic Ironists and Goethe* (Cambridge: Cambridge University Press, 1984), 1–27.

42 By "form," I do not mean the concept used in linguistics and literary studies pertaining to a level of analysis—that is, "form" as opposed to "content" or "meaning." This concept was soundly criticized by V. N. Volosinov in *Marxism and the Philosophy of Language*, trans. Ladislav Matejka and I. R. Titunik (New York: Seminar, 1973). Rather, I mean "form" in the sense used by cultural linguists Benveniste, Whorf, and Sapir: a "structure" of perception and understanding. It is this sense of "form," I believe, that is at the basis of Fredric Jameson's pertinent work, *Marxism and Form: Twentieth-Century Dialectical Theories of Literature* (Princeton, N.J.: Princeton University Press, 1971). See page xvi regarding form as the "pretext" of thinking.

43 OGTD, 29, 34, 178. Cf. Walter Benjamin, "A Berlin Chronicle," in *One-Way Street and Other Writings*, trans. Edmund Jephcott and Kingsley Shorter (London: NLB, 1979), 337.

44 OGTD, 33–35. See also Theodor W. Adorno, "The Actuality of Philosophy," *Telos* 31 (spring 1977): 125–128.

45 OGTD, 43.

46 Adorno, "Actuality," 131. See Buck-Morss, *Origin*, 101–103.

47 Adorno, *Kierkegaard*, 40–46.

48 Benjamin, "N," 48–50.

49 Ibid., 67.

50 Ibid., 47. Adorno's criticism of Benjamin prompted the so-called Benjamin–Adorno debates in the 1930s. See Adorno, "Letters," 110–120, and Benjamin, "Paris—the Capital of the Nineteenth Century," in *Charles Baudelaire*, 155–176. Benjamin scholars continue to debate whether or not his images are truly "dialectical" or mediated in any fashion; most sympathetic is Susan Buck-Morss, *The Dialectics of Seeing: Walter Benjamin and the Arcades Project* (Cambridge: MIT Press, 1989), 205–252. Peter Osborne argues that mediation occurs in the *experience* of the dialectical image insofar as it joins the Now-time and a moment of the past; see "Small-scale Victories, Large-scale Defeats: Walter Benjamin's Politics of Time," in *Walter Benjamin's Philosophy*, 85–89.

51 Benjamin, "N," 54f. See the discussion of montage by Andrew Benjamin, "Time and Task: Benjamin and Heidegger Showing the Present," in *Walter Benjamin's Philosophy*, 240–247. One writer who has used Benjamin's theories of history and montage with stunning insight is Michael Taussig, *Shamanism, Colonialism, and the Wild Man: A Study in Terror and Healing* (Chicago: University of Chicago Press, 1987), esp. 366–392, 435–446.

52 Adorno, "Actuality," 130–131. An excellent example of Adorno's method is the 1957 essay "Lyric Poetry and Society," *Telos* 20 (summer 1974): 56–71.

53 Theodor W. Adorno, "Reconciliation under Duress," in *Aesthetics and Politics*, 159–160.

54 Ibid., 168.

55 *OGTD*, 32.

56 Adorno, "Reconciliation," 163. Cf. *DOE*, 17–18.

57 Benjamin, "Edward Fuchs, Collector and Historian," in *One-Way Street*, 359–361; and "N," 72–73.

58 Adorno, "Letters," 111.

59 Benjamin, "Reply," in *Aesthetics and Politics*, 136–137. See also Richard Wolin, "Experience and Materialism in Benjamin's *Passagenwerk*," in *Benjamin: Philosophy, Aesthetics, History*, 210–227; and Richard Wolin, *Walter Benjamin: An Aesthetic of Redemption* (New York: Columbia University Press, 1982), 163–183.

60 Williams, *Journal*, 224f.

61 Aaron Haight Palmer, "Revised Plan for opening Japan . . . ," in *Documents and Facts Illustrating the Origin of the Mission to Japan, Authorized by Government of the United States, May 10th, 1851; and which finally resulted in the treaty concluded by Commodore M. C. Perry, U.S. Navy, with the Japanese Commissioners at Kanagawa, Bay of Yedo, on the 31st March, 1854* (Washington, D.C.: Henry Polkinhorn, 1857), 11. According to Peter Wiley, it was the report of the treatment of the shipwrecked crew of the whaler *Lagoda*, which reached Washington during 1850, that galvanized interest in an expedition

to Japan (see *Yankees*, 22–30, 78ff.). These reports are available in the U.S. Senate Executive Document No. 59 ["certain official documents relative to the empire of Japan"], 32nd Cong. 1st sess., 12 April 1852.

62  Palmer, "Revised Plan," 12–13; but see also U.S. Senate Executive Document No. 59, 80–82. According to Wiley, C. M. Conrad, the acting Secretary of State, gave Perry the official orders to secure (1) the protection of American sailors shipwrecked in Japan, (2) permission for ships to resupply in Japan and to establish coaling stations there, and (3) permission for ships to trade at designated ports in Japan. But there was some disagreement over this purpose of the mission, as Perry wanted to emphasize whaling rights and was less optimistic about opening diplomatic relations (see *Yankees*, 103f., 116f.).

63  Palmer, "Revised Plan," 10–11, 15. Williams printed his "Narrative of a voyage of the ship Morrison . . . ," in *The Chinese Repository* 6, no. 5 (September 1837): 209–229, and 6, no. 8 (December 1837): 353–380.

64  Williams, *Journal*, 47.

65  Ibid., 222. Cf. Williams's similar comments of 1837, "Narrative of a voyage of the ship Morrison," 377f.

66  Williams, *Journal*, 120.

67  Ibid., 148, 208, 225f.

68  Ibid., 151.

69  Luo, *Riben riji*, 28.

70  Ibid., 33.

71  Ibid., 42.

72  Ibid., 28.

73  Williams, *Journal*, 222f.

74  Ibid., 3f., 227ff.

75  A sign may also be an *index* of some larger process. As we have already seen, the introduction of the "useful and curious specimens of Western art"—the steam engine, telegraph, and so on—were said to manifest the spread of Western civilization. In this regard, the sign perhaps most powerfully repeated in the imaginations of members of the expedition was the singular act of "opening" Japan: where admission had long been denied, the U.S. Navy had entered, profoundly exposing the Japanese to superior American civilization. See ibid., 224–225; and Hawks, *Narrative*, 1: 4.

76  Williams, *Journal*, 224; Luo, *Riben riji*, 28.

77  *Edinburgh Review*, 96 (1852), 383, quoted in W. G. Beasley, *The Rise of Modern Japan* (New York: St. Martin's, 1990), 28. U.S. Secretary of State Daniel Webster reiterated the same conclusions in a letter of 10 June 1851, reprinted in U.S. Senate Executive Document No. 59, 80f.

78  Palmer intends his comprehensive plan for the independent "Oriental Nations" in *Documents and Facts*, 5–10. See also Commodore Glynn's 1851 report to the shipping firm of Howland and Aspinwall, in U.S. Senate Executive Document No. 59, 57–62.

79  Luo, *Riben riji*, 31.

80  Matthew C. Perry, *The Japan Expedition, 1852–1854: The Personal Journal of Commodore Matthew C. Perry*, ed. Robert Pineau (Washington, D.C.: Smithsonian Institution Press, 1968), 159. It was a U.S. naval policy to accept no "presents" from foreign powers; see U.S. Senate Executive Document No. 59, 30.

81  Williams, *Journal*, 190, 210f; Luo, *Riben riji*, 39. Ashmead relates that Townsend Harris, the subsequent U.S. envoy to Japan, made an annual profit of $6,000 from a yearly salary of $5,000 (see *Idea of Japan*, 353).

82  Williams, *Journal*, 195; Luo, *Riben riji*, 38, 42.

83  Compare Williams, *Journal*, 195; and John R. C. Lewis, *Bluejackets with Perry in Japan: A day-by-day account kept by Master's Mate John R. C. Lewis and Cabin Boy William B. Allen*, ed. Henry F. Graff (New York: New York Public Library, 1952), 154f.

84  William, *Journal*, 224f.

85  Luo, *Riben riji*, 32.

86  Ibid., 33.

87  Williams, *Journal*, 151.

88  Ibid., 166, 170.

89  Ibid., 184; Luo, *Riben riji*, 37.

90  Japanese officials were shocked to find a map of Edo in Williams's possession, even though it was copied from a Dutch map made eighty-six years earlier (see Williams, *Journal*, 69).

91  Hawks, *Narrative*, 2:400.

92  Ibid., 1:8, 165, 192, 421.

93  Williams, *Journal*, 104, 120, 126, 142.

94  On "brushtalking" generally and the interpenetration of Chinese and Japanese languages, see Douglas Howland, "The Japanese Borders of the Chinese Empire" (Ph.D. diss., University of Chicago, 1989), 72–95.

95  Williams, *Journal*, 137–139.

96  Luo, *Riben riji*, 35f., 39f., 41.

97  Howland, "Japanese Borders," 95–112. Can we not read Hirayama's invocation of the moral society, coming from a man clearly aware of Japan's commercialized economy, as just such an erudite overture to Luo Sen?

98  "Meitoku" appears to be a "literary name"—what the Chinese call *zi* and the Japanese *azana*.

99  Luo, *Riben riji*, 42.

100  Williams, *Journal*, 193, 210.

101  Ibid., 211, 214.

102  "Additional Regulations" (Article 7), rpt. in Wiley, *Yankees*, 504f.

103  Williams, *Journal*, 131–134; Hawks, *Narrative*, 1:356f.; and Perry, *Japan Expedition*, 176f., 233f.

104  Williams, *Journal*, 145–147; Hawks, *Narrative*, 1:359f.; Perry, *Japan Expedition*, 194–196.

105 Pierre Bourdieu, *Outline of a Theory of Practice*, trans. Richard Nice (Cambridge: Cambridge University Press, 1977), 4–8. See also Marshall Sahlins's pertinent comments on the role of "relative cultural logics" in intercultural relations: "Cosmologies of Capitalism: The Trans-Pacific Sector of 'The World System'," in *Culture/Power/History: A Reader in Contemporary Social Theory*, ed. Nicholas B. Dirks, Geoff Eley, and Sherry B. Ortner (Princeton, N.J.: Princeton University Press, 1994), 412–455.

106 Perry, *Japan Expedition*, 194.

107 Williams, *Journal*, 153.

108 Ibid., 145.

109 Perry, *Japan Expedition*, 190–194; Williams, *Journal*, 147f.; Hawks, *Narrative*, 1: 369f.; and Morrow, *Scientist*, 146. See also the comments of naval officer Edward Yorke McCauley, who disdained the banquet, presents, and entertainment, like most of what he witnessed in Japan: *With Perry in Japan: The Diary of Edward Yorke McCauley*, ed. Allan B. Cole (Princeton, N.J.: Princeton University Press, 1942), 96–100.

110 Perry, *Japan Expedition*, 190–194; and Williams, *Journal*, 147f.

111 Perry, *Japan Expedition*, 194.

112 Ibid., 196.

113 Ibid., 198.

114 Luo, *Riben riji*, 35.

115 Ibid., 34; Williams, *Journal*, 159; and Williams, *Life and Letters*, 219.

116 Williams, *Journal*, 154–157.

117 Ibid., 153, 213.

118 Clearly, an epistemological critique of the practice of construction is in order and might pursue the question: how do we evaluate the "logic of inner harmony" mentioned above?

119 For example, see Wolin, "Experience and Materialism," 212.

120 An attendant issue is the complicity of narrative in the truthfulness of historiography, explored perhaps most by Hayden White, who pairs an internal truth of coherence with an intertextual truth of correspondence in "The Fictions of Factual Representation," in *Tropics of Discourse: Essays in Cultural Criticism* (Baltimore, Md.: Johns Hopkins University Press, 1978), 121–134.

121 Benjamin's early manifesto, "On the Program of the Coming Philosophy," calls for such a redefinition of experience and truth; to that end, Benjamin undertakes a criticism of what he takes to be two problems in Kant's metaphysics: the dependence of knowledge on the opposition of subject and object, and the privileging of empirical consciousness over transcendental consciousness (in *Benjamin: Philosophy, Aesthetics, History*, 1–12). For a discussion of other early essays in which Benjamin began to formulate his understanding of truth as fleeting and fragmentary see Michael W. Jennings, *Dialectical Images: Walter Benjamin's Theory of Literary Criticism* (Ithaca, N.Y.: Cornell University Press, 1978), 128–132.

122 *OGTD*, 29–30.

123 Ibid., 32.

124 Ibid., 31.

125 Ibid., 35–36.

126 Ibid., 36; and Wolin, "Experience and Materialism," 213. Wolin elsewhere explicates nonintentionality as the union of the empirical and the intelligible (see *Walter Benjamin*, 92–95).

127 Benjamin, "N," 65. See also Wolin, "Experience and Materialism," 213; and Winfried Menninghaus, "Walter Benjamin's Theory of Myth," in *On Walter Benjamin: Critical Essays and Recollections*, ed. Gary Smith (Cambridge: MIT Press, 1988), 315.

128 Wolin, "Experience and Materialism," 210–211; and Max Pensky, *Melancholy Dialectics: Walter Benjamin and the Play of Mourning* (Amherst: University of Massachusetts Press, 1993), 216f., 223.

129 In discussing Adorno's aesthetics, critics typically ignore *Minima Moralia* and instead focus on the later writings, *Negative Dialectics* and *Aesthetic Theory*; hence my interest in looking more closely at the earlier formulation.

130 *MM*, 75.

131 Ibid., 224f.

132 Ibid., 76. Much later in his career, Adorno wrote a brilliant little essay that discusses the reciprocal determination of subject and object; see "Subject and Object," in *The Essential Frankfurt School Reader*, ed. Andrew Arato and Eike Gebhardt (New York: Continuum, 1982), 497–511.

133 *MM*, 224.

134 Ibid., 76.

135 Ibid., 94–95.

136 Ibid., 77. "Contemplation" here is *Anschauung*.

137 In the case of Benjamin's concept of the "aura" of the work of art, Rodolphe Gasché argues that auratic works of art are individual and presuppose an individual subject as viewer, and that nonauratic modern works of art presuppose mass audiences. See "Objective Diversions: On Some Kantian Themes in Benjamin's 'The Work of Art in the Age of Mechanical Reproduction,'" in *Walter Benjamin's Philosophy*, 182–204.

138 *MM*, 15.

139 Ibid., 142.

140 On Adorno's style see Gillian Rose, *The Melancholy Science: An Introduction to the Thought of Theodor W. Adorno* (New York: Columbia University Press, 1978), 11–14.

141 For a discussion of the "problem" of communication and intersubjectivity in Adorno see Albrecht Wellmer, "Truth, Semblance, Reconciliation: Adorno's Aesthetic Redemption of Modernity," *Telos* 62 (winter 1984–85): 98–100.

142 Theodor W. Adorno, "Resignation," *Telos* 35 (spring 1978): 168.

Redemption and Consumption:

Depicting Culture in the 1990s

### CULTURAL MAO ZEDONG

■ Of the social and cultural phenomena at the end of the 1980s and the beginning of the 1990s that most caught people's attention, one probably was "Mao Zedong fever." This was undoubtedly one of the social and cultural symptoms of both the mutual opposition between and the deconstruction of the employment of the ideological state apparatus and the first appearance of specific public space, the re-affirmation of prohibitions and the consumption of prohibitions, the reiteration of mainstream discourse and a voyeuristic desire to view political secrets, and so on. In other words, this was another interesting space, publicly used for multiple discourses. In some sense, while "Mao fever" attained a peak in 1990 and declined somewhat thereafter, it continued uninterrupted until it achieved yet a new climax on a grand scale during the organized activities of the 1993 centenary commemorations. It is in just this specific public space that "Mao Zedong fever," emerging out of several centers via multiple media, actually constructed an inscription of "the cultural Mao Zedong." This was a reconstruction and a parody, an employment of ideology and a consumption of ideology.

In fact, even though it was a classic method for employing mainstream discourse, the image of Mao Zedong appeared not only as simply the reproduction of classic revolutionary narrative, or as some may say, "the national narrative" of the initial "traumatic circumstances" representing the nation state, but also as a new narrative tactic, a retelling and reconstruction of the classic narrative discourse of divinity and revolution in the midst of deviation and dislocation. Such were the circumstances not only in the major "revolutionary epics" of the 1990s, also known to some as "the main melody" films (such as *Kai tian pi di* [The birth of new China], *Da jue zhan* [Decisive battles], *Kai guo da dian* [Founding the nation], and *Chongqing tanpan* [Conference in Chongqing]), but also in numerous feature film and television miniseries productions using biographical materials featuring Mao Zedong as the main character. In a certain sense, "Mao Zedong fever," both as the leading narrative, the narrative of revolutionary history that was the means of employing the dominant discourse, and as the debut of public space arising from the social stratum of urban residents, was not a discursive system of mutually opposed conflicts, or the struggle and opposition among cultural and discursive powers between center and margin. The fact is that already by the end of the 1980s, even before mainstream discourse and revolutionary canonical narrative returned to its reliance on Mao Zedong's image, a hint of "Mao Zedong fever" had already appeared within urban society. In what seemed to be a new fashion or fad, portraits of Mao Zedong (and occasionally portraits of Zhou Enlai)—what had been standard emblems of the divine—were now dangling decorations, beginning to be in great demand among taxi drivers and starting to appear on the windshields of cars and vans, replacing what had previously been so popular, that is, the fuzzy toys, the bottles of air freshener (which were something "foreign," an imaginary Western atmosphere), and the inverted lucky *fudao* pendants (the traditional talisman for a safe journey). Then the same illustrations appeared decorating leather beeper pouches, watch faces, and windproof lighters. This was quite in vogue for a time. Unlike what some overseas commentators have stressed, this did not simply express some form of discontent or attitude of political protest. In a certain sense, the promise of the fulfillment of the "Four Modernizations" at the end of the 1970s and the beginning of the 1980s, had once again ushered in a "Great Leap Forward" or fervid, utopian expectations. And for the entire decade of the 1980s the hot air balloon of optimism and idealism continued to rise with ever greater speed. When the gulf between imagination and reality showed up clearly at the beginning of the 1990s, it undoubtedly brought with it strong disappointment and discontent; at the same time, the continuous public exposure of high-level corruption deepened this sense of loss and dissatisfaction. Therefore, the onset and peak of "Mao Zedong fever" indeed has had political and real significance for the reiteration of canonical myth in the new social context. It signifies an imaginary redemption and road of return. Simultaneously, it is: an important social and cultural symptom, revealing to people an extremely important state of mind in the society of mainland China during its transformation; a recollection, not without sincere feeling, of people's faith in authority before the onset of gradual pluralization and the evaporation of the center; a look back on an age of idealism, neither without cynicism nor without sentimentality, before the great tide of pragmatism and commerce and the imminent victory of consumerism on all fronts; a calling out to heroes and myths that arose from the people in an age that "needed heroes"; and a lingering love of a nation losing divinity and prohibition, reluctant to part with a last symbol of the sacred and the taboo. It now and again conveys in the process of rewriting a desire for redemptive memory. Or, more accurately, the popular swelling of "Mao Zedong fever" signifies the longing of people for a sense of trust and of "security" in society, the memory of an age that, while not prosperous, still (at least in theory and imagination) neither knew hunger nor felt threatened. However, what the majority of commentators either ignore or overlook is precisely the "medium" of Mao Zedong's image at the onset of "Mao Zedong fever." Obviously, cars, beepers, and windproof lighters at the time were symbols of fashion, signifiers of consumerism. Therefore, it was more the revelation of a political unconscious than some kind of clearly conscious political behavior: the displacement and identification of political power with consumerism. Simultaneously it signified an ideological trend toward the quotidien and consumerization, precisely in a form that was not without irreverence and profanity, as it carried out the final dissolution of the taboo and the sacred.

By the end of the 1980s and the beginning of the 1990s, among thousands and tens of thousands of publications and audiovisual products, the most sustained of hot topics among hot topics was the book by Quan Yanchi titled *Zou xia shentan de Mao Zedong* [Mao Zedong off the altar], which took the form of the memoirs of Li Yinqiao, who for so many years followed Chairman Mao as the commander of his bodyguard. (Besides this, there were several other popular publications whose contents were largely similar to *Mao Zedong Off the Altar* and that took the same form, such as *Zou xiang shentan de Mao Zedong* [Mao Zedong ascending the altar], *Hong qiang nei wai* [Inside Beidaihe], *Lingxiu lei* [Tears of the leader], *Weishizhang tan Mao Zedong* [The commander of the bodyguard talks about Mao Zedong]). One hundred thousand copies were distributed for the first edition alone, and it continued as a best-seller through subsequent editions over the next four or five years (and that's not counting, for the moment, pirate editions and revisions). What is interesting is that *Mao Zedong Off the Altar* not only was an outstanding best-seller but also in some senses sounded the key note of "Mao Zedong fever" and constituted a set of observations for this important social and cultural phenomenon. And this work, which so many millions struggled to buy and wept over, in part intentionally and in part unintentionally, actually became the most successful example in the change of mainstream discourse and discursive tactics. *Off the Altar* is one true meaning of this instance of "Mao Zedong fever." If we follow the interpretation of Song Yifu and Zhang Zhanbin, who take the "Mao Zedong fever" of the 1950s as the beginning of the "deification" movement and the "Mao Zedong fever" of the 1960s as the frenzied pinnacle of the "deification" movement, then the "Mao Zedong fever" at the end of the 1980s and beginning of the 1990s was the process of narrating or renarrating a "deapotheosis."[1] Even though prior to this there had been titles that took similar forms, such as *Gensui Mao Zhuxi chang zheng* [Following Chairman Mao on the Long March], it was in *Off the Altar* that Mao Zedong appeared for the first time in a setting of daily life, a setting of husband and wife, of father and son, depicting the normal activities of eating and drinking. A great man, but one of flesh and blood, of feelings and of sorrow in his temperament and his logic. A man who, because he transcended ordinary people, had to accept more and greater suffering. A man made so lonely by his greatness even that he was beyond help. So many great historical events of New China have been endowed in this book with individualized and personalized motives and explanations. The leader of myriads, yet still with all the feelings of an ordinary person. So, because of what they learned when they read this book, people would revive and rewrite their sense of veneration in some entirely new mood of compassion and forgiveness. On account of this, *Off the Altar* became required source reading for nearly all the contemporary historical "large-scale revolutionary epics," biographical films, and television series on Mao Zedong, and nearly every film and television production of this kind had to contain situations and details taken from this book. In a narrative tone of emotiveness and individualization, which was handled in a relatively low key, the rewritten historical scenes repeatedly demanded of readers and audiences (the People?) a sense of understanding, forgiveness, and shared responsibility. In a sense, *Off the Altar* not only supplied so many "main melody" films with new source materials, new narrative strategies, new tone and distance, but also became the indispensable reference source to be consulted in the subsequent boom of writing, publishing, and marketing of best-sellers on Mao Zedong. Books like *Mao Zedong zhuan* [The biography of Mao Zedong], *Wo yan zhong de Mao Zedong* [Mao Zedong in my eyes], *Shenghuo zhong de Mao Zedong* [Mao Zedong in life], *1946–1976 Zedong shenghuo shilu* [Chronicle of the life of Mao Zedong, 1946–76], *Mao Zedong de ernümen* [Sons and daughters of Mao Zedong], *Mao Zedong yishi* [Anecdotes of Mao Zedong], *Mao Zedong yiwen lu* [A record of anecdotes about Mao Zedong], *Zoujin Mao Zedong* [Mao Zedong up close], and so forth and so on, were all best-sellers with first editions running anywhere from the tens of thousands to hundreds of thousands of copies, filling bookstores and bookstalls in every major city. Simultaneously, along with "Mao Zedong fever," the songs of the 1960s and its "Cultural Revolution" regained popularity performed by popular singers with electronic accompaniment. Taking their theme from "I Cherish You, *Mao Zedong Off the Altar*" (performed by Zhang Mi and Yang Zongqiang, Hubei Audiovisual Publishers), audiovisual publishers throughout the nation published hundreds of audio cassettes and CDs with odes to Mao Zedong and songs of his quotations.[2] This was true popularity, in cable broadcasts with classical trumpets, on the radio, on television, in concerts of every description, in variety programs, and in karaoke clubs, KTV booths, in the enthusiasm for home karaoke, on mass, open-air dance floors and in expensive, elegant dance spots. To youth, it was a new and different fad, and to middle-aged and older people, it was a fond and familiar, "personal" memory that spanned forty years. When in 1993 the French pianist Richard Clayderman visited China and performed in Beijing at the Capital Stadium with its capacity of tens of thousands, his pastiche style, a style of performance that was simultaneously both extremely elegant and comic, and his rendition of the exquisite, moving "Autumn Whisper," known throughout China, certainly drew the most enthusiastic of responses from the youthful audience, but only when the melody of "Reddest of Suns, Mao Zedong Is Dearest to Me" was heard did the entire stadium truly enter a fanatic state.

If we say that the dominant discourse of authority, in the process of narrating a deapotheosization that centered on *Mao Zedong Off the Altar*, tried to conform, through new narrative strategies and tone, to "the time in which the myth is told (retold)"[3] (while in a new fad, urban residents expressed their actual morale and need for a sense of security), then among news features on these burning issues, two hot topics that stirred up a sensation revealed another significance that was often overlooked by people. One was the news feature report that every entertainment and gossip publication vied to print and reprint about a certain actor of a particular appearance who specialized in portrayals of the leader and who was demanding high appearance fees on evening arts and literary shows and cheating on his taxes.[4] The other was the subsequent report that the daughter of Li Jiefu, an important and famous composer of the 1960s and 1970s, was suing several audiovisual publishers for pirating Li's work and violating his copyright and right of acknowledgment. This case was decided in favor of the plaintiff and concluded with two of the companies publicly apologizing and paying damages. As a suit over copyright and right of acknowledgment to a cultural product that during the 1960s and 1970s had been a powerful instrument of political propaganda and ideology, the latter example, especially, peeled away the inertial imagination and cognitive mode which held the music to be "spiritual wealth" commonly owned by society, and it laid bare the music's value and price as privately owned property. These two news features revealed that behind "Mao Zedong fever" was the reality of a consumer culture and cultural consumption. In a certain sense, from the peak of "Mao Zedong fever" in 1990 down to the present, this is a fact that was all too clear. The vulgar Mao Zedong badge, once taken by people as the product of ignorance and authoritarianism, now became a personal collectors' item of great value and was also reproduced and sold. All sorts of "precious red books" of that era—*The Quotations of Chairman Mao,* the four-in-one-volume pocket edition of Mao Zedong's *Selected Works,* and Mao's portrait— went for unheard-of prices in places frequented by foreign tourists and travelers. "Cultural Revolution" postage stamps were traded up in value by stamp collectors until they reached phenomenal prices. Even various kinds of mimeographed circulars from the Cultural Revolution were snapped up like rare valuables. If we say that the birth of "Mao Zedong fever" had its profound and pluralistic social, cultural, and psychological components, then its proliferation simultaneously contained a relationship of supply and demand in the consumption of contemporary Chinese political exhibitionism and voyeurism. It truly was a process of ideological production and reproduction and at the same time a very typical process of production/consumption—very much a consumer-culture fad with the most Chinese of characteristics. In it, mainstream discourse and consumer culture clashed with each other, relied on each other, mutually deconstructed each other, and constantly merged with each other. If we say that the process of "deapotheosization" on which the mainstream narrative of the 1990s relied repeatedly tried to fashion a new cultural conformity out of converting divinity, worship, and dread or loathing into understanding, compassion, and forgiveness, then the flaw in this strategy was that these feelings of compassion erased the last of the aura of divinity from the idol. If we say that "ruined temples are still shrines, toppled idols are still divinities," then the heat wave of "Mao Zedong fever," which consumed prohibitions, memory, and ideology, also eliminated the canyon between "the loftiness of the palace" and "the vastness of the realm," between the transcendence of the divine and the mundane world of the urban residents. Perhaps it could be said that this is something special to mainland China—sunset and dawn overlapping each other, the conclusion and the beginning of yet another age.

The gala artistic performance held on 26 December 1993 by China Central Television at Mao Zedong's hometown, Shaoshan, to commemorate the one hundredth anniversary of his birth seems to be an interesting case in point. The first half of the performance was a series of odes to Mao Zedong from the 1960s and 1970s sung by a grand chorus—majestic, powerful, manifesting again and again the magnificence and fascination of socialist choral art. Yet in a child's solo, written especially for this occasion, the following lines appear: "I asked Mama, Who is he? / Mama said: He is the clouds in the sky; / He is the lamp on the wall; / He is the brave old eagle in the mountains; / He is the busy bee." In the pluralistic, yet shared writing of the "Cultural Mao Zedong," a social and cultural transformation, an entirely new shift of power and change of direction, is taking place.

## THE REAPPEARANCE OF THE ORIGINAL PICTURE

Among the many social and cultural phenomena in the consumption of memory and ideology, those unique products of the "Cultural Revolution" era—the community of educated youth, the culture and writings of educated youth, and the transformations and shifts in the discourse about educated youth—form yet another rich set of symptoms in culture and the consumption of culture.

In one sense, the term *educated youth literature* that flourished in the mid- and late 1980s does not just refer to a particular group of writers or a particular set of narrated events but also to a narrative mode of multiple sutures, an extremely particular cultural space penetrated by a pluralistically determined discourse. It was unadorned confession and also a spiritual mask, an exhibition of wounds and a showing off of spiritual wealth. It was the writing of the special memories of a generation, whether expurgated, unaffected, or fictionalized. At the same time, it was "seeking roots"—a pursuit and questioning of the sorrow and despair in the national cultural memory. It was a place in which avant-garde literature at times set foot, and it was space that women's writing often entered. Like the 1980s movement reflecting on history and culture, it actually was the cultural extension of stillborn political reflection or its transformation into metaphor. "Educated youth literature" unquestionably continued, in the wake of "wound literature" and "reflection literature," to assume directly the ponderous and onerous memory of the politics of the Cultural Revolution/reality.

However, unlike "wound literature" and "reflection literature," this specially designated space of educated youth literature contains profoundly complex emotions and declarations. It is more like endlessly coiling memories and recollections than yet another accusation; more approaching something like a record of dreams and glory than penitence; more an inability either to resign itself or to control its own feelings than a deep reflection on history. Consequently, "educated youth literature" appears to be a special case, with a special license to link memories of the Cultural Revolution, of the Red Guard movement, and of the rustication movement of educated youth "up the mountains and down to the countryside" with mainstream ideology, forming subtle shifts and convergences. In fact, from "Lü ye" [Green night] to "Da lin mang" [Forest primeval], from "Zhe shi yipian shenqi de tudi" [This is a piece of miraculous earth] to "Jin muchang" [Golden pastures]—even to "Maijie duo" [Haystacks] and "Gang shang de shiji" [A century on duty]—from first to last, educated youth literature, whether typical or less typical, had a basic tone: of remorse during one's youth (yet with no regrets for one's youth), of sorrow and pain, or of high spirits or guilty reflection—all of which were out of place with the mainstream discourse, which thoroughly repudiated the "The Great Cultural Revolution."[5] However, the reason it could form such a special category, obtain such special license, is precisely because it held on doggedly, passionately, and irrationally to a fervor for idealism and for a heroism that harbors no regrets for having suffered terrible wounds. Unquestionably, this is the spirit and the fundamental narrative tone that won (and today still wins) the strong approval of mainstream ideology. In fact, as far as educated youth literature goes, it is less that it refuses to purge the era of the Cultural Revolution than that it refuses to purge the memories of the writers' own youth. Where Milan Kundera described the cultural situation of Eastern Europe during the 1960s as one in which "a generation erased their own youth," what happened in mainland China during the 1980s would seem to present just the opposite situation.[6] To a generation of people who went through their youth during the ten years of the Cultural Revolution, slogans like "Make the Gang of Four give back our youth" or "Subtract ten years from our age" sounded excessively glib and cheap, while purging or negating their own extraordinary youth was too cruel and desperate. If what the masses of the 1980s were longing for was a discourse that to the imagination was an "awakening from a nightmare to the morning," a farewell to what had suddenly become an unbearable memory of history, and a fantasy in which, while laughing heartily to forget, they consolidated a "new beginning" or new life; if the "wound literature" that stirred up such an incessantly fervid reaction sought, through fictive heroes and tender sentiments, to rescue the individual person from history; then what educated youth literature sought was to redeem the self from the calamity, the pillaging, the evil that was history—it was the memory of youth as substitute. Consequently, they tried with near desperation to rip away the memory of their youth from history and the discourse of history. Undoubtedly, it was all in vain. Consequently, the intensity of a thoroughly scarred idealism unexpectedly caused the generation of educated youth and the literature of educated youth not only to converge with classic mainstream discourse but also to echo the "idealism of suffering" of the 1950s generation. Yet it was in just this process of stripping off, within the memory of youth—or rather in the process of redeeming for a generation the value of the self from despair—that the accounts of heroism and idealism gradually intruded into the discourse of individualism, even though constrained by the circumstances, the reality, and the terms of collectivism.

By the late 1980s, educated youth literature and the representation of educated youth no longer formed a cultural space pluralistically governed and crossed by multiple discourses, but, in the course of gradually splitting away, became a field of pluralistic discourse. A portion of this finally entered mainstream discourse to become an important part of it; another portion, in the increasingly apparent culture and reality of utilitarianism, became, on account of the dogged persistence of their faith and the purity and fragility of their idealism, the declarations of so-called losers and outcasts. The most extreme among these adopted a fanatical fervor for cultural heroism, and during constant encounters and displacements of mainstream discourse, gradually became marginalized. In fact, during the decade of the 1980s, the generation that had thrown itself into the educated youth movement ("up to the hills and down to the countryside"), through various channels (principally the restored university entrance examination system), mounted the political and economic stage and gradually came into control in Chinese society, and it was people of this generation who became the principal cadres and the core of elite culture during the 1980s. Here the discourse about the so-called third generation and fourth generation constantly developed and proliferated, actually becoming something of an ideologically "legalized" practice.[7] A work of this period that was situated between fact and fiction— Lao Gui's *Xuese huanghun* [Blood red sunset] (1987)—unexpectedly became a sign of the break between the culture of the 1980s and that of the 1990s and at the same time constituted a floating bridge linking these newly separated shores. The narrative tone of the work (a biography approaching the style of a diary) and the unity and identification of the narrator with the other characters, leaving no distance between them, gives *Blood Red Sunset* a special characteristic that makes it seem a naked, severe, nearly savage "original picture reappearing." Manifested in this reappearing picture of the years of the Cultural Revolution and educated youth are: the jumbled substances and stuff specific to that discourse of idealism, as well as the cruelty and violence that by necessity it contains; the mauling of heroism and its puniness in encountering reality; and the desperate resistance and struggle of individualism, but only for the sake of approval and admittance by the "collective." For this era it is almost a legendary "demon-haunted wall": one walks away, only to find oneself returning again and again to the entirely outrageous circumstances encountered by a generation. But all this appears openly, without concealment, only in a personal, individual memory that is unreflective, or rather, that refuses reflection and remorse. In a certain sense, this work, which appeared only after repeated delays, constituted the master copy for so many educated youth writings; it constituted an original picture whose color had peeled away and then was made to reappear—the familiar, the gorgeous, the famed picture-scroll. It was obviously unlike "wounds," or "reflections," or "seeking roots." It was only the discourse of an individual—merely a naked, or rather, an utterly sincere statement of idealistic purity and devout sincerity (unexpectedly completing the transformation from the social ideal of heroism to cultural heroism)—calling on the "collective"/society to give belated recognition to the heroic conduct of the individual who has endured humiliation and exile. It would seem to be the necessary compensation for the persistence and the insistence of some youthful feelings.

However, the interesting point is that when *Blood Red Sunset* was a hot topic, going through one printing after another, what it aroused was not shock over the work's blind lack of reflectiveness, its refusal of remorse, and its fanaticism. Instead, a heat wave of powerful nostalgia and lingering affection was suddenly stirred up by the reappearance of an original picture. In fact, *Blood Red Sunset* incited the memory of a generation and its longing to "rectify names" more directly than any previous educated youth literature or discourse on the "third generation" and the "fourth generation." Consequently, next to another impassioned scene at Tiananmen Square, and alongside the furor over the "Exhibition of Modern Art," a large-scale display of illustrations and objects titled "My Soul Belongs to the Black Earth" opened solemnly at the Museum of History, next to Tiananmen Square. It was a time and place that, not by coincidence, indicated plainly that a generation persisted in maintaining the memory and the record of its youth, when it had stubbornly and tortuously tried to enter the moment and the circuit of history. The same theme of refusing remorse, of "no remorse for one's youth," again and again resoundingly repeated the main melody of the "battle of the century," which was tragically moving and blindly carried to extremes. The subsequent reminiscences and songs on the "black earth," the "yellow earth," and the "red earth," which continued throughout the 1980s and into the 1990s, and the large number of memoirs, reportage, and "historically faithful" writings on the educated youth movement following *Blood Red Sunset* and the exhibition of "My Soul Belongs to the Black Earth" created a new kind of best-selling book and best-selling author. Among those that drew people's notice were: *Revelations of the Grasslands, The Tide of Chinese Educated Youth, The Tribe of Chinese Educated Youth, Through Storm and Stress: The History of the Chinese Educated Youth Movement,* and several dozen other titles. As a new cultural symptom, from beginning to end there persisted in it most deeply a debate and a conflict between "youth unrepentent"—a memory of youth, a confirmation of self and history, an ideologically legalized practice promoted by the strength of what was already deemed correct and dominated the stage of society— and "the memory of blood and tears"—the reflective, accusatory practices of elitist culture that placed doubt on history. Obviously, however, the latter was rapidly reduced to an inferior position. It was not merely that the former was supported by some form of mainstream discourse, but it was also tacitly premised on the macropolitical economy of utilitarianism and the economic and political power of those who adopted such a position. At the same time, converging with the main trend in the reportage literature of the late 1980s, it responded to a special voyeuristic demand on the Chinese mainland for political secrets and thus became a harbinger of the consumerist culture that was about to erupt. In a certain sense, it happened that the writers of the historical accusation form (or rather, the appropriators of the signs of that position) were more successful converting the history of educated youth into one of the best vehicles for violence and even sex. Accompanying this was a "fad for educated youth returning to the countryside," which for a time surged until it nearly became a cult. It is evident that this was not a returning in the same sense as those recorded in *The Southern Coast* or *Spiritual History*,[8] but was more like a self-confirmation in the sense of revisiting home after one has left home and become a success, or like the rise of a new type of item on travel itineraries. In this field, consumer culture repeatedly showed off its ability to adopt ways of consumer ideology.

This cultural symptom and social fashion of nostalgia among educated youth and veterans of the rural commune teams, together with the reappearing memories of youth, were directly transformed, in the Beijing of the 1990s, into a mode of consumption and consumer fashion in the wave of consumer culture. Early in the 1990s, at various thriving locations in Beijing, there appeared middle- and high-priced taverns and restaurants with names like "Black Earth," "Sunflower Village," and the "Inn of the Former Rural Team Workers." With ingenious creativity, the original proprietors of these establishments set up several rural-style brick beds (*kang*), had the customers sit cross-legged on them, and served them the sort of fare never before admitted to elegant establishments—potato-noodle pork stew, corn flour cakes, cornmeal congee, "ants climbing a tree," and peppery "tiger food"—while of course not overlooking a wide variety of dishes from the exquisite and elegant northeastern-style cuisine. Even the plainest dishes from backwater counties had an impressive price. Opening nights at Black Earth, Sunflower Village, and the others were lively, impressive events, and as jammed as a marketplace. These establishments not only created a new fad and new social meeting spots that were the height of popularity and fashion but, in the aftermath of the popularity of Shandong, Cantonese, and Sichuan food, they also actually established the reputation and popularity of northeastern food. A notice pasted up everywhere soliciting people to compose scrolls of antithetical couplets for Inn of the Former Rural Team Workers read: "The ideal spot for the nostalgia and dreams of those who once worked in rural production teams." When the former educated youth (or rather, the "successful" among them) found a meeting place for "dreams and nostalgia," what they got was no longer the reappearance of the "original picture" nor the time of their memories, but signs that had been duplicated and sold, ceremony and "flavor," a mode of consumption, and nothing more. A "memory" with the price clearly marked. There is an interesting example at the Black Earth restaurant, where they have set aside a wall for people who spent time in the Great Northern Wilderness of the northeast to stick up their calling cards. Certainly there are a lot of names from all walks of life, but the majority have positions and titles like chairman of the board, general manager, and the like at numerous and as yet unfamiliar companies in trade, goods and materials, real estate, advertising, and so forth. Consequently, the historical memory of life on the black earth, which is not devoid of what can stir the soul, together with modern, urban modes of communication; the fervent, heartfelt experience of nostalgia and recollection, together with realistic utilitarian goals; the imaginary return to a youth for which one has no regrets, together with the display and authentication of being on the road of struggle/to success (for which money and consumption are the absolute and only standards)—all are not without a "postmodern" significance, sutured or brought together in one pastiche. A new culture and reality of utilitarianism and consumerism has transcended even the transformation from "the spirit of the Great Northern Wilderness" to "the miracle of big-bowl tea."[9]

Winning popularity throughout urban and rural China at this time, Li Chunbo's song "Xiaofang" appears to be an even more interesting example, indicating the rise and development of a deep social and cultural shift. As a "post–educated youth" song, the straightforward lyrics and simple tune of "Xiaofang" imitate and revise the educated youth songs of those years. Eliminating the fervor, the grief, and the despair of those years, "Xiaofang" is easygoing but not insincere, simplistic perhaps but not without heartfelt sentiments. Obviously this is not the reappearance of an "original picture," but more a matter of taste and consumption on the order of "Black Earth" or "Sunflower Village." Rather than any actual, painful memory, it is more accurately described as a sense of security, approaching even superiority and extravagance, that comes from being at some remove. However, what is more interesting is that this song, created for the sake of popularity/consumption, actually was extremely popular nationwide for some time, but not for the reasons that its creators expected nor in the way that they expected. The original intent was, through "a girl named Xiaofang," to enter the cult of consuming memory and look back on the years of one's youth from a position of security and superiority: "Thank you for the love you've given me. I'll never forget it in this life. Thank you for the tenderness you've shown me. It helped me through those years." What the song's creators hadn't counted on was that it was a different sort of people who made this song popular and a different sort of need for cultural consumption of social space that was taking shape. The people who were taken by the straightforward, simple, but genuine "Xiaofang," who were moved by the natural young village girl with braids in the song, turned out to be the peasants who were leaving their villages and flooding into the cities at the end of the 1980s and the beginning of the 1990s, along with a new generation of urbanites who had no more than an imaginary experience of rural China. It was among these newly arrived people who were on the margins of urban society and among these urban youth that "Xiaofang" received its greatest welcome. Easygoing recollections of distant days long gone were replaced by feelings being experienced on the spot. The narration, which did not require any memory, and the traditional image of a young girl, together with a love situation of the sort flooding pop music, simultaneously gratified the cultural demands of the marginal populace of the cities and filled some unmet psychological need among urban youth. Then, too, the straightforward lyrics and the simple melody gave the song a distinctive flavor, which responded to the longings of somewhat cynical minds to recover naturalness and sincerity. No one thought of words like "helping me through those years" as having any specific reference. Subsequently, another successful song by Li Chunbo, "A Letter Home," which was created for these specific consumer demands, no longer relied on memory or imaginary pretext and was composed of common, even daily circumstances, as in an ordinary letter home. Retaining not even the simplest rhyme scheme, in this instance Li directly employed the most commonplace language and formulas, such as "I send you best regards," so that to the urban workers and their kind, it evoked immediate circumstances and sensations like those they experienced, while to urban youth, what it conveyed was sarcastic, bored, and bold. No longer burdened by such transcendent aims as providing unsettling recollections, reflections, and the rectification of names, or "letting history inform the future" and the like, all that was left was the emergence of a new psyche, constructing and joining into the culture of a "new psyche." Subsequently,

Li Chunbo's songs and others, such as Ai Jing's "My 1997," together formed an important new type of indigenous popular music: urban folksongs.[10] The city and consumption began to replace the consumption of ideology and memory, and their gradually familiar forms occupied the new cultural space. It was an era that died out as quickly as it was born. Again and again, in the forms of their consumption and entertainment, people deconstructed the prohibited and the sacred, consuming memory and ideology. A future that is no longer an unbearable burden must lift people's spirits, and the prospect that it will no longer be limited to the expression of official views is a relief. Yet does an era completely shorn of taboos and reverence present an optimistic picture? I still have only the authority and capacity to describe.

NOTES

This essay was translated by Edward Gunn. [This is the second in a two-part essay. Trans.]

1 Song Yifu and Zhang Zhanbin, *Zhongguo: Mao Zedong re* [China: Mao Zedong fever] (Beiyue wenyi, 1991).

2 By March 1992 there were twelve audiocassette titles on Mao Zedong that were major best-sellers. [The Chinese text lists the twelve titles and their publishers. Trans.]

3 American film theorist Brian Henderson comments on the meaning of narrative works: "Finally the operation of a myth . . . always has to do with the time in which the myth is told, not with the time that it tells of" (see Brian Henderson, "*The Searchers:* An American Dilemma," in *Movies and Methods: An Anthology,* ed. Bill Nichols [Berkeley and Los Angeles: University of California Press, 1976], 434; Dai Jinhua, trans., "*Sousuozhe*--yige Meiguo de kunjing," *Dangdai dianying* [Contemporary film] 4 [1987]: 68).

4 [The actor referred to is Gu Yue, celebrated for his portrayals of Mao Zedong. Trans.]

5 See Zhang Chengzhi, "Green Night" and "Golden Pastures"; Kong Jiesheng, "Forest Primeval"; Liang Xiaosheng, "This Is a Piece of Miraculous Earth"; Tie Ning, "Haystacks"; and Wang Anyi, "Century on Duty."

6 Milan Kundera, *The Book of Laughter and Forgetting* (1978). The novel begins by describing multiple acts of private and public "erasure" of the past in Czechoslovakia following the Soviet invasion in 1968.

7 [The terms *third generation* and *fourth generation* appear in several sources of the late 1980s. The third generation refers to people who reached maturity between the late 1940s and the late 1950s, and the fourth generation refers to those who reached maturity during the 1960s and the early 1970s. Alternatively, the third generation refers to those people who were in university or senior middle school and joined the Red Guards at the outset

of the Cultural Revolution, and the fourth generation refers to those who came of age as educated youth during the succeeding ten years. Trans.]

8  Kong Jiesheng, *Nanfang de an* [The southern coast] (1982); Zhang Cheng-zhi, *Xinling shi* [Spiritual history] (1991). [These are accounts of how men's identities have been reshaped by living in remote locations of Hainan and southern Ningxia. Trans.]

9  During the 1980s a story was promulgated about a group of educated youth who returned to the city from a construction corps in the northeast, and who began selling large bowls of tea on the street for a few pennies, eventually moving up to large-scale enterprises.

10  Ai Jing's "My 1997" is another interesting example. Adopting an extremely colloquial language and folk style in the same fashion, it places the recovery of Hong Kong in 1997, which is sometimes referred to as the "big deadline," within the realm of Ai Jing's own personal fortunes, so that it no longer appears as a historical moment: "Hurry up, 1997," merely so that "I can go to Hong Kong, too."

Making Time: Historic Preservation

and the Space of Nationality


## ISLANDS OF MEANING

■ Jean-Yves Guiomar's contribution to *Les lieux de mémoire* takes us
back to the last turn-of-century eruption of nation-states, to the geographer Vidal de La Blache's uneasy musing on borders:

> Comment un fragment de surface terrestre qui n'est ni péninsule
> ni île, et que la géographie physique ne saurait considérer propre-
> ment comme un tout, s'est-il à l'état de contrée politique, et est-il
> devenu enfin une patrie?

> [How can a fragment of the earth's surface that is not an island or
> a peninsula, nor a singularity in the eyes of physical geographers,
> have risen to the state of a political country and finally became a
> fatherland?][1]

The problem of nation-space in this article is the still fresh assumption that makes his question possible: that there *are* divisions in nature
mandating divisions between people, that the nation-state could be a
state of nature. Given this foundational prenotion, a century of anoma-
lies confirms by exception: the Alsace deformation of the French octa-
gon, the leavings in the wide Dutch net that made Indonesia, or the
existence of a Bosnia-Herzegovina are cognized as deviations from
and thereby affirmations of the ideal case in which nature issues the
nation—a peninsula, an island, a Taiwan.

There on Taiwan in the political geographer's prized naturally discrete space, only one in every thirteen persons assents to ascription of

Taiwanese nationality. At this writing, only one in seventeen envisions a correspondence between a People of the island and a State of the island, a Taiwanese nation-state.[2] Four-fifths of Taiwanese questioned want the Republic of China Foreign Ministry to negotiate a territorial dispute between Taiwan and Japan, despite the fact that as far as Japan and the other nation-states are concerned, there is no such thing as a Republic of China, much less a Republic of China Foreign Ministry. Nationality rooted in the absent space, the absent time of China—while increasingly the object of questioning—continues not simply to buffalo but to inhabit, to constitute most people on the island as Chinese. And so from Vidal de La Blache's perspective, from the social science and state orthodoxy perspectives, there is a problem here: How does a political and physical singularity, at once among the world's stronger states and largest islands, *not become a fatherland?*

Cut off from Taiwan for generations, absent China's space could only exist for the great majority by "re"cognizing of what had not been experienced directly, an allegation, a Past. That alone seems to set Taiwan apart, yet insofar as we adopt the standpoint of the living, nationalism's territorial imperative in *every* nation-state is the institutional production of its pastness, its apparent spatial extension from over the horizon where the dead are, and we are not yet toward that place where those who will be born must live as nationals. The reality of national territory depends on the construction of a unified time-space stream of history, a seriality from which there is no escape.[3] That time-space where geological space melts and cannot constrain social classification is national memory—embodied, objectified, and institutionalized.

*Memory, Space, and Interrogation*

With Maurice Halbwachs we begin at the heart of memory, in the practice of interrogation: "We appeal to our memory only in order to answer questions which others have asked us, or that we suppose they could have asked us." Consequently, "there is no point in seeking where they are preserved in my brain or in some nook of my mind to which I alone have access: for they are recalled to me externally, and the groups of which I am a part at any time give me the means to reconstruct them."[4] A Past *takes place* in interrogation.

Going beyond Halbwachs, I place interrogation and memory in what Eric Hobsbawm calls the nation-state's "institutional or procedural 'landscape' which is unlike any other such landscape."[5] In this landscape new institutions become a technology of memory without precedent. Across the life course schools, standing armies, markets, professions, marriages, courts, and media interrogate an ever larger proportion of persons while licensing a small range of imaginable responses—homogenized memories of categorical identity. Nationality is partially a response to institutional interrogation of our extension through identicals in time over a common space, a response with two aspects: recognition of a codified classification within the taxonomy of nation-state person categories and disposition to see and act as if nationality in that first sense were a natural attribute.[6]

Contents of racial memories "recovered" on the institutional couch are themselves products of this unprecedented landscape. Codified national antiquity is an innovation forged in the modern workshops of history and, newer still, the subordinate custodial institutions that preserve the materiality of the past—public museums and the field of national historic preservation, where technicians operate at the end of the production chain on a self-evident Past. Here in the neutrality of the object world, space is made contiguous and persons absent in time are made copresent and identical; nations are remembered and authenticated.

This article analyzes nation-products of this new and specialized memory field, *national historic preservation,* through its institutionalizing and objectifying work. Making and unmaking China's absent space and time is presented as two mutually constitutive aspects of practice: consecrating nationality in a body of memory fetish sites, and struggle over the meaning of the game within the institutional field delegated to consecrate, a struggle in which I have participated.

*Institution and Objectification: Historic Preservation*

The analysis will flow through two sections organized around the master field of power. The first takes up instituting historic preservation and objectifying nation through sites in a regime of primitive domination, the martial law state. The second analyzes transformation of the field and its memory sites as dictatorship crumbles.

Through both periods we examine how sites are made and made to testify through heterotopy (here, displacement of absent space into a present space) and anachronism (displacement of a present necessity into an absent time), first for the Chinese nation and now increasingly for a Taiwanese nation. The meaning of island, emblem of a nation created by nature, gives way in preservation practice to Taiwan as an *island of meaning,* the nation as defined by socially made cognitive borders. That social production is in part a struggle in the field to uphold or change the rules of the game, a struggle in which all sides rely increasingly on a neutralized science-voiced authenticity. Authenticity in turn takes on several forms—national, techno-orthodox, and critical—and in this struggle Chinese and Taiwanese, orthodox and heterodox nationalism employ their shared doxa, the self-evidence of nationality as a mode of vision and di-vision. To effect the mis-recognition of nation as nature, nationalists are busy *making time,* literally and in the pejorative sense.

In the end we will be brought back to the misguided geographer Vidal de La Blache and the work of social science. The career of historic preservation in Taiwan suggests the experienced compulsion of national space and time is a fetish, a collective mis-*re*cognition genetically structured by social divisions of power, and potentially subverted. Taiwan's "national question" becomes significant not in its failure to fit global common sense, but rather in its demonstration that the naturalized framework of nationalism itself is, in Charles Tilly's phrase, a bloody fiction.

## CONCEPTS: NATION/ALITY/ISM

Terms slip and slide the moment talk about nations begins. One well-intentioned response is striving to standardize concepts of nation, nationality, and nationalism through a search for their essences. That project cannot succeed because nation/ality/ism is not the thing, the essence, in search of its name. This is a general problem in studies of social classification that Pierre Bourdieu has well explained:

> The social sciences deal with pre-named, pre-classified realities which bear proper nouns and common nouns, titles, signs and acronyms. At the risk of unwittingly assuming responsibility for the acts of social constitution of whose logic and necessity they are unaware, the social sciences must take as their object of study the social operations of *naming* and the rites of institution through which they are accomplished. But on a deeper level, they must examine the part played by words in the construction of social reality and the contribution which the struggle over classifications, a dimension of all class struggles, makes to the constitution of classes —classes defined in terms of age, sex, or social position, but also clans, tribes, ethnic groups or nations.[7]

Contending meanings of nation are typically assumed; when forced into talk, they face off as conflicting lists of objective and subjective attributes.[8] The sets of attribute lists do not match, and each list has its embarrassing exceptions in which decreed nonnations posture as venerable entities and ought-to-be nations fail to realize their destinies. In Tilly's words, "As a description of the way countries actually are, the idea of the nation-state has remained a myth."[9] Findings from a body of social historical studies now enable us to shift the nation onto new conceptual ground.

First, the meanings of "nation" as Westerners know them today are recent transformations of terms, chiefly in the Romance languages, that had previously denoted place of origin and/or status group. Nation only begins to assume its current status as a people with "their" corresponding state with the rise of modern warfare, capitalism, the transformation of relations between elites and people, and the spread of imperialism.

Second, the subjective commonalities in the scholarship of the lists (common sensibilities, collective character or personality, worldview) often come to characterize people only after they have been subjected to the homogenizing processes of the capitalist modernity and the nation-state.

Third, criteria sufficient to the objective list makers (common language, common history, common economic interests) are also products of nation-state construction. In Hobsbawm's words, "Nations are more often the consequences of setting up a state than they are its foundation."[10] Although research outside the core is less developed, the prenational states, rhetorics, and protonational collectivites are far from the Western experience, still work on the dominance of the nation and nation-state in the colonial modernity of Indonesia, Malaysia, Thailand, and India conforms with these findings.

Given that nations, far from being natural and inevitable things, are constructs of recent, complex, and contingent processes implicated in the making of modernities,[11] our definition is not *the* list, the list to end all lists, but a definition of the nation as practiced: again with Hobsbawm, "Any sufficiently large body of people whose members regard themselves as members of a 'nation,' will be treated as such."[12]

*Nationalism*

Nationalism in scholarly discourse is similarly fogged, and any attempt to define a "real" nationalism must fail. As Tilly put it, "Since coherent, unified peoples almost never exist on the large scale, and since states almost never serve as their instruments, nationalism rests on fictions."[13] Extending the social definition of nation, nationalism is a discursive formation, not a thing but a doctrine asserting natural correspondence between "nations" and sovereign states.

The pervasive quality of the fictions and the fact that they are indeed bloody fictions, give urgency to Hobsbawm's words on the responsibility of scholarship: "No serious historian of nations and nationalism can be a committed political nationalist. . . . Nationalism requires too much belief in what is patently not so." And if, as he quotes Renan, getting history wrong is part of being a nation, "historians are professionally obliged not to get it wrong, or at least to make an effort not to." Analysis of historic preservation will show how the structure of the field bears on the ability of intellectuals to "get it right."[14]

## Nationality: Social Classification and Disposition

To the extent that nationality stands apart in conventional usage from nation and nationalism, it does so as an attribute. All God's children have nationality, with the exception so rare ("stateless person," "man without a country"), like the child born without a limb or an organ, that its absence underlines the normal. Recent work exemplified by Rogers Brubaker's study of France and Germany continues in the arena of nationality what others have done with respect to nation and nationalism: the taken-for-granted "natural attribution" of nationality is a fiction. Case study evidence shows criteria for attribution of nationality at birth, not to mention the far more contentious issue of naturalization, are again recent inventions that vary from state to state and over time—hardly a reflex of nature.[15]

Nationality is a fiction, a powerful fiction. In critical instances we see agents act as if they were possessed. We need to treat nationality as more than a legal category or attribution and conceptualize it as a social classification linking person to nation-state and a disposition to perceive and orient action as if one were a part of a nation, a peculiarly national aspect of *habitus*.[16] Nationality as a codified system or as embedded in habitus is, like all other social classifications, at once cognitive and evaluative—in Phillip Corrigan and Derek Sayer's phrase "simultaneously descriptive and moral."[17] The politico-cognitive system, particularly taxonomies and the relationships among their elements, already contains embedded in the means of perception the outline of the things that can and often must be perceived.

## HISTORIC PRESERVATION UNDER THE DICTATORSHIP

Harmonizing with Edmund Burke's view that the nation is "an idea of continuity in time as well as in numbers and space," Chiang Kai-shek proclaimed that "promotion of civic education must pay special attention to the teaching of 'Chinese History' and 'Chinese Geography,' for it is only through them that the student's patriotic fervor and national pride can really be aroused, that he can be made to realize the fundamental significance of the basic virtues of loyalty . . . a citizen who loves his country more than his own life."[18]

By the time of writing his students were Taiwanese students, Chiang and his state having been driven out of China. They ruled by an ever-present potential (that certain uncertainty of which Michael Taussig speaks) to torture, imprison and kill, and by a spatiotemporal symbolic violence: the KMT (Kuomintang) ran the world's longest-lived martial law regime as China's *delegate*. Another armed group temporarily usurped the space of China, and so elections were matters of other past and future times, past and future space. To replace the 1947 delegates before that other time, that future time of return to the alienated space, would be profoundly undemocratic because only Taiwan Province would delegate the Chinese state.

Here we reach the constitution of the nation-state in both the sociological and legal senses, the compounding of physical and symbolic violence. Direct and violent control, "primitive domination," is a most uneconomic mode of mastery that Chiang sought to replace in part through constructing nationality in both of the senses outlined above, a molding of his subjects into colluding agents of the absent place/time through this civic education. As Corrigan and Sayer said of English nation-state making, civic education was "*moral regulation:* a project of normalizing, rendering natural, taken for granted, in a word 'obvious,' what are in fact ontological and epistemological premises of a particular and historical form of social order."[19]

The crucial product of moral regulation is not opinion and explicit subscription to a credo, but *doxa,* an invisible dark-star knowledge, and to its gravity both heterodoxy and orthodoxy incline.[20] The opposition of heterodox to orthodox (Taiwanese nationalism to Chinese nationalism) implies a true nationalism, as a perturbed orbit implies the massive dark companion with its irresistible system of possibilities—in short, the National structure of the prenotional world. Outside the field of opinion, doxic knowledge rests on historical relations deposited in bodies, and thereby embodied in the means of perceiving, cognizing, naming, and operating on the world where "otherwise" is literally unthinkable. Unthinkable it remains until objective crisis conjoins an effective heretical discourse, revealing as logical or factual faults the union of specific knowing to specific dominion that was always there.

## Chinese Preservation's Basic Problems: Autochthony and the Grateful Dead

Nationalism, the doctrine of correspondence between state and nation, always begins with a declaration of temporal priority in space, including "a claim of autochthony, origin inseparable from that very territory" that owes nothing to Others.[21] Nationality is contiguous, a coextension in space, and continuous, a temporal seriality coextending a person toward dead identicals with whom the relation is frequently the asymmetry of "debt." Deploying these principles as Chinese nationality on Taiwan creates two remarkable problems and suggests to nationalists their "solutions."

### CHINA: PRESENT ABSENCE AND ABSENT PRESENCE

Official nation/ality/ism on Taiwan stands as the extreme case, a nation-state existing in the absence of the national territory. Arrival of the Republic of China (ROC) central authority on Taiwan was the reflex of its expulsion from China, and other states have come to recognize China as the People's Republic of China (PRC). By selling arms, trading, and making binding legal agreements, they in practice recognize Taiwan in the ROC state. Survival of the ROC as a nation-state within the island, however, hinged on denial: one of the most successful nation-states explicitly credited its achievements to its nonbeing. Taiwan is China, not Taiwan, and yet the condition of it remaining so was isolation from China—exactly the condition of its prior Japanese nationality. Like the Japanese, the ROC succeeded where the Ch'ing had failed: they turned the Taiwan Straits into a giant moat and sealed out the Chinese. In this act of self-preservation, the state created a problem for contiguity in space and serial incorporation, the coextension of China in time.

Taiwan was never part of the national experience of Republican China. The island was traveling along the trajectory of Okinawa, on its way to becoming the southernmost island in the Japanese archipelago, when the interstate system handed it to the ROC in its last moments in Republican China. The final efforts to make a Chinese nation and state—the new constitution and national elections—did not include the Taiwanese, who would nevertheless become the only persons subjected. Neither elections nor a past in the Republic of China offered support to the project of domination through denial of China's absence.

## ANTIQUE NATION, NEW SPACE

As the prizewinning advertisement (above) shows, the weight of nation-state claims to sovereignty over space is proportional to depth in time.

A young architect-teacher with important responsibilities in historic preservation put the matter bluntly: "Basically Taiwan is a place without history. Although we often say China has a history of five thousand years, Taiwan itself has a history of only three hundred years. This island does not have its own cultural roots, and its culture has been influenced by the Han Chinese, the Dutch, and the Japanese."[22]

Isolated in space and weakly connected in time, the refugee state employed the defining technologies of modernity to push ahead incorporation into the absent presence. Technologies uniting those separated in space but copresent in time, most notably radio, daily newspapers, and later television, made for a strange simultaneity with China. Technologies uniting those separated in time but claiming the same space—photography, motion pictures, museums, and maps—mimetically infused daily life with a past China.

These means of modernity conjured relatively few pasts for an ever greater number of nationals and fostered an unprecedented extension and homogenization of a collective Past. Technologies of nationalization embedded in social institutions of common interrogation —school, talk, production-consumption, military conscription, and spaces-made-places—to resolve the problems of absence and newness.

### THE PALEONTOLOGY OF KNOWLEDGE

The dead are the first and most compliant conscripts in the armies of nationalism. On Taiwan, however, the official demand for dead, Chinese dead, far outstrips the supply. Since thousands of years of non-Han dead are useless to the project at hand, the shallowness of Chinese peopling in time gives rise to two instances of heterotopy, or mis-*place*ment, here a misplacement of the past.

The first and garden variety heterotopy is a foray into a mute human past. Like other states and would-be nation-states concerned with establishing priority in a space—excavation in today's newspaper throws up a Jewish priority on the Golan Heights against peace with Syria—the ROC attended to archaeology. Unable to do much with Taiwan, the space of control, Chinese national archaeology displaced the site of prehistory to the place where Chineseness originated, and from which it diffused to Taiwan. This type of scholarship reached its apex in fascist Germany as bits of rubbish were paraded to prove an origin on the North German plain and then priority in the "Ostmark" and beyond by early diffusion. Kossina's 1940 map of arrows carrying civilization from *das Heimatgebiet* across Europe (foretelling the movement of Nazi armies the following year) bears an uncanny resemblance to a textbook map interrogating every elementary school student in Taiwan. Arrows spread out from the center of China to embody waves of civilization (later, migrants) moving from China to Taiwan. The logic, however, inverts fascist archeo-logic. For *Deutsche Vorgeschichte*, the vector ran outward from the space controlled, along the series of sites to the place to be controlled in the future. For the KMT, the map ran from the space controlled backward in time and space into the absent and antique space that had been the center and whose cultural legacy fills the alleged vacuum of frontier Taiwan.

However hyped, fascist and KMT political archaeology at least maintained a connection between supposed persons and space. The unprecedented absent presence of China and the newness of Taiwan led official categorization beyond Nazi science into an entirely new heterotopia, the world's only paleontology of the nation-state.

From the early 1950s into the present, the most popular official reference, commemorative, and background works assert Chinese sovereignty with these words: "Taiwan has close historical and cultural ties with Mainland China. Fossils discovered in archaeological excavations in western Taiwan and Penghu (the Pescadores) demonstrate the islands were physically connected with the mainland in prehistoric times."[23] Nowhere else do fossils testify to the legitimacy of the state. In another Taiwan Miracle, nature is mobilized to enforce Taiwan's incorporation into the Chinese nation-state, even before there were Chinese.

Even before there were *people*—here paleontology dissolves into geology as the earth sciences testify to the "meaning of the island." While some geology locates Taiwan as a volcanic island on the Ring of Fire, ROC Chinese geology speaks of a disjuncture between Taiwan and the arc running from Alaska, Siberia, and Japan down through the Ryukus. Chinese geology sees Taiwan as cut off relatively "recently" from China—by glaciation and tectonic shift (the view instituted in the Chiang Kai-shek Memorial Hall) or by a "rift" during the Pleistocene.[24] Problems posed by absence and newness to the "normal" nation-state mode of naturalization—notably a *people without China*—were worked through to a most extreme natural state formation by a *China without people*. The ROC on Taiwan has been "delegated" by a pure geological space, by Pan Ku.

EMBODIED CHINA

A second technology addressing the spatiotemporal separation of China from Taiwan is embodiment of state classification. This goes beyond official discourse's usual metaphorical treatment of the nation as a body. The genetic trope of descent mis-places historical construct into the body. The normal translation of the commonly used *t'ung-*

*pao* as "compatriot" obscures the natural (nonvolitional) compulsion of the body inscribed in the characters and in the Greek *adelphós*—of the same womb.[25]

Below the distinctions Chinese/non-Chinese and then citizen/noncitizen, ROC nationals are classed as being from a place with two components, province and locality. Native Place *(chi-kuan)*, a spatial notion in other polities, is another time-space construct on Taiwan. Under the dictatorship, coordinates of the space of individual birth had nothing to do with place of origin; origin devolved through the patrilineage so that one's place of origin was actually that of the father. But that space was not necessarily the birthplace of the father since his *chi-kuan* was actually that of *his* father, and so on in an infinite regression.

The relation between state *chi-kuan* and gender/family domination, the logical flaws, and distance from historic practice—after all, without change in *chi-kuan*, everyone would be "from" a handful of places—posed no major problems to the institution of native place. Elsewhere I've discussed how enforced silence, Chineseness flowing from the entire ensemble of memory machines, and the correspondence between a simplified *chi-kuan* (Mainlander and Taiwanese) and social division was sufficient to turn what was on one level an entirely artificial state code into an aspect of habitus, a basic prenotion ordering the differences produced by KMT domination into the inclusive hierarchy of the Chinese nation.[26] In respect to time and space technology, however, two additional points bear emphasis.

First, the abstract code was literally embodied. For first-generation migrants and the second-generation Mainlanders (who had not seen the mainland) born to two Mainlander parents, the category *wai-sheng* is probabilistically associated with a distinctive bodily hexis, most notable in the absence of the Min-nan language and its marked phonological influences on spoken National Language. This is not simply something happening in the brain's language sites; linguistic hexis entails the mouth, the glottis—all the bodily machinery of sound making—in time-space–marked speech that eased the way into preferred places in the social division of labor. National language standardization, coupled with differentials in the ability to approximate the standard, inscribes on the body a relation to the absent space of the language center and the "place of origin." Viewed from the other side, the inability to produce native quality Min-nan or Hakka speech (exemplary of a range of bodily dispositions) implicates the Mainlander in a relation of some distance from Taiwan time and Taiwan space, affecting access to social and cultural capital. In the matrix of *sheng-chi* (provincial origin) as official classification, both the marked and the unmarked bodies became memories of the China that encompassed their opposition.

Second, the unequal incorporation of the classifications into the division of labor was, from the beginning, a stimulus to heresy met with guns, reforms, more history, and more biology. Although he bumped off his first Taiwan military governor, Chen-i, Chiang Kai-shek retained Chen's basic discursive strategy first enunciated in the February 28 massacre of tens of thousands of Taiwanese: "Enemy agents and rebels use the terms Taiwanese and Mainlanders to stir up trouble and turn people against each other. We must not be tricked by this lie. *We all come from the same root,* and we are all compatriots [*t'ung-pao*] in the Republic of China."[27]

NATIONALIZING CULTURE

In official talk, the flesh of this root is part culture. This is hardly unique to the ROC, or even to Nationalists. Walter Benjamin reminds us that "whoever has emerged victorious participates to this day in the triumphal procession in which the present rulers step over those who are lying prostrate. According to traditional practice, the spoils are carried along in the procession. These are called cultural treasures, and a historical materialist views them with cautious detachment."[28]

In addition to paleontology and embodiment, heterotopy on Taiwan also proceeds through the world's most extensive nationalization of the spoils into a state cultural capitol as capital. With a collection pilfered from the Forbidden City, the island's premier national museum is the only national museum in the world virtually without anything from the space of nation-state control. Temporally and spatially specific mainland Chinese genre were renamed and thereby transformed into National Painting, National Language, National Theater, National Opera, and so on. The indicative becomes imperative through nation-state power to make words efficacious, a power over objects anchored simultaneously in force and in the force of the "solemn act of categorization which tends to produce what it designates."[29] Interrogating a named architectural style or a mode of painting made visible by state control over the acts of construction, exhibition, and the asking of common questions recalls seemingly without effort the absent presence of China while marginalizing or actively suppressing forms not nationalized.

· The place of historic preservation in this procession of the spoils was codified over thirty years into the ROC on Taiwan in the Law on the

Preservation of Cultural Assets. A key figure involved explained historical preservation as part of a broader policy of preserving "cultural heritage," including "historical sites, antiquities, natural landmarks of cultural significance, ethnic arts, folk customs and related arts and crafts." Ch'iu K'un-liang contended that "all these constitute the life-orbit of our people and the crystallization of our people's wisdom. Through them we understand the spiritual substance of our people and the ways of life of our ancestors."[30] Through their practice, the subject "our people" is constructed, naturalized, and made the inevitable category of future life: "When our offspring thousands of years from now can appreciate their forefathers' art, their national feelings will be roused, and they may become artistically inspired to create a better, more beautiful national art."[31]

THE COLLAPSED "FIELD" OF HISTORIC PRESERVATION

Historic preservation, like the discipline of history, national language, national culture, statistics, and so many others, is a very new knowledge construct, having emerged with its fellows during the national and capitalist transformation of the West. More than discourse or profession, preservation is practice in a social field. The *field* heuristic refers to a set of objective relations between positions, their locations in field space determined by the amount and types of power (capital), and the regulative procedures that structure conditions under which participants access the stakes of the field.

Through this conceptual glass, the historic preservation field during the dictatorship resolves as an extremely simple space, an apparatus. A relative handful of persons occupied a few positions — for example, a housing officer in the provincial government, part of a job description within a municipal civic affairs bureau. Collapsed into the near singularity of party and army power, historical preservation was a protofield. Regardless of anyone's intention, field conditions made it most difficult to, in Hobsbawm's phrase, "get it right."

The main work of the apparatus — instituting historic sites — was an original work in both Chinese and Indo-European states, that of the *rex,* the priest-protoruler, drawer of boundaries between social categories. Transforming spaces and objects into memory-bearers through language, the "delegated" employed a sacred logic and, as Emile Benveniste generalized, "The magical character of this operation is evident: what is involved is the delimitation of the interior and the exterior, the realm of the sacred and the realm of the profane, the national territory and foreign territory."[32]

The current overlay of bureaucratic and scientific forms obscures the magical/arbitrary basis of these operations today, making it difficult to imagine them during martial law. Some islands adjacent to Taiwan, however, are history reserves, living museums far more realistic than the social Jurassic Park at Williamsburg. To move back in time we move outward in space to islands abutting China, where martial law had not ended. There the small potential power of capital was subordinated to military power so that "development has been retarded," and there are proportionally more older buildings than on the mainland (mainland Taiwan!).

For this reason, it is a favorite destination of preservation planners, academics, and architects. On a recent trip, the local military ruler introduced visiting professionals to a special historic site. He dreamed of a woman abused by the communists and when a woman's body washed up on the beach he connected his dream to the dead stranger. The warlord solemnly consecrated the space as a historic site, a *ku-chi*.

Change and danger later in the dictatorship encouraged codification of what had been entrusted to habitus. Historic sites, *ku-chi*, were defined to include historic buildings, spaces where something important had happened, and a residual "others" category. The Cultural Assets Preservation Law of 1982 placed *ku-chi* along with folk arts, handicrafts, and scenic sites in Benjamin's "procession of spoils" and entrusted them to different retainers. *Ku-chi* were placed under jurisdiction of the Ministry of the Interior; folk arts and handicrafts went to the Ministry of Education; scenic resources were charged to the Ministry of Economics.[33] The Council for Cultural Planning and Development (CCPD) became the locus for declaring sites (*chih-ting*) and maintaining them once they were instituted.[34]

## Lieux de mémoire *as* Mémoire de lieux:
### Chinese Chronotopes on Taiwan

Framed in these state-time technologies and institutions, the sites of memory could memorialize other sites, the absent presence of China. Under martial law, key *ku-chi* could be nationalized or controlled by fiat. The martial law apparatus instituted 250 *ku-chi*. Article 38 of the bylaws implementing the 1982 act specified eight diagnostic criteria. The first is possession of historical, cultural, artistic, scientific, memorial, or scholarly value. The second requires the site be of some unspecified antiquity. A site that expresses the particularities of a time and/or a place is made eligible under the third guideline. The fourth is that sites lacking in all these values may be eligible if an important actor was associated with or if a historical event took place in that space. The remaining four minor criteria—scale, state of preservation, local environment, and number—had little impact. Because weights were not calibrated for the different criteria and because the memory managers judged few sites qualified on most of the grounds, the logical control implied by codification was only a "possibility." As the field developed, technicians targeted "vague" and unordered formal criteria. In practice, however, the criteria were straightforward.

Analyzing how sites were instituted and represented in discourse, along with the semantics of the site/time relation, suggests several operative principles for making sites. First, historic sites are not places, nor are they disembodied times; they exist only in the perceived union of time and place. These time-places where time is imagined to persist in a bounded space require a word to distinguish them from other spaces and from the conventions of national historic preservation. Following Jonathan Boyarin from Mikhail Bakhtin, they will be called *chronotopes*, or time-places.[35] We shall see in the following discussion that the single most important criterion for an official chronotope was never directly stated: does the space refer to the Chinese state, nation, or signs of officialized culture in such a way as to embody the eternal unity in both time and space of Taiwan with absent China? In some instances antiquity would be highlighted; in others the aesthetic value or association with a local notable would be highlighted; in others the aesthetic value would be highlighted. The stated criteria amplify the mis-placement of space and time into a Chinese chronotope, through the operators of object classes, construction material, tactile effect, organized forgetting, and hierarchical inclusion. Memory sites remembered the absent site of China, metonyms of the nation-state.

OBJECTIFYING CHINA IN FIRST RANK SITES
Once consecrated, the sites were themselves ordered in a three-tier system distinguishing relative degrees of value. Sites of modest value were designated Rank 3 and left to the financially strapped localities. Moderately valuable sites were assigned to the provincial government. As late as 1988, fewer than 10 percent of the sites were deemed "First Rank" and placed in the relatively wealthy purview of the national government. The pattern of inclusion and exclusion in Rank 1 reveals practical logic separating a national history to be preserved from the undistinguished spaces of oblivion.

By 1985, 460 chronotopes had been examined, and nearly half were authorized as *ku-chi*. Only eighteen sites made the First Rank cut. First Rank sites stood out by their uneven distribution across the fourteen site categories. Half of the categories—categories with lower levels of state, absent space, and Chinese time potential—had no place in the First Rank.[36] The following sections analyze the inclusion and exclusion of sites grouped in the included half of the categories.

*Domestic Statements: Grave, Memorial Arch, and House* The "house museum" and domestic sites constitute a major portion of Western historic sites, a small proportion of ROC sites, and an even smaller proportion of First Rank sites; however, one dead authentic Chinese body marches in the First Rank of domestic sites. Wang Te-lu was born in Taiwan's Chiayi County and moved upward (to the rank of demigod) and inward (military chief of Chekiang Province), embodying Taiwan's officialized historical trajectory from beyond the pale to the Chinese center.

Wang was an instrument of state violence asserting Ch'ing sovereignty over Taiwan from the suppression of the internal challenge of the Lin Shuang-wen Rebellion to the external threat of the Opium War. Under the strict sumptuary laws of the Ch'ing, the state-mandated scale of his funeral and the form of his tomb instituted it as a National chronotope; the KMT Interior Ministry designation of *ku-chi* 139 years later simply reaffirmed the Ch'ing with a nation-state trope.

On its surface, the single memorial arch in the First Rank recognizes a woman and establishes a homology between family, filiality, and "glorification" of women through subjection on one side and violence/loyalty to the nation on the other. She has no real identity apart from being mother of the real subject; she was "Ch'iu Liang-kung's Mother." Not just anyone could express filial piety in such a manner that it survives today in monumental form. The arch exists not because of Ch'iu's mother (she could have given birth to a bandit or a beggar) but because of a relation, the relation between Ch'iu Liang-kung (more accurately his position in social space) and a Chinese state.

That relation is carved into the arch itself. In the central position under the eaves and over the main inscription is the imperial mandate, without which it could not be erected, let alone preserved. The reasons for granting the mandate are spelled out below the declaration of filial piety in a series of carvings representing General Ch'iu Liang-kung's triumphant, if apocryphal, return to Chin-men after a life of service in the state's organs of violence.

Concluding the abbreviated domestic theme, only one residential chronotope became a First Rank site. This particular "residence" was included not because of beauty, craftsmanship, or representativeness of the object, nor even association with a resident like General Wang. The Chin Kuang-fu House was actually a *kung-kuan,* a state house built as part of a base system from which a privately raised but state-mandated fund was administered to support the conquest of aboriginal lands between Hsinchu and the mountains. Its name, Chin Kuan-fu Kung-kuan, referred to the "eternal wealth" of the mainland provinces of Kuantung and Fukien, *chi-kuan* (native places) of the "Taiwanese" who provided the funds. The descriptive documents belie the censorship imposed by the field through the importance of the residence class to architecture and international preservation. Official commentary reveals this site not as a residence (*chai-ti*) but as a part of the *kuan-sai,* or strategic pass class.

*Monuments to State Violence: Borders and Transgressions* These *kuan-sai,* together with city walls (*ch'eng-kuo*) and structures protecting state offices (*wei-shu*), are separate object classes in the official code. In respect to their origins and functions, however, the three are a single analytic class of state military chronotopes. In 1985, military sites accounted for only 13 percent of the *ku-chi* as a whole, but almost half of the First Rank structures. These eight sites of the highest category had no pretense to cultural or aesthetic merit (the first formal dimension of value in the code).

Nor, even by Taiwan standards, are they particularly ancient. The Er-sha-wan gun emplacement dates from 1840. Three of the sites—the Hsi-t'ai gun emplacement, the North Gate remnant of the Taipei city wall, and the Er-k'un-shen emplacement—were constructed within a few years of each other: 1886, 1882, and 1875, respectively. Why these spaces and these times? The answer is the binding of nation time to the space of control: each chronotope stands at a double boundary.

The battlements stand on the edge of Taiwan space and at a temporal edge between China state time and non-China state time. In the 1880s French, British, and Japanese troops threatened the boundary and were met with a commitment to bind the space with modern weapons and by categorizing Taiwan as a province of China. Both partial successes and failure that delivered Taiwan to Japan glorify in heroic and tragic modes the nation into the violence separating in from out, a debt owed by the present to those who remained loyal to the nation and suffered defeat.

At the Er-k'un-shen fortification, one can read the inscription arching over the entrance of what in our present is known to have been doomed then, and perhaps redeemable now with the return of Taiwan to China: *I-sui-chin-ch'eng* (Golden bastion for a hundred million years). The Er-sha-wan gun site at Keelung also comes from and potentially keeps alive the tension of that moment of danger at the border by the subject it makes: China, Taiwan Province. The emplacement helped drive off the British during the Opium War but was destroyed in the Sino-French War. Official representations of Hsi-t'ai fort's value speak of boundary maintenance and its patron, the first governor of Taiwan Province. Signifying Taiwan's categorical transformation, the governor's personal cult, and Ch'ing failure despite able subordinates, the time of the fort is matched to the contest for space, one that could only be resolved in nationalist discourse by going beyond the flawed empire to the era of the nation-state.

That these sites are good to think dangerous and make danger subject to the Chinese nation comes through in discourse about the North Gate to Taipei. In 1882 masons imported from Canton erected the long-planned wall around the administrative center of Taipei. Japanese students of Baron von Hausmann destroyed the walls; the North Gate is the last element surviving in something like its original condition — if one can ignore the jumble of roads that swirl around and over the gate. Its quasi-authentic appearance leaks into the authentication of the story signified by its time-place. An important architect-teacher in the field today explains that the site is valuable because it is "intact and it alone authentically reflects the historical background of why Ch'ing dynasty Emperor Kwanghsu ordered the building of city gates. The landmark also serves to remind us of the Japanese invaders who climbed the city walls to enter Taipei."[37]

The gate "reflects" and "reminds." What is reflected through the "emperor ordered" is the embodiment of the nation, rex, who in the face of external danger commanded separation of a natural inside and outside. What is recalled is that the separation was insufficient and breached by another nation. To those who have heard the story in its other incarnations the next step, the debt of shame (to the ready-to-be-grateful dead) and the need for the more effective violence in the National border, falls into place without much prompting to insinuate a subject of debt and danger, a China.

This North Gate story exemplifies the fetish logic of nation-state chronotopes. The object is an agent that "reflects" and "reminds"; what is left out is the social condition of its effectiveness, the real magic of the nation-state fetish. The North Gate gets up and starts pontificating only in ensemble, among its fellows for the initiates or in the state socialization institutions. To the extent that the ensemble of sites exerts a theory effect, a compelling account of social reality, the stones speak. If, however, the theory effect falters, the stones can be trained to tell other stories or fall silent, and then as ruins of ruins ridicule the whole effort—an Ozymandias effect.

Like the sites from the 1880s, the other four First Rank state violence spaces are not described as aesthetically or culturally valuable. Unlike the preceding four, they do allege a much earlier time. The walls around Fengshan are unlike the previous four in another respect: although sites from the 1880s invested time and space tracing out the external frontier, the Fengshan object confronts the internal frontier. No less an invocation of state violence, Fengshan was rebuilt several times against its enemy, rebellion. Its difficulties and relative age can be made to signify both the effort and the failure/danger—the majesty and the pathos of national power before the nation-state. A story attached to the structure says restoration was awaiting a particularly auspicious day for symbolic completion when the local magistrate suddenly died.

Fort Santo Domingo controlled the Tamsui harbor above Taipei and is a rare example of a First Rank military site that is relatively old and bears some resemblance to the original (1629) structure. The fort's relative physical integrity offers a buttress to the key signifier, the name. By its original name or by its Chinese name (the Red-hairs' Fort) it is a transgression sign that Other nations controlled Chinese space in the past and could again in one lave, one potential future. The CCPD texts describing the site devote only a few sentences to the building itself, focusing instead on the succession of foreign conquerors, first as a fort and in the end as another sort of extraterritoriality, a consulate. During the 1970s the Red-hair's fort passed from Britain to Australia and then to the United States as these states successively recognized the Chinese nation-state as the PRC. When the Americans jumped ship, the ROC state "recaptured" the fort. Later history runs symmetrically alongside early history. Spanish troops constructed the site in a state vacuum only to be ousted by the Dutch imperialists. The brief Dutch rule ended in expulsion by the former Ming remnants led by Koxinga.

A major component of orthodox history lodges in persons of the state, signifiers who are in turn signified by the chronotopes. We have already encountered Wang Te-lu and the first governor, but the most important figures are Chiang Kai-shek and his preincarnation, Koxinga (Cheng Ch'eng-kung). Koxinga-Chiang's recapture of Taiwan for China inhabits the remaining two First Rank military sites, rendering them valuable despite their lack of any other redeeming features. Now known as the "ruins of the An-p'ing Fort," the earliest such structure on Taiwan was built by the Dutch from 1624 to 1634. Originally called Fort Orange and then Fort Zeelandia, the present naming was accomplished by Koxinga on the expulsion of the Dutch. Apart from a few bricks, only the name and the empty coordinates of foreign intrusion and Koxinga's victory remain, and that is sufficient for a First Rank national chronotope.

Visitors to Fort Zeelandia can contemplate the Dutch in ruins. Crossing the street to the last military site, even the trace is displaced. Fort Provintia's official history began with construction by the Dutch and reached its goal when Koxinga renamed it to signify its subordination to the ruler of China. Since then, the fort was felled by earthquakes, scavenged for construction materials, and completely built over. Today the Dutch trace is a gate embedded in the base of a patently Chinese building, a temple to the Sea God. Its fragments swallowed by an architectural non sequitur, Fort Provintia is perhaps a "negative *ku-chi*" in every respect except one: the political euphemized as historical. No history-shaping event took place here, just Koxinga (Chiang) renaming, resignifying—exactly the same sort of performative magic now attempted by state historic preservation.

Koxinga looms large because interrogating textbooks, comic books, television, and chronotopes make known to all the homology Koxinga : Ch'ing :: Chiang Kai-shek : PRC. At the same time that Koxinga (Chiang) expelled the barbarians (Japanese) from Chinese Taiwan, he refused to accept the rule of the Manchu (communist) usurpers who controlled the mainland. One popular heterotope has Koxinga sailing up the Tamsui as far as the Yüan-shan. There, where the Americans subdued the Japanese by bombing the island's most sacred Shinto shrine and Koxinga stilled the waves with his sword, the Chiang clan built a hotel.

*Temple, State, and State Temple* Temples accounted for half of the *ku-chi* after the first round of nomination but constituted little more than a third of the First Rank sites. Despite their clear superiority over military sites in craftsmanship, "aesthetic and cultural value," and representation of the era or locality's distinctive features, only one in twenty *ku-chi* temples (compared to one in four city walls and almost half of *wei-shu* fortifications) ranked first. The seven temples that made the top grade could be qualified on any of the three major grounds and this "overdetermination" in turn makes possible additive or conflicting effects.

Heterodox and orthodox preservationists alike praise the materials, craft, and relative simplicity of the Tainan Confucius Temple. Restoring the temple began with one preservationist and the temple's place in his autobiographical, not state, history. In both these respects, the temple escapes the nation. At the same time, inclusion in the codified ensnares the temple in nationalist discourse. Of the eleven statements of fact regarding the temple in a widely circulated official description, nine refer to political time/person/event markers.[38] Changhua's Confucian Temple, though on a larger scale and with less critical acclaim for its form, is similarly located. A main point in its official description is subordination under sumptuary laws that reserved the closed four-sided courtyard form for prefectural-level schools.[39]

Military connections are inherent in the Tainan temple to Kuan-ti, the loyal general, but it is also demonstrably old and accepted as one of the best realizations of temple architecture; the CCPD describes the temple's swallow-tailed roof as evidence of high craftsmanship in its ability to combine "rigor and ease." Combining rigor with ease, control with relaxation, the marks of a superior architectural talent are also the very description of the most-qualified, best-capitalized linguistic productions and their producers. Nothing is forced; there is no urgency — only competence acquired over a long time by those who could afford, or be afforded by patrons, the opportunity to perfect.

The temple's official name speaks the third level of qualification, association with events or persons of historic significance. In 1725 the Ch'ing bestowed the name *Ssu-tien wu-miao* (Military Temple for State Sacrificial Rites) and made the loyal general's temple sacred space for the spring and autumn rituals of a political-natural institution. Placement further articulates the political; an official description notes that from this temple one can see the roof of Fort Zeelandia, which as I just noted is no more than a Chinese building on the coordinates of absent Fort Zeelandia.[40]

The goddess Matsu seems hardly the vehicle for nation-state abstractions. She has in fact been implicated in all sorts of state-ignoring activities. Before the legalization of travel to the mainland, police intercepted Taiwanese returning from the home temple in Fukien. The helmsman claimed no legal responsibility as "Matsu had taken control" of their boat and forced them to the mainland. Despite lapses by her devotees, two of her temples were consecrated as First Rank historic sites.[41]

Penghu's Matsu Temple, the first Han religious structure in the space controlled by the ROC, is distinguished by its simple supporting columns, high elevation of the main hall, intricately carved hanging pots, and delicate woodwork. It is also well qualified on political grounds, and the sequence of restorations embeds the nation in the architecture as it conscripts Matsu: her shrine was altered for the first time to commemorate, to institute in stone, a Ming victory over the Japanese. Another victory over the Japanese in 1592 occasioned a remodeling. In 1622 the state restored the temple to fix into memory the expulsion of the Dutch. Since the Ch'ing claimed Matsu's assistance in wresting Penghu from the Ming-in-exile, she was "promoted" to Queen of Heaven, and the temple space and name were again altered to embody the time-place whereby Taiwan is revealed as Chinese.

The *Ta tien-hou-kung* (Great Matsu Temple) also registers the promotion and is officially distinguished as "the earliest Matsu sanctuary to have its name officially changed" from Temple of the Princess of Heaven to reflect her career change.[42] Just as one name displaced the other in step with the extension of the fatherland, so the architectural object itself had displaced another chronotope. The temple site is the erased palace of the last Ming prince.

The end of the Ming in Prince Ning-ching's suicide occasioned yet another First Rank site, the Temple of the Five Concubines (*Wu-fei miao*). Euphemized for foreigners as the Shrine of the Five Noble Ladies, this site praises the "suicide" of Ning-ching's five concubines who supposedly hung themselves in the palace out of loyalty to the prince. Ch'ing inspectors ordered a shrine built adjoining the grave. The Ming may have been their enemy, but the Manchu paid tribute to the allegation of doxa without which no nation-state could exist.

A few women are admitted to the 1985 First Rank chronotopes according to the principle of hierarchical inclusion. Women appear in two guises: young widows who renounce sexuality in supposed deference to the dead and suicidal concubines, alleged to have measured up to Chiang Kai-shek's standard for others, "loving her country more than her own life." The reality of the nation is further generated by inserting the image of loyalty to "it" in a family-based sequence of loyalty, obligation, and virtuous suffering. Each familiar object asks of the viewer or the reader, "What am I?" and then as metonym discloses the other metonyms such as filiality, other aspects of the abstract Chinese time and space materialize in an arch or a shrine as an answer—not in the Ming or the Ch'ing but in 1985 as Min-kuo 74 (seventy-fourth year of the ROC).

The meaning-dependence of *ku-chi* on encompassing social practice is evident in the last of the First Rank temples, the Lukang Lung-shan Temple. The preservation movement began early in Lukang, joining artisans, temple associations, folklorists, and intellectuals into a relative autonomy from state-sponsored work. Begun in the 1970s when Lukang's sites were devalued in the center as lacking in national significance, the loose alliance linked with local governments and later began to search for cultural tourism markets among the urban professionals. Brought into the national system and at the same time encompassed in the Lukang local scene, the Lung-shan Temple can be made to tell very different stories.

State invasion of the chronotope begins by fixing time of construction during the reign years of the Ch'ien-lung Emperor, "at a time when Lukang had become an important exchange point for trade between the mainland and Taiwan." An act of mimesis, the temple is said to be a "direct copy" of the Kai-yüan Temple in Chüan-chou.[43] Construction material, statues, a bell, and technical knowledge came from China, the temple being "both copying *and* sensuous materiality" in the sense that Taussig has recalled Benjamin.[44] Thus is it subsumed through heterotopy into China and China realized in it, "a fine example of late eighteenth-century *Chüan-chou* (a mainland county) temple architecture"—just as the language commonly called *T'ai-yü* (Taiwanese) is mis-placed as *Min-nan hua,* the language located in the space south of Fukien's Min River in the absent origin-space.

Countermemories begin in a present because the Lung-shan Temple is still alive. A base for *Nan-kuan* and *Pei-kuan* troupes and the site for performances in the annual folk arts festival, the temple is also a locus of local struggle, most notably the environmental campaign that defied the center and thwarted Dupont's plan to stick a hazard in the community. This Lung-shan Temple of the present has an alternate narrative lodged in social memory about its past that includes the mainland, but is not focused on the state.

Looking back on the original group of First Rank sites, from both the classes of objects included and the official consecration stories, crucial diacritica that distinguish nonsites from sites and First Rank from the less valuable center on national time-space. The time-space of the objects is a Chinese place marked in a time of reign years, filial life spans, military victories, and chronotopes of danger on the border.

Spaces of no other merit rank first because they materialize as Past the control of movement and boundaries, city walls, gun emplacements, forts, proper relationships, and Chüan-chou style; by making them stick despite time, they were extended into the likely future by means of an implicit creative prediction. Together with the other operators of memory construction, they work in ensemble to make into the future what they describe as past, to the end that life in the now contains that absent space and is locked into series. When they work, they work in the same mode that "realist" American social science works over Taiwan. They transform nation into nature; they fatalize. Take the example of Ralph Clough's predictive diagnosis of "most people" on Taiwan in his aptly titled *Island China:* "It would be a psychological wrench for most people on Taiwan to accept the view that they and their descendants would no longer be part of the stream of history now represented by the 850 Million [1978] people on the China mainland."[45] Repeated and interrogated not for subscription but rather in the dailiness of life by buildings, empty spaces, television, textbooks, and authorities foreign and domestic, the nationalization of persons presents a force flowing through a stream channel, a seriality and spatiality from which there seems no escape. The successful chronotope "absorbs into itself that which it represents," and the nation is objectified both as intersubjectively verifiable reality and as fetish.

## MATERIALIZING CHINA

The Government Information Office (GIO) defends preservation, saying "history is easier to embed in the mind if there are tangible objects that bring the past into focus."[46] The tangible lens always assumes the image has been prepared by words, that words coil in reserve, freeing the object to do what language alone cannot. The tangible once properly known reveals in a glance and as a whole. The tangible is above all amenable to tactile knowledge. Memory is interrogated into being, authority says, by "running fingers along the grooves of a carved door, or brushing dust out of the recessed Chinese characters on a stone stele. Tactile experience of the past is a tremendous stimulus to cultural awareness." The official account notes everyone "knows" about the An-p'ing Fort, the Dutch and Koxinga through language in school interrogation, but "while students and teachers are familiar with the story about how the Dutch first built the fort in 1623 (they called it Fort Zeelandia), they are encouraged to have altogether different thoughts about this period of history after running their hands over the wall's rough surface. Touch and the other senses combine to stimulate the imagination, and encourage them to learn more."[47]

Where would stimulus to the imagination from touching seventeenth-century Dutch bricks lead? What "more" ought to be learned? I will return to this question and the bricks of this Dutch wall in the final section of this article; for now, tactile knowledge gives a push down the path already broken by interrogation through stones and timbers, the constituents of buildings. Being more raw and prior to intention than the buildings they bear, materials and labor appear more disinterested and therefore more reliable informants about the state-positioned subject of history. Finished buildings may speak about China, but timbers and stones from the mainland "are" China, and so official discourse takes each opportunity to memorize and recall that "most building materials were brought in from the mainland at considerable cost."[48] The "process of institution consists in assigning properties of a *social* nature in a way that makes them seem like properties of natural nature," and as the Lukang Lung-shan Temple discussion suggests, the naturalizing of social properties through *ku-chi* builds on the mimetic potential invested in the object's constituent materials.[49] The masons who built Taipei's North Gate came from Kuantung. Lung-shan Temple is supported by fir timber and bricks from Fukien; its bell was cast in Ningpo. The materials are even more disposed than their aggregations to affect the erasure of representation, so that we are "absorbed into the object's emptiness."[50]

Since 1839 when the French archaeologist Didron said, "it is better to preserve than to restore and better to restore than to reconstruct," authenticity of material has been a cornerstone of the Western invention, historic preservation.[51] Regulations implementing the basic law on preservation for the ROC spell out four principles to guide the protection and restoration of sites, the second being repair with original materials or, if the original is not available, the closest possible substitute.[52] Since the space of China was technically inaccessible (this did not prevent the Mao Zedong Memorial Hall from obtaining wood from Taiwan Province), what constituted the closest possible substitute was open to dispute. In dispute and questioning, the "authenticity" of materials reveals a strictly nation-state dimension.

This continues, even after mainland materials have begun to enter the market. The Ch'eng-huang Temple in Chia-i was known among preservationists for its ancient wooden archway. Interviewing the temple's managers, I noted that the wooden arch was gone and in its place there was a new stone structure. They explained that, yes, they had finally raised the money to get rid of the ugly old thing and in the spirit of preservation replace it with "original materials"—very expensive stone from China. *Original* meant of the place of origin, not the original molecular structure.

While original material originally smuggled in naturalness, the priority of national political space in raw material guise runs not only through what was selected and how it was repaired but also in what was *not* selected. The place of material in objectifying China is also the place of forgetting.

## THE ORGANIZATION OF FORGETTING

Writing of English nationality, Corrigan and Sayer explain that "such classifications are means for a project of social integration which is also, inseparably, an active *dis*integration of other focuses of identity and conceptions of subjectivity. They provide a basis for construction and organization of collective memory—the writing of history, the manufacture of 'tradition'—which is inseparably an active organization of forgetting."[53]

Slowly being encircled by cement apartment towers, the Li family residence in Lü-chou is one of the last and best remaining Japanese-era farmhouses in northern Taiwan. After years of battle, the house was finally declared a *ku-chi,* but of the third and lowest rank. With each year runoff water from the surrounding apartment sprawl threatens to undermine the building beyond a point of no return, yet problems persist and the farmhouse crumbles under the weight of red tape. This building lacked one quality that could have immediately saved it: nation-state significance.[54] This was simply a landlord's farmhouse (or so it seemed) from the Japanese era and had nothing to do with China.

*Taiwanese* What was not said in public until the last few years was that this was no ordinary landlord, but a very unusual Taiwanese. During the war against Japan he was one of the few who left Japanese Taiwan for China and fought in the Nationalist armies. There he married a mainlander and returned to Taiwan with the Chinese forces. With these unusual credentials, his strong criticism of KMT abuses on Taiwan were initially hard to silence. After his silencing, his widowed mainlander wife became the practical head of the extended Lü-chou Li family. She established a very successful translation business and has spent most of her remaining energies fighting to preserve this site.

A major problem at Lü-chou is not a lack of national historical significance but rather that it signifies two aspects of national history that were organized into oblivion: the Japanese era and the February 28 Incident. From the official standpoint, this chronotope would call attention to the very object of forgetting. The conflict was euphemized in several ways, most interestingly into the construction materials. On one occasion, a high Chinese official concluded his inspection of the site with "you know, there's not one stone, not one piece of wood from the mainland!"

The 250-site system in the late 1980s is meaningful through what it excluded as well as what it included, and the Lü-chou Li family residence is one of many examples of parts of the Taiwanese past excluded because they lent no energy to the national project. The nonconsecrated sites joined Taiwanese literature, orthography, literary pronunciation, folk music, and accounts of abuse and more in the nonculture.

*Aboriginal* As in South Africa, the most direct challenge to priority and autochthony of the settler nation-state comes from the existence of aboriginal peoples. Historic preservation saw no aboriginal chronotopes to include when the system was established in 1982–1985. That a leading preservationist would publicly declare that "basically, Taiwan is a place without history" (see page 113) and contains only Dutch, Japanese, and Han cultural elements, testifies to the effectiveness of organized forgetting. It also reflects the power of national time-space making, for where else outside of a Chinese building on once Dutch coordinates, some bricks, and a dozen textbooks is there any trace of the few years of Dutch presence in Taiwan culture? As for the residents of thousands of years, they are categorically domesticated as *shan-pao* (mountain brethren), as if they were always on the periphery just out of the Han brothers' way and never expropriated. Despite the logical and legal obligation to protect sites that evidence their former place in Taiwan, erasure was the order of the day, and Han priority was protected during the dictatorship.

Forgetting the aboriginal clears space for the re-cognized extension of China. The memory masters declare "these [included] sites testify to the *extension* of Chinese culture in the architectural objects of Taiwan, Penghu and Chin-men." [55] In the choice of sites we saw the hyperconcern for moments in which others might occupy Taiwan, a shadow of Chinese spatial "extension" in time that underlies official discourse. Chinese culture, the Chinese state extended to Taiwan, colonized it. Like the other external powers fearing those whose pasts it sought to erase, the ensemble posturing as China excludes the fullness of the space/time it displaced and so defines a relation to the island by invasion, the nightmare coming over the horizon which, as it closes in, reveals China itself as the feared invader.

*Japanese* A peace treaty ended the military war with Japan, but another war broke out, this one against the memory, the re-cognition of the alien ensconced in the body of Taiwan. Officially labeled by *kuo-chi* (legal nationality), Japanese colonists were tangible objects that could be removed. Signs of Japanese nationality, however, were in the institutional, topographic, and bodily landscape of Taiwan itself.

The KMT was not completely mad in asserting that Taiwanese resistance during the February 28 Incident "was caused not by the demand for political reform . . . but by the Taiwanese who had received the evil spirit of the Japanese."[56] The twisted truth of the matter is that by many measures—language competence, education, labor migration patterns—a portion of the Taiwanese colonial subject elite was being nationalized (in the sense of formal classification and disposition previously discussed) as Japanese.[57] These people were not the totally defenseless, "really, most sincerely dead" Dutch imperialists buried in historical memory under the Tainan Temple to the Sea God. The Japanese and the liminal Taiwanese lived, copresent and in autobiographical memory. Under the Chinese dictatorship, a demonizing discourse aimed to exorcise this evil spirit.

Most vivid are the images of ruptures in the natural order that rightfully constrain both beast and barbarian (*fan*) in their allowed but bounded spaces. Taiwan is home to a large variety and number of poisonous snakes, but a portion of the first generation raised under KMT rule thinks this long-standing natural fact is a recent and nefarious plot. In this story, the Japanese figure as an anti–St. Patrick who bred poisonous snakes in the mountains of Taiwan and then released them just before "Retrocession" to plague "Chinese" people for all time.

The position of the Taiwanese in relation to abomination is ambiguous. On one hand, the state bases its rhetoric of legitimation on an assertion that the Taiwanese and all others under the control of the Chinese state are *t'ung-pao* (of the same womb). In practice, however, the Taiwanese had lived for fifty years in a Japanese world, speaking their way through it in the Japanese language, while the Japanese released snakes in Taiwan and massacred Chinese on the mainland. Habituation to the beastly Japanese made an alternate time, a past and a future without the KMT, a real presence, and such conditions are notably intolerable to the dominant during incorporation. Pollution and the need for cleansing were never far from the surface of post-Incident state policy.

The Chronotope Campaign scraped away at the Japanese national memory with the unavoidable outcome of genesis amnesia. With aboriginals and Taiwanese, negative inclusion and exclusion worked best. Unlike war against aboriginal and Taiwanese pasts, erasure of Japan has a more active side: defacing or destroying chronotopes.

A 1974 Interior Ministry edict entitled "Main Points on the Elimination of Taiwan Japanese Era Colonial Rule Memorials and Historical Remains Manifesting Japanese Imperialism's Sense of Superiority" codified what had been the reflex of political habitus. Japanese-era maps and guides to the island posit the thirty Shinto shrines as landscape anchors: Taipei's Chung-shan Road, for example, was a major Japanese physical reorientation of urban space organized along an axis running from the eastern edge of the old city center toward the island's premier Shinto temple on the Yüan-shan. The edict commanded that Shinto shrines be destroyed. Today only part of one, the Taoyüan shrine, remains, and that because it had been defaced and turned into an antishrine. Second, the apparatus decreed complete elimination of memorials and tablets "manifesting Japanese imperialism's sense of superiority."

Entwining the national/aesthetic, all Japanese stone lanterns and similar fixtures in temples and other public buildings were to be altered (removing the aesthetic quality making them nationally Japanese) or else destroyed. Reframing the Past, Japanese calendrical inscriptions dating buildings and monuments were effaced and replaced with Chinese Republican calendrical markers. Memorials to Japanese persons not showing this sense of superiority and deemed valuable by local governments were left to the local organs. Grave markers of Japanese persons and other "innocent" date inscriptions using Meiji reign years could be exempted, though in practice much was destroyed.[58]

The nonpresence of these three pasts—Taiwanese, aboriginal, and Japanese—in the official reality called Historic Sites is forgetting, not the absence entailed in being-in-the-world but the institutionalized symbolic violence that erases pasts to fatalize a national future. That forgetting is never complete and memories of resistance now threaten memories of the absent site, China, in the sites of memory, the *lieux de mémoire*.

## MAKING TIME AFTER THE DICTATORSHIP: "WHAT PLACE IS THIS TIME?"

In Taiwan of the 1990s, the rush of the new, eruptions of the unprecedented are such that a distinct present seems to insist on recognition. A question once seldom posed is now speakable, new groups of agents contend for state power and in respect of both problems the contenders answer the questions "Is this place a nation? If so, which one?"—with and in a struggle over chronotopes. Here I will highlight several changes relevant to institutions of historic preservation that have begun in and act back on the master field, the field of power.

Stand by the emergency room door on the west side of the Veterans' General Hospital in Taipei and you can see the first transformation. The first generation of mainlanders, the Chinese of autobiographical memory, the soldiers who whispered (and they had not been interrogated about Koxinga) about the old man's dark powers, the ones who held fast to the deeds to China—they are coming in the hospital doors and leaving the world. Many have taken a detour through an unexpected China. The barrier to the extension of ROC state space remains, but the absence of China is remade if not gone. They returned to the origin place as tourists from a different social formation; a very few— but many more Taiwanese—are welcomed back to China, armed not with their old m-1's and deeds but with dollars. The membrane, however, is permeable in only one direction, and it is easier for the grandchildren of Stalin or Enver Hoxha to get into the Republic of China than for a "Chinese." Where Taiwanese capital sees Chinese as a class category of cheap labor and seeks to let some in, Taiwanese nationalists make electoral profit contending the new mainlanders ought to be classified as *wai-chi-lao-kung,* or foreign laborers, *Gastarbeiter.*

The passing of Chinese migrants over the spatial border into China and over the temporal border into death changes politics on the island. As the handful who had ruled as "delegates" of China since 1947 verged on extinction, the principle of delegation began to shift to selection by Taiwanese voters and the Chinese diaspora. And for the generation about to come into the world, the embodiment device of *chi-kuan* will now use place of birth.

A second transformation is what others call the Taiwan Miracle, the relentless commodification of life, including space and time. Capitalist development since the policy shift of 1961 creates new social structures and millions of daily relations in which the state is shoved to the background. In the process, space as commodity is not as easily subjected to state designations like *ku-chi.* Further, the speedup in the circuits of production and consumption engenders new "use values"— cultural consumables like nostalgia, truth, and natural space, as well as land speculation's big profit.

A third change of consequence for historic preservation's relation to nationality is a decline in unmediated nation-knowledge relations that opens doxa to challenge. These changes open up several plausible futures for the past. One is an ever more inclusive and "benign" extension of China's five-thousand-year space. Another is the production of a Taiwanese nation, in part through a Taiwanese past fetishized in chronotopes. Against these national pasts, the present opens up space in which nonnational chronotopes, "cultures," and polities can contend, a possible Taiwan Miracle where other nation-states seem hopelessly trapped in nationalism's logos.

*Historic Preservation: From Memory Apparatus to Field*

Historic preservation is a field, a "set of objective relations between positions, their locations in field space determined by the amount and types of power (capital) and the regulative procedures that structure conditions under which participants access the stakes of the field." The performative power of buildings and utterances about buildings are its products, the misrecognized power of agents and their positions in social space.

Because of concentration in the master field of power, historic preservation had been a collapsed field, a point space coinciding with the field of power. The decisive change for chronotopes beginning in the mid-1980s was the gradual complication of social space in response to the major transformations noted here, and change in the form of the state from an apparatus to a field of struggle for power. Ironically, codification in 1982 and logical control provided the immediate impetus to historic preservation's field expansion. Space expanded; the code had to be implemented. A military officer's dreams were no longer sufficient on the main islands, and new positions emerged claiming competence to do the job evidenced by possessing different forms of capital. Moreover, by making the logic explicit, historic preservation became much more an object of struggle. Before examining in detail the particularities of the new instruments of appropriation based on state, social, "economic," and knowledge capital, a word on their common currency: language.

In large part the struggle to be described is a struggle to institute a world with words; for this to succeed, the words must be authoritative—delegated or empowered by embodied disinterest—and in modernity that boils down to the Nation, the Public, Efficiency, or Science. In the discussion that follows, two signs of authority recur: credential and cant. Authoritative language, that spoken by those who can claim the credentials required by the field (Ph.D., civil service rank, architect's license, spokesperson, journalist's name card), at once states the basic ground rules and silences those who do not control the credential code. In addition, authoritative language is jargon, a specialized language of the field that uses ordinary language while (often falsely) claiming a break with it, an autonomy from ordinary language. Contrast the mathematical concept of group from the use of "a group of buildings" or note the smuggled power when statistics appropriates the ordinary language connotations of "significance," and we have some sense of the power of symbolic violence invested in jargon's second-order appropriation of "authentic," "conserve," "restore," and "the people." Authoritative talk rushed in where the state faltered.

### FIELD OF THE STATE

Field change in Taiwan is not so much the "withering away of the state" as it is the empowerment of land as capital, the invention of the public, and technical knowledge. Power to enforce preservation is now a matter of central law—law that honors property, rather than decree. Centralized yet circumscribed, the weight of the state unit oscillates around this contradiction: ultimate power resides in the center yet is increasingly separated from the persons of the center delegated as mini-rex.

By itself, codification would be expected to dramatically increase the number and field locations of state-delegated agents, but reforming historical preservation came as the center attempted to restrict the growth of personnel. Rather than hire a permanent body of experts from different fields or set up a national institute to certify in-house experts, numbers were kept in check by relying at all levels on contracting, especially *wei-t'uo* (commissioned) research to establish the validity of nomination claims, evaluate policy, and suggest future directions. By May 1992, the invitation list for a gathering of the field included sixty names, and less than half were state employees.[59] Deducting those whose preservation work is secondary to other responsibilities, the state share of people in the field drops to about one-quarter.

The significance of the state positions, however, does not decline in proportion to the percentage of its agents. Because major resources are delegated by and administrative decisions are made at the center, positions in the center continue to carry a certain if circumscribed power. The most active day-to-day workers managing state preservation are very aware of the "overly" nationalized heritage of the state segment. Within the constraints posed by their political overseers, they have generally tried to professionalize that part of the field in their custody and to decrease attention to "political" considerations in favor of more "objective" criteria. Both of these trends have increased the weight of technical and social capital.

Last, with a shift from apparatus to field, the capital of other positions grows in importance, and the state becomes the common object of complaint, for it alone holds in autobiographical memory not only the power to undo its old failings but also the only possible power to restrain the threat to the other positions posed by a new capital, economic capital.

LAND AS CAPITAL

Living *ku-chi,* almost always temples, have an institutional structure and claim to space; these sites have clear incentives for continuity. Dead sites are different. An individual who wishes to spend a hour amid the ruins has no need to possess title to the site to consume. She is a free rider; an institution is required to construct a public interest in *ku-chi,* and then on that basis find a means either through ownership or state power to remove chronotopes from the space of potential commodities.

Market logic now with the force of law seems irresistible. If the residents of the old Taipei marketing center of Ti-hua Street can turn a quick and major profit by widening the street and then selling out to apartment developers, what is to stop them? The doxa of the state is such that the only conceivable alternative is assertion of a public interest in preserving-instituting the object-form of neighborhood and then invoking state power to suppress individual property rights.[60]

What politics had sundered—preservationists and the state—capital forces back together, and in the process a new nationality is a little more "real." The problem is experienced as the Taiwanese as a people, and that paradoxically tends to separate them out as a subject, a public apart from China. As Yen Ya-ning put the matter so frankly, "People here are more or less opportunists. We have no sense of history."[61] This twisted theory is taken as adequate to the fact; there is an explanation of a whole range of behaviors intolerable to the academics, technicians, social movement participants, and, ironically, the far right of the KMT.

SOCIAL CAPITAL AND THE PRESERVATION MOVEMENT

A historical preservation movement gradually emerged in the 1970s in response to the destruction of the built environment and pushed for the Cultural Assets Preservation Law that passed in 1982. The term *movement* might be a little confusing to outsiders. It was a movement that developed with a dictatorship that suppressed all independent organizations and speech; the movement by definition was of those who had voice to which the dictatorship would listen unthreatened. By 1987, a new form of power (capital) had been recognized in the field, the power of nonstate persons to declare themselves delegates, spokespersons for a public. The year 1987 saw the loosening of the law on organizations in such a way as to encourage both activists and capitalists to place their respective political and tax-reduction agendas into the foundation format. Several foundations delegated themselves as defenders of *ku-chi* and spokespersons for the public.

Some, most notably Alice Ru-Hwa Chiu of the Yaoshan Foundation, successfully mobilized economic and academic capital, and even persons within official organs in campaigns to restrict property rights and prod state action to preserve. In the late 1980s a new world of electoral delegation and heterodox politicians, the image of a public segment pressing for preservation, congealed as a social capital in the hands of the spokespersons who, unlike the certified expert, could offer no more capital than the fruits of their own organizing might generate. Lacking the economic capital necessary to sustain a large-scale movement or the credentials to enforce a vision of what historic preservation is (after all, only a certified [Ph.D.] wizard can distinguish a genuine chronotope from a heterotope!), the preservation movement is contained in the lower reaches of field space. The movement is compelled to collaborate with other forms of capital to succeed in the game—that is, credit for nominations, secure funding, heeded alarms, and recognition as spokespersons for the chronotopes.

The fact that the ROC claim to being of China is not recognized by other nation-states presents nongovernmental organizations (NGOs) with the opportunity to do what elsewhere would be done by a state body like the CCPD. Preservation NGOs are free to act in international contexts from which the ROC is excluded. From quasi-official bodies like ICOMOS (the International Council on Monuments and Sites) to European ministries of culture, NGOs act on a case-by-case basis as delegates of the state. As in its collaboration with academics, the movement leadership constantly faces the possibility that it is being used (its social capital bringing return to the other field positions); yet, given the regulative principles of the game, without collaboration with political power or authorized academic language, there is little return to social capital.

Over its first century, the knowledge-capital region of historic preservation fields has resolved into two moments, two segments of space; in terms of the symbolic forms on which they act, one (historic) deals with signifieds, what took place, and the semantics of the past's representation, while the other (preservation) acts only on the signifiers. Paradoxically, where the nation-state is in serious question, relative dilution of direct nation-state power over the field has further fetishized the chronotope, setting off a flight from the political nation—signified into the properties of the signifier—exactly the fetish-site that has completely absorbed the referent of the nation. The site is received, unquestioned, and the work of preservation is restricted to the materials of representation, but this is hardly the same as "depoliticizing." Shoring up a set assembled by interested symbolic violence through engineering that treats the set as a self-evident and unconstructed collective treasure is a highly political act on the part of those who feel they despise the political. This trend, which some call *formalism* and I will label *techno-orthodoxy,* is a meaning of preservation and inseparably a trend in the field's construction: What are the positions in space? How many agents are there? What is the power of their knowledge claims?

The meaningful flight into the fetish is realized in the field by equating knowledge capital with engineering credentials. Returning to the CCPD 1992 roster of the field, we find twenty-one professionally certified knowledge workers operating outside the state preservation units. Of these, over two-thirds are architects. Only one person works in aesthetics; only one does sociology, and he's in Wisconsin. Three are historians, while over five times as many are graduates of engineering programs.

In the following sections, I examine the effects of engineering's dominance of preservation space and language. Here, however, the sketch of the field after the dictatorship would be misleading if we simply stopped with an assumed categorical imperative of architect. In Taiwan, the connotation of architect differs in an important respect from that which obtains elsewhere. This difference is a consequence of the ROC's construction of the field of academic knowledge.

Fixed on the threat posed by words, by counterinterpretations of the social world, the migrant state attacked the disciplines associated with criticism. After Chiang Kai-shek's death squads visited the Tai-ta men's dormitories, attention shifted to the social sciences, literature, and philosophy. Disciplines associated elsewhere with more critical approaches remained relatively orthodox; students with critical dispositions were often attracted (or pushed by the entrance by exam system) to other disciplines. The theory of professions, apart from an attendance to fields, needs a shot of chaos theory, for small differences at key points can be magnified over time. Such is the case with the emergence of a critical center from an unlikely place, the "Earth and Wood Institute" of an engineering school. This space within the field of architecture became known quite early as more amenable to critical discourse and action.

It helped to be in an engineering school. The image of engineering within the KMT party-state since the flight contrasted with disastrous policies of the past. The 1961 policy switch that launched the so-called Taiwan Miracle was designed not by economists as much as by engineers from Westinghouse. When faculty and students within the School of Engineering began to phrase the new urban mess in engineering terms and, in the mode of engineering, took on visible projects, they became a pole. Historic preservation, including the semantic/social aspect, fell within the purview of the program, and students were exposed, later even required, to do coursework or qualify out of studies of the social aspects of space. Although still only a minority in the profession, the diffusion of graduates to posts in private practice, the state, and teaching positions around the island gave architects dealing with preservation as a whole a greater willingness to see the entire range of chronotope making, not just the molecular structure of the fetish.

The second qualification to the image of knowledge capital as engineering turns on the institutions in which architects deploy their capital. The great majority of preservation architects are also academics — faculty in universities, colleges, and technical schools. These work locations limit architects' time available to concentrate in historic preservation, but they also provide potential resources for sponsored research, the authoritative metalanguage of the academy, and partial independence from market forces, notably clients and the state. The leading critical center's technical capital has accumulated primarily not from preservation but from urban planning. Interests are diversified, allowing them to move in and out, potentially reducing their investments in the collective taken-for-granted of preservation.

Position in the highest reaches of academic space is central to critical preservation. There academic architects have special access to labor power: graduate students needing projects. Another advantage of academic space is access to the virtual community of international academics. Given the official position that cultural life had to catch up with capitalist development, access to the imperial centers with their relatively extensive historic preservation systems adds to the highest ranking academics' capital. Changes desired by the academics are made more authority-dense by invoking expert voices in the United States and Europe, including those most critical of core country preservation; voices of authenticity, cultural pluralism, stewardship, the supposed benefits of cultural tourism, and community participation transfer symbolic resources to the benefit of the dominated fraction of the dominant (academics and movement preservationists) at the expense of purely nation-state preservation. This internationalization of authority is also a struggle over the shape of the field and the relative value of the different forms of capital.

This foreign currency can be used not to undermine domination but to simply shift the locus of domination to a new space of the field. Consider how a professor-consultant to Taipei City uses the power of broker in the international circulation of specialized information to distort: "In Europe, every street, every block, even every corner has a committee handling [historic preservation] matters."[62] Recognizing this power to distort inherent in the position is not to say that new demands from "experts" for citizen responsibility, an honest accounting of history, or raising "aesthetic value" over national content are just smoke screens put up in front of cap and gown smash and grab. Rather, there exists a homology between positional struggle in the field and other struggles, specifically between the position of the dominated in the field and the dominated outside, made all the more powerful by and reinforcing the sense of ethical obligation.

Not locked into a single field, invested with both technical and academic capitals, and prepared for the crisis of authoritative language precipitated by the state's transformation, this most autonomous segment of the field has moved to redefine the interests of the field and the practice of preservation, my two remaining topics.

HISTORIC PRESERVATION AND ILLUSIO

We cannot deduce practice or even the interests of agents in the preservation business from a map of objective positions. First, situations must be perceived and recognized, classed through the organizing power of habitus, leading different sets of agents to respond to the same circumstances in very dissimilar ways. Second, the relative values of capitals and the regulative principles of the field described at any moment in structural (positional) language are not permanent; to the contrary, the distribution of powers within the field is at once antecedent to and at the same time an object of struggle. Last, given the contradictions and ambiguity of the "game" and its articulation with other fields, outcomes are always less than certain.

A "game" is a useful simile, though we should start out by noting places where the correspondence breaks down. The game gives all the appearance of being self-contained—that is, its starting points and outcomes are internal to it. The field, however, interlocks with other fields, and this one is clumsily encompassed by the field of power. The game has fixed rules, while the conditions governing success in a field are the object of struggle.

With this caveat, a field, like a game, depends on embodied practical logic: a feel for the struggle. As an aspect of habitus specific to the field of preservation, this practical sense enables a ready response to contingency without reference to the intellectualist machinery that rational choice theory mistakenly infers into the intelligibility of practice. Because the players in the field occupy unequal positions in field space and their ability to effectively cognize and respond is limited by position, differences in disposition and evaluation are not random. There is, however, one aspect of habitus that is necessarily shared across all positions: a prereflexive commitment to the worth of historic preservation as constituted in the field. Historic sites are good. Any attempt to specify the valuation ends quickly in vacuous talk about "collective treasures" or "the spiritual substance of our people." In the non-stop euphemizing (interpreting the site, unlocking national memories, public interest, managerial efficiency) the compact of denial is sealed: above all, refuse the terrible truth that the objects are themselves silent, that the work of each and every person in the field, for better or worse, is a redoubled ventriloquism, thus making the inanimate appear to move the lips of the dead.

Put another way, everyone in the field is "interested" in both ordinary language senses—no one can be indifferent, everyone is invested into—and there is no surer sign of this interest than the pretense of disinterest, of merely being the mechanic of nation, history, truth, or beauty. Shared and contradictory, interests, like outcomes, are not a strict function of the distribution of power within the field, but exist in a more complicated state. Here I prefer Bourdieu's concept, *illusio,* from *ludens* and game.[63] Illusio as the investment of self into the game is keyed to the specific arena in question, and on this point it stands distinguished from the ahistorical interest of the maximizing individual, or its twins writ large, the proletariat and progress. Illusio as a commitment to the field's worth has another interesting property by virtue of being a prenotion. It is belief at the doxic level functioning without explicit interrogation; in fact, it and the field are most stable to the extent that it stays on the far side of discourse, taken up into habitus.

The commitment to the field uniting all positions stands out more clearly when we look at the authoritative language that fills the space vacated by retreating nationalist rhetoric. Uniting engineering and sociocritical field segments is the self-evident good called *authenticity*. A very modern break from a Chinese aesthetic blending real and copy, authenticity's elevation of a real over a false gives authoritative leverage to the knowledge producers who have filled much of the expanded space, both the technicians who deny they are signifying and the critics of power's separation of spaces and abuse of the dead. The same word can be deployed in microattention to the authenticity of fetish components and the authenticity of time-place narratives because both kinds of professionals claim through Science the authoritative means to substantiate.

The compromise between "expressive interest" and the limits inscribed in the field uniting the two types of authoritative language are realized in the recommendations from the Interior Ministry–commissioned study intended to be the basis for historic preservation's legal reform. Three of our six conclusions address problems from the standpoint of materials, their technology, and their management. The other three address the sociopolitical contradictions of the field: historic preservation is not a purely technical or innocent problem; participation of civic organizations in preservation work could increase the likelihood of satisfactory outcomes; exchange of ideas and policy development should not be confined to the borders of the nation-state but expanded to be a part of international discourse.[64]

Concrete recommendations, however, emphasized professionalization, the great common ground of the credentialed. The first suggestion was the establishment of an official yet somehow independent expert body responsible for preservation of cultural resources. Next came the suggestion that administrative personnel within the state system receive specialized training. On the critical question of site nomination by the center, the report advised incorporating the opinions of scholars into the process; power is to be shared with the credentialed. The remaining recommendations encourage designation of preservation districts and suggest how private owners might be encouraged to preserve by tax breaks and management bodies. State-delegated research tends to quietly limit what can be said since those involved are normally invested into the field, by implicit common interest.

Given that a particular illusio can be defined in relation to the illusio of other segments of field space, one way to assess the distribution of these interests, collusion and conflict between positions, is to analyze the field materialized in rare instants as a whole. Now with state power weakened and CCPD professionals depending on the authoritative language of engineers and academics, one way for the CCPD to do preservation is to grant space, money, and prestige—and by so doing maintain the uniquely official power to define. In May 1992, the CCPD did just that, constituting the field through invitation to discuss issues as they defined them. Two hundred and fifty-five persons defined as working in cultural preservation assembled into units responsible for archaeology, folk arts, scenic resources, and historic sites. The CCPD raised three thematic questions, each reflecting some difference within the field.

Expressing the shared assumptions of almost everyone in the field, the first question asked, How might state units increase administrative efficiency? If the state's primary fault had been too much arbitrary action, a shared criticism meshing nicely with the illusio of the engineering wing argued the state had become too passive: possible sites remain unevaluated; trained preservation technicians are in short supply; regulations are poorly enforced. Entailed in each criticism is silent recognition that the field continues to depend on organizations of the nation-state. It is the nation-state that consecrates spaces into chronotopes; the nation-state organizes the transmission of knowledge and certifies professionals; nation-state organs of "order" are the last line of defense for vulnerable chronotopes in the face of the money-grubbing unwashed (euphemized under the sign of progress as those whose "cultural level has not caught up with their economic level").

This last assumption informs the second conference question: What legal changes are needed? Techno-orthodoxy, dedicated as it is to the material of the signifier, to buildings and their constituents, sees Taiwanese property rights and culture of opportunity as a basic danger. A basic component of doxa underlying historic preservation is the presumption that only the center can constrain commodification before it eats up the past; this doxic presumption promotes more laws and is integral to the illusio shared across field space.

The final question, a concession to the academic-critical and social movement zones, concerns the relationship between historic preservation, local identity, local culture, and local autonomy. It is along this local axis that the struggle over chronotopes and over the very nature of the field directly confronts nation-state doxa lodged in both the state region and the new techno-orthodox regions of field space. A concise introduction to that struggle is Hsia Chu-joe's talk to the May meeting and the responses it engendered. The heart of the talk was a challenge to part of the unspoken limit condition that constitutes the field. Entitled by possession of both technical capital and the capital that critical knowledge embodies in the extraordinary moment of crisis, he could say what techno-orthodoxy could not, and what others lacking the proper types and amounts of capital can say but cannot make heard: "Preservation is not an innocent or technical problem."[65]

The talk politely called attention to the "apolitical" means by which the techno-orthodox and nation-state sanitize preservation. The outline of a critique develops by focusing on the central work of the field, the rex-work that had been kept off the official agenda. Hsia acknowledged that the nomination process remains a key unsolved problem—decision power belongs entirely to the state, which need only consult with "experts"—and that present political and social considerations made preservation work a "nightmare."[66] Participants were told restructuring the field ought to be a key topic for preservation discourse, which in turn implies the dreaded questions, For whom? For what? A partial answer at odds with both techno-orthodox and nation-state interests suggested that historic preservation is in fact part of the transformation of today's world in which people could inventively and consciously grasp their own history. In this mode, the doxic assumption that the people are the problem must be inverted: success in preservation would be enabled (and in part measured) by the ability to make memory with (rather than overpower) people at the local level.[67]

Such a basic inversion of the regulative principles (governing how the stakes of the field are obtained and the relative weights of different forms of capital) collided with the illusio of the nation-state and techno-orthodox regions of the field. It is precisely here, and not in a Habermasian failure of the communicative process, that the field-wide conversation broke down. One of the most famous figures in the field, an architect-professor who had been trained by a pioneer in the field, countered that these things could be talked about endlessly and still there would be no conclusion. Better that the time when everyone is in the same room be spent on the real-world work that is piling up.

Eventually the surface world of techno-orthodoxy filled dialogic space: local officials seized the moment to explain why the latest abysmal failure in project x was not really the speaker's fault. In turn, nation-state orthodoxy dismissed their talk as petty provincial concern with what is, after all, only one province of the great Chinese nation-state. Instead they tried (without success) to center discussion on threats posed to Chinese historic preservation by the mainland Sanxia dam project. Economic development, they declared, threatens China's treasures, and now that the space of China is no longer absented, preservation authorities from Taiwan have a national duty to perform. For the first time, not only the discourse of historic preservation would be mis-placed, even the technicians (like the Palace Museum) would become heterotopic, Odysseus returning to Ithaca and finding himself in upstate New York.

The difficulty of reception was anticipated. It was not that the speech was incomprehensible; rather, imposing a different mode of perceiving the chronotopes as signifiers of the social was received by the techno-orthodox as inappropriate—like an insufficiently euphemized reference to a bodily function, or a malapropism—a violation of the standards of good form to mention the political underside, the censorship imposed by the structure of the field. The moment in which the virtual and actual fields coincided was brief. The struggle to make chronotopes, however, is ongoing, and we now turn to how the field is realized in struggle, a struggle that is remaking the past and futures.

*Struggle over Sites as the Site of Struggle*

Once consecrated as objects to behold and institutionalized into the interrogations of socialization, memory technology works with little effort and continues to institute the Chinese nation-state as a natural fact into habitus as nationality. Memory technology can be redirected only by changing the object set, the institutional world in which it is interrogated, or remaking the historic preservation field itself. Struggle on all three fronts has focused on the rex-work, separating spaces from places through the nomination of new sites. With a common investment in authenticity, both the critical academic and techno-orthodox segments are interested in broadening the field and can do so by invoking secondary criteria included in the 1982 codification. By May 1992 another 21 chronotopes had been added to the original 250, slightly diluting the substantiation of nation-state claims.

If duration and primacy alone mattered, the time-space of the Han on Taiwan would seem quite shallow and small. That a leading preservationist can say "This island does not have its own cultural roots" (see page 114) and find virtually no opposition is the result of a classification struggle, denouement to a three-hundred-year Chinese colonial expedition.

The former dirt-barbarians who had become *shan-pao* with the dictatorship could now also be properly described (separated) as the nine tribes. Against their categorical subordination, aboriginal intellectuals have offered a new sign— *Yüan-chu-min,* or primordial inhabitant.[68] Aboriginal peoples had been inserted into the historical series "migrant," just as Taiwanese Han were inserted into the series "Chinese," as a means of hierarchical incorporation into the nation. Official history went so far as to suggest the "earlier migrants," like the geological fact of the island itself, originated on the mainland. The clear separation is inverted to index a prior unity.

Hierarchical inclusion and suppression of spatiotemporal difference also proceeds through nation-state memory technology; again we see the tag team of elementary school text interrogation and historic preservation. The single well-known site memorializing the aboriginal beyond the First Rank "frontier station" of subjugation is the Wu-feng Temple in Chia-i County. The racist fabrication, known as fact by virtually everyone who has attended school in Taiwan, describes the sacrifice of a Chinese that led the aboriginal *fan* toward civilization. Despairing of the barbarians' head-hunting, their dear friend Wu-feng (*in partibus infidelium*) devised to teach them a lesson. Concealing his identity, Wu-feng allowed himself to be captured and killed. The *fan* then pulled back his cloak. Seeing they had wasted their benefactor, they abandoned head-hunting in shame. They had taken a first step on the road to civilization, absorption into the Chinese nation—all officialized and substantiated by the body of the temple. As far as the historic preservation system in the mid-1980s was concerned, aboriginal history was contact with the Chinese as conquerors (Chin Kuan-fu Residence) and saviors (Wu-feng Temple).

Systematic exclusion of chronotopes that did not involve China complemented the inclusions. Most notable was the Shih-san-hang site near the mouth of the Tamsui. For some time archaeologists had been aware of an extensive site bearing traces of iron making and global trade. Shih-san-hang suggested that Taiwan had had contact with peoples to the west, had developed significant technologies, and had supported a sizable population—all independent of China. By law, the site should have been protected. Archaeologists and activists properly reported the situation; Premier Hao inspected the site. In the end, law was openly disregarded and the greater part of the site was obliterated—"forgotten" in the active voice.

Field shift, however, enabled a change in aboriginal chronotopes, even as most of Shih-san-hang was being obliterated. Archaeological knowledge producers staked a claim on expanded field space, and by necessity they fed on aboriginals. Again under the banner of authenticity, aboriginal *i-chih* (ruined sites) began to enter the system. All four of the First Rank sites invested after the first round of selection were *i-chih*.

The career of Taiwanese artist Milo Chang is an indicator of the changing fortunes of an aboriginal past. When he began to collect *Yüan-chu-min* "artifacts" he was regarded as an eccentric with a taste for junk. By the time of the transformation he had sold his Pei-t'ou folk arts museum to the trendsetting Ploughman group that now runs the popular museum in conjunction with a teahouse and an extremely popular Mongolian barbecue. The past of the people without a past has entered the market for cultural consumption.

The most important sign of change is Old Hao-cha Village in the mountains above P'ing-tung. The village had gradually emptied out during the Japanese colonial period as residents sought wage labor in the plains below. In what has become a recurring pattern, graduate students involved in the academic-critical center's planning research for the P'ing-tung area made serendipitous contact with *Yüan-chu-min*. People from the critical center provided authoritative language to the *Yüan-chu-min*, wishing to preserve and revive the village. A breakthrough came in 1991 when the state field segment under pressure designated Old Hao-cha as *ku-chi* of the Second Rank and implicitly recognized a measure of *Yüan-chu-min* autonomy.[69] Two other aspects of this case marked an important contribution of the aboriginal peoples to the struggle over sites: Old Hao-cha is a village, not a building or an empty site, and is moving from a dead to a living village. Before turning to the implications of these two facts, let us first consider the return of another past that had been excluded.

JAPANESE SITES: TRACES OF A PAST'S INTERIOR

As noted earlier, the accusation against the Taiwanese that they had internalized the "spirit of the Japanese" refracted a truth that terrified

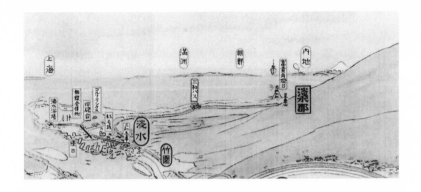

the KMT: the supposedly natural and unalterable character of nationality is in fact open to reconstruction. Consider the map from a time in which Taiwan was Japan (above).[70] Looking down, the relations among places making up Taipei are themselves located in national space by the heterotopy of horizons. Where the curve of the earth offers up only water, the cartographer misplaces land from beyond the island. This segment of the map moves from Shanghai to Manchuria and Korea, and suddenly, quite out of place at the center of horizoning, Mount Fuji appears alongside the label *nei-ti* (the interior). Vidal de La Blache's original assumption-question, which I reformulated as how does an island not become a nation, gets one answer: it becomes one of a series of islands in a nation-archipelago. Political power, finance, career paths, education, language, public health, for some even the sense of nationality—in all these respects the map properly locates the center, the interior of Taiwan's nation-state life on yet another island, Honshu.

As the suppression of Japanese language and even memory of the Japanese past diminishes, all but a handful of preservationists now call for including Japanese-era chronotopes in the system. Techno-orthodoxy phrases the matter as antiquity: "About eighty percent of the *old* buildings in Taipei were erected during the Japanese occupation. It is not right that these buildings are not included in the 1982 Cultural Assets Preservation Law."[71] The key characteristic here is a natural property called "old," a relational term. It says something about the state of the field that in two years these buildings had become "old." More important than the passage of a few hundred days is the passing of the party-military dictatorship that techno-orthodoxy, euphemizing politics into nature, is loath to mention.

Lacking legal protection, Japanese buildings became a public issue as they were targeted for demolition. Struggles led by the most energetic and effective movement-foundation and techno-orthodox scholars were unevenly successful, but extensive newspaper coverage and community organizing declared for the first time a value in traces of the Japanese past. A bank, a Tai-ta Medical School building, the Shih-fan University Library, and the Tainan Courthouse—with the exception of a railway building in the south, all these Japanese sites shared one distinctive characteristic: all were exemplars of the Euro-centered genre of stately architecture, stately in the sense of connection to the state and in the sense of ministerial majesty seemingly internal to the mutated Classic forms.

The buildings were attacked both for metonymic and mimetic reference to the Japanese nation-state and as impediments to progress. In their defense came a blending of Taiwanese nostalgia and aesthetic evocation of European majesty working the vector along which European stateliness acts as antidote to "a lack of culture." Even as one mythology rolled back through the inclusion of monumental colonial architecture, the exclusion of the nonstately is being fought on another front, community preservation. It is to this preservation that we now turn.

### LOCALITY AND OTHER AXES OF CLASSIFICATION

Halbwachs noted that "just as people are members of many different groups at the same time, so the memory of the same fact can be placed within many frameworks, which result from distinct collective memories."[72] Shifting the memory framework could lead to many collectivities: ethnicity, gender, class, descent, and taste. The list goes on, but in Taiwan *locality* and *community* increasingly appear alongside exemplary buildings as the mode of memory materialization. Localities, districts, ties between towns, working-class space, vernacular architecture: all these disparate spaces are united first by what they are not. They are not stately—Japanese, European, American, or Chinese—either in architectural form or in the species of power that caused them to be. They are spatial forms more amenable to recalling other kinds of time and social relations and as such are sites of struggle to denationalize space-time.

These new preservation categories originated in codification designed to rationalize and protect statist memory technology. Article 36 of the Cultural Assets Preservation Law incorporates notions from the homelands of historic preservation allowing whole areas to be instituted as historic districts.[73] Once designated, change within the boundaries would be subject to some state control. This imported convention mitigated against Chinese nation-state preservation because the perceived locality of the preservation object increases as it expands beyond a single edifice. The structure of a building may be more easily described as relations among its constituent materials, but the structure of a district, or a whole town like Old Hao-cha, includes its interrelations between buildings and spaces, agents and other agents, within the boundaries. Referents become internal to the locality—a market, a temple, the street of the coffin makers—rather than the abstractions of a different order obtaining between a gun emplacement and the national military in Beijing that caused it to be.

Unlike residents of newer districts in the largest cities, residents of older and architecturally homogeneous districts are fairly class homogeneous. In these districts where the age and style of buildings attract the preserving eye, position in topological space is highly correlated with position in social space, the analytic relational grid in which positions are grouped according to the quantity and forms of power. To the extent that geographic contiguity increases the classificatory homogeneity of agents, sense of place memory indexed by features of topologic space can coincide with habitus as "immanent law, *lex insita,* inscribed in bodies by identical histories, which is the precondition not only for the coordination of practices but also for practices of coordination."[74]

Critical preservation (and community planning) tries to build on the affinities of habitus to organize "practices of co-ordination" defending the spatial integrity of locales associated in social memories with an imagined state and capital and to dilute Taiwan. Community preservation, in its most fundamental sense of objectifying classification through totems, is no different from nation-state historic preservation, yet it is unique in several dimensions of practice.

Like nation-state memory, local time-space is not dependent on literal continuity in time or contiguity in space. Sense of place can be evoked by attaching a group narrative to space where an authoritative voice insists the group took place. In the case perhaps most closely resembling invocation of the absent China, former residents and descendants of a village destroyed by flood gather yearly on an empty space that is said to have once been the village site. Other memories of origins span space through ties among migrants and narratives of connection, such as the relationship between the Taipei suburb of San-chung and the origin point for many residents, Yuanlin. A historical claim to descent from a founding Matsu temple unites the collective identities of Pei-kang and Lu-kang with (now only somewhat) absent space of the mainland town of Meixian without any reference to a China or a Taiwan.

The intentions of critical preservation and the metric it uses to indicate success are at odds with much of the rest of the field's prenotion of itself. First is the neodoxa of empowerment in the present. Second is the restoration of other levels of memory, a defense of the abused dead. Third is the hope that "as long as it is possible to manipulate a category so as to emphasize the past while negating the present it is still possible to use the category in creating a future."[75] The fate of that intention depends on the struggle in which the changing sense of the game and capital distributions within the game are decisive. Here the messy reality indexed by "community" has to be put in terms of a struggle to impose a theory effect. Depending on the state of the field, practice has resulted in communities defined through or against historic preservation.

*The Community Unites—Against Preservation*  One of the key field transformations noted earlier is a shockwave of the Economic Miracle, the emergence of economic capital as a major force in preservation. In the absence of a vigorous market for labor and strong demand for land as a commodity, patrilineal self-preservation along the merchant streets of Ti-hua Chieh in Taipei and Min-ch'üan Road in San-hsia was synonymous with preserving the physical and social integrity of the districts. Rising land prices in the 1980s led to what Hsia identified as a central problem of preservation: antagonism between preservation and development focusing on the traditional towns.

Initial local support for preservation faded as the land price boom swept metropolitan areas. Initial successes (blocking road widening in Taipei, declaring the Min-chüan Road district in San-hsia to be a Second Rank chronotope) led into a struggle transformed by economic capital, a struggle that united the communities, but not in the way that the movement and academic-critical preservation had planned. By late 1993, the more visible movement spokespersons and academics were being vilified in public meetings and "big character posters." Delegation has become a central issue. On whose behalf do the movement leaders speak? For propertied residents, preservation had come to mean being locked into dark, uncomfortable homes and unprofitable business while others became rich. Media rhetoric of preservation described preservationists, state and public, as disinterested and cultured while residents were deemed interested, selfish, and uncultured.

*Lukang and Old Hao-Cha: Authentic Agents, Authentic Material*  Outside the centers of land price explosion, economic capital wreaked less havoc. Lukang, its harbor long blocked by silt, is far from its days as a gateway between China and Taiwan. Virtually ignored in precodified historic preservation, the Lukang movement sought to restore an older residential area. With local and county government help, residents were offered financial assistance for much-needed repair, with the stipulation that restoration faithfully reproduce "authentic" Lukang. The project was completed, and the streets were entered into Lukang's modest cultural tourism industry.

Problems emerged and, as in the two cases just mentioned, took the form of conflict between residents and preservationists. At a meeting presided over by the progressive magistrate of Chang-hua County, the conflict was embodied in the problem of roofs. To preserve authentic Lukang, the technical specialists insisted on reproducing the original roof slope. Unfortunately, the original was a mistake; the authentic slope ensured that water would leak into the structure during heavy rains. The magistrate, her staff, and preservationists decided that adjustments had to be made to meet the needs of people who lived within these buildings. Techno-orthodox authenticity could not be allowed to turn a local preservation movement into a movement of locals against being "preserved," bottled up in social formaldehyde.

Many of these problems could have erupted as people moved back to Old Hao-cha. With a focus on the social rather than microauthenticity, local activists and the group's delegated memory recorders working closely with university-based preservationists have avoided many of the conflicts that might arise in simultaneous preservation and revivication.

With the market for preservation (including the value of state and techno-orthodox positions) threatened by economic capital, this "participatory design" appeals to some workers invested in the field, as what was written in respect to linguistic markets applies equally here: "One cannot save the *value* of a competence unless one saves the market, in other words, the whole set of political and social conditions of production of the producers/consumers."[76] One way to "save the market" is illustrated next in what has become through the representational space of a movie the world's most (mis)recognized Taiwan space, not Taipei's space of the Miracle, but the image of old Chiu-fen.

*Commodity Form and Preservation as Praxis: A Mining Town*  Making chronotopes had been a struggle to invest the Chinese nation-state in totemic spaces. Struggles in the transformed field are increasingly defining memory against another fetish, the commodity. A most interesting project combines social capital of the movement and residents with academic-critical preservation at Chiu-fen in the mountains above Keelung. There the conversion of space into a speculative or leisure commodity is the target of struggle, not the basis of a struggle against preservation.

Chiu-fen was a mining town and, like mining, is in economic decline. Stunning views of the Pacific, notoriety as a site for the memory film "City of Sadness," and the architecturally signed sense of pre-Miracle Taiwan make it a choice weekend house site for Taipei and Keelung's nostalgia-consuming professionals. As land and buildings were swept up by speculators, the alliance of residents and academic-critical forces supported by CCPD progressives launched a counter-attack through the authoritative languages of historic preservation and comprehensive planning, followed by an on-site training program and international discussion.

The Chiu-fen campaign is the first historic preservation to frame itself as heresy. In the words of the design team, it is defined against the "object-obsessed outlook of the profession" and "nostalgic simulation."[77] The team presented preservation as "one part of social practice as a whole" aimed at constructing "local subjectivities" and developing local autonomy against the commodity form and implicitly against the time-space claims of both orthodox Chinese and heterodox Taiwanese nationalisms. Heretical talk about practice was part of heretical practice. For the first time, the planning team was required to live in the locale to be preserved, get to know the people, and analyze the social questions confronting the area. The plan was developed through a participatory design strategy that mobilized local memory in the context of a larger plan to deal with Chiu-fen's class and political-economic incorporation into a larger system. The key element of the resulting plan is social. A local preservation organization is to supervise development and institutionalize autonomy. The original layout of cultural space is to be preserved, while specific areas are marked to service (and bring in money from) the cultural tourism industry. The longer-term aim of the plan is to enable local people to "rediscover the use value of the settlement space. This value will later supersede the value of commodity exchange." This claim is ambitious, but what is worth noting from the standpoint of a theory of practice and nationality is that questions do not revolve around how this chronotope substantiates the Taiwanese Nation and denaturalizes the Chinese Nation, or vice versa. Rather, the object of practice is historically specific domination, autonomy, and the commodity form, raised and made integral to the struggle over historic preservation.

The significance of the Chiu-fen case to the field is proportional to the reflexivity of its practice. Relatively aware of the field in which it works, the team sought to use it to change the field. A training conference at Chiu-fen (supported by key people at the CCPD) brought dozens of students from several architecture and social science programs into the project. Like the design team, students lodged in the town and went out with local residents to get a grasp of social memory lodged in places and how this sense of what Chiu-fen has been help constitute what it is now.

The most antidoxic of conference talks questioned whether there was any defensible reason to teach an old horse new tricks. Under what circumstances could historic preservation, could a building, be more than a spatial prop to the reproduction of existing social relations? For the memory master Pierre Nora, asking this question places one on the edge of the field: "If we penetrate the object, we liberate it but we destroy it; and if we acknowledge its full weight, we respect it, but we restore it to a state in which it is still mystified."[78] This talk dragged the tacit into the open and revealed the speaker's deficit of illusio, of investment in the field as constituted that would in a more normal field be the condition of being heard; for some the deficit, the violence to the object, made the question literally unthinkable. For others, it made the basic presuppositions of the field debatable and therefore subject to critical analysis, pointing toward leaving the field or transforming the representations of space and the spaces of representation in its social practices.

We have seen that an essential feature of this field is the way in which it overlaps with academics. The process of conversion and reconversion of capital and profits between academics and historic preservation provides strong incentives for representation of the Chiu-fen case. The project was among twenty-nine winners out of hundreds of entries in the 1993 international "What Is Socially Responsible Design?" competition held in New York by the Pratt Institute. Judged exemplary in its collective, participatory, and social character, the Chiu-fen case has become a vehicle for international discussion of preservation and design's potential contribution to empowerment. No matter how "progressive," fields necessarily require a certain investment to play the game—even the laudable game—and impose a certain amount of structural censorship, so it is understandable that the limited representational space of the new approach was not focused on certain problems: What is community? How does preservation break with social reproduction? What becomes of the capital differences between professionals and the "community"? These issues that deeply concerned those involved in the Chiu-fen struggle are more clearly addressed in the final case study, the Hou-chu-wei neighborhood.

*Memory and Fractals of Domination* Hou-chu-wei, the "bamboo patch out back," began during the Ch'ing as a small peasant community and became a neighborhood by virtue of being swallowed up by the Taipei sprawl of Sanchung. On seizing Taiwan, the KMT sought to break connection with the non-Chinese nation-state past by changing the name to a Taiwanese homonym with an orthodox political flavor. During the following forty years, Hou-chu-wei was engulfed by the unplanned growth of Taipei and its attendant nightmarish disorder of space, pollution, and alienation. The bamboo patch became a dividing line between long-standing residents and recent migrants. The bamboo grove entered the 1990s as a garbage dump.

On one of his first trips into the neighborhood, Yang Pei-ju asked a man how long he had lived there. He replied, "Oh, about two hundred years." The spatial and social remnants of a long-standing community stood out in the present of bamboo patch remembered in the dump. Unlike Chiu-fen, no application was made to officialize Hou-chu-wei as a historic district; nevertheless, we can grasp something of the direction in which the postnational approach to chronotopes is developing at the margin of the field.

Offering their technical capital, the students joined local activists in calling on the whole community to jointly design a park, displace the dominated dump-present with a transfigured memory of the bamboo grove past as an opening to a future. The coordinating practices of planning began with a community cleanup, an exemplary practice that materialized a different version of the world in which residents could take matters into their own hands. Through practice they began to bring into discourse what it meant to live with that dump, to live without autonomy. Institutionalizing joint action, they were theorizing into being a collectivity, the community.

A second move was interrogating time-place memories. A long sheet of paper was divided into times of day and posted in the newly cleared past-future space. Residents drew scenes keyed to daily routine on the sheet labeled "A Day in Hou-chu-wei." The planning group asked older residents to spend an evening in the future park telling stories about the pre-KMT neighborhood. While members of the design team took notes, residents of all ages came to listen to and be questioned about autobiographical time.

A sense of place emerged that noted Hou-chu-wei's relative lack of status in the past; residents parried that memory with irony. The neighborhood had been adjacent to a dung hole. Because essentially the same sounds in Taiwanese mean "university" and "dung hole," locals young and old alike continue to refer to "Hou-chu-wei University" even though the dung heap is a distant memory. In another interrogation, the design team brought a Polaroid camera to the neighborhood. People on the street were asked to photograph something of special beauty in Hou-chu-wei. In one instance an elderly man searched for a remembered delight and then recovered it—the green mountains that are now almost totally occluded by the cement walls of the present Hou-chu-wei.

Another activity linked definition of community and its memory to redefinition of the encompassing society through a new form of the *Chung-yüan p'u-tu,* the annual Festival of the Ghosts. Despised by outsiders from the Christian missionaries to the Japanese colonialists to the KMT, Ghost Month became a vehicle for local resistance to nation-state claims. With a cash infusion from the new reform Taipei County Magistrate, local temple associations, artists, and intellectuals focused the placating ritual on the Tamsui River that separates Taipei and the town encompassing Hou-chu-wei. The river has been left lifeless by pollution and the political silence in which no one could object. The river and its spirits were also connected to the February 28 massacres. Many victims of nation-state death squads were sewn into rice sacks and then dumped into the river to drown. On both counts, the river was the object of political and ritual appeasement confronting the memory foundation of domination in rituals of institution, rather than materializing it in buildings.

In memory practice the team became more sensitive to the constructedness of the new social classification displacing nation-state memory. "Community" tended to conceal the fractal-like reproduction of domination on different scales. Young people and a young woman teacher from the neighborhood started the struggle. Many on the design team were women. The doxa-shattering Taipei County *Chung-yüan p'u-tu* was the creation of Ch'en Wen-ch'ien and a group (mainly women) that came to be called *Ku-niang-miao* (after temples built to contain or appease the dark power of women who had died before producing sons) in a playful and yet deadly serious commentary on gender, memory, and domination. Despite the importance of young people and women, older males from the temple committee, from the neighborhood council, and from the "Two-Hundred-Year Families" were the voices heard. Community may be the source of delegation in contrast to the Chinese nation-state because of the structure of both the preservation and planning fields, but it also tends to reify a singularity that makes invisible class, age, and gender domination. Struggling with these problems, the final park design was conducted in separate groups containing residents of the "Ch'ing Dynasty community" and the newer immigrants—women, older men, middle-aged and young men, and children. Each group produced a plan, and these plans were merged in a meeting of the whole.

In the same mode, the new frame of participatory planning should not obscure the truth that professionals and residents are not equally capitalized. Though they were students speaking in Taiwanese, dressed like the residents, it was still the capital of National Taiwan University, of the particular institute, of certified knowledge that provided an opening into the community. The means of entry also reproduced the boundary.

It was difficult for the more recent migrants to feel comfortable attending activities in the old bamboo site since that was the territory of the "two-hundred-year-old people," and when an older man from the other side of the tracks showed up and began to chat, I felt that he was more disposed than most to cross all sorts of boundaries. He had strong opinions on the political life of the island, but when we asked his opinions about the park design, his demeanor changed and with his entire body he demurred—he couldn't say, he "wasn't well educated." Despite intentions of preservationists and planners, the authority's interrogation tends to key the "sense of limits," a sense of place that includes an appreciation of one's place in social space, a "correspondence between the objective classes and the internalized classes, social structures and mental structures, which is the basis of the most ineradicable adherence to the established order."[79]

Aiming to break just that adherence, the team made what efforts it could to demystify the authoritative language, their sign of delegated power. The four resident design teams were given nontechnical tools to map out their ideas for how to use the former bamboo/future park space. The children's design group used crackers and candy to represent on the model surface what they wanted to put where. The resultant plan, also a winning entry in the international Socially Responsible Design competition, did more than counter nationalist memory with community. For many, the name of the community quietly changed back to its pre–Chinese Nationalist name through the plan. Just as important, it raised the problems and fought to limit the symbolic violence structured into the fields through the unequal distribution of power within the "community" along gender, age, and class lines and between community and its allies with authority. These are the issues that will confront critical historic preservation and planning in the turn from national scale histories.

## "EVEN THE DEAD ARE NOT SAFE"

Each of these cases since chronotope 250 shows state memory technology being revalued, but they are a small part of the institutional practice of chronotope making. The original sites instituted when preservation was an apparatus remain, their materiality reproducing national memory in the interrogations of universal schooling and conventional discourse. Persistence of memory is grounded in precisely this mode of genetic linkage, historic preservation being only one, between the structure of domination in a nation-state form and embodied as habitus.

What had seemed on the surface as another Taiwan Miracle, bounding within an absent space and insertion into the lockstep seriality of absent Chinese time, is in fact typical of nation-state classification. Neither the presence of the world's clearest geographic and political boundaries nor the absence of the Past's space exert anything like the persuasive power of doxa. If we accept that the reification of *nation*, itself a recent and arbitrary invention keyed to the mobilization of modern powers, is no less fantastic anywhere else, the fact that the Republic of China on Taiwan exists without the crutch of national space demonstrates the material power of institutionalized classification to make worlds. As meaning, nationality appears to bound itself in nature, but these islands of social classification are everywhere products of homogenizing practices of coordination (see figure above right).

This article emphasizes the site of struggle over *lieux de mémoire*, historic preservation as a field. The fetishes exist because they are instituted, carved out by power operating in a field and represented by power as having absorbed the referent China into their materiality. Chronotopes were produced here not simply through discourse or through an abstract power of a monolith state, but rather through the field whose imagined imperatives—positions, capital, and how the

黃帝子孫都是同根生

game is supposed to work—invest ways of making objects and the objects themselves. It is not intention or ideological subscription of the historian or architect alone but the juncture of their habitus with conditions of the field that disposes them to produce in a definite mode. Objective demands of the field—demands on buildings and on agents—are themselves the object of strategic action to uphold or transform the rules of the game. Codification of state memory institutions through the Western form called historic preservation encouraged the expansion of field space, increasingly linked the power of different positions within that space with authenticity and technical authority, and thereby diluted the products' national character. Given this mix of reproduction and transformation, we can now ask, What sorts of futures beyond the Chinese nationalism are possible for the space of the Past?

Structural crisis when conjoined with an effective heretical theory can be a means for breaking a specific domination. It can just as easily be a context of great danger. Nationalism, the doctrine of correspondence between the state and the "nation," is a program of domination, nationalism of the dominated not excepted. After nearly a century of experimentation, it is clear that the proposition that national liberation is the first step toward social liberation is untenable. Assertion of a natural basis for the state in a social classification that includes by excluding is not a first step toward undermining other forms of domination. The danger posed by nationalism, not simply Chinese nationalism, as Benjamin wrote of all forms of domination, is that everyone, everything is at risk and *even the dead* will not be safe from the enemy if he wins. And this enemy has not ceased to be victorious."[80]

## Doxic Redux: *Taiwanizing Chronotopes as* *"Rectification of Names"*

If we were to take seriously American commentators and KMT social science up until the late 1980s, the nation-state question was settled by Clough's nationalization of the dead and insertion of the Taiwanese in the "stream" of Chinese history. Convention had it that the Taiwanese "could not escape the ties of language, tradition, and custom that have *made them Chinese* [my emphasis]."[81] Despite imperial academics who misused their authority to immortalize the seeming winners, Taiwanese nationalism is posing a new basis for the state, one not dependent on heterotopy, that fits better with Vidal de La Blache's orthodoxy on the natural basis of the nation.

Taiwanese nationalism has no need to undo the entire time-space representational system of the Chinese. Like the Japanese Colonial Governor's Office becoming the ROC Presidential Palace, Taiwanese nationalism can move right in. It is happening now. A major condition of nationalism's performative efficacy is the mis-recognized power of the positions from which it is spoken. The extremely high value of academic capital and the ease with which it is converted in different fields—the very condition of the nonnationalist academic-critical center's success within the fields of planning and historic preservation— lends force to nationalist retheorizing social classification. The primary institutional form for the exercise is journalism imposturing through scholarly credentials. Short columns in which academic stars reveal opinions as moral lessons to society-pupils (necessarily bereft of the quality of their justification or lack of it in the academic field) offer a quick payoff on scientific credentials in the currencies of honor and money. In the process, nationalist sociologists invest the authority of science, by which they claim delegation to speak, into their invented nationality, the "New Taiwanese" (*Hsin-t'ai-wan-jen*).

The symbolic basis for a fairly simple appropriation of Chinese historic preservation lies in the unity of orthodox and heterodox nationalisms. They share the same unspoken prenotions: political order is a correspondence between a people in a historically bounded space and a state. If the imagined historical bounding can be relocated, the naturalizing forms of nationality—even the former chronotopes of another nation—can switch masters and be incorporated into institutions substantiating yet another "inescapable" seriality, this one called Taiwanese instead of Chinese.

Some liabilities in the Chinese system become assets in the prospective Taiwanese system. Tension between antiquity implied by historic preservation and the newness of Han presence that had been "resolved" through heterotopy and material insertion in Chinese hierarchy is displaced in one stroke; Yen's comments cited on pages 113–14 regarding Taiwan's poverty of culture assume an entirely new meaning. The Chinese claim of autochthony is reversed, and the national culture becomes a mix of the memorialized Dutch, Chinese, and Japanese (but note, not *Yüan-chu-min*). China becomes just one of the tutors.

Taiwan's "poverty of history" is likewise recast. In a newspaper section entitled "I Love Taiwan," the techno-orthodox field issues of re-educating an unappreciative nation, financial support, and state policy are reconstructed by an introduction making a new nation steward of its relics: "Historic sites are a common asset for humankind and are spiritual signs of the Nation as 'heir of the sages and teacher of posterity.' Taiwan's history is very short and precisely because of this, the preservation and protection of historic sites is even more important." [82]

Even the supposed aesthetic deficits of the Taiwanese are levers for appropriating the sites of ROC historic preservation. If the objects in Taiwan are less majestic, we are told that "culture is a product dependent upon history and geography," so it is not right to compare the Great Wall with the European fort at Tamsui. Comparison is an injury to pride and fair play. Sufficiently indignant, our preservationist author finds part of the fault for such egregious talk and the money disease in a national educational system that never introduced an appreciation of Taiwan. [83] All the more reason to preserve sites officialized by the ROC.

What Taiwanese nationalism requires is a rectification of names (*cheng-ming*). Consecrated sites where the military marked out frontiers were overrepresented among the Chinese First Rank chronotopes, but this presents no problem of principle to Taiwanese nationalism. The Hsi-t'ai gun emplacement and the Er-k'un-shen emplacement are silent about whom it is that they repel. They simply point outward, with Vidal de La Blache, toward the sea that defines the experienced borders of the island. And if, as Yen says, the North Gate recalls both the imperial edict to build it and the Japanese victory over it, it can be used to go beyond the Ch'ing, beyond the KMT to the Taiwanese who alone suffered occupation as a result of the failure. The dead defended Taiwan; the tragedy befell Taiwan; the debt is owed to the Taiwanese dead. In this new past as in the old past, national time aggressively *takes place*.

Nationalism rummages about in graveyards and feeds on the dead. Chinese nationalism on Taiwan always faced an embarrassing supply problem—not enough dead of historic stature to prop up the ranks of monuments. The Taiwanese dead, however, are like a newly discovered oil field, a national(ist) resource having sufficiently decomposed underground. At the hands of aboriginals, Dutch, Spaniards, Manchu, and Japanese, the violently dispatched stretch out into historical memory, defenseless against the coming call to arms, the anachronistic proclamation that they died "for Taiwan."

More powerful, however, are the dead just barely over the horizon, the tens of thousands murdered by the KMT. Now KMT censorship of their mention is broken and they are back; how shall they be protected? In the struggle to create a chronotope memorializing the February 28 massacres, most involved are struggling to remember the dead, their struggle, and the forces of domination; however, for some the same nationalist logic is at work (for a Taiwanese nation) that lives in the Martyr's Shrine (for a Chinese nation). In another act of violence against the dead, the martyrs are made to say they died for a nation. The victims of the KMT are appropriated to impose a new theory effect, the revelation that all along what has been suppressed and even murdered has been the Taiwanese nation. Chinese heterotopy gives way to Taiwanese heteropathy, attempting to cure one disease by inducing another.

*Subjunctive Constructions: Archipelagoes of Meaning*

Discussing possible futures for the technology of national past making, I have here suggested that, nationalism being nationalism, Taiwanese nationalism can work quite well with the chronotopes of the Chinese field. After all, Taiwanese nationalism is not directed against the domination of women (the arch for Ch'iu Liang-kung's Mother can stay) nor against class domination (the general's grave can remain a chronotope) or ethnic oppression (the Wu-feng Temple remains sacred).

Although it has emerged from silence, the new nationalism faces constraints ranging from the threat of Chinese military intervention to the rise of nonnational memories. With strong forces mitigating against the plausibility and practicality of yet another nation-state, the possibility exists for what Tilly calls "creative political redefinition"—the separation of cultural distinctness from the principle of statehood.[84]

The conditions of historic preservation as a social field in Hobsbawm's institutional landscape make possible a gradual creative timespace redefinition as well. Beyond the trend toward new distinctly local units, class memories, and gender memory, even the old forms are open to nonnational subversion. Like the last Shinto shrine that was "preserved" to denounce Japan, consider what might be done to the Temple of the Five Concubines. Let's re-cognize the wall from Fort Zeelandia. If the tactile experience of contemplation or distraction were able to break the doxic straitjacket, Dutch stones could be made to do some interesting work. And so, a story:

One afternoon in Chia-i a visitor asked us to imagine the offices of the Dutch East India Company one day in the early seventeenth century.[85] On an official's desk there sat reports on two island colonies and several problems of the day. One of the most pressing problems was what to do with dissenters, heretics, and Jews in a time of increasing persecution. Sending Jews off to one of the island colonies was a favored option. In the end, with a push from a French sea captain and twenty-three Jewish refugees, New Amsterdam was chosen over Fort Provintia, Manhattan over Taiwan.

Immersed in this writing I head south from my office at the New School, down Broadway to New York's earliest space in continuous use, the seventeenth-century cemetery of the Congregation Shearith Israel. Those stones in the Jewish graveyard, traces of what had happened and not happened in two Dutch colonies, they could just as well be in the tangle of flowers and vines back of Tamsui's foreign buildings. Facing the Goddess of Mercy Mountain or Chatham Square, they offer no substance to those who would find in nature the fatality of national division and national space. The tactile reality of the two sets of "Dutch" stones on opposite sides of the earth forms an antidoxic chronotope: preservation in the subjunctive.

Upholding Hobsbawm's injunction to "get it right," to get beyond power's mystifications of "what happened," our fields must allow for the contingency of the pasts, an antidote to the fatalist conceit that what has happened (and by definition "can no longer happen") was always the "irresistible future of the acts which made them happen."[86] Past is present in making social categories, "islands of meaning," because agents struggle to make sense of the world and overcome its fatality. If we have a preference for one of those futures, for modes of classification and action that at the least decrease the naturalization of domination, workers in the field would do well to transpose undoing the dualities of objective and subjective, of space and time, into a solidarity with those who are, in Boyarin's image, contemporary but distant in space and those who are distant in time. It seems possible in the conjuncture of fields and habitus to make a different time and link islands of classification into new configurations—archipelagoes of meaning.

NOTES

The notion of social categories as "islands of meaning" is drawn from Eviatar Zerubavel's elegant book on everyday distinction making, *The Fine Line* (New York: Free Press, 1991). Thanks for this article go to Tani E. Barlow, Donald Lowe, Carol M. Johnson, Kristin Dunn, Kaleigh Dunn, and two anonymous reviewers. The work itself was possible through the help of many friends, too many to list here. You know who you are and I thank you.

1  Jean-Yves Guiomar, "Le *Tableau de la géographie de la France* de Vidal de La Blache," in *Les lieux de mémoire, La nation 2. Pt. 1*, ed. Pierre Nora (Paris: Gallimard, 1986), 565. Thanks to Eric Hobsbawm, whose work directed me to Vidal de La Blache and the *Les lieux de Mémoire* project (Hobsbawm, *Nations and Nationalism* [Cambridge: Canto, 1991], 90–91).

2  Calculated from *Taiwan ti-ch'u shih-hui pien-ch'ien tiao-ch'a*, 1991, machine-readable data file; results are almost exactly the same as reported in Ch'iu Hai-yüan, ed., *Taiwan ti-ch'u shih-hui pien-ch'ien tiao-ch'a, ti erh ch'i, ti yi-er-ts'e tiao-ch'a chih-hsing pao-kao* (Taipei: Institute of Ethnology, 1991), 133.

3  Jonathan Boyarin suggests that "our reified notions of objective space and time are particularly linked to the modern identification of a nation with a sharply-bounded continuously occupied space controlled by a single sovereign state, comprising a set of autonomous yet essentially identical individuals" ("Space, Time, and the Politics of Memory," Working Paper Series no. 122 [New York: Center for Studies of Social Change, New School for Social Research, 1991], 1).

4  Halbwachs, *On Collective Memory*, ed. and trans. Lewis A. Coser (Chicago: University of Chicago Press, 1992), 38. Halbwachs, though way off the mark in treating social memory as an ahistorical object and euphemizing power into "society," offers powerful arguments for the social basis of memory.

5  Hobsbawm, *Nations and Nationalism*, 86.

6  The fact that the Kuomintang (KMT) does not falsify nationality as much as it hides the truth that there is no true nationality, this I have accepted only with great difficulty. As my own work developed through a confron-

tation with Chinese mythology, each unraveling of KMT symbolic violence seemed to demand the recognition of a corporate victim, a genuine *Taiwanese* nation. Only with difficulty have I come to see the common doxic ground conceded by both Chinese and Taiwanese nationalisms, and the menace this mobilizational quick fix poses (and has historically posed around the world) to women, men, workers, farmers, children, "minorities," and the 99 percent of the world that by necessity becomes foreign.

7  Pierre Bourdieu, "Introduction to 'The Social Institution of Symbolic Power,'" in *Language and Symbolic Power*, ed. John B. Thompson (Cambridge: Harvard University Press, 1991), 105.

8  A sample from the lists of attributes supposed to scientifically define the nation: "geographical contiguity, historical and cultural tradition, and economic interest"; "men in a definite territory, with common feelings developed in common history"; "mental community"; "national mind"; "distinct personality"; "national character"; "people sharing a common language, a common history, a sense of kinship"; "co-present and contemporary persons in contiguous space"; and perhaps most famous, Stalin's five characteristics—"A nation is a historically evolved, stable community of language, territory, economic life and psychological makeup manifested in a community of culture." Examples are taken from Karl Deutsch, *Nationalism and Social Communication* (Cambridge: MIT Press, 1966), and Hobsbawm, *Nations and Nationalism*.

9  Charles Tilly, "Past, Present and Future Nationalisms," *New School Commentator* 4 (1992): 3.

10  Hobsbawm, *Nations and Nationalism*, 78.

11  Stephen Toulmin, *Cosmopolis* (Chicago: University of Chicago Press, 1990), 7.

12  Hobsbawm, *Nations and Nationalism*, 8.

13  Tilly, "Past, Present, and Future Nationalisms," 1.

14  Hobsbawm, *Nations and Nationalism*, 12–13.

15  Rogers Brubaker, *Citizenship and Nationhood in Germany and France* (Cambridge: Harvard University Press, 1992).

16  *Habitus* is the set of dispositions—inculcated, durable, generative, and transposable—that incorporate class (age, gender, nation, relation to production and consumption . . .) circumstances into the body and adjust cognition and practice to a prereflexive anticipation of what is possible for the class-constituted agent in specific domains. Habitus does not generate practice (i.e., mechanically reproduce the circumstances of its acquisition). It is not the execution of a rule, although it tends to create a sense of limits from the correspondence of disposition and apprehension of arenas of action; instead it provides a rough means of categorization/evaluation to strategic *practice* in fields often changing and ambiguous. For a critique of the reductionist, intentionalist, and utilitarian misreadings of habitus and the economy of practices, see Loïc Wacquant, "The Structure and Logic of

Bourdieu's Sociology," in *An Invitation to Reflexive Sociology*, Pierre Bourdieu and Loïc Wacquant (Chicago: University of Chicago Press, 1992), 24–25.

17 Phillip Corrigan and Derek Sayer, *The Great Arch* (London: Basil Blackwell, 1985), 6; Bourdieu, "Description and Prescription," in *Language and Symbolic Power*, ed. Thompson.

18 Quoted in Richard Wilson, *Learning to Be Chinese: The Political Socialization of Children in Taiwan* (Cambridge: MIT Press, 1970), 276.

19 Corrigan and Sayer, *Great Arch*, 4.

20 *Doxa* here goes beyond Husserl's modernized opposition to emphasize the social underpinnings and consequences of the lifeworld's facticity: homogeneity of institutionalized life in the first respect and domination in the latter (see Edmund Husserl, *The Crisis of European Sciences and Transcendental Phenomenology* [Evanston, Ill.: Northwestern University Press, 1970], 65).

21 Boyarin, "Space, Time, and the Politics of Memory," 10.

22 Ya-ning Yen, "Perception Problems," *Free China Review* (November 1990): 53.

23 Virtually the same words are found in the following: Tina Lin, "Background: Taiwan Province," *Free China Review* (August 1988); *Republic of China 1987: A Reference Book* (Taipei: Hilit, 1987); and *China Yearbook 1965–66* (Taipei: China Publishing, 1966). A slight variation appears in *In Remembrance of the Late President Chiang's Benevolence* (introduction to slide show given at the Chiang Kai-shek Memorial Hall in 1992) and in *Taiwan kuang-fu erh-shih nien* (Taipei: Taiwan Provincial Government Information Office, 1965), 1.

24 Chiao-min Hsieh, *Taiwan — Ihla Formosa: A Geography in Perspective* (Washington, D.C.: Butterworths, 1964).

25 Emile Benveniste, *Indo-European Language and Society*, trans. Elizabeth Palmer (1969; rpt., Coral Gables, Fla.: University of Miami Press, 1973), 175.

26 Marshall Johnson, "Classification, Power, and Markets: The Waning of the Ethnic Division of Labor," in *Beyond the Economic Miracle*, ed. Denis Simon and Michael Y. M. Kau (Armonk, N.Y.: M. E. Sharpe, 1992).

27 Ch'en-i, "Message from Ch'en-i, Commander of the Taiwan Garrison Command," *Taiwan hsin-sheng pao*, 16 March 1947, 3.

28 Walter Benjamin, "Theses on the Philosophy of History," in *Illuminations: Essays and Reflections*, ed. Hannah Arendt, trans. Harry Zohn (1964; rpt., New York: Schocken, 1969), 256.

29 Bourdieu, "Rites of Institution," in *Language and Symbolic Power*, ed. Thompson, 121.

30 All quotes in this paragraph are from K'un-liang Ch'iu, *On Preserving Folk Art* (Taipei: Council for Cultural Planning and Development, Executive Yüan, 1989), 4.

31 Ibid., 42.

32 Benveniste, *Indo-European Language and Society*, 312.

33 Li-fa Yüan, *Wen-hua ts'e-ch'an pao-ts'un fa* (Taipei: 1982).

34 A particularly valuable piece of authoritative discourse on the general prob-
    lem is Chi-lu Chen, *T'ai-min ti-ch'u ku-chi hsun-li* [Pilgrimage to historical
    sites in the Taiwan-Fukien area] (Taipei: CCPD, 1986).

35 See Boyarin, *Storm from Paradise* (Minneapolis: University of Minnesota
    Press, 1992); Bakhtin, *The Dialogic Imagination* (Austin: University of Texas
    Press, 1981).

36 Calculated from the Nei-cheng-pu, *Tai-min ti-ch'ü ku-chi i-lan-biao* (Taipei:
    November 1990). The classes without First Rank representatives were old
    wells, schools, beacons, churches, gardens, stele, and *i-chih*—ruined or
    "empty" sites.

37 Yen, "Perception Problems," 51.

38 CCPD, *Historical Sites of the First Rank in Taiwan and Kinmen* (Taipei:
    1987), 56.

39 Ibid., 142.

40 The description is accurate in a sense, the same sense that my daughter's
    track training site was described as affording a "view of four states." What
    can be seen is landscape that is under the control of four institutions called
    states. As the landscape from that vantage point now signifies state, so the
    Tainan Temple of the Sea God, visible from the Kuan-ti miao signifies the
    Dutch (Chuang Fang-jung, Huang Su-chüan, and Wu Shu-ying, eds., *Tai-
    min ti-ch'ü ti-i-chi ku-chi* [Taipei: CCPD, 1987], 90).

41 The Japanese colonial authorities understood the game differently and in
    their militarist phase dispatched police to arrest gods in their statues.

42 *Tai-min ti-ch'ü ti-i-chi ku-chi*, 180.

43 Quotes on the Lung-shan Temple come from CCPD, *Historical Sites of the
    First Rank in Taiwan and Kinmen*, 70–71.

44 Michael Taussig, *The Nervous System* (New York: Routledge, 1992), 145.

45 Ralph Clough, *Island China* (Cambridge: Harvard University Press, 1978),
    124.

46 Free China Review, "Touching the Past" (November 1990): 1.

47 Ibid.

48 Chen, *T'ai-min ti-ch'u ku-chi hsun-li*, 4.

49 Bourdieu, "Rites of Institution," 118.

50 Taussig, *Nervous System*, 139.

51 The quote is from William J. Murtagh's *Keeping Time: The History and
    Theory of Preservation in America* (Pittstown, N.J.: Main Street Press, 1988),
    18. My title "Making Time" plays on the title of his wonderful book.

52 Nei-cheng pu, *Wen-hua ts'e-ch'an pao-ts'un fa shih-hsing-hsi-tse* (Taipei: 1984),
    Article 46.

53 Corrigan and Sayer, *Great Arch*, 195.

54 "Lu-chou Li-tsai pu-yüan tang ku-chi," *Chung-kuo Shih-pao* (19 May 1991).

55  Chen, *T'ai-min ti-ch'u ku-chi hsun-li*, 4.

56  Hsin-sheng Pao editorial quoted in Su Bing, *Taiwan's Four-Hundred-Year History* (Washington, D.C.: Taiwanese Cultural Grassroots Association, 1986), 134.

57  See Chen, "The Japanese Ideal and Ideas of Assimilation in Taiwan, 1895–1945."

58  Nei-cheng-pu, *Ch'ing-ch'u Taiwan Jih-chiü shih-tai piao-hsien Jih-pen ti-kuo-chu-i yu-yüeh-k'an chih i-min t'ung-chih chi-nien i-chi yao-tien* (Taipei: 1974).

59  This and subsequent calculations are drawn from Executive Yüan, *Wen-hua ts'ai-ch'an wei-hu yü pao-ts'un tsuo-t'an-hui ts'an-ju jen-yüan ming-ts'e* (Taipei: CCPD, 1992).

60  See the final report from our team to the Ministry of the Interior, *Ku-chi kuan-li yu wei-hu-pan-fa chih yen-chiu (Ch'i-mo pao-kao)* (Taipei: Yaoshan Foundation, 1992). I am one of the three coinvestigators.

61  Yen, "Perception Problems," 53.

62  Ibid., 51.

63  Illusio denotes the general class of interests, a class in which economic interest is simply one (usually poorly specified) among many. Illusio is more than an overarching name for a shopping list of "utilities" for it recognizes that there is interest only to the extent that something matters. The range of "somethings" is theoretically infinite whereas interest in its current usage is rather impoverished. See Bourdieu and Wacquant, *An Invitation to Reflexive Sociology*, 115–117.

64  *Ku-chi kuan-li yu wei-hu-pan-fa chih yen-chiu (Ch'i-mo pao-kao)*, 98–99.

65  Hsia Chu-joe, "Hsien chie-tuan ku-chi pao-ts'un chih chung-yao k'e-t'i," in *Wen-hua ts'e-ch'an wei-hu yü pao-ts'un tsuo-t'an-hui yi-yen-jen pao-kao* (Taipei: CCPD, 1992), 7.

66  Ibid., 12.

67  Ibid., 18.

68  See Fred Y. L. Chiu, "Some Observations on Social Discourse Regarding Taiwan's Primordial Inhabitants," *Unbound*, 1994.

69  "Hao-ch'a Chiu-she puo-ting erh-chi-ku-chi," *Lien-ho Pao*, 3 April 1991. Work continues as one of the very best young scholars (now in the doctoral program) combines thesis research and collaboration with residents.

70  Thanks to Lai Tse-chang for tracking down this map.

71  Yen, "Perception Problems," 52.

72  Halbwachs, *On Collective Memory*, 52.

73  Li-fa Yüan, *Wen-hua ts'e-ch'an pao-ts'un fa* (Taipei: 1982).

74  Pierre Bourdieu, *The Logic of Practice*, trans. Richard Nice (Stanford, Calif.: Stanford University Press, 1990), 59.

75  Chiu, "Some Observations on Social Discourse," 21.

76  Bourdieu, "The Production and Reproduction of Legitimate Language," in *Language and Symbolic Power*, ed. Thompson, 57.

77 Gallery exhibit, "What Is Socially Responsible Design?" (New York: Pratt Institute, 1993).

78 Pierre Nora, "Between Memory and History: *Les lieux de mémoire*," *Representations* 26 (1989): 159.

79 Bourdieu, *Outline of a Theory of Practice* (1977; rpt., Cambridge: Cambridge University Press, 1979), 164.

80 Benjamin, "Theses on the Philosophy of History," 255.

81 Clough, *Island China*, 124.

82 *Tse-li tsao-pao*, 17 May 1991, 5.

83 Kan-lang Li, "Hang-t'ung-ti kan-ch'u," *Chung-kuo Shih-pao*, 24 September 1990.

84 Tilly, "Past, Present, and Future Nationalisms," 5.

85 The visitor was Dean Leonard Schneiderman from UCLA.

86 Bourdieu, *Outline of a Theory of Practice*, 8–9.

Aesthetics and Chinese Marxism

■ Marxist Aesthetics has been a central concern in China's cultural scene for much of the twentieth century. Obviously, Mao Zedong's foundational emphasis on cultural politics or revolutionary hegemony surfaced spectacularly in the disastrous Cultural Revolution (1966–1976). Equally importantly, there has also persisted a non-Maoist tradition of "aesthetic Marxism" ever since Hu Feng's theory of the "subjective fighting spirit" emerged in the 1940s to contend that subjective experience was one appropriate site of revolution and resistance. Little known outside its own locale, Marxist aesthetics in China has a long track record, with significant implications for international Marxism and cultural criticism.[1] Controversies debated intensely in the 1950s and 1960s among Chinese academic Marxists were quite similar to problems in contemporary European critical theory, specifically: subjectivity in aesthetic experience; praxis/practice in the cultural terrain; the relationship of humanity and Nature; and aesthetics as ideology.

However, Chinese "aesthetic Marxists" like Zhu Guangqian and Li Zehou, whose works are my main concern here, were not familiar with Western Marxist agendas despite the fact that what we customarily call "Western Marxism" (diverse Western European and North American Marxist intellectual enterprises) has also been preoccupied with "culture" and "aesthetics."[2] Moreover, save for a partial knowledge of Maoism, Western Marxists have had little grasp of what Chinese colleagues were doing in a different context. Thus, although Maoism undoubtedly transformed the way Europeans thought about Marxism, it also seems to me valuable to compare Chinese "aesthetic Marxism" and Western Marxism as a means of understanding the historical development of modern Marxist cultural theories. Chinese aesthetic Marxism and Western Marxism have both created a theoretical space for critical interventions by empowering cultural politics.

I will argue here that while European and North American cultural politics have fostered an oppositional vision centered largely on the problems of domination and resistance, manipulation and self-government, consent and coercion in modern capitalist society, aesthetic Marxism in China served a twofold mission of criticizing the intrinsic contradictions within the revolutionary hegemony and offering a constructive vision of culture in a postrevolutionary society. Herein lies the value of Chinese aesthetic Marxism, a value that I think reaches beyond China proper into the world of global cultural critique. As a non-Western Marxism, Chinese aesthetic Marxism has from the start had to question the Eurocentrism inhering in Marxism itself. If this inherent Eurocentrism is challenged or problematized, then, it is my belief that the questions that Chinese aesthetic Marxism poses take on their full significance. I choose to study Chinese aesthetic Marxism because of its originality and despite its historical and structural limitations, and because I believe that it has made, and is still making, a critical difference in real-world struggles.

In what follows, I offer a narrative of the Chinese aesthetic Marxists' debates during the 1950s and 1960s, situating these in the historical conjuncture of global developments and "local" movements. My recontextualization focuses on points linking the aesthetic debates of the 1950s and 1960s and the "Cultural Reflection" of the late 1980s, for the ideological underpinnings of the latter are traceable not just to the "Cultural Revolution," but, as importantly, to overlooked moments in the 1950s and 1960s. My purpose in this essay, however, is not merely historical. I also wish to present here some preliminary notes on rethinking an even earlier rethinking of culture, politics, and ideology in a theoretical manner, commenting on both the historical events and the less tangible historicity of the concepts and categories by which the events are mapped. And of course, my own critical position, informed by the theories I discuss here, is also subject to the rigorous scrutiny of History. Insofar as the dialectic of history (or "practice") and "theory" constitutes the very problematic of Marxism (or the "principal contradiction"), the reinscription of "self-reflexivity" as a proper Marxist problematic is an integral part of our renewed efforts of cultural critique.

Modern Chinese aesthetic discourse is loaded with a mélange of ideological presuppositions. As a historical concept derived from Western

Enlightenment thought, it speaks at once for the political and ideological hegemony of the bourgeoisie and, in a utopian vein, for true humanity in opposition to bourgeois utility. Aesthetics is primarily a concept of modernity, in the sense that it bespeaks the autonomy and separation of spheres and presupposes a self-determining and self-sufficient subjectivity.[3] The internal contradictions became most apparent when intellectuals appropriated aesthetics into China as an essential constituent of modernity. Liang Qichao (1873–1929), an eminent reformist and cultural enlightenment figure, extolled "beauty" or aesthetics as "the most important element of human life" and insisted that "*meishu*" or the art of beauty, or fine arts, "generates science."[4] Cai Yuanpei (1868–1940), founding president of Peking University, even proposed substituting "aesthetic education" for older religious doctrines.[5] Chinese Marxism, too, from Li Dazhao and Chen Duxiu to Qu Qiubai and Mao Zedong, invariably stressed the importance of class struggle in aesthetic and cultural realms.

However, aesthetics in modern China is related to the creation of a new language of modernity and revolution. As Arif Dirlik has observed, "Learning a new language and forgetting the old has been a basic problem in Chinese politics, as is evident in the radical shifts in the language of socialist revolution." In a fundamental sense, Dirlik continued, "it is a problem of what Antonio Gramsci described as 'hegemony.' The struggle to create a new language of revolution is but a struggle to assert the hegemony of revolution over its historical inheritance."[6] Mao had transformed the aesthetic into a discourse of revolutionary hegemony, but in doing so, he politicized and instrumentalized the aesthetic, stripping away its function as an affective, subjective domain of culture within which hegemony operates by diffusing its values and gaining consensus from the ruled. Aesthetics itself then becomes alienated under Mao's collapsing of political apparatuses and ideological means, which has resulted in the wholesale aestheticization of politics as well as the politicization of aesthetics.

The transformation or "alienation" of the aesthetic in Mao's revolutionary hegemony is symptomatic of a fundamental contradiction in Mao's project of alternative modernity in which "culture" and "cultural revolution" figured most prominently. To put it very crudely, cultural revolution was first conceived by Mao as a counterhegemonic, antideterminist strategy of constructing an alternative modernity, against the Eurocentric teleology of modernity and economic determinism inherent in classical Marxism. But in the course of Chinese revolution, the antideterministic strategy gradually lapsed into a rigidly deterministic "objective law" of incessant superstructural and cultural revolution. Such a structural transformation of "cultural revolution" had severe consequences, especially in a postrevolutionary society in which the antinomy of revolution and reconstruction as the central problematic of China's alternative modernity was exacerbated, rather than resolved, by Mao's "continued revolution" in the cultural terrain.[7]

Thus, in the most general compass one can say that the Chinese debate over aesthetics occurred within the context of the complex process of establishing revolutionary hegemony and modernizing the economy. It began in 1956, triggered by a self-critical essay by China's leading aesthetician, Zhu Guangqian, on his "idealist aesthetics."[8] In his 1956 essay "The Reactionary Aspects of My Literary Thoughts," published in the widely circulated journal *Wenyi bao* [Literary gazette], Zhu Guangqian criticized his own "subjective idealist views" on aesthetics and literature and arts to "break with old, bourgeois ideas and to build new Marxist views." Now, Zhu had been China's foremost advocate of Western modern aesthetics, especially Benedetto Croce's intuitive-expressive theory. His first encounter with Croce had, as he put it, "enabled me to see Kant, Hegel, Schopenhauer, Nietzsche, and Bergson through a Crocian lens."[9]

Still, it was Kantian aesthetics that provided the larger framework in which Zhu, like most other Chinese intellectuals in a variety of time periods, apprehended modern Western aesthetic theories. Kantianism bridged classical, Enlightenment, and modernist aesthetics in Europe, and it featured prominently in the Chinese aesthetic Marxists' call to reconstruct a subjectivity in Chinese culture in the 1980s. This era in turn had its roots in much earlier cultural discussions, including the May Fourth enlightenment and the 1950s and 1960s debates over aesthetics. But writers and critics in the Republican period had hardly ever interrogated Western modernism on philosophical and theoretical levels. In this respect, Zhu Guangqian's assiduous efforts in the 1930s and 1940s, first to introduce modern Western aesthetics and then to incorporate them creatively into Chinese aesthetic tradition, broke new ground for the eventual convergence of Marxist cultural theory, Chinese tradition, and Western modernism. His encounter with Western aesthetics, though described in the 1956 essay in a negative vein in accord with the official discourse, actually verifies Zhu's vanguard position vis-à-vis Western modernist aesthetics, and thus it is worth pursuing here at greater length.

Croce, Zhu Guangqian maintained, "comes closer to Kant than to Hegel in his aesthetics," because "Kant . . . first formulated the notions such as 'disinterestedness,' 'purposiveness without purposes' as well as 'pure form,'" and Croce stretched Kantian aesthetics to a "reactionary extreme to defend formalist arts of the bourgeoisie in decline."[10] Zhu had adopted Croce's theory of intuition-expression in two ways. First, rather than focusing on Croce's language-oriented theory of symbolic representation of both logical and intuitive conception, Zhu mainly appropriated the Kantian implications of Croce's formulation of aesthetic experience as a detached, autonomous, and purely imaginary process. This, in fact, reflects Zhu's concern with the problems of modernity, captured by Kantian and post-Kantian aesthetic theories precisely as the self-conscious separation and autonomy of arts from other spheres of life. Second, Croce's emphasis on the expressive and psychological dimensions of aesthetic experience, as well as on the lyrical mode as the quintessential expression of emotion, indicates a possible point of convergence of modern Western and classical Chinese aesthetics. Taking Croce's position as a cue, Zhu incorporated a variety of modern Western aesthetic theories, from Kant's "disinterested contemplation" to Schopenhauer's notion of aesthetic experience as a "forgetfulness," with the Chinese Taoist notion of "forgetting both self and matter" as the ultimate goal of aesthetic contemplation. In particular, Zhu was drawn to the psychological theories of "aesthetic distance" represented by English psychologist Bullough, as well as to Lipps' theory of *Einfühlung*, or "empathy." Trained as a psychologist, Zhu was well versed in Freudian psychoanalysis and was in fact among the first Chinese to study it systematically. Unimpressed by its central belief in an isolated individual psyche and repelled by its parochialism, he was also among the first Chinese to criticize Freudianism.

There is undeniably a modernist tendency in Zhu Guangqian's aesthetic theory, but his earliest work exhibited a fundamental ambivalence. On the one hand, he was drawn to modernist, Kantian-Crocean notions of the autonomy of arts. Committed to the task of "contending for an independent space for literature and arts," he also voiced criticism of the Confucian pragmatic and didactical tradition that used literature as a vehicle for conveying political and ideological messages.[11] Interestingly, Zhu was critical of Confucian pragmatic and deterministic views and of the tendency in modern Chinese enlightenment intellectuals that perpetuate rather than undermine Confucian cultural determinism. On the other hand, he was troubled by Western modernist celebrations of the separation of art from life and the valorization of art. Zhu sought to complement what he took to be the Western modernist notion of the autonomy of art by emphasizing "identity of self and matter" in aesthetic experience; to do so, he drew on Chinese classical Taoist aesthetics. "Identity" for Zhu was not simply a moment of *Einfühlung* in aesthetic contemplation, although he toyed with the correspondence between Lipps' theory and Taoist aesthetics. Rather, Zhu's invocation of the concept of "identity" signaled his ambivalence toward Western modernist aesthetics. In this regard, what he held to be incongruous was the modernist notion of disinterestedness specifically in light of China's political reality, a reality devastated by violence and saturated with corruption.

Zhu Guangqian insisted that his main disagreement with Croce was the latter's formalist propensity to totally separate aesthetic judgment from cognitive and moral political activities.[12] By focusing on "identity" in aesthetic judgment, Zhu demonstrated his uneasiness with the Western modernist aesthetics of artistic autonomy and the separation of arts and reality. (As I will elaborate below, Zhu's Marxist period modified and extended, rather than entirely abandoned, his earlier "identity" theory by substituting the dialectic notion of "unity" for the more static one of "identity." When measured against Adorno's celebrated concept of "nonidentity," Zhu's distance from Western modernism becomes apparent. Though Adorno's "nonidentity" cannot be simply equated with modernist notions of aesthetic autonomy, it is arguable that Adorno's insistence on nonidentity as a central concept is closely linked to his theory of aesthetic experience as a site of resistance to the capitalist conceptual domination. In any case, Adorno's view is as much a critical response to as a product of the Western modernist movements. His "nonidentity" and Zhu's "unity" mark a major difference between the Frankfurt School and Chinese aesthetic Marxism, to which I shall return.)

Contrary to the rather misleading essentialist language he often used in his theoretical writings, Zhu Guangqian's notion of "identity" is not a metaphysical category postulating an invariable "essence of beauty" with mind and matter are identified. Rather, the "essence of beauty" in Zhu's view was totally relational: "Beauty does not lie in the matter, nor in the mind; rather, it lies in the relationship between mind and matter. But unlike the Kantian assumption and the common sense that conceives such a relationship in terms of matter as a stimulus and mind as reaction, it is the mind's expression of emotion through the image of the matter. . . . Beauty must be created by mind and soul."[13] Irrespective of its Crocian overtones, Zhu's formulation of the aesthetic (or "beauty") touched on a crucial problematic:

the subject-object relationship in aesthetic judgment. Even as he renounced his own "bourgeois idealism" in 1956, Zhu continued to insist that his relational concept of the aesthetic "is basically correct" because "to solve the question of the aesthetic, a unity of the subject and object must be achieved."[14] His defense of this crucial position immediately drew criticism that charged that his attempt at formulating a Marxist notion of "the unity of subject and object" was but a reassertion of his previous "subjective and idealist" position derived from Kantian-Crocean idealism. To this kind of criticism Zhu made quick response, using notions acquired from Marx's *1844 Manuscripts* to further his new concept of the aesthetic. The exchanges between Zhu and other critics on the problem of the "essence of beauty," which is in effect an issue of the subject-object relationship in the aesthetic experience, kindled a controversy which was to last for eight years. Most important, this controversy evolved into a theoretical debate that somehow, ironically, fulfilled Zhu's earlier pre-Marxist wish to create an "independent cultural space," this time in a Marxist symbolic world.

From the outset, the 1956 debate was a testimony to the resilience and ambiguity of its topic—aesthetics. It not only effectively reopened a key subject of the May Fourth enlightenment cultural critique but also generated a series of theoretical positions for an emergent aesthetic Marxism. Subtly, the debate continued and developed Hu Feng's views of "subjective fighting spirit." The debate also initiated in China for the first time discussions of Marx's *1844 Manuscripts*, which constitutes nothing less than a foundational text for much of Western Marxism as well as for Chinese humanist Marxist thought, that, in the beginning of the 1980s, stormed China's cultural scene with its powerful critique of "alienation" and "reification" in socialist society. Moreover, for aesthetic Marxists, the debate was central to the establishment of a positive and constructive vision of the future, especially for Li Zehou's theory of "aesthetic subjectivity" as a major force in the cultural ferment of the 1980s. Li Zehou first surfaced when he criticized Zhu Guangqian in the debates of the 1950s. It was in fact Li who first brought Marx's *1844 Manuscripts* to the attention of Chinese intellectual circles during that formative debate.

Subjectivity, the subject-object relation, is crucial to modern aesthetics, for it encapsulates basic tensions inherent in modernity. Since Marxism claims the only viable solution to this tension, it becomes especially important for modern Marxists to reaffirm their positions on this subject-object relationship. In this regard, Chinese Marxists have been conspicuously incoherent and nonchalant. Early Marxist intellectuals of the May Fourth cultural enlightenment, like Li Dazhao and Chen Duxiu, held that their first obligation was to wage a social revolution that would reverse China's backwardness, thus bringing it in line with the evolution of history as a progressive telos.[15] Since the central concept of revolution, class struggle, requires a revolutionary agent—a working class—the earlier Chinese Marxists tended to posit a metasubjectivity or collective subject of revolution without differentiating the individual subject from the social collectivity. Nor did they bother to attend to the philosophical distinctions of subjectivity-objectivity, which involve an ensemble of epistemological and ontological questions of mind and matter, universality and particularity, and so on.

Mao then overdeveloped the Chinese Marxist emphasis on class struggle at the expense of other Marxist categories, especially Marx's philosophical reflections. Mao's notion of class struggle departed from the classic Marxist definition by identifying the popular "masses" as the primary revolutionary force in lieu of the genuine proletariat that only existed, according to classic definition, within a capitalist mode of production. But Mao was no populist in a strictly political sense. Antielitist predisposition notwithstanding, Mao tended to default to Leninist vanguardism and centralized party politics when the question of ultimate political authority was raised. In effect, he took it for granted that the CCP and its cadres formed the decisive revolutionary agent or subject. On the other hand, Mao oscillated back and forth between a notion of revolution that stressed "subjective initiative" and "self-conscious ability" (winning him the name of "voluntarist") and an objectivist view that held Marxism to be a universal, truthful "objective law."[16] Mao's philosophical essays, "On Contradiction" and "On Practice," tend to ontologize "contradiction" as the universal and objective law generating and governing the totality of the world, from society to nature. Objectivity thus became synonymous with the universal law of contradiction in Mao Zedong Thought. The subjectivity of the revolutionary agent who must initiate practice was curiously conflated with the prior, objective truth of contradiction.[17]

"Objectivity" was further codified into a pervasive ideological system legitimizing Mao's political rule after the founding of the People's Republic. Maoist cultural bureaucrats made objectivity a socialist-realist aesthetic principle, while they denounced subjectivity as a bourgeois and idealist concept. In spite of Mao's efforts to bring about the democratic participation of the masses, a hierarchy emerged in the cultural institutions and the ideological state apparatuses that created crudely political exigencies, subordinating culture to politics. Mao not only remained oblivious to the conceptual ambiguity of the relations of subjectivity and objectivity, he also ignored the complexity of subject-formation in revolutionary practice. That is, despite his emphasis on "thought-reform" to foster revolutionary consciousness, Mao had little understanding of, and less interest in, the complex fabric of the individual psyche that enables an individual consciousness to negotiate with social determinations.

Hu Feng did venture deeply into the psychic realm, which he conceived to be a crucial site of resistance. Hu Feng's formulation of "subjective fighting spirit" attempted to capture the relationship of subjective experience or class consciousness on the one hand and representation on the other. Specifically, in the late 1940s, he contended that to represent social reality and revolution, a realism rooted in "subjective fighting spirit" was necessary. This spirit would have to be able to resist both dogmatic adherence to ideological formulas ("subjective formulaism"), and equally dogmatic submission to the narrow-minded, utilitarian propaganda of the Red Army's political commissars ("objectivism"). Of central importance to my thesis is Hu's argument that the "subjective fighting spirit" stems from an "interfusion of the subject with the object." The "subject" in Hu Feng's theory referred to the revolutionary writer, while the "object" was synonymous with social life itself. Thus, for Hu Feng, revolutionary practice at once constituted and was constituted by a revolutionary subjectivity that emerged out of the immediate struggle of "opposing fascism and feudalism, lashing out at all forms and measures of slavish ethics," and from "fostering a critical power in combating the content of the life of the people," who had been subject to "thousands of years of spiritual slavery."[18]

In the 1940s, Hu Feng broached the crucial issue of subjectivity in revolutionary practice and aesthetic representation. Renounced by Mao as "bourgeois idealist" and "counterrevolutionary" in the 1950s, the thorny question Hu Feng raised still remains, especially in the field of aesthetics: who, after all, can judge what is beautiful? If one ascribes to the reflection theory that "objective reality" determines the "beautiful," and human consciousness only reflects beauty in objective reality, the answer surely squares well with the principle of "socialist realism" that fetishizes objectivity and disavows subjectivity. This was precisely the position taken by many critics of Zhu Guangqian in the Chinese debate. But the discussions never resolved the problem of *who* had the final authority for knowing objective reality, let alone judging that most evasive and ambiguous thing called "beauty." Mao simply displaced the question by assuming an a priori revolutionary metasubjectivity embodied by the Party, with indisputable authority, because it alone understands objective, universal law. Although arguably sufficient in a political sense, this tautology is nonsense insofar as literature and arts are not the equivalent of objective reality. They are artifacts that must necessarily be created by a subject—a writer or artist—who can hardly be equated with a metasubject like the Party. Hu Feng's theory worked to unravel the constitutive aspects of subjectivity in cultural and aesthetic realms, thereby pointing to a space different from political and economic sectors. Moreover, foregrounding the category of the subject itself revealed the inherent paradox in Mao's simultaneous valorization of objectivity as the "universal law" and his insistence on the metasubjectivity of the Communist Party.

In subsequent debates of the 1950s and 1960s, Zhu Guangqian's formulation of the "unity of subjectivity and objectivity in aesthetic experience" sparked further interest in examining culture and aesthetics as independent and autonomous spheres and had far-reaching philosophical and ideological ramifications. First, the notion problematized the Maoist hierarchy of objectivity and subjectivity, and threatened to unmask many other critical lacunae in the Maoist hegemony. Second, by identifying aesthetic subjectivity as the ultimate Marxist ideal, the Chinese debate reaffirmed a constructive dimension of Marxism in the cultural realm. In this latter project of expanding the cultural realm of action within Marxism, Zhu Guangqian formulated the theses enumerated below on the "unity of the subjective and objective": (1) "Beauty" is a false concept that perpetuates the mechanical materialist conflation of "beauty" with objective reality, and should therefore be redefined as the "beautiful" or "aesthetic experience," which signifies the subject-object dialectic. In other words, to equate "beauty" with objective reality only essentializes what is in fact a dynamic process of mediation on the subjective and objective. (2) Because aesthetic experience is derived primarily from the creative and imaginary work of art and literature, the characteristics of art and literature should be central to aesthetic inquiry. (3) Just as art and literature are ideological forms, aesthetic experience by its very nature is ideological. As an ideological form, aesthetic experience is subjective, but is determined objectively by social conditions just as ideology is objectively determined. (This is a version of Zhu's earlier thesis of the "unity of the subjective and objective.") (4) The central issue of aesthetic inquiry is "practice," through which the unity of the subjective and objective are potentially materialized.

By forcefully insisting on "aesthetic experience" as the true aesthetic issue, Zhu Guangqian underscored the problematic nature of subjectivity, and consequently was accused of harboring a "remnant bourgeois idealism." The most prominent of his critics, Cai Yi and Li Zehou, engaged in extensive debates with him on the subject-object relationship. Cai Yi, a veteran Marxist aesthetician who adhered to Lenin's reflection theory, insisted on the existence of "beauty" as an objective entity in the material, natural world, and on the concept of aesthetic experience as only a reflection or recognition of the "essence" of the "objective law of beauty." Cai Yi defined the "objective law of beauty" as the "law of typicality": what is beautiful is what is typical in nature. Cai Yi never equivocated on the absolute primacy of objectivity in aesthetics, and he continuously opposed Marx's *1844 Manuscripts* for its "residual bourgeois humanism and subjectivism." Of course, Cai Yi found Zhu Guangqian's theory objectionable in principle, because in his view the insistence on "aesthetic experience" as such connoted "bourgeois subjective idealism."[19]

Li Zehou, then a fledging philosopher, criticized Zhu Guangqian from a more complex perspective. Li argued for the primacy of objectivity with no less passion than Cai Yi, but his description of the "objective" was far more subtle. Briefly, Li Zehou's "objectivity" refers to social existence, which determines the objective nature of beauty. Li contended that because objectivity means the "sociality of beauty," Zhu Guangqian was wrong to identify the social aspects of beauty as subjective. Li also criticized Cai Yi's metaphysical proposition attributing to beauty an essentialist "natural property" as simply collapsing the natural object with "beauty," a social phenomenon. Li's view of "objective social existence" is primarily relational and structural: beauty as a social phenomenon must be objective, since social being is determined by structures of social relationship that lie beyond human consciousness and feelings, which are "physically intangible and imperceptible but objectively existent."[20]

Zhu Guangqian tirelessly defended his views on aesthetic subjectivity. He defined "subject" and "object" as epistemological rather than ontological categories, and then critiqued the radical separation of the two in what he called "metaphysical thinking." His argument is worth quoting at some length:

In terms of knowledge of the external world, man is the "subject" and the external world the "object" [keti/duixiang]. From the subject's point of view it is "subjective," while from the object's point of view it is "objective." Hence, consciousness and general psychological phenomena are subjective, and the external world to which consciousness relates itself is objective. It is undeniable that there is an apparent opposition between the subjective and the objective, but to see the two as absolutely opposed and separate is metaphysical thinking. . . . *The subjective also has an objective basis and an objective effect.* On the other hand, is there any objectivity [keguan] that has nothing to do with subjectivity? Having nothing to do with subjectivity means having nothing to do with mankind, and even if one assumes that it exists, it is out of our concern here. *Insofar as it becomes an object [duixiang] of our discussion, it then turns into an object [duixiang] of our knowledge and practice.* And as such it must be the object [duixiang] of an subject. It is an oxymoron to say "object [duixiang] without subject" or "subject without object [duixiang]." One can say that knowledge means that objective existence determines subjective consciousness, and practice means that subjective consciousness affects objective existence. This is precisely what Marx means, as we analyzed before, by the "objectification [duixiang hua] of man" or the "humanization of nature," as the unity of the subjective [zhuguan] and objective [keguan].[21]

Philosophically, what is at issue is the conceptual ambiguity and polysemic indecisiveness both of the concepts and related terms of "subject"/"object," "subjectivity"/"objectivity," "subjective"/"objective." In Chinese, there are two terms for "object": *keti* and *duixiang*. As a noun, *keti* refers to the object as matter, the external world, nature, the opposite of mind and consciousness. But the related adjective, *keguan* [objective], and the related noun, *keguan xing* [objectivity], also refer to that which is general and universal, including specifically social totality. This is Li Zehou's meaning, one that was sharply criticized by Zhu Guangqian for collapsing two different realms—society and Nature—into one single concept. The other Chinese term for "object," *duixiang*, refers to the object of the subject's knowledge, and therefore is more epistemological and phenomenological than ontological. Zhu grappled strenuously with the slippage of the concepts in his argument, for he believed that the resolution to the aesthetic problematic lay in the subject-object relation.

Adorno, in a different context, tackled a very similar set of ambiguities. In his seminal essay entitled "Subject-Object," Adorno calls attention to precisely the dialectic relationship between subject and object that cannot be resolved at one stroke by privileging one over the other. He regards Western thought's separation of subject and object as "both real and illusory. True, because in the cognitive realm it serves to express the real separation, the dichotomy of the human condition, a coercive development. False, because the resulting separation must not be hypostatized, not magically transformed into an invariant."[22] The preoccupation with the dialectical tension between subject and object leads to Adorno's critical principle of negative dialectics, or the "nonidentity" of subject and object. While insisting on "the preponderance of the object" irreducible to an active subjectivity, Adorno cautioned in *Negative Dialectics* that "it is not the purpose of critical thought to place the object on the orphaned royal throne once occupied by the subject. On that throne the object would be nothing but an idol. The purpose of critical thought is to abolish the hierarchy."[23] In the essay "Subject-Object," Adorno contended that "since primacy of the object requires reflection of the subject and subjective reflection, subjectivity—as distinct from primitive materialism, which really does not permit dialectics—becomes a moment that lasts."[24]

It is in the same sense that Zhu Guangqian addressed the "unity of the subjective and objective" in which the moment of subjectivity is ineradicable. Moreover, Zhu similarly wished "to abolish the hierarchy": "The error that [Chinese] aestheticians presently commit is to *absolutize the object while kicking out the subject at one stroke*" (emphasis in original). This error, he added, stems from "eradicating the unity of the opposites between the objective and the subjective, for superstitiously fearing the subjective and absolutizing the objective. The redundant and scholastic reasoning, like a mouse jabbing inside an ox horn, is predestined to be metaphysical in its method. This is why aesthetics at present comes to a dead-end. It is time to decide on a road for aesthetics."[25] Zhu's message is unmistakable and it took courage to articulate at that time, when the sheer mention of "subjectivity" would be not simply "politically incorrect" but dangerous. Set against Marcuse's more assertive statements, Zhu's words may appear rather unassuming, but the sentiment is quite similar: "Even in its most distinguished representatives Marxist aesthetics has shared in the devaluation of subjectivity. . . . And in contrast to the rather dialectical formulations of Marx and Engels, the [base-superstructure] conception has been made into a rigid schema, a schematization that has had devastating consequences for aesthetics. The schema implies a normative notion of the material base as the true reality and a political devaluation of nonmaterial forces particularly of the individual consciousness and their political function."[26] While Marcuse maintained that "liberating subjectivity constitutes itself in the inner history of the individuals—their own history, which is not identical with their social existence," thus emphasizing the irreconcilable schism between the subject and object,[27] Zhu envisioned greater links, or unity, between the two by way of practice.

It should be noted that Zhu's notion of "unity" is not to be confused with "identity." On the contrary, Zhu's proposition of "unity of subject and object" was articulated against, albeit indirectly, the theory of "identity of thought and existence," then triumphant in the controversy over the identity issue so prominent in China's philosophical circles, which occurred roughly at the same time as the aesthetic debate. In 1958, the philosopher Yang Xianzhen criticized the *Soviet Concise Dictionary of Philosophy*'s confusion of two kinds of identity as Marxist propositions: the identity of thought and existence, and the identity of contradictions. Yang Xianzhen contended that the notion of identity of thought and existence was derived from Hegelian idealism, while the identity of contradictions was dialectical materialist. His view was rebuked by Ai Siqi, a veteran philosopher and a close associate of Mao from the Yan'an period, who insisted that the concept of identity was materialist. The heated exchange between Yang and Ai then developed into a major debate in the Chinese academy. In 1960, Mao saw that it was necessary to intervene, declaring that a rejection of the identity of thought and existence would inevitably lead to Kantian dualism. Accordingly, Yang Xianzhen was attacked as a "revisionist" and a "right-wing opportunist." The philosophical debate amounted to nothing less than an assessment of Mao's Great Leap Forward campaign of the late 1950s, which ended up as a scandalous fiasco. Yang saw behind the notion of identity of thought and existence a voluntaristic impulse that precipitated Mao's disastrous "grand revolutionary praxis." Although apparently defending Mao's concept of contradiction, which the Soviet *Dictionary* attacks, Yang in fact took the question of identity as an opportunity to criticize Maoism.[28]

Adorno, as we know, rejected relentlessly the identity theory, but his rejection was occasioned by the historical conditions of modern capitalism. The sociohistorical underpinning of the identity theory may be the exchange value in capitalist society which generates facile sameness or identity among radically different things.[29] By the same token, the Chinese debates, especially Yang Xianzhen's notion of nonidentity, were politically motivated. In a 1960 response to Cai Yi's criticism, Zhu Guangqian maintained that the philosophical debate over identity of thought and existence "touched upon the fundamental philosophical problem. Once this problem is solved, then the difference between metaphysical and dialectical modes of thinking becomes clear. In the meantime, it will solve the subquestion of whether beauty stems from the unity of subject and object under the general question [of the identity of thought and existence]."[30] Although Zhu's notion of unity may give the impression of being aligned with the identity theory, in fact, the crucial difference between "unity of subject and object" and "identity of thought and existence" lies in the latter's cancellation of the difference between thought and existence and the former's insistence on the indispensable *difference* between subject and object in aesthetic experience. Hence Zhu was prescient in his unremitting refusal to absolutize and essentialize "beauty" as objective existence and his tireless insistence on the *relational* nature of "beauty" and the "beautiful."

The question of practice also emerged in these heated arguments about the relation of subject-object. Following Marx's *1844 Manuscripts,* Chinese Marxists generally considered practice a key link that mediated subject and object. In this respect, most telling is Li Zehou's shift of positions from an earlier insistence on objectivity to his later passionate plea in the 1980s for a construction of aesthetic subjectivity. This later notion that "aesthetic subjectivity" constituted a redefinition of the intellectual self and the deployment of an autonomous and self-determining subject came to be formulated in response to the profound intellectual crisis that followed the Cultural Revolution; I would also argue that the shift did not really constitute an abrupt break with his earlier positions. The foundational position of practice has featured prominently in Li's work from early on. Young Li Zehou, though an ardent advocate of "objectivity," was never committed to essentialist views like Cai Yi's. Instead, his parastructuralist notion of "objective social existence," understood subjectivity as indispensable social agency. Like Gramsci, who argued that objectivity always means "humanly objective" or "universally subjective," Li's shift of positions on subjectivity is grounded in historical considerations.[31] In his 1956 essay "On Aesthetic Experience, Beauty, and the Arts," Li introduced the *1844 Manuscripts* to Chinese intellectuals, arguing that it constituted a crucial work in Marxist cultural and aesthetic theory. Evincing little interest in the notion of alienation, Li focused on young Marx's idea of the "humanized nature," and made this notion the foundation of his Chinese Marxist aesthetics. This link between subjectivity and practice makes possible a constructivist view of culture and society which, though itself a utopian vision, is nevertheless quite significantly different from Maoist radical revolutionary utopianism.

Li Zehou's utopian vision is similar in some pertinent ways to the utopianism of the Frankfurt School. Adorno inscribed a utopian hope in a certain subjective experience that he defined essentially in aesthetic terms: "Approaching knowledge of the object is the act in which the subject rends the veil it is weaving around the object. It can do this only where, fearlessly passive, it entrusts itself to its own experience. . . . The subject is the object's agent, not its constituent; this fact has consequences for the relation of theory and practice."[32] While implying that the individual subjective experience can resist the domination of rationalist discourse by sensuous receptivity, Adorno was never certain about how "the relation of theory and practice" can be affected by such an experience which remains "fearlessly passive." As Martin Jay reminds us, Adorno's aesthetic experience "is hardly a formula for political activism."[33] Adorno, of course, was not at all optimistic in his projection of a utopia, for the profound pessimism encapsulated in his axiomatic phrase, "To write poetry after Auschwitz is barbaric," seriously contorts his utopian vision.

Like most Western Marxists, Adorno was preoccupied with the issues of alienation and reification. He feared more than anything the domination of subject over object, or vice versa; and accordingly, he opposed any attempt to suppress heterogeneity in the name of identity. His hostility towards the privileging of production in "vulgar Marxism" has to be understood in conjunction with his attempts to resist the subject's domination over nature and to restore the irreducible differences and heterogeneity in the material world. Admittedly, Adorno's celebrated posture of perpetually playing off difference against identity makes him eminently amenable to poststructuralist thinking generally, and deconstructionism in particular. While the trenchant critique of Western culture and capitalist domination that Adorno and the poststructuralists have mounted is certainly invaluable, how plausible is the possibility of utopian peace in the real world after the deconstruction of all values, by theory at least, if not by physical force? Nor is Marcuse's assertion of art as a radical revolutionary praxis any more viable. Marcuse's affirmation of aesthetic remembrance as the revolutionary agent simply recasts Adorno's concern that "all reification is a forgetting" in a Hegelian foreclosure, taking remembrance as the reinternalization or retrieval of a lost subjectivity vis-à-vis an externalized objective world. In other words, Marcuse is reluctant to go beyond the subjective realm and to ground artistic creativity in material practice. In this respect, Li Zehou's critique of the Frankfurt School's "idealist" notion of praxis is well taken. The Frankfurt School philosophers' tenacious refusal to grant material practice any constructive or positive status in Critical Theory, as well as their persistent denigration of "productivist" vulgar Marxism, is in sharp contrast to Chinese Marxism. Chinese views of practice and practical subjectivity, on the other hand, are imbued with an optimism about the projected future of "humanized nature." Chinese Marxist thinking insists that material and creative practices enable human beings both to objectify their essential powers—to realize fully their potential—and to humanize the natural world, signifying the unity of subject (mankind) and object (nature).

Chinese aesthetic Marxism's reinvention of practice does not start from Mao's famous notion of practice integrating theory with action. Ideologically, of course, Mao's view has been very influential; outside China its significance contributed to the notion that Maoism "sinified" Marxism somehow. Thanks to the very ambiguity of Mao's usage, "practice" also became a powerful weapon for the pragmatic leaders of post-Mao China when they turned to debunking Maoist doctrines in 1978 under the slogan "practice as the sole criterion for evaluating truth." There is plenty of room for the argument forwarded more recently that Mao's view lacks theoretical coherence in light of Western Marxists' notion of praxis.[34] But aesthetic Marxists like Li Zehou find that Maoist notions of practice lean too far in the direction of the voluntarist and idealist views of praxis that characterize Western Marxism. In the context of post-Mao rethinking, Li has sharply criticized both Maoist radicalism, responsible for the catastrophic Great Leap Forward and the Cultural Revolution, and a Western Marxism that privileges cultural praxis over material production or practice.

Even in the debates of the 1950s and 1960s, Zhu Guangqian and Li Zehou remained adamant that "praxis" and "practice" were different entities and that the latter was the historical materialist core notion on which Marxist aesthetics could be erected. In Zhu's argument, Marxist aesthetics can be extrapolated from the first of Marx's 1845 "Theses on Feuerbach." Marx, Zhu argued, regards practice as the link, or unity, between subjective activity and objective reality, in the sense that "the thing, reality, sensuousness" must be understood as "human sensuous activity, practice."[35] Critical to aesthetic theory, practice should be grasped as "human sensuous activity," for aesthetic experience must be defined as the concrete, sensuous experience of human beings. But Zhu was not content with the obvious connection between aesthetics and sensuousness. Practice as the cornerstone of Marxist aesthetics is explicit in the *1844 Manuscripts*. There, Marx makes one of his very few remarks on the "laws of beauty:"

> In creating an *objective world* by his practical activity, in *working-up* inorganic nature, man [*sic*] proves himself a conscious species being, i.e. as a being that treats the species as its own essential being, or that treats itself as a species being. Admittedly animals also produce. . . .[An animal] produces one-sidedly, whilst man produces universally. It produces only under the dominion of immediate physical need, whilst man produces even when he is free from physical need and only truly produces in freedom therefrom. An animal produces only itself, whilst man reproduces the whole of nature. . . . An animal forms things in accordance with the standard and the need of the species to which it belongs, whilst man knows how to produce in accordance with the standard of every species, and knows how to apply everywhere the inherent standard to the object. Man therefore also forms things in accordance with the laws of beauty.[36]

Zhu insisted that the two theses, namely, "man [*sic*] produces universally" and "man [*sic*] forms things in accordance with the laws of beauty," are indissolubly at one. This is not simply because "the laws of beauty" imply the creative labor, or objective material practice, that produces in freedom and in universal terms. Indeed, the Schillerian overtone of freedom and universality in Marx's passage was accentuated by the Chinese aesthetic Marxists in the 1980s, especially by Li Zehou; but in the 1950s and 1960s, the emphasis was rather on material practice that "humanizes nature." Marx stated that "for not only the five senses but also the so-called spiritual senses, the practical senses (will, love, etc,) in a word, *human* sense—the humanity of the senses—comes into being by virtue of its object, by virtue of *humanized* nature."[37] In his 1960 essay on Marxist practical aesthetics, Zhu Guangqian detected in the concept of "humanized nature" a vital connection between artistic creativity and material labor:

> No matter whether it is creativity of labor or artistic creativity there is only one principle: "humanized nature" or "objectified essential

powers of man." There is also only one fundamental experience: one experiences joy and pleasure when one sees an object as one's own "work," which embodies one's essence as a social being, or one's "essential powers." . . . *Productive labor is humanity's grasp of the world in practical spirits, and it is thus humanity's grasp of the world in artistic ways.*[38]

Zhu Guangqian saw aesthetic and material production as mutually dependent. The elimination of "alienated labor" enables an aesthetic state of playful and joyful productive labor. Zhu's notion of aesthetic practice seems to be reaffirmed by Terry Eagleton's interpretation of Marx's aesthetics as a materialist rethinking of the body: to the extent that the humanized *senses* of the body as naturally given constitute the paramount aesthetic experience, the material practice of labor is aesthetic in terms of somatic pleasure or bodily experience.[39] But Zhu's concern was not so much with the bodily and sensuous experience as with cultural and aesthetic work itself. His conception of cultural and aesthetic work as part of the Marxian notion of practice can be construed as a trope for cultural construction, which as a distinct kind of practice of artists, must be valued the same way as the material practices of workers and peasants.

However, on this score, Zhu has been severely criticized by Li Zehou in particular. Li argues that there are two distinct categories of practice—material and spiritual—that cannot be confused, and humanized nature does not simply mean human senses; it refers first and foremost to the objective material world as the precondition of human existence.[40] Li tirelessly insists on the fundamental distinction and precedence of objective, material practice over intellectual and artistic practice:

> When I talk about "humanized nature," I am referring to the productive labor of making and using tools or the concrete material activity that changes the objective world. I think this is the real origin of beauty. . . . It is not the individual's "essential powers" of feelings, consciousness, thoughts, wills, etc., that create beauty; on the contrary, it is the essential powers of the *socio-historical* practice of the *totality of humankind* that create beauty.[41]

From this fundamental definition of practice as concrete material activity, Li Zehou elaborates on his constructive philosophy, arguing that to transcend the idealist enclave, the primacy of material production must be preserved as the absolute precondition of the aesthetic state, or "humanized nature." In other words, to humanize nature means to change the objective material world through material practice, or the development of productive forces. Marx stated in the *Grundrisse,* "the highest development of the forces of production, hence also the richest development of individuals."[42] Marx's productivist and anthropomorphic views have been rejected by many Western Marxists in the face of the troubled relationship between human beings and the ecological environment consequent on modernization. But for Li, the distinction has to be made between a productivist notion or economic determinism and material practice itself. For Western Marxists, on the other hand, alienation and reification constitute the central categories for their *critique* of capitalism. The antagonistic aspects of human beings and Nature are perceived as a part of capitalist alienation.

These differing views confirm that even such a widely accepted wisdom in the West is also historically conditioned and partial; it cannot exhaust all other alternatives, either conceptual or real. Insofar as Marx's notion of "humanized nature" is eschewed by Western Marxism for its outmoded productivist tendency, a constructive view of practice as a utopian vision is unlikely to emerge. Terry Eagleton, for example, on the one hand concedes that Marxism remains "the single most creative aspect of the aesthetic tradition," and on the other hand, cautions against the "premature aestheticization" of aesthetic experience that Marx's "romantic humanist" views may entail, and against "premature utopianism," which is either "desirable but unfeasible" or "inevitable but not necessarily desirable."[43] Eagleton's concern, however, emerges from a specific understanding of "material practice" in Marx's aesthetic view that somehow constricts its rich meaning to the body and senses as material realm. Mostly concerned with the problems of representation and communication, Eagleton offers only a hazy identification of Marx's economic categories with the aesthetic ones. If, as in Eagleton's theorization, aesthetic experience and utopianism remain locked within conceptual and/or sensuous realms of culture, a positive utopianism that does not risk being self-complacently illusory is hardly possible.[44]

But it should be added that Li Zehou's emphasis on material practice as the precondition of aesthetic fulfillment is not simply productivist. His somewhat crude positions of the earlier period developed into a psychologically oriented theory of aesthetic subjectivity. In his major philosophical work of 1979, *Critique of the Critical Philosophy: A Study of Kant,* which tries to connect historical materialist categories and Kant's reflections on human rationality and subjectivity, Li expatiates on his "aesthetics of practical subjectivity":

> Marx's "humanized nature" . . . means productive labor as the fundamental social practice of mankind. . . . Man [*sic*] becomes the master of nature . . . through active social practice that unifies the oppositions of man and Nature concretely and historically. Only then the real unity of contradictions, between man and Nature, truth and virtue, sensuousness and rationality, laws and purposes, necessity and freedom, becomes possible. . . . Rationality can thus become sedimented or congealed into sensuousness, form into content, and the form of Nature then becomes the form of freedom—which is also Beauty.[45]

Drawing on Kant and Piaget, Li Zehou here conceives of a grand historical process of material practice that transforms humanity from its natural form to a "form of freedom," an internalized, or sedimented rationality embodied by a creative subjectivity. How exactly the material practice of productive labor transforms mankind into beings fully developed both in sensuousness and rationality is never clearly described, and the overemphasis on rationality inherent in Li's theory is certainly problematic. However, what emerges from Li's theory are the contours of a constructive utopianism of freedom and beauty which lies not in nonmaterial forms of thought but in concrete material practice. That is, Li envisions a positive and constructive alternative "post-Marxism," distinct from the various negative and pessimistic post-Marxisms and Western Marxism. Because Marxism, from Marx and Engels through Lenin, Trotsky, and Mao all the way to Lukács and Gramsci, has always been a "theory of revolution and a theory of critique," Li asserts an urgent need to "creatively transform Marxism from a critical philosophy and revolutionary theory to a *constructive* philosophy. It is precisely for such a reason that my philosophy has nothing to do with the entire Marxist theory of class struggle and proletarian dictatorship, and that mine is a 'post-Marxism.' "[46]

Li Zehou's insistence on the primacy of material production as practice also contradicts his overall vision of aesthetic subjectivity that takes culture, rather than material production or economic development, as its central site of reconstruction. The aesthetic also serves cognitive and heuristic functions in Li's project of reforming education and psychology. In this respect, his ambitious project coincided with Zhu Guangqian's. But their differences are quite revealing, too. Li was primarily concerned about the Cultural Revolution's impediment to economic development. In the 1980s, Li criticized Mao's "idealist tendency" by privileging dialectical materialism over historical materialism. Yet in the 1950s and 1960s when he might very well have sensed the danger of excessive stress on cultural revolution at the expense of economic development, he could still only express his disagreement obliquely by critiquing the "idealist tendency" in other scholars, such as Zhu Guangqian. Zhu, on the other hand, envisioned the need for an independent and autonomous cultural space as the most pressing issue. It is arguable that both Li and Zhu grasped the contradictions in Mao's revolutionary hegemony from different angles. Both the neglect of economic development and politicization of culture and aesthetics were equally serious problems that undermined the project of China's alternative modernity. In hindsight, the questions raised in the aesthetic debates during the 1950s and 1960s were in one way or another tied to the increasingly intense and frequent ideological and political campaigns in the terrain of culture and aesthetics. The relationship between aesthetics and ideology, then, became a compelling issue in the debates.

The debates over the ideology-aesthetic relation should be understood both as a criticism of ideology and as an endeavor to examine productively the tangled relationship between ideology and aesthetics. The interrogation of ideology in the debates challenged and problematized the official concept, and the difficulties encountered by aesthetic Marxists in their attempt to constitute an original ideological critique are themselves quite revealing.

The project of Chinese aesthetic Marxists parallels Althusser's undertaking of roughly the same period. There is, of course, a remarkable irony in Althusser's Chinese connection. Althusser was more than an admirer of Mao and the Chinese Cultural Revolution, like many French radicals of the 1960s. His theoretical works bear significant imprints of Mao, especially his central concepts of "contradiction and overdetermination" and "structural causality." But Althusser's work has been viewed in China quite unfavorably, by both the orthodox Marxists who categorically relegate Western Marxism to the ranks of bourgeois social democrats and the oppositional intellectuals who condemn Althusser's sympathies for Maoist radicalism. During the humanist Marxist protests against "alienation under socialism" in the 1980s, however, Althusser's antihumanist Marxist view was smuggled in by Hu Qiaomu, a member of the Politburo of the CCP and the official ideological spokesman, who reproached the humanist "distortions" by referring to the earlier "unscientific" Marx of the *1844 Manuscripts*. These complex conceptual transmigrations reaffirm the sociohistorical determinations of thought, an empirical fact often obscured by voracious aspirations for theoretical sophistication and poststructuralist obsession with language. These kinds of border-crossings are especially relevant in the case of the inquiries into ideology in which Althusser and Chinese aesthetic Marxists were engaged under similar historical conditions.

The historical conjuncture in which these theoretical inquiries took place was the crisis of socialist ideology prompted by the process of de-Stalinization in the Soviet Union. Althusser was devoted to the search for productive answers to the questions raised by the denunciation of Stalinism at the twentieth Congress of the Soviet Communist Party in 1956. Toward that end, as Valentino Gerratana has written, Althusser felt it "necessary to draw up a Marxist balance sheet of Marxism itself—of its far-from-linear history and its largely unexplored potential for further development. The main stress was on the philosophical aspects of the undertaking."[47] One major contribution is Althusser's celebrated notion of ideology as a representation of imaginary relationship of individuals to real conditions. Althusser's objective was to differentiate "ideology" from "science" "in order to dare to be the beginning of a scientific (i.e., subject-less) discourse on ideology."[48] Clearly, Althusser wanted to defend Marxism as a true science vis-à-vis ideology and "Ideological State Apparatuses" (ISAs). But most valuable in his work is not his tenacious distinction between the "ideological" and the "scientific" Marx as a result of the so-called epistemological break; rather, it is his original analysis of the workings of ideology. The Chinese, such as Zhu Guangqian, also intended to revive a true Marxist notion of ideology and art, not so much against anti-Marxist, bourgeois humanist distortions as against "mechanical materialism" or "metaphysical thinking," as coded terms signifying Mao's ideological orthodoxy.

Zhu Guangqian begins his discussion of ideology by saying that "the distortions of Marxism have created great obstacles to the aesthetic path."[49] These "distortions," he suggests, are caused by one of the sacrosanct tenets of the orthodoxy: Lenin's reflection theory. Lenin, of course, cannot be criticized explicitly, but the misappropriations of his view can and are: "The aesthetic inquiries in China," Zhu writes, "invariably apply Lenin's reflection theory simplistically and uncritically, based on his 'Materialism and Empiriocriticism' as the sole classic text."[50] To say that our consciousness reflects objective reality is a correct materialist statement, Zhu maintains, but only to a certain extent: insofar as "red" is a sensation caused by the material property of things as objective existence, it is correct to say that our senses reflect reality; but when we say art is a reflection of reality, it is altogether a different matter. Art reflects reality in much more complex ways than mere sensory and scientific reflection, for art is historically and socially conditioned, whereas sensory and scientific reflections are not. Art is a refraction of reality as ideology. To bolster his argument, Zhu quotes the famous passage from Marx and Engels's *German Ideology:* "If in all ideology men and their circumstances appear up-side down as in *camera obscura,* this phenomenon arises just as much from their life-process as the inversion of objects on the retina does from their physical life-process."[51] Zhu's emphasis is on ideology as a relatively autonomous realm with particular sociohistorical determinations:

> Ideology does not simply reflect the [economic] base of the same historical period, for superstructure may lag behind base. That is to say, ideology at a given historical period contains both new and old strata, the new reflecting the contemporary base, and the old, the residual influence of the previous one or more historical periods. This simple fact has much to do with many critical issues in literature and the arts, including traditional form, traditional ideas, the continuity of and opposition to tradition, the limits and immanent contradictions of authors, etc. Finally, as a superstructure of the same base, one ideology can influence another ideology. For example, literature and the arts can reflect legal, political, religious, and philosophic views of the time.[52]

Anticipating Raymond Williams's distinctions among the cultural "dominant," "residual," and "emergent" in complex ideological formations, Zhu unremittingly insists on the necessary differentiations and correlations among ideology, superstructure, and economic base.[53] In his 1979 preface to *A History of Western Aesthetics,* Zhu Guangqian revises his earlier position on ideology by underscoring the relative independent and autonomous position on ideology vis-à-vis the general superstructure. He argues that such a view can be found in Marx's seminal formulation of "base" and "superstructure": "The sum total of these relations of production constitutes the economic structures of society, the real foundation, on which rises a legal and political superstructure and to which correspond definite forms of social consciousness."[54] The relationship between "legal and political superstructure" and ideology ("social consciousness") is, in Marx's definition, parallel rather than hierarchical. In other words, ideology neither merely belongs to nor is subjugated to superstructure. Zhu asserts that the distinction of ideology and superstructure sustains the Marxist notion of the social division of labor: "the ideology of each different realm has its distinct historical continuity and relative autonomy in the historical the process."[55] Moreover, Zhu insists that the concepts of "superstructure" and "base" are relational and metaphoric: " 'Superstructure' is relative to 'economic structure' or the 'real foundation,' and these terms are all metaphors. The gist of it lies not so much in terminology as in three essentially different driving forces of history. These are: (1) economic structure or real foundation; (2) legal and political superstructure; and (3) ideology in a broad sense as a system of ideas and values."[56] Analogous to Althusser, Zhu substitutes the doctrine of linear historical causality or determinism with a notion of multilinearity or overdetermination.

The Chinese reinvention of the Marxian notion of ideology clearly evidences what Pierre Bourdieu calls the struggle for "symbolic capital," or the battle against "symbolic violence."[57] If ideology is a heavily contested battlefield of such symbolic warfare, then the debate about ideology itself strikes at the very center of the contention. The significance of Zhu's advocacy of the relative autonomy of ideology from the "legal and political superstructure" must be understood in this light: when everything is politicized by the absolute authority of the Party or monologic ISAS, the relative autonomy of culture is no small symbolic capital to gain.

Aesthetic reflection is ideological rather than scientific, not only because of its historical and social determinations but also because of the constitutive role played by subjectivity in the formation of ideology and aesthetic experience. Zhu's insistence that subjectivity is ineradicable in aesthetic experience, contrary to Althusser's theory of subjectivity through interpellation, argues that ideology requires the active force of subjectivity in its formation. The workings of ideology are "extremely complicated," Zhu writes, and the process of ideological formation is "often unconscious. The ideological totality of the individual's lived experience and cultural upbringing, his worldview, his view of life, and his class consciousness, etc., is fraught with emotional colors. . . . Ideology and lived experience are inseparable to the extent that ideology works through the individual's lived experience." Because "ideology is an emotional, affective system of thought which determines the individual's attitudes towards things and his ideals about life and art," aesthetic experience is ideology par excellence.[58] Althusser similarly emphasizes the emotional, affective, and unconscious aspects of ideology, and as Terry Eagleton points out, if ideological statements by Althusserian definition are both subjective and universally valid, ideology has a certain affinity with the Kantian notion of aesthetics.[59] In this respect, the similarity between Zhu's and Althusser's concepts is obvious. Interestingly, however, they differ markedly on the question of subjectivity. If Althusser's view of subjectivity and ideology smacks of a certain "political pessimism," as Eagleton observes, Zhu's more optimistic view of subjectivity cannot be interpreted simply as an expression of radical idealist utopianism.[60]

Ironically, Zhu Guangqian and his Chinese colleagues may arguably be more justified than Althusser in asserting the repressiveness of the political mechanism of interpellated Subjectivity under Mao's rule. Their recognition of the constructive possibilities inhering in material practice, however, have directed them away from remaining locked into the issues of consciousness and ideas. In fact, Zhu Guangqian has been repeatedly criticized by Li Zehou and others for his lingering idealist influence, which resulted in his ambiguity about material practice. Li views material practice first and foremost as the productive labor of making and using tools in changing the material reality—in other words, economic activity as the "real foundation" for change in a historical materialist sense.

Yet Li himself is far from consistent on this issue. His concept of the objectivity of social existence is, as we know, parastructuralist. His view of ideology also reflects this structuralist propensity. Li regards ideology as some Janus-faced thing, subjective insofar as ideology is a social consciousness reflecting an objective economic base; and, as a given fact in the social reality partaking of that very process of social formation, it is part of the objective, material social existence. It is worth noting that Li maintains a strong aversion to the language-centered modern Western philosophy and aesthetics. Certain Western Marxists or post-Marxists identify language as the very material form and substance of ideology, drawing on structuralist and poststructuralist notions. But in Li's theory, it is unclear what constitutes the mediating link between the material practice of productive labor and cultural formations, because materiality does not denote language or the process of signification in his notion of practice.

A difficulty arises, then, concerning the problem of representation. Zhu Guangqian had already broached the issue of mediation and signification in the 1960s, by proposing (and drawing on Henri Lefebvre's differentiation of *l'object present* and *l'object presenté*) a distinction between a "thing" (thing A) and the "image of a thing" (thing B) in aesthetic experience. "Thing A" is a natural object unrelated to human beings, whereas "thing B" is a socially and ideologically determined and mediated human perception.[61] Between the late 1970s and early 1980s the heated debate about "imaginary thinking" or "imagination" became a major event in the circles of literary and art criticism. The debate was essentially concerned with the issue of representation: the Chinese phrase *xingxiang siwei*, literally meaning "imaginary thinking" or "think in images," concisely summarized the search for new forms of literary and artistic representation that would free literature and the arts from the straitjacket of nonimaginative, formulaic "socialist realism." Zhu, then already more than eighty years old, was most energetic in the debate, promoting "imaginary thinking."[62]

Representation was also a major issue in the humanist Marxist protests against "alienation under socialism." The question of representation was brought to bear on the phenomenon of ideological alienation, referring to the Maoist hegemony that had turned a revolutionary theory into a quasi-religious dogma. Wang Ruoshui, an outspoken critic of socialist alienation, accused the Maoist ISA of manipulating of representation to cultivate Mao's personality cult. Invoking Marx's seminal semiotic analysis in *The Eighteenth Brumaire,* which stated that the small peasants "cannot represent themselves, they must be represented," Wang Ruoshui poignantly pointed out that in Mao's China, too, the peasants had to be represented by the "new masters," as Marx put it, "as an authority over them, as an unlimited governmental power that protects them against the other class and sends them rain and sunshine from above."[63]

The humanist Marxist upheavals in the early 1980s, reproved and crushed by the Party as "bourgeois spiritual pollution," brought the crisis of Maoist ideological representation into sharp relief. It reemerged as a central issue in the "Cultural Reflection" of the late 1980s, only to be registered on the other side of the problematic: representation was then less about installing new voices than about finding an audience not only responsive to but also constitutive of its new forms. Chinese aesthetic Marxism, and Li Zehou's theoretical formulations in particular, proved to be immensely successful in this regard. Li's "aesthetics of practical subjectivity" had captured the imagination of hundreds of thousands of young Chinese intellectuals. That his abstract philosophical monograph on Kant sold nearly one hundred thousand copies, inducing a "Kant Fever" of no small scale in

China's intellectual circles in the 1980s, cannot be explained as merely a result of interest in "theory." It is no coincidence that the Chinese aesthetic Marxists, Li in particular, played leading roles in this intellectual movement that signaled a watershed in China's cultural scene. Although Chinese aesthetic Marxism no longer has the centrality in China's intellectual scene it once enjoyed, the critical space and the momentum it created has had lasting impacts, not the least of which is the problematic that it formulated in the "Cultural Reflection." In the 1990s, the problematic of cultural transformation and reconstruction becomes more complicated as it must now confront capitalism in its current phase of transnational/flexible production, which inevitably involves China in a process of globalization that makes any self-sufficient, enclosed socialism meaningless.

That Li Zehou's original work has offered rich "symbolic capital" to an audience in need of spiritual nourishment is obvious enough; the point is that in Chinese aesthetic Marxists' undertakings lies the powerful appeal of their reinvention of Marxism, which not only unsettles the monolithic orthodoxy of Maoism but, more significantly, breeds a constructive alternative that is at once utopian and practical. In China at least, Marxism remains a vitally productive and positive discourse. Apart from being a predominantly critical theory of capitalism, Marxism in China can mean something positive and productive, against the Party's instrumentalization of Marxism as an ISA. This vocation, however, is socially and historically grounded, just as Marxism in the West today sees the critique of the postmodern condition, or "late capitalism," as both its historical occasion and mission. Since the strength of Marxism lies primarily in its fundamental conviction of the dynamic process of history as a totality, in which the economic, or the material practice of productive labor, is the ultimate determinant, it offers an epistemological horizon that confronts and counterposes the political, ideological, and intellectual fragmentations in the present world. Of course, in contemporary Marxism the homogenizing inclinations, especially with respect to the issues of race, gender, and nationhood, and other internal contradictions such as the culturalist tendencies in theorizing culture, must be rigorously confronted, too. It is the impassioned drive of seeking alternatives that has characterized the historical fortunes and misfortunes of diverse Marxist projects. As a self-conscious inquiry of alternative modernity, the vitality of Chinese aesthetic Marxism depends on its ability to insist on both its critical and constructive vision in this rapidly changing world, and to continue its searches for alternatives.

1  For a preliminary discussion of Marxist cultural and aesthetic theories in 1980s China, see Liu Kang, "Subjectivity, Marxism, and Culture Theory in China," *Social Text* 31/32 (spring–summer 1992): 114–140.

2  For a classic account of Western Marxism, see Perry Anderson, *Considerations on Western Marxism* (London: NLB, 1971); also see Fredric Jameson, *Marxism and Form* (Princeton, N.J.: Princeton University Press, 1971).

3  For an analysis of the ideological nature of the aesthetic concept from a Western Marxist perspective, see Terry Eagleton, *The Ideology of the Aesthetic* (Oxford: Basil Blackwell, 1990). Also see Josef Chytry, *The Aesthetic State: A Quest in Modern German Thought* (Berkeley: University of California Press, 1989); and J. M. Bernstein, *The Fate of Art: Aesthetic Alienation from Kant to Derrida and Adorno* (University Park: Pennsylvania State University Press, 1992).

4  Liang Qichao, *Yinbin shi heji* (Shanghai: Zhonghuan shuju, 1964), 176.

5  Cai Yuanpei, *Cai Yuanpei xuanji* (Beijing: Zhonghua shuju, 1963), 328.

6  Arif Dirlik, "Revolutionary Hegemony and the Language of Revolution: Chinese Socialism Between Present and Future," in *Marxism and the Chinese Experience*, ed. Arif Dirlik and Maurice Meisner (Armonk, N.Y.: M. E. Sharpe, 1989), 27.

7  For fuller accounts of Mao's revolutionary hegemony and cultural revolution, see Liu Kang, "The Problematics of Mao and Althusser: Dialectics, Alternative Modernity, and Cultural Revolution," *Rethinking Marxism* 8, no. 3 (1995): 1–25.

8  Zhu Guangqian (also known as K. C. Chu) was born in 1897 in Tongcheng, Anhui Province. He studied English at the University of Hong Kong, and in 1925 went to study in England and France. He received his Ph.D. in 1933 at the University of Strasbourg. Back in China the same year, he taught at many Chinese universities, and especially at Peking University, where he taught until his death in 1986. Criticism of Zhu Guangqian's idealism was part of an ongoing campaign in ideological and cultural realms. In 1955, shortly after the Korean War (1951–1953) ended, Hu Feng (1902–1985), an unorthodox Marxist literary theorist critical of Mao, was singled out for attack. Hu had outraged Mao with a direct critique of Maoist cultural policy. Mao, for his part, condemned Ha's literary theory of "subjective fighting spirit" and accused him of engaging in "counterrevolutionary activities." Hu Feng was imprisoned for over two decades and "rehabilitated" only in 1980. A significant casualty was Hu Feng's Marxist cultural theory that dealt with the issues of constructing an independent cultural space in a postrevolutionary society.

9  Zhu Guangqian, "Wode wenyi sixiang de fandong xing" [The reactionary aspects of my literary thoughts], in *Meixue wenti taolun ji* [Essays of the debate about aesthetic problems], vol. 1 (Beijing: Zuojia chubanshe, 1957), 1.

10  Ibid., 7.

11  Zhu Guangqian, "Zuozhe shuoming" (Author's note), in *Zhu Guangqian meixue wenji* [Collected aesthetic essays of Zhu Guangqian], vol. 1 (Shanghai: Shanghai wenyi chubanshe, 1982), 17.

12  Zhu Guangqian, "Keluoqi pai meixue de piping" [Critique of the Crocean school of aesthetics], in Zhu, *Collected aesthetic essays*, 1:165.

13  Ibid., 153.

14  Zhu, "Wode wenyi sixiang de fandong xing," 22.

15  For Li Dazhao's Marxism, see Maurice Meisner, *Li Ta-chao and the Origins of Chinese Marxism* (Cambridge: Harvard University Press, 1967).

16  For discussions of Maoism see Fredric Wakeman, *History and Will: Philosophical Perspectives of Mao Tse-tung's Thought* (Berkeley: University of California Press, 1973), and Maurice Meisner, *Marxism, Maoism, and Utopianism* (Madison: University of Wisconsin Press, 1982).

17  Mao's concepts of "contradiction" and "practice" have been subject to criticism by Chinese Marxists in the Post-Mao period (see Bill Brugger and David Kelly, *Chinese Marxism in the Post-Mao Era* [Stanford, Calif.: Stanford University Press, 1990]).

18  Hu Feng, "Zhishen zai wei minzhu de douzheng limian" [Situating ourselves in the struggle for democracy], in *Hu Feng pinglun ji* [A collection of Hu Feng's literary criticism], vol. 3 (Beijing: Renmin wenxue chubanshe, 1985), 17–22.

19  See Cai Yi, *Meixue lunzhu chubian* [Primary essays on aesthetics] (Shanghai: Shanghai wenyi chubanshe, 1982).

20  Li Zehou, "Mei de keguan xing he shehui xing—ping Zhu Guangqian, Cai Yi de meixue guan" [The objectivity and sociality of beauty—comments on the aesthetic views of Zhu Guangqian and Cai Yi], in *Meixue wenti taolun ji*, 2:31–45.

21  Zhu Guangqian, "Lun mei shi keguan yu zhuguan de tongyi" [On beauty as the unity of the subjective and objective], in *Meixue wenti taolun ji*, 3:26, emphasis in original.

22  Theodore Adorno, "Subject-Object," in *The Essential Frankfurt School Reader*, ed. Andrew Arato and Eike Gebhardt (New York: Urizen Books, 1978), 498–499.

23  Theodore Adorno, *Negative Dialectics*, trans. E. B. Ashton (New York: Pantheon, 1973), 181.

24  Adorno, "Subject-Object," 504.

25  Zhu, "Lun mei shi keguan yu zhuguan de tongyi," 28–29.

26  Herbert Marcuse, *The Aesthetic Dimension: Towards a Critique of Marxist Aesthetics* (Boston: Beacon, 1978), 3–6.

27  Ibid., 5.

28  For a brief discussion in English of the identity debate, see Brugger and Kelly, *Chinese Marxism*, 89–93. Also useful is Yang Xianzhen's own recol-

lection of the debate in his *Wo de zhexue "zui'an"* [My philosophical "criminal records"] (Beijing: Renmin chubanshe, 1981).

29  Fredric Jameson argues that Adorno's notion of "nonidentity" must be understood in connection with the form of economy: nonidentity is a refutation of money as exchange value that erases critical differences of social relationship (see Jameson, *Late Marxism: Adorno, or, The Persistence of the Dialectic* [London: Verso, 1990], 15–24).

30  Zhu Guangqian, "Meixue de xin guandian bu neng shi 'zhuguan yu keguan xiang fenlie' de guandian" [The new aesthetic view cannot be one of 'a split between subject and object'], in Zhu, *Collected Aesthetic Essays*, 3:312.

31  Gramsci's words are quoted from Terry Eagleton, *Ideology: An Introduction* (London: Verso, 1991), 121.

32  Adorno, "Subject-Object," 506.

33  Martin Jay, *Adorno* (Cambridge: Harvard University Press, 1984), 78.

34  Brugger and Kelly, *Chinese Marxism*, 119–138.

35  Karl Marx, "Theses on Feuerbach," in *Marx-Engels Reader*, ed. Robert C. Tucker, 2d ed. (New York: Norton, 1987), 107.

36  Ibid., 62.

37  Ibid., 75.

38  Zhu Guangqian, "Shengchan laodong yu ren dui shijie de yishu zhangwo— Makesi zhuyi meixue de shijian guandian" [Productive labor and man's artistic grasp of the world—the view of practice in Marxist aesthetics], in Zhu, *Collected Aesthetic Essays*, 3:290; emphasis in original.

39  Eagleton, *Ideology of the Aesthetic*, 196–234.

40  Li Zehou, *Meixue lunji* [Essays on aesthetics] (Shanghai: Shanghai wenyi chubanshe, 1980), 153–159.

41  Li Zehou, *Li Zehou zhexue meixue wenxuan* [Collected essays of philosophy and aesthetics by Li Zehou] (Changsha: Hunan renmin chubanshe, 1985), 464–465; emphasis in original.

42  Karl Marx, *Grundrisse*, trans. Martin Nicolaus, (Harmondsworth: Penguin, 1973), 541.

43  Eagleton, *Ideology of the Aesthetic*, 229–230.

44  Ibid., 208–209.

45  Li Zehou, *Pipan zhexue de pipan: Kande shuping* [A critique of critical philosophy: a study of Kant] (Beijing: Renmin chubanshe, 1979), 402–403.

46  Li Zehou, "Zhexue dawen lu" [Philosophical dialogues], in *Wo de zhexue tigang* [Outlines of my philosophy] (Taipei: Fengyun shidai chuban gongsi, 1990), 4–6.

47  Valentino Gerratana, "Althusser and Stalinism," *New Left Review* 101/102 (1977): 112.

48  Louis Althusser, "Ideology and Ideological State Apparatuses," in *Lenin and Philosophy and Other Essays*, trans. Ben Brewster (London: New Left Books, 1971), 182.

49  Zhu, "Lun mei shi keguan yu zhuguan de tongyi," 14.

50  Ibid.

51  Karl Marx and Frederick Engels, *The German Ideology*, ed. C. J. Arthur (New York: International Publishers, 1974), 47.

52  Zhu, "Lun mei shi keguan yu zhuguan de tongyi," 17.

53  Raymond Williams, *Marxism and Literature* (London: Oxford University Press, 1977), 121–128.

54  Marx, *Marx-Engels Reader,* 4.

55  Zhu Guangqian, *Xifang meixue shi* [A history of Western aesthetics], vol. 1 (Beijing: Renmin wenxue chubanshe, 1979), 18.

56  Ibid., 16–17.

57  Pierre Bourdieu, *Outline of a Theory of Practice* (Cambridge: Cambridge University Press, 1977).

58  Zhu Guangqian, "Lun mei shi keguan yu zhuguan de tongyi," 34.

59  Eagleton, *Ideology,* 18–20.

60  Ibid., 146.

61  Zhu Guangqian, "Lun mei shi keguan yu zhuguan de tongyi," 36–37.

62  See, for instance, Zhu Guangqian's conclusion of *A History of Western Aesthetics,* in which he applies "imaginary thinking" to the key problems of aesthetics.

63  Quoted in Brugger and Kelly, *Chinese Marxism,* 143.

The World Conception of Japanese Social Science:

The *Kōza* Faction, the Ōtsuka School, and the

Uno School of Economics

■ The influence of Marxism on the social sciences in Japan has been strong, especially when compared with the United States and Western Europe, and this is particularly so in economics. Until quite recently, the economics departments of top schools such as Tokyo University and Kyoto University were dominated by professors who taught Marxist economics rather than so-called modern economics (*kindai keizaigaku*)—by which is meant neoclassical and Keynesian economics—a term generally applied to differentiate postwar non-Marxian economists from their Marxist counterparts. Marxist scholars became a minority in economics departments in Japan only in the 1980s.

To understand the dominant influence of Marxism in the Japanese academic world during the past half-century, one must look to the history of the social sciences in Japan before 1945. When economics departments were established at the leading national universities in the 1920s, lecturers were recruited from the highest ranks of the bureaucracy and the business world. These new academics, who had studied government administration (*kokkagaku*, a neologism for the German *Staatslehre*) and national finance (*zaiseigaku*) in the law departments of Japan's major universities, tended to advocate ideas that were considered progressive for their time. Many were sent by the Education Ministry to conduct research in Germany, where they came into contact with the new theoretical developments in Marxism that followed

Hilferding's theory of finance capital. At the same time, a young labor union movement in Japan was experiencing a surge in strength in the wake of the Russian Revolution, and socially concerned scholars and students began to turn almost exclusively to Marxist thought in their exploration of the Japanese economy's various problems.

It was into this academic environment that *Nihon shihonshugi hattatsu shi kōza* [Symposium on the history of the development of Japanese capitalism, 1932] emerged, marking the high point of Japanese Marxist research in the prewar period. At the same time, however, a confrontation emerged within the Marxist world between those who supported the analysis presented in *Nihon shihonshugi hattatsu shi kōza* and those who did not. The debates between these two camps were eventually silenced by a military and a government that were expanding their war of aggression against China and strengthening their totalitarian system of power at home.

When freedom of speech and academic liberties were restored by the Occupation following World War II, Marxists resumed their earlier explorations. The incrimination of scholars who had played leading roles in the production of ideas supporting East Asia Co-Prosperity Sphere ideology, the institution of land reform, and the passage of laws to dismantle the *zaibatsu* during the Occupation seemed to bolster the analysis of Japanese political economy that earlier had been conducted by Marxist scholars. The prestige of Marxism, consequently, grew immensely, in both academia and society as a whole. Thus began the dominance of Marxism in postwar Japan, not only in economics but also in history, political science, and sociology.

Given the overwhelming academic and social influence of Marxism, how might we compare the developments in Marxist thought in Japan to those of Marxism in the United States and Western Europe? What independent theoretical developments, what autochthonous lines of analysis have emerged within Japanese Marxism? This essay will explore these questions, showing how scholars of the Japanese economy first focused solely on analysis of capitalism within national boundaries and later moved to developing theoretical frameworks for treating capitalism as one interconnected world system.

As we will see, some Marxist scholars actively cooperated in the war policies of the Japanese government and military, and some only feigned support while attempting to critique the prosecution of the war. The line between cooperation and criticism was often a fine one. Setting aside the entire issue of wartime scholars' culpability for the war, however, it is clear that in the course of the research conducted by Japanese Marxists under the extraordinary conditions of the war years, new perspectives were introduced to Marxist analysis that then gave impetus to the development of various new lines of theoretical exploration after the war. Whereas Japanese scholars had asserted the special nature of capitalism in Japan in comparison to capitalism in Western nations, before long they instead began to define Japanese capitalism in terms of its relation to a wider system of world capitalism. The new theories that followed from this global vision of capitalism in Japan share much in common with the dependency theories of Andre Gunder Frank and the world system analysis of Immanuel Wallerstein, yet are significant in that they nevertheless developed along independent lines.

## THE WORLD CONCEPTION OF BUNSEKI

What became known as the debates on Japanese capitalism began with the writings of Noro Eitarō and Inomata Tsunao in the late 1920s and, following the publication in 1932 of the earlier-mentioned *Nihon shihonshugi hattatsu shi kōza* (hereafter *Kōza*), soon flared into a hot dispute between the intellectuals who formed the *Kōza* faction (*Kōza-ha*) and those in the opposing *Rōnō* faction (*Rōnō-ha*). After raging for several years, the debates were stifled in the People's Front and the *Rōnō* Faction Professors' Group arrests in 1937 and 1938, which marked the end of free expression in prewar Japan. After the war, the debates on capitalism began again with the rebirth of Marxist social science in Japan. Most of the prewar participants also figured prominently in the postwar debates, and the issues they fought over were nearly identical to those that had been central to the battles of the 1930s. Although these renewed debates would become the basis for many later developments in postwar social science, we will not examine them in detail here, since they already have received generous attention.[1] Rather, in this section of the essay I would like to focus on the world conception (*sekai ninshiki*) held by intellectuals of the *Kōza* faction, an issue that has received almost no attention from those who have attempted to evaluate the historical significance of the debates on capitalism that took place in the 1930s. In particular, I will attempt to elucidate this world conception as it appears in Yamada Moritarō's *Nihon shihonshugi bunseki* [An analysis of Japanese capitalism; hereafter *Bunseki*].[2]

The points of debate were many in the disputes that erupted following the publication of *Kōza*. The question of how to interpret the structure of Japanese capitalism, which at its base consisted of a broad layer of small-scale tenant farmers paying extraordinarily high land rents, was one point of sharp contention. As is well known, *Kōza* faction writers believed that a refeudalized system of social relations took shape during the Meiji period, and they blamed high land rents on these feudal (i.e., extra-economic) factors. In contrast, *Rōnō* faction writers believed that the land rent system had become modern when restrictions on the buying and selling of land were ended after the Meiji Restoration (1868). They thought that high land rents could be explained by high levels of demand. Beyond this issue, there was the problem of defining the nature of the Meiji Restoration itself, the starting point of capitalism in Japan. Specifically, writers sharply debated whether the Meiji Restoration was a bourgeois revolution or whether it represented the reorganization of absolutism, an issue that continues to be a point of contention even today. The strategies by which Marxists hoped to bring about social revolution were influenced by the ways they interpreted current conditions. The ways Marxists defined the Meiji Restoration and the capitalist society that was born of that event, therefore, directly affected whether they believed that a socialist revolution was immediately possible or that a bourgeois revolution would first be required. Marxists also debated more detailed questions, such as whether Japanese industry during the end of the Tokugawa period (1603–1867) had reached the manufacturing stage of development in the strict sense of the word. In these and many other related debates, the real battle between the opposing *Kōza* and *Rōnō* factions was always over defining the overall structure of Japanese capitalism. Yamada Moritarō's *Bunseki*, which succinctly described the overall organization of capitalism in Japan, would become the focus of this battle.

In *Bunseki*, Yamada tries to "concretize theories of reproduction in Japanese capitalism."[3] His analysis is based on his unique vision of Marx's theory of the schema of reproduction, which consisted of a sector in which production of commodities for production took place (that is, a capital-goods production sector, dubbed Sector I) and a sector in which the production of commodities for consumption took place (Sector II). Yamada believed that the organization of capitalism within any given country could be understood by analyzing the formation of the various industries involved in each of these two sectors. He argued that once a certain level of development had been attained in the relation between the values of Sector I and Sector II within any given country ($\text{I.v} + \text{s} = \text{II.c}$ and the relations of accumulation), then the capitalist system within that country would theoretically have reached

a certain coherent completion.[4] In Japan, these processes were established during the fourth decade of the Meiji period (between 1897
and 1907), and they determined the pattern in which Japanese capitalism would develop thereafter. During that ten-year period, the Japanese model of capitalism became one in which a highly industrial,
militarist-monopolist sector stood atop an economic foundation consisting of semi-feudal land ownership and a semi-serflike pattern of
petty farming.

During the same period, capitalism in other countries around the
world became increasingly characterized by imperialism. Inextricably
implicated in this global shift, the process of industrial capital formation in Japan was instantly transformed into an imperialist process in
which industrial capital formation manifested itself as finance capital.
Unlike the usual interpretation of imperialism, which had been based
on the idea of overaccumulation and bank control of investment capital, Yamada treated imperialism and finance capital in terms of their
relation to the process of reproduction. As the scale of capital circulation increased in any given country, Yamada argued, a stable, complete
system of economic circulation could no longer be sustained. This led
to the search for colonial areas through which a new, complete system of capital circulation was successfully reestablished, only now in
an expanded region beyond the borders of the former domestic economy. Yamada believed that the imperialist partitioning of the globe at
work in the Boer War was an example of just such expanding systems
of capital circulation.

The decade between 1897 and 1907, which Yamada saw as the formative period of Japanese capitalism, was roughly delimited by the
first Sino-Japanese War at the beginning and the Russo-Japanese War
at the end. With its victory in the Sino-Japanese War, Japan acquired
Korea and Taiwan, as well as Chinese cities such as Shanghai and Nan-
jing as markets for its spinning-mill exports. It also secured steel supplies from the mainland. The establishment of the Yahata steelworks,
which processed this steel using domestic coal, marked the beginning
of modern steel production in Japan. Victory in the Russo-Japanese
War then gave Japan control over the Manchurian market and enabled
it to secure access to the coal and steel of northern Korea, both of which
had a defining effect on the establishment of the capital-goods sector (Sector I) of the Japanese economy. With each victory in war, new
economic benefits redounded to Japan. It is surely to this history that
Yamada referred when he stated that the formation of Japanese industrial capital occurred simultaneously with the emergence of imperial-

ism, and concluded that the pattern of reproduction that took shape during this period determined the nature of economic development in Japan thereafter.

We must also note the relation that Yamada saw between absolutism and the particular pattern of Japanese capitalism. To ensure that Japan would not become a colony of one of the capitalist powers, the Meiji government set out to construct a modern economy. The only means by which the authorities could secure the resources required for this undertaking was the levying of a tax on land. Following the institution of a national land tax, land rents became so high that they absorbed the labor power required to ensure the subsistence of farmers. Yamada argued that the result was the reemergence of the landlord and tenancy system. In response to these conditions, resistance movements, such as the Freedom and People's Rights Movement (*Jiyū minken undō*), and revolts by former samurai (*shizoku*) followed in quick succession. To safeguard their modernization strategy, however, the Restoration government wielded absolute power to suppress the masses. Both domestically and externally, then, great emphasis was placed on the maintenance of order, through either military or police organs. And capitalism in Japan, argued Yamada, formed in such a pattern that the feudal relations that were allowed to develop by the Meiji authorities came to determine the shape in which capitalist industry took shape.

It should not escape our attention that the sort of Japanese capitalism described by Yamada is quite similar to the standard image of Russian capitalism before the 1917 revolution. In the Russian case, a peculiar militarist-feudalistic capitalist system developed in which an advanced monopolistic capitalist structure rested atop both a vast system of mir and labor relations that were a vestige of the serf system. The peculiar characteristics of capitalism in Japan and in Russia before the revolution, therefore, clearly had much in common.[5]

Returning to the world conception of *Bunseki*, we must now touch on the relation between Yamada's vision of the structure of Japanese capitalism and the Comintern's *1932 Thesis*. As has been frequently noted, a number of conceptual differences exist between the Comintern's *1932 Thesis* and its earlier *1927 Thesis* and, accordingly, between the revolutionary strategies stressed in each. In the period between the release of these two works, Japan's continental strategy of aggression became clear to all, first with the advance on Shandong in 1927, followed by the eruption of the Manchurian Incident in September 1931. The Comintern's changing analysis of Japan clearly reflected recent events in China. Whereas the 1927 *Thesis* was concerned with the rapid growth of capitalism, the concentration of finance capital, and the new power of large industrial concerns in post–World War I Japan, the 1932 *Thesis*, written after the Manchurian Incident, stressed the absolutist rule in Japan of the bourgeoisie, which it said was represented by the landlord-supported emperor system. In fact, the 1932 *Thesis* begins with these words in regard to Japan: "The thieving war unleashed by Japanese imperialism has thrown the popular masses into a new historical crisis." It continues: "The occupation of Manchuria, the bloody incidents in Shanghai and in assorted other locations in China, and in general all of the militaristic activities plotted by Japan's thieving imperialism represent the first militaristic advances of a vast plan by the large imperialist powers suffering under the current depression."[6]

The result of the aggressive continental expansion of Japanese imperialism was the development of "an extraordinarily complicated international situation," claimed the 1932 *Thesis*, in which "the great imperial powers planned to construct a united front to wage war against the Soviet Union." Specifically, argued the 1932 *Thesis*, the world powers were working to achieve this plan by launching assaults "from the Far East by means of Japanese imperialism" and assaults "from the West by France and its dependent countries." This situation meant that the Japanese proletariat carried "the highest responsibility" to fulfill its pivotal role in the battle against imperialism.[7] The external war being waged by Japan was exacerbating the opposition between the Japanese classes. The Japanese proletariat and its vanguard had a duty to tie the antiwar struggle of the workers to the struggle for daily survival of all laborers and farmers, the 1932 *Thesis* argued: "The proletariat must combine its fight against the war with its own economic struggle, with the fight against its total enslavement. Its duty is to cause the revolutionary overthrow of the bourgeois- and the landlord-supported emperor system by turning the imperialist war abroad into an internal rebellion."[8]

The 1932 *Thesis* called for a revolution, then, that would topple the Japanese ruling structure, which it described as a plundering capitalist system consisting of *zaibatsu* (large industrial and financial conglomerates), a semi-feudal system of land ownership, and the absolutist, bourgeois rule of the landlord-supported emperor system.

But there the parallels between *Bunseki* and the 1932 *Thesis* end. Unlike *Bunseki*, the 1932 *Thesis* includes analysis of the tensions in the international system. Its opening discusses the formation by the imperialist powers of a united front against the Soviet Union and describes the struggle between what it saw as a rotting capitalism and a prosperous socialism. It also points out the oppositions between the imperialist powers themselves, especially the rivalry among Japan, England, and the United States over control of China. It portrays the ways in which the imperialist countries strove to carve up world markets into areas of monopoly control, describes the mutual frustration of each other's global designs, and links Japanese imperialist activity to this international contest.

*Bunseki,* on the other hand, reveals very little concern with the world system as such. It ignores the interrelations within the imperialist world economy between the capitalisms of England, France, Germany, the former Russia, and the United States, the countries that Yamada uses as models for analyzing the special characteristics of Japanese capitalism.

A look at his writings after World War II, however, seems to indicate that the later Yamada did not completely lack a vision of the wider, international economic relations between the various capitalist countries. After the war, he noted, for example, an interest in understanding "the disruption of world economic flows during World War II,"[9] a comment significant for its emphasis on the traffic between nations rather than on the discrete economic circulations occurring within individual national economies. He argued in these postwar writings that the logic of imperialism meant that the reproduction process of each capitalist country had developed within the international framework of colonialism. That is, the overall economic process, which revolved around the relationship described by the formula $I.v + m = II.c$ (the process of accumulation), was governed by "the characteristic domestic process of capital expansion in which labor and capital stand opposed"; at the same time, however, this economic process "had to be supplemented by the surplus returns gained through colonial holdings and the exploitation of subject laborers." This possession of colonial lands to augment domestic capital formation was the hallmark of the prewar period, when Japanese capitalism acquired Korea and Taiwan and, "in addition to attempting to manage the supply and demand of rice in Japan by importing roughly 15 million koku from those two areas, controlled iron and coal production in Korea as well as the sugar supply in Taiwan."[10]

Here is at least one example of Yamada extending his analysis of capitalism beyond the boundaries of the nation. Yet how far beyond Yamada's prewar theory of reproduction *within* national boundaries did this postwar idea of extra-national economic circulation really go?

Although he pays lip service to a new world vision of capital circulation, Yamada's analysis, in reality, never develops beyond the comment that "once the imperialist-capitalist nations reached the appropriate stage of development, they entered into relations with each other characterized by an international division of labor that then determined the patterns of worldwide economic circulation."[11] Yamada was making this argument in 1966, after the expansion of the Soviet Union and the Eastern bloc following the end of World War II, by which time most former colonies had already gained independence, when it seemed that democratic forces were faltering in most advanced countries, and when postwar recovery and high growth were underway. He was well aware, therefore, that, given the hegemony of the United States in the capitalist world, imperialist confrontations between capitalist nations over monopoly control of world markets were ending. Under these radically different world conditions, one would have expected that Yamada's vision of capitalism and the confrontations within the capitalist world system would have undergone significant change. Yet, although a new concern with economic circulation in world perspective is not entirely absent in his postwar writings, Yamada's fundamental approach remained unchanged from that of his work in the prewar period. Because Yamada's analysis in the postwar period continued to be rooted in an idea of a unitary structure of capitalist reproduction within each individual country, his treatment of the relation between capitalism in Japan and capitalism in other nations is forever abstract. His writings on postwar developments indicate that he believed that the root cause of Japanese economic recovery and growth was the development of a process that he dubbed "re–primitive accumulation" (saihan genchiku). Yamada pointed out that while wages and prices in March 1946 were five and ten times higher, respectively, than the prewar benchmarks, they rose to twenty-seven and sixty-five times higher in response to the new wage and price system of July 1947. He argues that the controls that held wages so far below rising prices were evidence that it was "inevitable" that the postwar economy "would redevelop as a system of monopoly capital."[12] At the same time, Yamada noted, this postwar phenomenon also meant that the reemergence of monopoly capital in Japan was linked to monopoly capitalism in the United States. Yet although Japanese postwar recovery was unarguably aided by U.S. assistance, Yamada never concretely explains his understanding of the connection between reaccumulation in Japan and U.S. monopoly capital. Yamada's idea of the schema of reproduction was effective in elucidating the capitalist system within Japan, but was deficient as an approach to understanding the world economy as a whole.

## JAPANESE MARXISTS AND THE EAST ASIA CO-PROSPERITY SPHERE

Having explored *Bunseki*'s vision of the processes of world history, I will examine in the following two sections of this essay the ways in which the world conception represented in *Bunseki* informed the ideas expressed by *Kōza* faction academics in two later debates. After government suppression silenced the debates on capitalism in the late 1930s, many former *Kōza* faction academics helped produce reports on the material resources problem of the Greater East Asia Co-Prosperity Sphere, as members of the East Asia Research Institute (Tōa Kenkyūjo) and related organizations. The approaches *Kōza* faction writers took to the economic problems of the Co-Prosperity Sphere were often shaped by the vision of the global system that had been described in *Bunseki*. Then after the war, the social sciences in Japan turned to the problem of the third world, a topic we will examine in the third section of this essay. Here again, I believe that the vision of the world system in *Bunseki* found expression in *Kōza* faction studies on this issue as well.

The Communist Academy Incident of 1936, with its mass arrests of intellectuals, was one of the events that marked the end of the prewar debates on capitalism. In the wake of the publication of *Kōza*, its editors, Yamada Moritaro and Hirano Yoshitaro, and contributing writers, such as Kobayashi Ryosei and Aikawa Haruki, continued their research into the feudal character of Japanese society and made plans to release a study titled *Nihon hōkensei kōza* [Symposium on the Japanese feudal system], forming a collaborative research group toward that end. These scholars engaged not only in academic research but also in activities like those carried out in the Communist Academy in the Soviet Union, studying Communist Party strategies and tactics.[13] In response, the authorities charged the scholars associated with the new project with subverting the Peace Preservation Law and arrested them. The scholars rounded up in the *Rōnō* Faction Professors' Group Incident of 1938 were not engaged in activities such as those of the members of the *Nihon hōkensei kōza*. In fact, they were first categorized by the authorities as an anti–Communist Party group and later as members of the legal left wing. Their eventual arrest was described by the authorities as a move intended to prevent the group from engaging in potential future socialist activities.[14]

Despite the suppression of the scholars, the indictments of members of the *Nihon hōkensei kōza,* including Hirano Yoshitaro and Aikawa Haruki, were set aside, and academics such as Uno Kōzō, arrested in the second *Rōnō* Faction Professors' Group Incident of 1938, were found not guilty and set free. Still, those released did not return to their former university positions.

With the beginning of the Sino-Japanese War, Japanese expectations of war with the United States and England rose. The Japanese government began to make plans for a wider conflict by establishing numerous research organizations to investigate Japan's material-resources supply problem. The South Manchurian Railway Research Bureau is one such organization that is well known; others included the East Asia Research Institute, set up under the Planning Agency, and the Pacific Cooperation Council (Taiheiyō Kyōkai), of which Hirano Yoshitarō was a member. The vast organization of the East Asia Research Institute conducted research on all of Asia, including not only China but also the Soviet Union, the Middle East, and Southeast Asia. Topics ranged from the natural sciences to society, economics, and politics, and extensive projects were also commissioned by outside organizations. Not only did the planning section of the Pacific Cooperation Council conduct research and "formulate relevant proposals both for domestic and foreign measures by which to achieve national aims in the Pacific,"[15] it even dispatched national goodwill missions overseas. The scholars who had lost their jobs in the Communist Academy (Komu Akademi) and the *Rōnō* Faction Professors' Group Incidents became members of these very national policy and research organizations in various capacities.

In their new positions, these scholars underwent a dramatic shift —from formulating theories and practical strategies for overturning what they saw as a militaristic, semifeudal ruling system to conducting national policy research for the prosecution of an imperialist war. In fact, the release by the authorities of those who had been charged with violating the Peace Preservation Law was not unrelated to their political apostasies (*tenkō*). Early in the postwar period, the war responsibility of those implicated in the work of the national policy research organizations became an issue of debate. Those who came under scrutiny attempted to disown any links to research groups perceived as having cooperated in the war effort.

Because in many ways the foundation of postwar research on Asia (*Ajia kenkyū*) had been laid in the studies conducted in national policy research organizations during the war, I now would like to turn to the framework of analysis and the world conception that can be found in that wartime research. From a Marxist perspective, the Greater East Asia Co-Prosperity Sphere was an attempt by Japanese imperialism to redivide the East Asian colonial holdings of the imperialist powers, particularly of England and the United States. But former Marxists working within the national research organizations could not, of course, describe the war in such overt terms. Even in the introduction to an otherwise objective analysis of the Chinese spinning industry, for example, a Marxist scholar then conducting research in a national agency felt obliged to insert language that painted a benign picture of the Greater East Asia Co-Prosperity Sphere.

Because the pressure to lend support to official expansionary policies was so great, those scholars who did attempt to express subversive opinions in the context of their national policy research took great risks. In *Busshitsu senryaku to gaikō seisaku* [Material resources strategy and diplomatic policy], Gushima Kensaburō, a member of the Manchurian Railroad Research Bureau, investigated the ability of the nations of the world to supply the materials necessary for modern total war. He argued that if Japan, Germany, and Italy were to enter a confrontation with the world powers, they would suffer material resource shortages. From a purely military perspective, it would be disadvantageous for Japan to join the Axis countries. He also pointed out the limits that this reality imposed on Japan's potential diplomatic policies. Although these were dangerous opinions, Gushima was not arrested, only because more than likely the military did not fully grasp the importance of what he had argued.[16] Yet even if we allow that there were instances in which men such as Gushima resisted the militarists, the mere fact that scholars held official positions within these national policy organizations meant that they, in effect, played a role in supporting the system.

However, the issue of culpability in the production of wartime ideology remains an ambiguous one. These intellectuals, in fact, played a range of roles within the Japanese system, from resistance carried out under the political protection offered by *tenkō* to support by those such as Hirano Yoshitarō who exhibited a positive commitment to the Japanese system and to the Greater East Asia Co-Prosperity Sphere. Under these conditions, scholars who previously had studied capitalism within the Japanese context alone now were forced to extend their sights to East Asia and the Western Pacific. How were their conceptions of the world affected?

Yamada Moritarō's "Shina inasaku no konpon meidai" [Thesis on the basis of rice cultivation in China], which appeared in *Tōa kenkyūjo hō* [Report of the East Asia Research Institute], begins: "Given current international tensions and the steadfast posture of the Japanese people, both of which are fueling the creation of the Greater East Asia Co-Prosperity Sphere, it is time to reflect on the state of Japanese agricultural science and rice cultivation technology. We have a great responsibility to fulfill positive leadership role over Chinese agriculture."[17]

Yamada argued that the success of the East Asia Co-Prosperity Sphere depended on whether or not Japan could successfully assume leadership for increasing the technological level of Chinese agriculture. But he also warned that there was a risk that Chinese agriculture might achieve increased productivity independent of Japanese guidance: "If scientific methods were to be successfully applied under Chinese leadership alone, then the future of Chinese agriculture would take a path independent of Japan altogether."[18]

The remainder of the "Thesis on the Basis of Rice Cultivation in China" consists mainly of detailed analysis of the many tables of statistics appearing in *Bunseki*. Yamada begins his argument by pointing out that rice production in China was 65 percent of Japanese domestic yields. This meant that Chinese agriculture yields per equivalent unit of land at the time that Yamada was writing only equaled those in Japan roughly at the end of the Tokugawa era (1603–1867). Yields in Korea and Taiwan surpassed those in China, but those achieved by native agricultural practices before the introduction of advanced techniques by the Japanese were far below the level achieved in Japan around the end of the Tokugawa period and the beginning of the Meiji period.

Yamada then compared the income levels of Chinese and Japanese farmers. Although their yields were two-thirds of those of Japanese farmers, the average wet-paddy rice farming family in China at the time earned only 42 yen per year, compared to 228 yen per year for a family in Japan, or a mere 18 percent of the Japanese average. "It is impossible to ignore the destitution of Chinese farming families," wrote Yamada. Given these conditions, Yamada went on to make two additional points. First, because it was difficult for Chinese families to survive independently, familial relations based on powerful, primordial blood bonds formed the basis of farming life; second, there were huge numbers of coolies and transients who existed outside of the village system.[19] Yamada believed that these conditions in China were caused by technical deficiencies in seed stock and growing methods.

Yamada's presentation makes the case that Japanese technical assistance and leadership were required in Chinese agriculture. Yamada argued that compared to Japanese agriculture, which had recovered from depression and become strong and stable through a process in which a new type of appropriately sized farm holdings had emerged, Chinese agriculture was unstable, characterized by frequent financial ruin even among prosperous and middle-level farmers. Yamada had struck quite a different note only ten years earlier in *Bunseki,* however, when he described the Japanese system of semi-slave and petty farming as one in which "there is opportunity neither for independent farmers nor for the category of small farmers" to develop and in which "middling farmers themselves become like semi-slaves, falling into destitution."[20] Since Yamada carried over his later, positive view of Japanese agriculture into postwar works such as *Nōchi kaikaku tenmatsu gaiyō* [A detailed overview of land reform], it is evident that this shift from his earlier views was not made to comply with wartime national policy orthodoxies. Rather, Yamada simply was applying his own honest interpretation of the facts at the time.

Now, how did Yamada explain the fact that Chinese agriculture was so unstable that "farming [there] was characterized by the decline of wealthy and middle-level farmers, the backbone of the farming class,"[21] while in Japan the nucleus of the farming classes consisted of households farming one to three hectares of land, a structure which provided a firm foundation to farming society? And why were tenant rates lower in China than in Japan? According to Yamada, the reasons were to be found in the differences in the distribution of wealthy, middle-level, and petty farmers within the social structure of the countryside in each country. Many local patterns existed in China, of course, and some were similar to the Japanese case. Yet, in general, unlike in Japan, where neither very large nor very small holdings existed, but medium-sized farming operations were the norm, in China the large operations of wealthy farmers, who owned many draft animals and kept many indentured servants, were surrounded by vast numbers of poor and tenant farmers.[22] Individual farm holdings were generally being reorganized downward into a greater number of smaller holdings; medium-sized farms were not able to survive. The source of the instability of Chinese agriculture, then, was this overall downward trend toward ever smaller farm holdings. For Yamada, this meant that if Japanese agricultural science were to take responsibility for reforming Chinese rice farming practices, it would have to introduce not only technical guidance but also measures to confront this imbalance in the social structure of the countryside.

Uchida Yoshihiko, another scholar whose research appeared in the *Tōa kenkyūjo hō* [Report of the East Asia Research Institute], is also of interest to us here, precisely because he knew Yamada's theories better than anyone else. Running throughout his essay "Marai no kome" [Rice in Malaysia] is a concern with determining how self-sufficiency in rice production might be achieved in that country.

Rice, along with rubber and coconuts, was one of Malaysia's three most important products. While rubber and coconuts were "global products that played a significant role in the world economy," Malaysian rice was not.[23] Nor was it a major crop in terms of area of land under cultivation: the acreage of rice land was surpassed by that of rubber in Malaysia. If "the issue of how to increase the fighting strength of East Asia so that it might achieve autonomy," as Hirano Yoshitarō put it, was at heart a problem of material resources acquisition, then Malaysian rice did not figure as an important crop.[24] But Uchida points out that, considered from the perspective of the political and economic administration of Malaysia, rice was decidedly important. First, rice was a staple of the diet of all Malaysia's inhabitants, and nearly two-thirds of the rice required to fill this need had to be imported. Second, even though rice production was not significant in terms of its role in the Malaysian economy as a whole, from the point of view of Malay-asians themselves, it remained centrally important. This second point relates to the structure of the economy that emerged as Malaysia was developed as a source of raw materials under British imperialism.

According to Uchida:

Colonial raw materials industries such as tin, coconuts, and especially rubber operated outside of the traditional Malaysian economy of self-sufficiency, and as these were rapidly developed they soon formed the basis of the entire Malaysian economy. This stimulated the immigration of a vast new class of laborers who worked in these foreign-imposed industries (and the immigration of the workers in the industries required to support this colonial industrial labor force). These population shifts in turn spawned new demand for rice. The development of traditional rice cultivation in Malaysia before colonialization was slow, and it could not meet these new levels of demand.[25]

As a result of the inflow of Chinese and Indian workers brought by the colonial monoculturization of Malaysian society, over half of Malaysian inhabitants were immigrants. This problem was complicated by the fact that rice cultivation was carried out not by the immigrants but by Malaysians themselves. At the time that Uchida Yoshi-hiko wrote his report, only 35 percent of the rice consumed in Malaysia was domestically grown, with the rest imported from Thailand and elsewhere. This situation could be seen as a natural result of Malaysia's development as a colonial source of raw materials. But the problem did not end there. In fact, "during normal times, the supply of rice was supplemented by imports of cheap foreign rice, which were financed by the receipts derived from exports of rubber and other products." During economic downturns or wars, however, Uchida pointed out, this arrangement became unstable: "During economic recession, export industries stagnate[d], and the rice imports necessary to support the workers employed in those industries place[d] severe pressure on the Malaysian economy. During wartime, rice imports [were] disturbed either for political reasons or because sufficient shipping [was] not available for transport."[26] Within the old British colonial government, there were two competing visions with respect to the balance-of-payments problem: One favored a laissez-faire policy toward rice imports, and the other a policy that aimed to achieve self-sufficiency in rice production. With the onset of depression in 1931, the government instituted a positive policy to increase domestic production of rice, while in 1933 an import tariff was levied on rice, only to be ended a year and a half later. Such policy shifts stemmed from the fundamental difficulty of finding a suitable solution to the balance-of-payments problem. Uchida pointed out that policies such as these, which only tinkered around the edges of the problem, would bring no lasting resolution: "A solution to the problem [could] not be found without to some extent changing Malaysia's position as a colony for raw materials production."[27]

Even if the language in the research Yamada Moritarō and Uchida Yoshihiko conducted as members of national policy institutions potentially may have lent support to the Greater East Asia Co-Prosperity Sphere, one must still credit these scholars for their strong grasp of economic conditions. And as Ogura Toshimaru has argued, one must not forget that the wartime criticism of American and British imperialism, exploitation, and racism by apostate former Marxist scholars was, in fact, often based on Marxist critiques of imperialism. Of course, in levying their critiques, these scholars also made nationalist claims that Japan's Greater East Asia Co-Prosperity Sphere was different from the imperialism of England and the United States. These arguments, moreover, functioned to legitimize Japan's control of East Asia. Yamada Moritarō and Uchida Yoshihiko did, in effect, then, support Japanese policies in East Asia through their research, although this was not their intention. On the other hand, the works produced by Hirano Yoshitarō—who had been a central figure in the *Kōza* group of intellectuals—while he was at the Pacific Cooperation Council represented genuine, active support of Co-Prosperity Sphere goals. During his time at the Pacific Cooperation Council, Hirano had become a Pan-Asianism ideologue. I will not trace here the path Hirano took in his shift from *Nihon shihonshugi shakai no kikō* [The structure of Japanese capitalist society] to his later *Dai Aziashugi no rekishiteki kiso* [The historical basis of Pan-Asianism]. Rather, I wish to examine how Hirano's research, although it constituted only one small part of national wartime planning, nevertheless contributed to Co-Prosperity Sphere ideology.

Hirano's work reveals just how it was that agricultural studies such as those by Yamada and Uchida could be used to legitimize the idea of a Greater East Asia under Japanese rule. For Hirano, "constructing a Greater East Asian sphere meant that the people of Asia would create an organically united military, economic, and cultural system centered around Japan." And he believed that the foundation of just such a system already existed in the form of "rice cultivation based on paddy irrigation and family-based intensive growing operations, which both constitute[d] the East Asian agricultural system." This East Asian system "fundamentally differ[ed]" from the agricultural practices at the heart of the economic structures of Europe and the United States. Of course, the East Asia Co-Prosperity Sphere encompassed a wide area, and no single form of agriculture prevailed throughout. In addition to rice cultivation, there was the upland dry-field cultivation of barley and other less important grains in the northern part of the continent, "the backward, petty subsistence stick-hoe farming of native peoples in tropical areas," and the farming practices that resulted from "colonial agricultural institutions operated by white capital and colored labor." Wet-paddy rice cultivation, however, Hirano argued, still represented the main agricultural system in East Asia. It subsumed the other two patterns of cultivation within the region and provided an organic structure to East Asian agriculture in general.[28]

Hirano believed that agriculture in East Asia should move in the direction of the medium-sized farms that we earlier saw Yamada Moritarō argued had developed during the process of Japan's emergence from the depression in the first half of the 1930s and that were closely connected to values of familialism and communal co-operatism. Hirano wrote:

In contrast to the East Asian agricultural development policies carried out by Europe and the United States, which relied solely on exploitation by capitalist corporations, and that of the Soviet Union, which attempted to carry out land reform based solely on a concern with the poorest class of farmers, Japan's East Asian agricultural policy focuses on nurturing the middle-level class of farmers in an attempt to promote the overall development of the countryside.[29]

Hirano further offered a concrete proposal to support the middle-class farmers not by land reform but by "a land policy aimed at returning absentee landlords to their farms . . . reforms to rationalize distribution networks through cooperative unions and collaborative corporations," and "reforms to establish a technological foundation for middle-level farming and communal cooperatism."[30] These proposals marked a significant retreat from the reforms earlier advocated by *Kōza* faction scholars. At the same time, it was clear that Hirano was also inspired by ideas on agricultural policy that had been expressed in the Soviet Union, when the prospects for constructing a socialist society still seemed bright.

The influence of Soviet policies on Hirano's thinking becomes clear when we examine his proposals for East Asian agricultural policy in more detail. He speaks of the necessity for national assistance in the installation of irrigation systems and of raising agricultural productivity in the northern continent by establishing scientific, large-scale mechanized farming techniques in strategic locations, in parallel with measures to more generally establish farming by animal power. He also asserts that in tropical areas, where British and U.S. capital had previously developed monoculture agriculture, Japanese profit-based enterprises that had been reconfigured to operate under a planning control system should be utilized both to fortify East Asian wartime strength and to secure a dominant position in the world economy. Hirano hoped to institute Soviet-style collective farming practices in the areas captured by Japan early in the war.

In Hirano's case, these arguments for an East Asian agricultural policy were not merely formal expressions of support for national wartime policy that masked some underlying resistance. Hirano held that scientifically mechanized agriculture and planned control were essentially distinct from the modern experience of Western Europe and properly belonged to the East Asian version of modernity, which would, in the end, become the dominant model. How did Hirano reach the conclusion that the East Asian model of the modern would gain eventual supremacy? He bases his argument on the idea that the unity of East Asian society could be found in the village communitarianism (*kyōdō shakai*) that was born of the necessity for flood control and irrigation systems in the cultivation of wet-paddy rice. Familial groups gave form to a social system of local villages tied to each other by regional bonds, and they fostered a communitarian spirit, constituting a society of local self-governance. Hirano acknowledged that throughout the various countries of East Asia one could find a wide range of local practices. Nevertheless, he argued, at their heart all societies in East Asia were based not on contracts or individual rights and responsibilities but on the pursuit of common benefits brought by a social solidarity that was forged in a spirit of communitarianism and mutual support. According to Hirano, because of these distinct characteristics, East Asian society would win out over Western European society. The recent changes witnessed in this essential East Asian society, Hirano said, had been caused by the penetration of the modern economy based on a Western model. He argued that this dominance of a Western-style modern economy had to be stopped before "individualism became firmly established" even in East Asia.[31]

Yet earlier, in an article titled "Burujoa minshushugishi" [Bourgeois democracy] that appeared in *Nihon shihonshugi shakai no kikō*, Hirano had written in regard to the historical significance of the French Revolution: "The citizen's revolution restored the autonomous individual as the basis of a society of citizens by excising the ruling class of the old order and by reforming national institutions, which had been based on the profit of the remote feudal-lord minority."[32] Hirano's idea of the world historical significance of the autonomous individual as a modern citizen had undergone a 180-degree shift by the time he made his arguments for a shared East Asian heritage of communitarianism and collective responsibility. Not only did his position on the autonomous individual change, so, too, did his position on the emperor system. While in his earlier *Nihon shihonshugi shakai no kikō* Hirano had castigated the emperor system (*tennōsei*) as an absolutist power system, in his *Dai Ajiashugi no rekishiteki kiso* of 1945 he positively praised "the epochal significance of the Meiji Restoration for all the peoples of East Asia" and "the movement in Japan for an independent constitution."[33]

Unlike the work of Hirano, the studies of Chinese and Malaysian rice cultivation by Yamada Moritar and Uchida Yoshihiko did not represent a complete turn away from the positions they took in *Kōza*. Contrary to the intentions of the authors, however, those studies were believed to have represented a positive expression of Greater East Asia Co-Prosperity Sphere ideology.

## THE ŌTSUKA SCHOOL AND THE THIRD WORLD

In July 1965, *Shisō no kagaku* [The science of thought] ran a special edition, "Social Science Thought," that included an article entitled "Sengo shakai kagaku jūyō bunken nenpyō" [Time line of the important literature of postwar social science]. Looking at this time line today, one is first surprised by the fact that almost all of the works listed are about the politics, economics, and society of Japan: none deal with the world in a global perspective. Of course, separate studies appeared on various foreign topics, such as modern German politics or the diplomacy of the United States. But these, too, fail to include a truly world perspective.

Surely one explanation for this almost singular focus on recent Japanese history in the postwar period can be found in the Cold War. The division of the world into two spheres of power must have played a significant role in turning the perspective of the social sciences in Japan inward. The most important reason for the directions the social sciences in Japan took, however, was that research had resumed after the war by returning to the old debates on Japanese capitalism that earlier had been suspended by official repression. With the opposing camps of the *Kōza* faction and *Rōnō* faction again facing off against each other, these debates were reopened along lines more or less similar to their prewar antecedents.

But new lines of thinking began to take shape on both sides as well. Within the *Kōza* faction there was a concern with interpreting the meaning of the occupation of Japan and of the dependent relationship of Japanese society to the United States. Those who gained influence in the *Rōnō* faction wanted to restructure Marxist economics along the lines of the three levels of analysis—*sandankairon:* pure theory, stage theory, and analysis of history—advocated by Uno Kōzō. Other schools of thought related to the debates on capitalism developed after the war as well. Ōtsuka Hisao, whose position was in many ways similar to that of the *Kōza* faction, carved out an independent position for himself and gained many followers with his work on the classical development of capitalism within the separate national environments in which it historically had emerged. Despite these new investigations, however, social science research during the period from 1945 to 1950 continued to be shaped by its prewar and wartime antecedents. Its chief concerns were to understand the postwar period by revisiting the interrupted prewar debates on capitalism (albeit from a postwar perspective) and, at the same time, to further develop and systematize the theoretical perspectives that had informed those earlier debates.

This situation changed, however, as the 1960s opened. The second of Uno Kōzō's three levels of analysis, the so-called stage theory (dan-kairon), led Uno school scholars to pursue detailed research on imperialism and finance capital accumulation as it occurred in the domestic economies of various countries. A theory of world capitalism eventually emerged from the debates stimulated by this research. At the same time, Ōtsuka Hisao and his followers developed a view of history that was less concerned with the shift from feudalism to capitalism than with the specific relation between capitalism and the industrial revolution. Their vision of capitalism emphasized an idea of the uneven development of the various areas of the world. They rejected former ideas of capitalist development as a vertical structure in which capitalism spread over time from advanced countries to later-developing countries, in favor of a horizontal structure in which advanced and underdeveloped regions of the world existed simultaneously as part of the systemic structure of the capitalist system. Not only theoretical developments within Japan, but also world events themselves stimulated Japanese social scientists to turn their eyes to a wider world perspective. In the 1960s, the former colonial countries of Asia, Africa, and Latin America, which prior to 1960 had been locked into their subordinate positions by the rigid structure of the Cold War, began to win independence in quick succession. These independence movements received attention because the nations of the "south," born with the fall of the colonial system, constituted an autonomous political power center that gave its support neither to the United States nor to the Soviet Union. These new nations began pressing their own economic demands on the northern nations in international venues, such as the 1964 United Nations conference on trade development. While the nations of the south had achieved political independence, the condition of underdevelopment under which they suffered went unchanged. In fact, economic conditions worsened, a situation brought into sharp relief by the successive coups d'état that erupted in many of these countries.

Encouraged to turn their attention to a wider world context by both recent theoretical developments and world events, Japanese social scientists began to link the problems of underdevelopment in the former colonial countries to theories of imperialism. The research on imperialism and finance capital touched off by Uno Kōzō's work focused on the late-nineteenth-century movement toward participation in a world system by Germany and the United States in the wake of England's extraordinary economic development. These studies were specifically concerned with the confrontations between the capitalist countries, in which, for example, England attempted to defend its position as the leading nation against the advancements of Germany. They also advocated a research methodology in which the imperialist stage of capitalism was examined through "comparison of the German and U.S. model to that of England."[34] After all, Germany and the United States did not simply repeat the same developmental process that England had undergone. Uno school studies were concerned with understanding, therefore, unequal global relations, requiring later-developing countries to compete with advanced countries, a process that, in turn, determined the form of finance capital in each country.

Similarly, Ōtsuka historical studies argued that the separate, national economic structures that arose in each of the countries of the world during the formation of global capitalism, "when seen in world perspective, existed in various, unequal stages and mutually influenced one another's development."[35] Unlike the Uno school, which focused on the nineteenth century, Ōtsuka looked at an earlier period, from the eighteenth century to the 1870s. England, the leading capitalist country during this period, either forced other countries to take measures to compete or else colonized them, thereby ensuring that these countries could not form national economic systems similar to its own. "Modernization and capitalism in the true sense of the words," said Ōtsuka, were possible only in England and the United States. In the cases of Germany and Japan, he said, "the industrial structures were distorted by the international environment,"[36] and he thus focused his research on trying to understand capitalist development, not as having occurred along a single path but as one that involved three models: the English, the Dutch, and that of colonial monoculture. In this way, the Ōtsuka school became the first to turn its academic sights to the underdevelopment of the Southern Hemisphere.

Ōtsuka's idea of the simultaneous existence of differing levels of development can be taken in two ways: either as describing a certain, inevitable unequal structure in world capitalism that was simply one effect of English capitalism's continued position as the leader of the capitalist world or, as seen from the perspective of the underdeveloped countries of the south, as describing the mechanism, forced into being by England and the other advanced capitalist countries, that posed the biggest obstacle to their own economic development. The first interpretation is argued according to the idea of free trade imperialism, the second according to underdevelopment economics.

It is interesting to note that the idea of free trade imperialism developed out of the interaction between Ōtsuka's historical studies and the theory of dependent development expressed by those such as Andre Gunder Frank. Dependent development theory did not believe that underdevelopment in Asian, African, and Latin American countries in the postwar period was an essential aspect of those countries; rather, it grew out of a deficiency in the developmental process of the modern history of Europe and the United States. Frank argued that the distorted structural development that caused countries to become stuck in a pattern of underdevelopment and stagnation was caused by a mechanism whereby world capitalism made these countries satellites of the core countries. As such, the underdeveloped countries became the very source of capital accumulation and economic development in the central countries. Furthermore, this mechanism did not begin when the imperialist countries began dividing up the world at the end of the nineteenth century and making colonies of these now underdeveloped areas. Frank contended that it had operated continuously, from the inception of liberal trade policies by core nations and continuing up to the present. Rather than argue for rupture—that is, that imperialism had begun suddenly at the end of the nineteenth century—Frank argued in favor of continuity, saying that imperialism had existed from long before that time.

Frank's vision of world history invited, of course, a reconsideration of the role of Britain's free-trade system. But it also called into question Marx's view that the breakdown of old, small, fixed social institutions in colonial India as a result of the British introduction of steam power and free trade was socially revolutionary. This critique was part of a general attack by many dependence-theory scholars on Marx's notion of the civilizing effect of capital. Mōri Kenzō, however, who undertook a detailed study of Marx's work in the face of these criticisms, argues that Marx was not unaware of the socially destructive capacity of capital. According to Mōri, Marx recognized that the expansion of English industrial capital in Ireland after 1846, the year by which the free-trade system is thought to have been fully formed, constituted a system in which Irish business was quietly driven to extinction and indicated that this was an important event for understanding the process of world history. Late in his life, says Mōri, Marx also realized that as the various regions and countries of the world were forcefully incorporated into the world market by the English free-trade system, they were robbed of any mechanism for systematically developing their own manufacturing strength.

Mōri went on to point out that one could answer the question of how the free-trade system of England—the country that until the 1870s was simultaneously the world's factory, the world's bank, the world's shipper, and the world's distributor—distorted the independently developing economic structures of other countries, by looking to the cases of Germany's tariff problem and Brazil's coffee economy. In English parliamentary debates in the first part of the nineteenth century, one finds numerous arguments urging the sale of English exports at a loss if need be to crush U.S. manufacturing export competition, which was then gaining strength. These statements revealed clearly where the true interests of free-trade imperialism lay: they expressed the belief that it was in the natural order of things that England's industries should have an exclusive monopoly in world markets from Europe to India and South America and that an international division of labor should prevail in which other regions and countries of the world were merely satellites for the provision of food and raw materials.[37] This was the sort of environment that greeted the late developing countries as they attempted to undertake capitalist development during the nineteenth century. And in the twentieth century, only the countries that were able to resist the world division of labor and to achieve their own domestic sphere of reproduction were able themselves to become advanced capitalist countries along with England. Mōri's argument, sparked by the emergence of dependency theory, succeeds in its coverage of an aspect of the free-trade system missed by theories, beginning with Lenin and Hobson, that saw imperialism as a new development marking a rupture with previous history.

Analysis of economic underdevelopment grew out of attempts to understand why development theories based on the historical record of advanced countries did not prove successful when actually applied to underdeveloped countries. In the postwar confrontation between the United States and the Soviet Union, it became a matter of urgent concern to produce an efficacious model of development. From the 1950s on, various, often competing models were proposed. Prasanta Chandra Mahalanobis of India advocated a focus on heavy industry, an idea opposed by the theories of some, such as Millican Rostow. None of these models, however, produced extraordinary results. Ōtsuka Hisao blamed these failures on the distortions of a world capitalist system in which regions of unequal development must necessarily exist simultaneously for the capitalist system to exist at all. Rather than seeing the difficulty of raising up underdeveloped countries as merely caused by the internal economic system of each nation, Ōtsuka argued that it was a natural effect of the horizontal structure of capitalism as a global system.[38] He argued that some aspects of underdeveloped countries were linked with the advanced countries, but that other aspects were not. It made sense, he said therefore, to apply theories about advanced country development to underdeveloped countries when they shared aspects in common; but at the same time, effective results could not be expected to follow when they were applied to situations — such as the economic foundation of the tribal system in African countries or the caste system in India — in which there is no connection between underdeveloped and developed countries. Ōtsuka pointed out that the economic aspects of the tribe or caste system, for example, were often not taken into account in underdevelopment theory, and were even actively ignored by scholars in advanced countries. At their root, argued Ōtsuka, economic phenomena in underdeveloped countries "operated according to completely different, independent laws of motion" from the imperialist laws at work in the advanced countries. Ōtsuka believed that not only did these independent laws of motion work counter to the progress of development as predicted in theories of manufacturing growth proposed in the advanced countries, but also they could be expected to "mount a counterattack to the imperialism" that invariably emerged in the wake of that initial development.[39]

Ōtsuka's own concrete proposals for how to overcome obstacles to development in underdeveloped countries were few. He did note the importance of two factors working against development: the structural distortions that arose in the extreme monocultural economies of colonial countries and the premodern, traditional landowning systems that lay at the heart of those economic distortions. He also advocated that to construct appropriate economies from positions of political independence, underdeveloped countries first had to expel colonial rulers themselves and then had to remove the obstacles hindering their development. Ōtsuka's positive recommendations, however, went no further than this.

Akabane Hiroshi, on the other hand, extended the analysis of underdevelopment begun by Ōtsuka. Because imperialism not only acted to keep premodern, traditional social institutions in place but also actively made use of them, monoculture and dual economic structures remained intractable problems. To promote industrialization within the traditional structures that dominated agricultural production, Akabane believed that measures would have to be put in place to deal with these problems. Akabane found the key to these challenges in the work of Paul Bairoch and Michael M. Postan, who argued that the driving force behind European economic development during the eighteenth and nineteenth centuries was the rising productivity of agricultural labor. High productivity in the agricultural sector meant that sufficient food supplies could be provided to the manufacturing labor population and that the buying power of farmers rose, which in turn stimulated the effective demand for manufactured goods in particular. This virtuous circle, therefore, eliminated the domestic market formation dilemma. From the point of view of this idea of economic growth, Mahalanobis's heavy industrialization model in India was mistaken in its neglect of agricultural production, which was the very engine that drove manufacturing expansion. In the hands of Akabane, the arguments of Bairoch and Postan begin to approach Ōtsuka Hisao's theory of local market areas.

Akabane proposed that the way to escape traditional social structures in order to promote a shift to manufacturing was to enact agricultural land reform (*nōchi kaikaku*). Other researchers of underdevelopment had also expressed the opinion that land reform was necessary, but feared that it might also result in the atomization of farm holdings and an actual worsening of rural economic stagnation. Akabane, on the other hand, said that whether those unwanted results occurred or not would depend on how the necessary dismantling of colonial monoculture economic structures and the creation of a new industrial structure were carried out following the implementation of land reform. He believed that the first problem that would be encountered by underdeveloped countries beginning an industrialization strategy would be a deficit of capital. Initially, imports could be expected to be secured through the export products of the monoculture economic base; thus the monoculture economy should be maintained at first to promote the manufacturing sector. This strategy would be delivered a setback, however, by the competition that the technological revolution in advanced countries would bring. This revolution would allow advanced countries to begin manufacturing products domestically to replace the monoculture exports of the underdeveloped countries. Yet Akabane argued that, even if those foreign markets temporarily were lost, the best policy for underdeveloped countries was to move toward manufacturing production by completely reforming the monoculture structure of the economy.

How could economic independence and a shift to manufacturing production be achieved in underdeveloped countries if these countries could not gain entry into the primary products markets of the advanced industrial powers? The answer lay in the path followed by the United States as it gained industrial independence from England. The United States gave birth to what Ōtsuka had called local market areas (*kyokuchiteki shijō ken*) that then grew into one large national economy (*kokumin keizai*) acting as a coherent sphere of reproduction independent of outside economies. To achieve this sort of national economy, said Akabane, "a mix of industries making domestic self-sufficiency possible, the organization of those industries into one coherent national market in which there is a balanced division of labor, and the active development of each of the industries themselves" must all occur following the implementation of land reform.[40] No particular conflict exists between this idea and the heavy industrialization policies actually implemented by any number of underdeveloped nations. The Ōtsuka school believed that agriculture could be liberated from premodern, traditional social structures by land reform, so that it might then proceed along a development path in which it was incorporated into a self-sufficient industrial system. In this way, underdeveloped countries would be able to win economic independence. Rather than the familiar export-led model of industrial growth often cited in discussions of recent East and Southeast Asian economic history, Akabane's vision of development is clearly closer to an import-substitution model.

Given the history of the social sciences in Japan, it seems natural that Japanese intellectuals during the war, working from within a conception of an East Asia Co-Prosperity Sphere, should advocate that former colonial countries, isolated from their colonial masters and from world markets, should move toward the creation of their own spheres of self-sufficiency as a remedy to underdevelopment. In regard to Southeast Asia, Hirano Yoshitarō argued for "reform of the lopsided, monoculture economic systems caused by English and U.S. capital and for the promotion of food supply self-sufficiency and an autonomous agricultural system."[41] Uchida Yoshihiko, too, conducted his research on Malaysian rice supplies with an eye toward how that country might achieve rice self-sufficiency. Because control of the supply of water is critically important in irrigation, Uchida argued that water systems set up by the cooperative efforts of the local people themselves were on a scale too small to be efficient. Instead, larger systems needed to be coordinated by the government, Uchida claimed. In regard to the distribution of rice itself, he noted that "rice-processing plants in Malaysia were all owned by Chinese." In response, Uchida called for the colonial government to "abolish the middleman profits of the Chinese, to ease the losses of Malaysian farmers, and to promote increases in rice crop yields."[42] In addition, he wanted the government itself to set up rice-processing plants and worried that it was becoming common in various regions of Malaysia for farmers to borrow money to pay for mortgages on their land. He wrote: "One can surmise that this is resulting in the forfeiture of land by some debtors and the emergence of a tenancy problem."[43] Uchida's discussion of all of these issues was based on the understanding that each would become important in any strategy for achieving Malaysian economic self-sufficiency.

The development policies later actually applied in Southeast Asian nations cannot be summed up in the usual dichotomy drawn between export-led growth and growth based on import-subsitution. Rather, they have been a mix of these two, combining both light and heavy manufacturing, industrialization, and the promotion of agricultural development, as well as openness toward and restrictions on foreign capital in various degrees, depending on the comparative priorities and guiding philosophies of each country. Large differences can be seen, therefore, between the policies of various countries. The Malaysian government, pursuing a noninterventionist policy, at first welcomed foreign capital and followed a model of heavy industrialization through export-led growth. British and Chinese profited from this industrialization, however, while Malaysians themselves did not, an imbalance that resulted in the race riots of May 1965. In the wake of this unrest was born the Bumiputra policy, in which Malaysians were favored, development policies that achieved a balance between rural and urban sectors were to be pursued, and the gum plantations and tin mines formerly owned by British and the banks formerly run by Chinese were nationalized. Thailand, on the other hand, appears to have achieved success by growing the import-substitution industrial sector based on exports of newly strengthened agricultural, fishing, and livestock industries.

Although Southeast Asian economic success is often thought to be the result of policies similar to those of the South Korean and Taiwan models of export-led growth, it can also be said, as is clear from this discussion, that many aspects of the underdevelopment theories of the Ōtsuka school are evident in the experiences of these countries.

In the previous section of this paper, we saw that the focus of Japanese social scientists changed from capitalism within national contexts to capitalism in a global context, a shift in thought roughly delineated on one hand by Yamada and on the other by Ōtsuka. But there were other voices in the social sciences in Japan calling for similar reconceptualizations of capitalism during the 1960s. A split began to emerge within the Uno school of economics as scholars, led by Iwata Hiroshi, began to criticize the standard Uno version of the history of capitalist development. In the stage theory portion of his tripartite levels-of-analysis approach to capitalism, Uno had argued that in the era of imperialist development in the early part of the twentieth century, England and Germany formed two contrasting models of finance capital. He had then compared and contrasted capitalism in the United States, Japan, and France with these models. Iwata and others came to believe that the understanding of capitalism that underlay Uno's analysis, one that treated capitalism as discrete systems operating within separate countries, was inadequate. Rather, he argued for a conception of the world economy as a whole (*sekai keizai ron*).

Others in Japan also began to see capitalism in terms of one world system. Kawano Kenji and his group believed that the reasons why imperialism, postcolonial nationalism, and underdevelopment characterized the contemporary world could only be understood if these issues were seen in terms of the structure of world capitalism.[44] Kawano said that the world economy had always consisted of individual national economies and the sites (*ba*) at which the relations and structural connections between these national economies were negotiated. Within the hundred years from the end of the nineteenth century, however, these sites of structural interaction became greater than the individual national economies themselves, growing into an autonomous entity. This independent, dominant structure, argued Kawano, governed the particular shape of each separate national economy.

Given the battle lines over these new visions of capitalism, what, more specifically, were the issues of contention during this period of postwar Japanese social science? How did the analysis of the historical development of capitalism change with these new definitions of the global economy as one worldwide system, rather than as the sum total of the mutual relations between separate national economies?

Ōuchi Tsutomu—who was aligned with Uno as a member of the main current of Uno school thinking, and not with those such as Iwata who began to critique the standard approaches of the school—said that the development of the Japanese economy since the formation of state monopoly capitalism, roughly after World War I, could only be understood by applying Uno's notion of an analysis of history (*genjō bunseki*). He argued that state monopoly capital did not emerge naturally out of the imperialist stage of capitalism, but rather evolved in response to the threat to the capitalist nation represented by the birth of socialism in the Soviet Union. The final goal of national policy, then, was on the one hand to achieve economic stability by regulating shifts in the economy in Keynesian fashion and on the other to smooth over, through the formation of the welfare state, the various social contradictions that naturally arise within capitalism itself. Ōuchi believed that this stage of the world economy differed greatly from the classical imperialist stage prevailing around the turn of the century. Before the beginning of the imperialist stage of development, the structure of the world economy was determined, as pointed out by those who made the free-trade imperialism argument, by English capital, Ōuchi argued. Once the classical period of imperialism had begun, the confrontation between Germany, which had developed along the imperialist model, and England became the pivotal relationship within the world economy. By the end of World War I, however, new, exceedingly complicated and confrontational relations between the nations of the world had taken shape. There was opposition between capitalism and socialism; opposition within the capitalist world between the United States, which was maneuvering to take the reins of world leadership, and the countries subordinate to it; and even opposition among these U.S.–dependent countries. Soon, too, conflict emerged between the rulers of colonial and semicolonial areas and the movements for national independence that began to grow up within those regions. Following World War II, the tensions running throughout the world international system increased as the relations of dependence and opposition within a capitalist world dominated by the United States grew more complex. Ōuchi argued that Uno's stage theory (the second of Uno's three levels of analysis), which was originally designed to be applied to the classical period of imperialism at the beginning of the twentieth century, was of no help in understanding these later structures in the history of capitalism.[45] To understand the rise of state monopoly capital and the hegemony of the United States, both of which followed the imperialist stage of capitalist development, it was necessary to employ Uno's analysis of history, the third of his three levels of analysis.

Signaling a rift within the Uno school, Iwata Hiroshi, however, argued against Uno's and Ōuchi's method of casting the English and German cases of finance capital as models by which to analyze the development of finance capital in other countries. He claimed that it was the very arrival of imperialism during the period of finance capital that made clear capitalism was a worldwide system. Iwata also saw imperialism as the colonial rule of one group of advanced countries over backward countries and the monopolistic control of world markets by those advanced countries. But Iwata believed that imperialism did not just take place between national economies; it also occurred within them. Even within advanced capitalist countries, all sectors of the economy did not achieve a complete capitalist transformation. Rather, the capitalist organizations within the few advanced industrial sectors of the domestic economy achieved monopolistic control over both slower-developing industrial sectors and the agricultural sector. These domestic relations then expanded to a worldwide scale. Imperialism, according to Iwata, works to create complex, unequal relations of dependence at both the international and domestic levels. At the heart of imperialism were the technologically advanced industries of a small number of advanced countries, which in turn arranged the remaining countries of the world as colonial holdings on the periphery. In this way, imperialism was a system in which one layer dominated all others.

But how did Iwata respond to the question of how imperialist war could have developed within a system that encompassed the entire world? He employed an idea of the contradictions of the world structure (*sekai hensei no mujun*). The emergence of imperialism clearly indicated that capitalism was a global system. This meant that the contradictions of capitalism were not the contradictions that arose with the domestic development of capitalism in each nation, but rather were the contradictions of the world system—of global economic structures as well as the political and military structures that emerged in response to those economic structures—as a whole. These contradictions gave birth to World War I. Moreover, the Russian Revolution was not the result of the internal contradictions of Russian capitalist development, but was, in reality, fundamentally governed by the international and domestic strategic operations of that imperialist World War I, argued Iwata. Here Iwata had in mind one world system, but it was not one of equal and uniform structure. Rather, it was marked by a center and a periphery that were linked by relations of domination. This structure of center and periphery was not confined to the domestic organization of countries, but extended across international borders, and was characterized by having many competing relations in operation at the same time. The contradictions of the world structure were located exactly at those sites of competition. Iwata saw World War II as a resumption of World War I. His vision was different from that of Ōuchi Tsutomu, who viewed the interwar period, which saw the formation of national monopoly capitalism, as a turning point in the history of capitalism. Iwata recognized that the world economy after World War II was in opposition to the socialist bloc and believed that the capitalist world, led by the United States, was engaged in a redivision of the globe. He believed that this redivision was taking place on the strength of the growth of a U.S. economy that was being bolstered by expanding government expenditures. U.S. economic expansion and the international spread of the dollar led to trade and financial support for European and Japanese industrial development, according to Iwata.

Although disagreements over theoretical approaches divided members of the Uno school, in the end those such as Ōuchi and Iwata who represented opposing ideas about the historical development of capitalism did not hold significantly different views of the postwar world economic system. Both critiqued what they saw as an unequal system of dominance and dependence that rested on U.S. hegemony.

In the end, though, despite the frequent similarity of their most fundamental interpretations of the contemporary capitalist system, basic differences still separated the ideas of those such as Iwata who argued that there was a world capitalist system and those such as Ōuchi who did not. At heart, what separated these two groups of scholars was whether or not they understood economics in terms of the individual capitalisms of separate countries. Why was it that Iwata Hiroshi went beyond the borders of the national economy in his analysis of capitalism?

Three mainstays of Iwata's reasoning in particular led him to conclude that a reasonable explanation of the history of capitalism could not be confined to the experiences of individual nations. First, he disagreed with the theoretical models of national capitalist development used in Uno school analysis, especially the notion that the development of the English economy had ever approached a complete and pure capitalism (*shihonshugi e no junka keikō*). Iwata argued that at the same time as England was becoming the most advanced industrial country in the world, a great portion of the population was still engaged in semi-handicraft, semi-agricultural activities. Despite this fact, England's exports consisted of factory-produced products. The incompleteness of capitalist development even within England seemed to Iwata to militate against Uno's application of England as a theoretical model of capitalist development.

The second reason Iwata moved beyond the borders of the nation in his interpretation of capitalism was related to his view of England as a central country, a view that held much in common with theories of free-trade imperialism. England constituted the center of the capitalist system, and France, Germany, and the United States were arranged in the periphery. At the same time, however, these peripheral countries had established factory manufacturing systems based on their spinning industries, just as England had done. Yet these countries were incorporated into the world division of labor based on the exports of their semi-handicraft, semi-agricultural sectors alone. Finally, Asia, Africa, and Central and South America, which only produced agricultural products, were positioned outside the system altogether. Again, these facts led Iwata to conceive of capitalism in global terms.

Yet if this were the extent of Iwata's conception, it would imply simply that the national economies of all countries were incorporated into various relations of dependence within the international division of labor. But Iwata went one step further by describing the system of financial circulation within world capitalism. He said that the reason that this sort of unified world system ever came into existence at all was precisely because of the robust economic circulation based on the strength of the English financial world. "The spinning industry that constituted the nucleus of production in England's domestic capitalist organization became at the same time the production center of a world capitalist marketplace that revolved around England," wrote Iwata. "All of the interrelations within the international division of labor depended on the internal profit logic of the English spinning industry and were governed by it as one united system."[46] This resulted in an economic mediation system in which the price of products in the world market responded to cost changes within the English spinning industry, so that England became the agent that determined international commerce and finance.

Iwata further explained the mechanism of economic circulation in world capitalism during the middle of the nineteenth century by describing the cycles of world financial expansion and contraction caused by the fluctuations of the London capital market. As wealth and production volume in the English spinning industry expanded, this caused an increase in international and domestic credit. This cycle eventually resulted in a countercycle in which the limit of credit expansion was reached, resulting in a contraction of the London capital market and causing a downturn in economic prosperity that spread to affect various other regions of the world.[47]

This system changed in the second half of the nineteenth century, when investment in railroads increased rapidly worldwide. This transformation caused disruption in global economic flows, and the huge outlays required for the steel industry and for construction of railways promoted the shift to the corporate stock system of raising industrial capital. By the 1880s, capital markets in the United States had gained independence from markets in England, and the steel industry in Germany was expanding rapidly. The result of all these changes was that the economic flows that ran throughout the world capitalist system became unregulated and ill-formed. More important, the relations between center and periphery became more complex and varied. Both the inequalities that arose in the domestic development of each country and the inequalities of international development alike were aggravated.

From the new perspectives of those such as Iwata, the idea of a world economy began to emerge in the social sciences in Japan, one that implied a quite particular view of capitalism. In this view, capitalism was a process of global exchange at the center of which always stood a specific industrial sector in a specific country that worked to position the various types of noncapitalistic social production at the periphery (either domestically or internationally) of the entire system. The process of expansion of this global system from center to periphery in turn led to the formation of multiple centers and peripheries and uneven relations of dominance and inequality.

In this conceptualization of capitalism, then, a center emerges and takes shape. Next, either capitalism spatially expands from that center, or a periphery is organized around that center. Either way, the center then splits and becomes pluralized, and the relations between center and periphery become more complex and diverse. It was to this variegated structure that Iwata referred when he used the phrase "the contradictions of the world structure."[48]

Baba Hiroji inherited Iwata's conception of center and periphery when he took up the issue of spreading affluence in the advanced countries during the postwar period. As a member of the Uno school of economics, he questioned whether the social sciences in Japan as they had previously existed were capable of dealing with new realities—such as the affluent society—that were emerging in Japan and across the world in the decades after the war. Applying explanations that owed much to the *Rōnō* school of Marxist thought, the Uno school had been able to explain issues such as high farm rents in Japan in the period prior to World War II. But, complained Baba, neither the Uno school nor its heirs had anything to say about postwar high economic growth. Indeed, they had claimed that high economic growth and income doubling would be theoretically impossible to achieve. Then, continues Baba, when it became impossible for these scholars to deny the reality of high economic growth any longer, they said that it was a peculiar type of high growth that had developed only because of Japan's original backwardness, adding that Japan's industrial structure and international competitiveness were fragile at any rate and therefore destined to crumble despite apparent recent successes. Finally, when the auto industry began successfully exporting, these critics spoke about the inadequacies of the government's pollution and social welfare policies. Baba criticized the Uno school for only reacting in this way to current conditions. The result of this stance, he said, was that the Uno school avoided wrestling head-on with the globally unprecedented accumulation of capital that occurred during the period of high growth.[49]

Baba's criticism was a product of his notion of "finance capital and the shift to affluence," his attempt, described in a book by the same name (*Fuyūka to kinyū shihon*), to understand economic growth and the affluent society resulting from it. In his theories of the affluent society, Baba extends the idea of capitalism as process.

After presenting an overview of the development of capitalism in *Fuyūka to kinyū shihon*, Baba offers a unique exploration of the affluent society in which he envisions the trend of rising affluence as a wave that expands from a center to a limited number of outer countries of the world that then form the peripheral boundary of affluence. He explains that the wave of development that brought the shift to capitalist factory production, beginning with the industrial revolution in England in the last part of the eighteenth century, was responsible for forming industrial capital by the middle of the nineteenth century. The result of this process was that England became the factory of the world. This capitalist wave then extended to the United States and to the countries of Western Europe, which Baba called the boundary zone of capitalism (*genkai shihonshugi chitai*). Next, in the imperialist stage of development, from the end of the nineteenth into the twentieth century, this wave resulted in the emergence of finance capital, at the center of which were the heavy industries of Germany and the United States. These two nations overtook England, the former center of the system, in terms of manufacturing productivity. And the capitalist system then expanded to subsume Eastern Europe, as well as Russia and Japan in the Far East, as its new boundary countries. During this stage, argues Baba, the placement of countries within the system underwent great change. The England-centered system that had existed up to this time was brought to an end, and the period of imperialist confrontation began. During the period around World War I, the United States became the productivity center of the world, and Russia was removed from the capitalist world altogether. This left Japan as the only nation at the time occupying the boundary position of the capitalist world. The wave of capitalist industrialization then expanded still further, "so that by the end of the 1960s, the boundary zone moved outward, as unprecedented high economic growth in Japan brought productivity levels rivaling those in Europe and the United States, and the capitalist system extended to include all the various countries of the newly industrializing world."[50] According to this view of capitalism, the newly industrializing economies of East and Southeast Asia would have to be considered the boundary zone countries of affluence today, although at some point Russia and the countries of Eastern Europe may have to be included as well.

In Baba's vision of the world economy and social change, a second wave then washed across countries that had already experienced the first wave of capitalist industrialization. This was the shift to affluence. But this affluence did not appear just anywhere within regions through which the tide of capitalist development had passed. Rather, it emerged where finance capital led to rapid capital accumulation and subsequent rises in the general level of income. More specifically, the origin of this shift to affluence can best be found in Germany, a nation that represents the classic case of finance capital formation. There, this new affluent society was shaped both by an increased complexity of social class relations—represented by the shift to middle-sized farms, the dual structure of the labor market, and the expansion of the middle class—and by the implementation of social reform from above, as for example in government social insurance policies. Yet "in terms of the relation between the shift to social affluence and finance capital," noted Baba, "it [was] less the complexity of class relations than the rise in productivity rates that [was] important."[51] Because it brought about an economic expansion far greater than what was achievable under industrial capital, capital accumulation under the finance-capital system characterized by large-scale stock corporations produced increases in both volume of production and productivity.

This second wave, originating in Germany, then spread to the United States and became even more pervasive. From the end of the nineteenth century, the United States experienced the formation of finance capital with the development of its iron ore, coal, and railroad industries. These economic shifts, in turn, brought a great social transformation. Although the United States did not become a classless society per se, a widespread, popular affluence (*taishūteki fuyūka*) was created, acting as a bulwark for the democratic system. By the 1920s, new industries such as automobiles, oil, electric power, electric machinery, chemicals, and artificial fibers were added. And the post–World War II era saw the birth of the petrochemical, aircraft, and electronics industries, one after the other. The interrelation between these new areas of production brought consistent rises in the rate of productivity. At the same time, a vast, strong mass market of consumption was created by the Fordist interplay between mass production and high wages. Baba writes: "The efficiencies gained in mass production brought the cost per unit of production down, which further widened the potential market for those goods. This, in turn, led to the expansion of industry and industrial labor markets. In the process, the purchasing power of workers was raised, bringing them into the middle class. A virtuous circle thus was created."[52]

It was this mechanism that created the world's first society of mass affluence (*taishūteki fuyū shakai*) in the United States. This wave of affluence spread next to Canada, then to Western Europe, which along with the United States witnessed the emergence of finance capital in the prewar period; and finally, although later and to a lesser extent, to Japan.

Of course, the path that Japan traveled in its rapid rise to inclusion within the borders of the nations of affluence was not identical to that taken by the United States. Rather, Japan took the opposite route, relying on a system that kept wages and consumption relatively low and that featured relatively cooperative labor relations during the period of high economic growth. As Yamada Moritarō points out in his *Sengo junkan no seikaku kitei* [Regulation of the character of postwar circulation], the system of reproduction during the high-growth period in Japan was based on a postwar economic recovery that was achieved through wage and price regulation, that is, through low wages (the burden of labor) and low rice prices (the burden of farmers). And the

French scholar Benjamin Coriat shows that the Japanese-style production control system, especially Toyota's adherence to Ōno's ideas, much vaunted as the secret to the high productivity of labor in Japan, could be introduced only after the postwar labor movement was finally defeated.[53] Relations between labor and management during the high growth period were marked, therefore, by more cooperation than in the United States, for example, where labor maintained an oppositional stance throughout that same period. Remarking on the alternative path taken by Japan, Baba argued that economic development in Japan tended to suppress mass-level affluence and social security, a condition that resulted in rising productivity levels.

Given the view of the shift to affluence that emerges from the idea of capitalism as process, what can be said about what will happen to this expanding wave of affluence in the future? If the levels of affluence achieved in the advanced countries were extended to all of the Southern Hemisphere and to the formerly underdeveloped countries of the East, we could expect that the scale of the global economy would increase fivefold and that, in turn, oil consumption, deforestation, and environmental pollution would all increase proportionately. The cost of increased global affluence seems high. On the other hand, because the current world capitalist system is one in which affluence and underdevelopment are both advancing at the same time, widespread famine remains an ever-present problem in the have-not countries of the Southern Hemisphere. Can we simply allow such conditions to continue without acting to remedy them? Some have argued that there is a surplus of affluence in the industrialized countries, a viewpoint that has given rise to the reverse argument that in Western Europe there is a surplus of welfare programs and other policies aimed at achieving economic equality. Because excessive social welfare and economic redistribution programs tend to dampen economic activity, such policies surely would be rejected in Japan. Baba Hiroji, however, argues that even if we assume that such welfare measures would slow the engine of economic growth, they still ought to be implemented when considered from the perspective of greater human welfare.[54]

Any discussion of the so-called wave of affluence must also include consideration of several reverse currents moving across the globe, including impoverishment and "third world–ization." As we saw in the writings of Iwata Hiroshi, world capitalism organizes the industries of each nation and the various processes of social production into relations of domination and subordination by creating a center-periphery structure. That the center of this world system is able to exist at all is due precisely to the existence of an expansive periphery; because a vast third world exists, the advanced countries are able to enjoy great abundance. Borders must always exist to separate the nations of affluence from the rest. This is why Baba Hiroji specifically made use of the term *boundary nation*. There are limits to the world's natural resources, however. A surplus of affluence cannot continue to exist in the advanced countries. If these disparities of wealth are not reduced by raising the level of affluence in underdeveloped countries, then the contradictions causing them will work themselves out, at least in part, through a continuation of the current process in which the third world is being brought within the boundaries of the advanced nations. Evidence for this trend can be seen now in the stream of foreign workers into Japan and Europe in recent years and the third world–ization of the United States so much commented on of late. Surely views of capitalism as world system and as global-market process such as we have touched on here can contribute to our future understanding of these serious issues.

NOTES

This essay was translated by Scott O'Bryan.

1 Important older works include Uchida Jōkichi, *Nihon shihon shugi ronsō* [The debates on Japanese capitalism] (Tokyo: Shinkō Shuppansha, 1949); and Koyama Hirotake, ed., *Nihon shihonshugi ronsō shi* [The history of the debates on Japanese capitalism], vols. 1 and 2 (Tokyo: Aoki Bunko, 1953). More recent works include Moriya Fumio, *Nihon marukusu shugi riron no keisei to hatten* [The formation and development of Japanese Marxist theory] (Tokyo: Aoki Shoten, 1967).

2 Some may find it strange that one would attempt to identify a particular world conception through an analysis of Yamada Moritarō's *Bunseki*, a work that, by comparing Japan to England, France, Germany, and Russia, is solely devoted to revealing the peculiar pattern of Japanese capitalism. Specifically, Yamada's essay describes the system of capital circulation—the system of reproduction—operating within capitalism in Japan. How can we hope to locate a general conception of the world, in a global sense, in a book dedicated to the processes of Japanese capitalism in particular?

Others may question my proposal to identify the particular world conception embedded in Yamada's analysis of Japanese capitalism from precisely the opposite point of view. That is, they may object that the problem of locating a world conception within Yamada's work is in reality no problem at all. It is well-known that *Bunseki* shares many of the major premises of the earlier *Kōza*, the seven-volume compendium of *Kōza* faction Marxist thought. The view of Japanese capitalism presented in *Kōza* places great emphasis on the semifeudal nature of the relationship between Japanese landlords and tenants, a view often thought to have been largely shaped by the analysis found in the Comintern's *1932 Thesis*, which was published prior to the release of *Kōza* in Japan. Should it not be easy to deduce the world conception underlying *Bunseki* itself, then, simply by analyzing the view of world history that emerges in the "Japanese Imperialism and War" section of the opening of the *1932 Thesis*?

While each of these reservations about my approach to the question under consideration in this section has merit, *Bunseki*, in truth, can be defined neither in terms of a sole focus on the internal structure of Japanese capitalism nor in terms of the similarities its idea of Japan in the world may share with the Comintern's *1932 Thesis*. As we shall see, Yamada's analysis considers capitalism as it operates within individual nations, but at the same time it is not completely lacking a larger concern with extranational economic processes.

3  Uchida Yoshihiko, *Nihon shihonshugi no shisōzō* [Thought on Japanese capitalism] (Tokyo: Iwanami Shoten), 85. This phrase was frequently used among Marxist scholars during the 1950s.

4  In the twentieth chapter ("Simple Reproduction") and the twenty-first chapter ("Accumulation and Reproduction on an Extended Scale") of the second volume of *Capital,* Marx divides reproduction in capitalist economies into two sectors—a capital-goods production sector (Sector I) and a consumer-goods production sector (Sector II)—and divides value into three sorts: convertible capital (c), unconvertible capital (v), and surplus value (m). He then relates these two schemata by these formulas: $I = c_1 + v_1 + m_1$ and $II = c_2 + v_2 + m_2$. The formula that Yamada uses, $I.v + m = II.c$, expresses the conditions under which simple reproduction repeats itself. For expanded reproduction (*kakudai saiseisan*) to occur, according to Yamada, relations must exist such that $I.v + m(v) + m(k) = II.c + m(c)$.

5  Yamada Moritarō, *Nihon shihonshugi bunseki* [An analysis of Japanese capitalism] (Tokyo: Iwanami Bunkohan), 236.

6  "Nihon ni okeru jōsei to Nihon kyōsantō no ninmu ni kansuru têzê ('32 têzê)" [Thesis regarding the current conditions in Japan and the responsibilities of the Japan Communist Party (The 1932 thesis)], in *Gendai shi shiryō* [Source materials in contemporary history], vol. 14 (Tokyo: Misuzu Shobō, 1964), 613.

7  Ibid., 614–616.

8  Ibid., 616.

9  Yamada Moritarō, "Sengo junkan no seikaku kitei," in *Yamada Moritarō chosaku shū, dai 5 kan* [The collected works of Yamada Moritarō, vol. 5] (Tokyo: Iwanami Shoten, 1984), 3.

10  Ibid., 3.

11  Ibid., 16–17.

12 Ibid., 5.

13 For a treatment of the Communist Academy incident, see Nagaoka Shin-kichi, *Nihon shihon shugi ronsō no gunzō* [The participants in the debates on Japanese capitalism] (Tokyo: Mineruva Shob, 1984), 244–248.

14 Ishidō Kiyotomi, *Waga itan no shōwa shi* [My heretical history of the Shōwa period] (Tokyo: Keisō Shobō, 1986), 205.

15 Nagaoka Shinkichi, *Nihon shihon shugi ronsō no gunzō*, 295.

16 Gushima's "Busshitsu senryaku to gaikō seisaku" appeared as an article in a 1939 issue of the *Mantetsu chōsa geppō* [South Manchurian Railway Company monthly research review] (the month of publication is unclear). For this discussion of Gushima, see Ishidō Kiyotomi, *Shōwa shi*, 222–223.

17 Yamada Moritarō, "Shina inasaku no gijutsu suijun—Shina inasaku no konpon meidai" [The technological level of Chinese rice cultivation—thesis on the basis of Chinese rice cultivation], in *Tōa kenkyūjo hō* [Report of the East Asia Research Institute] 11 (August 1941): 1.

18 Ibid., 2–3.

19 Ibid., 23.

20 Yamada Moritarō, *Bunseki*, 263.

21 Yamada Moritarō, "Shina inasaku nōka keizai no kichō" [The economy of family rice farming in China], in *Tōa kenkyūjo hō* [Report of the East Asia Research Institute] 15 (February 1942): 20–21.

22 Ibid.

23 Uchida Yoshihiko, "Marai no kome" [Rice in Malaysia], in *Tōa kenkyūjo hō* no. 212 (June 1943): 1–2.

24 Hirano Yoshitarō, *Minzoku seiji no kihon mondai* [Basic problems in national politics] (Tokyo: Koyama Shoten, 1944), 3.

25 Uchida Yoshihiko, "Marai no kome," 3.

26 Ibid., 5.

27 Ibid.

28 Hirano Yoshitarō, *Minzoku seiji no kihon mondai*, 10.

29 Ibid.

30 Ibid., 14.

31 Ibid.

32 Hirano Yoshitarō, *Nihon shihonshugi shakai no kikō* [The structure of Japanese capitalist society] (Tokyo: Iwanami Shoten, 1934), 156.

33 Hirano Yoshitarō, *Dai ajiashugi no rekishiteki kiso* [The historical basis of greater Asianism] (Tokyo: Kawade Shobō, 1945), 7–31.

34 Baba Hiroji, *Fuyūka to kinyū shihon* [Finance capital and the shift to afflu-ence] (Tokyo: Mineruva Shobō, 1986), 93.

35 Ōtsuka Hisao, "Kinyūshi ni okeru kokusai hikaku—sangyō kōzō, keizai kōzō, kinyū kōzō" [A comparative international history of finance: indus-trial structures, economic structures, and financial structures], in *Ōtsuka Hisao chosakushū* [The collected works of Ōtsuka Hisao], vol. 9 (Tokyo: Iwa-nami Shoten, 1969), 355.

36 Ōtsuka Hisao, "Kinyūshi ni okeru kokusaika no shikaku" [A perspective on the internationalization of finance], in *Ōtsuka Hisao chosakushū* [The collected works of Ōtsuka Hisao], vol. 9 (Tokyo: Iwanami Shoten, 1969), 359.

37 Mōri Kenji, *Jiyū bōeki teikokushugi* [Free trade imperialism] (Tokyo: Tōdai Shuppankai, 1978), 125–126.

38 Ōtsuka Hisao, "Yoken no tame no sekai shi" [Predictive world history], in *Tenbō* [Prospects] (December 1964). Reprinted in *Ōtsuka Hisao chosakushū, dai 9 kan*, 209.

39 Ibid., 202.

40 Akabane Hiroshi, *Teikaihatsu keizai bunseki josetsu* [An introductory analysis of underdevelopment] (Tokyo: Iwanami Shoten, 1971), 29.

41 Hirano Yoshitarō, *Minzoku seiji*, 14.

42 Uchida Yoshihiko, "Marai no kome," 63.

43 Ibid., 85.

44 Kawano Kenji and Inuma Jirō, eds., *Sekai shihonshugi no rekishi kōzō* [The historical structure of world capitalism] (Tokyo: Iwanami Shoten, 1970), iii.

45 Ōuchi Tsutomu, *Nihon keizai ron, jō* [Thesis on the Japanese economy] vol. 1, (Tokyo: Tokyo Daigaku Shuppankai, 1962), 6, 16, 39.

46 Iwata Hiroshi, *Sekai shihonshugi* [World capitalism] (Tokyo: Miraisha, 1964), 40.

47 Ibid., 42.

48 Ibid., 336.

49 Baba Hiroji, "Joron, ima, naze ōbei ka" [Why Europe and America now? — An introduction], in *Gendai nihon shakai, dai 2 kan, kokusai hikaku, 1* [Contemporary Japanese society. Vol. 2, International comparisons, 1] (Tokyo: Tokyo Daigaku Shakai Kagaku Kenkyūjo, 1991), 11–12.

50 See especially "Joron, fuyūka no tetsugaku" [The philosophy of the shift to affluence — an introduction] in Baba Hiroji, *Fuyūka to kinyū shihon*, 4.

51 Ibid., 5.

52 Ibid., 7.

53 Benjamin Coriat, *Gyakuten no shikō — Nihon kigyō no rōdō to soshiki* [A reverse view — labor and organization in Japanese enterprises], trans. Hanada Masanori and Saitō Yoshinori (Tokyo: Fujiwara Shoten, 1992), 41–43.

54 Baba Hiroji, *Fuyūka to kinyū shihon*, 15.

"And They Would Start Again": Women and Struggle

in Korean Nationalist Literature

■ I still remember the day in 1972 when I came home from school to find the whole house empty. I was twelve years old. The note my mother had left for me said that she was going to my grandparents' home because my grandfather had been arrested. That shocked me. In my twelve-year-old frame of reference, ingrained by public school education, prison was a place for people who committed heinous crimes; prison was probably forever, possibly even until death. I had only just overcome my fear of newspapers and accepted the fact that my grandfather's pictures appeared there not because he was a criminal but because he was president of the Korean Lawyers Association, cochair of the Korean Democratization Coalition, and a representative of the Korean division of AMNESTY.

My grandfather Yi Pyonglin was a leader of the Korean democratization movement in the 1960s and early 1970s.[1] He believed in law, democracy, and ironically, the United States. Although I have deliberately avoided studying the history of his struggle, I still remember one of his longest and fiercest battles against the South Korean government. He fought for legislation requiring the government to prove a danger of escape existed before anybody could be put in prison. He argued that such an act would protect people's basic rights and freedom, and also that developed countries, especially the United States, had implemented such measures long ago. He believed that his proposed legislation could extirpate what was a widespread practice in a dictatorial country where people who refused to be subservient to the state just mysteriously disappeared, to be tortured in secret places and perhaps found dead later.

It was one of numerous ironies of his life that he was arrested without any warrant or hearing because he was fighting for legislation requiring warrants and hearings. Another irony was that the United States played a crucial role in his defeat, which in turn more than symbolized the destiny of the whole Korean democratization movement at that time. When the U.S. government came to clarify its position toward the political situation in Korea, it made it very clear that America supported human rights, but not enough to jeopardize the loyalty of the military regime in Korea. My grandfather spent his last days in a small rural village, away from politics, acquaintances, and even most members of his family. He died at the age of seventy-six, still believing that juridical struggle should be the primary means for attaining democracy in Korea.

Ever since I was old enough to be aware of his struggles, the life history of my grandfather has dominated my life and decisions. I decided not to become a lawyer because I did not want to follow in his footsteps. What I believed I saw was betrayal, cruelty, and, more than anything else, despair. I became interested in legal discourse, not because it was the "religion" my grandfather proudly professed but because I could see it was a socially constructed discourse about power and struggle. I also started studying imperialism, past and present, to prove theoretically that my grandfather was wrong to trust the United States. I guess I was angry with him.

Looking back from my present vantage point, it would seem that I was still romanticizing my grandfather's history because it was the big man's history that made it into the headlines. While I was busy being obsessed by my grandfather, I forgot about my grandmother, who suffered because her husband took out his frustration on her, who was publicly humiliated when her husband was arrested on a trumped-up charge of adultery, who followed her husband to the little village where she died alone, a victim of wretched medical facilities. I also resisted remembering the life of my mother, who had to give up her education because her father believed that women were better off without one, who had to slave over housework as did most women in Korea, and who also suffered her husband's domestic violence. I am not claiming that the men in my family did *not* suffer. My oldest uncle, who everyone believed would have a bright future as a lawyer, died in his forties in a mental institution. Until his last day, he believed that he was being shadowed by the Korean CIA (Central Intelligence Agency).

Rather, what I am saying is that I myself accepted the dichotomy be-tween the public and the private, the political and the personal. What my unsung grandmother, mother, and uncle lived through was not considered worth being included in "history": what my grandfather did, said, and wrote—*that* was History. The movement my grandfather represented was remembered, discussed, and later even revived. What my grandmother and mother suffered from—domestic labor, male domination and violence, unequal opportunities—was forgotten, and remained unnoticed, unmarked, and unrepresented.

That is in the past now. What obtained in Korea in the 1980s was an explosion of labor movements, feminist movements, and resistance against neo-imperialism specifically targeting the United States.[2] Let us for a while put ourselves back into that historic modality. Workers are researching and writing, students are fighting, farmers are dem-onstrating. The participants in the democratization movement are not "big men" any more but nameless men and women. In "The Flag," a short narrative about women workers who gain mature political con-sciousness through armed struggle in the Kwangju Uprising and its aftermath, some female workers decide to compile a collection of their own writings because they are dissatisfied with the way established writers distort and obfuscate their history.

> So they made their own booklet. They included poems, autobio-graphical pieces, letters home, and essays. Hyongja suggested that they not sign them with their names.
> "Read these without names. They all seem to be yours."
> That was true. They all felt that they had written each piece them-selves. They found a thrust in the collection as a whole that they had not noticed when they read the writings separately. Individual discontent had gathered itself into collective anger.[3]

"The Flag" represents the Kwangju Uprising from the viewpoint of a young female worker, Sunbun. Sunbun and the other female workers participate in the uprising and survive the state's brutal massacre because they evacuate City Hall just before the military invasion of Kwangju. The surviving girls acquire political consciousness, which helps them recognize themselves as autonomous political agents, but this awakening is rendered tragic and urgent when their friend Hyongja is killed after she refuses to leave City Hall on the final day of the insurrection.

"The Flag" narrates one of the most tragic events of modern Korean history from a working-class woman's point of view, thereby opening a text that illuminates class structure, gender hierarchy, and neo-imperialism and represents Korean women workers who come to see that their positions are central, not marginal, to society. Once they recognize how the state, class system, and neo-imperialism operate together to mystify their existence, they are finally able to embrace their mission as the authors of history. The process in which female workers obtain this crucial knowledge and power (at the price of their own lives and the lives of their loved ones) actually also narrates the way Korea as a collective entity unlearned its faith in liberal humanism and painfully acknowledged the necessity and the centrality of class and anti-neo-imperialist struggle.

The events that "The Flag" narrates formed a pivotal point in the Korean democratization movement and modern Korean history at large. On 18 May 1980, civilians in the nation's fourth-largest city, Kwangju, were participating in a peaceful demonstration against the country's still-solidifying military regime. This event followed the October 1979 assassination of the tyrannical president who had held power for more than eighteen years. Though most Koreans were aware that the country was still dominated by the military, knowing we were free of that particular person, who had ruled us ruthlessly for nearly two decades, was liberating. May is the month traditionally associated with festivity in Korea, as it is in many other parts of the world. The people demonstrating on the street were happy and friendly. Those not actually participating in the demonstration stood applauding on the sidewalks, debating political and economic issues with demonstrators. Even the police officers sent to suppress the demonstration were not hostile.

Then, seemingly out of nowhere, a special army unit appeared. Children and elderly people were the first to die because they were slow and weak. The soldiers then massacred everyone—men and women, old and young. The estimated number of fatalities on that day alone was over two thousand. In total shock at the massacre, Kwangju citizens armed themselves, took power from the marauding soldiers, and ran the city themselves for a week until regular troops reinvaded and brutally suppressed the uprising with a second general massacre.

The Korean military state's massacre of Kwangju's citizens, unlike China's 1989 Tiananmen Square massacre, got virtually no positive worldwide media attention.[4] Following the massacre Korean masses were forced to rethink their relationship with intellectuals in the context of revolutionary struggle, and especially in light of neo-imperialism and the global order: Who and where were our true allies? Who were our potential allies? What should be the relationship of nationalism to the masses? Where could we find autonomous political agents? This paper is a part of that rethinking, which is why, in discussing "The Flag" here, it is not my object to lodge accusations against the forces of neo-imperialism but rather to review strategies for making decisions about who will author Korea's *future* history. Yet the way communal discourse about the United States is reported and reevaluated in the text is important because only after clearly discerning Korea's status in the neo-imperialist world order can the Korean masses start fighting their battles.

> People seemed to be tense because of the rumor of immediate invasion of the Martial Law Army.
> "Sis, look at the bulletin board."
> Sunbun was pointing to the big poster which read, "An American aircraft carrier is lying in Pusan Harbor. The United States is the country that advocates democracy and human rights. The carrier is in Pusan Harbor in order to protect Kwangju civilians who are fighting for democracy. Kwangju will not shed any more blood. There's no call for commotion. Let us gather at the City Hall."
> Some people seemed to relax a little. They might have had some expectations about a country which is symbolized by the Goddess of Liberty. (198–199)

Yet this familiar praise of the United States and the easy reliance on the democratic principles of the outside power are thoroughly weighed, contested, and discarded. After the principal characters talk to an old man who, because of his experiences in the Korean War, refuses to buy into such facile assurances and ideological complaisance, they examine the political and military situation in Korea not because they want the theory and the knowledge as such but because they have to figure it out to save their own lives and the lives of others. Ascertaining what is the international as well as the domestic political and economic situation is necessary to survive. Having fragmented knowledge means possibly losing one's life in a wasteful way.

> "Sis, America is still a good country. They've come to help us after all."
> "Well. I agree with grandpa. Our blood was shed by the military dictatorial government. The United States acknowledges and supports the same military dictatorial government. . . ."

"Think about this, Sunbun. Do you know who has power over military operations in Korea?"

Sunbun shook her head.

Hyongja continued, "The commander-in-chief of the ROK-U.S. Combined Forces has it, except in Seoul. And the commander-in-chief is American. . . ."

"What is certain is that Kwangju can only be invaded by the army under martial law with the permission of the United States."

"True."

"We have too many vague fantasies about the United States. Maybe we can get a clear sense of the real identity of the United States."

"How?"

"If . . . if we were to lose City Hall, if we were to be shot to death, then we would know what the United States is really about. . . ."

"You can sometimes win by losing, and it makes me sad to think that we might have to pay such a dear cost to learn the truth."

Hyongja's voice was tremulous. (199–200)

Lukács points out in *History and Class Consciousness* that "the totality of history is itself a real historical power—even though one that has not hitherto become conscious and has therefore unrecognized a power which is not to be separated from the reality (and hence of the knowledge) of the individual facts without at the same time annulling their reality and their factual existence."[5] Compared with the text I am discussing, Lukács's argument for the historical power of the totality sounds too apologetic. Hyongja, Sunbun, and other female workers see only one possible avenue to power: claiming the totality of history without annulling "their factual existence." In this case, not claiming power means not living.

Lukács also argues that "the historical knowledge of the proletariat begins with knowledge of the present, with the self-knowledge of its own social situation and with the elucidation of its necessity (i.e. its genesis)."[6] Even though I agree with him on the thesis of the historical knowledge of the proletariat, what seems to be missing in his theory of totality is the tragic inevitability of such knowledge when or as it is acquired by the proletariat. "The Flag," like the survivors of the Kwangju Uprising in general, testifies to the rigor of such knowledge obtained during struggles against the state and against imperialism.

Hyongja and Sunbun saw people holding a rally in front of the fountain on their way to the YWCA to fetch the *Warriors' Paper*. Citizens went up to the dais and said everything on their minds. Yet there were rigorous criteria to their "everything." The criteria were the need to avoid wasting the freedom they had obtained with their blood and the need to take clear retribution against their enemy. The standard of fierce armed struggle was the context of their battle. This was Freedom. Freedom was not choosing something out of infinite possibilities but the simple necessity imposed by the situation. There could be only one solution to each situation. (197)

The historical knowledge and power that protagonists in "The Flag" secure is not about an infinitude of possibilities nor about self-multiplying signifiers. Their freedom would not fit into the paradigm of "freedom, American style," as Gramsci suggested.[7] Theirs was a rigorous decision allowing for only one solution in each situation, mainly because they were forced to make irrevocable decisions about their lives. Yet they each knew that what they secured was freedom because they, and not the military government nor any neo-imperial forces, were making that decision.

Just before the army under martial law suppresses the citizen army and kills virtually every civilian remaining in City Hall, Hyongja enjoins Sunbun to never forget the knowledge, power, and freedom they had had in those days.

> "Listen to me. Somebody has to do this later. Maybe you are the one to do it," said Hyongja.
>
> Sunbun squeezed Hyongja's hand.
>
> Hyongja continued, "Remember the people who remained in the City Hall. You have to remember who participated in this revolution, who fought for it, and who died for it. . . ."
>
> "Then you will know who makes history. . . . That will be your power." (203)

Now, in an immediately preceding section, the text had explored conflicts arising between liberal intellectuals and proletarian participants of the "uprising."[8] Contrary to the desire of most intellectuals, who wanted to go back to the prerevolutionary reality by negotiating with the government and giving up their weapons, the proletariat wanted to expand their temporary power over the area and press forward to a larger-scale revolution. Although we have to remember that there were radical students and intellectuals who joined the mostly proletarian revolutionaries in those final days and who met their deaths, this particular uprising was significant for the way it clarified, for

Koreans who were working for change, the terms of the relationship between intellectuals and the masses and the distinction between reform and revolution. In the passage quoted above, Hyongja is arguing that knowledge acquired through revolutionary practice should become the ultimate critique of all other types of knowledge.

Following the suppression of the uprising and the slaughter of hundreds of civilians, Sunbun and the other surviving women workers go through the painful process of "knowing" their reality, their society, and the world.

> They scratched themselves, and each other. Scars bleeding, they stabbed with knives in the still-bleeding scars. Finally the most intimate parts of their bodies were torn out, leaving nothing to hide. It was as if their intestines, hooked on a saber, ended up on the street, distinctly revealing in broad daylight grains of rice swallowed a while ago. They could not help confronting reality and making diagnoses. It was a shame to be alive. They could not help thoroughly shattering their most intimate parts which had justified their lives.
>
> To be alive was a personal decision, a shame under the sun, a cowardice, and also a sin. They had to acknowledge that. And then they would start again. (210–211)

The original Korean text repeatedly uses the female plural pronoun *kunyodul* instead of the neutral *they* when it refers to the surviving women workers. What we have as a result is a passage that centers the discussion around the consciousness of women workers, always an integral part of Korean anti-imperialist struggles and class struggles, yet always marginalized and silenced in representations of those struggles. Women workers in Korea, who occupy the site where the oppressions concerning race, gender, and class intersect, together produce knowledge about social, economic, and political reality in the neo-imperial context.

That the imagery employed is about the human body, its depth, and the violence it sustains is telling. There is no doubt that the passage refers to what actually happened just before the Kwangju Uprising. After all, the bayonet was the weapon used most lavishly on Kwangju citizens in the state's suppression of the peaceful demonstration, probably because it produces the most gruesome visual effects, and thus translates the scene most readily into a signifier of terror.

Ironically, and maybe inevitably, survivors of the uprising ideologically replicate the state's violence against them. The difference is that they do not turn their bodies into mere signifiers and metaphors. They could not objectify or allegorize their bodies because they were confronting the bodies of their loved ones as well as their own, and not the bodies of the "mob," which belong only to public spectacle in the political discourse of the state. Actually, the hardest lesson the women workers learned in "The Flag" was that, when it comes to their bodies, the distinction between the private and the public spheres is a spurious and arbitrary, if not a violent one. They were not allowed to hide "their most intimate parts," and "their intestines" were revealed in broad daylight, in the public arena. By once again going through the violence the state had wreaked on them instead of covering up each other's shame and guilt in a "humanistic" way, they refused to return to the "normality" of prerevolutionary reality. They accepted the significance of their bodies in the public sphere in a way which refuses to nullify its materiality so that "they would start again."

As I have already pointed out, the author makes it clear that the subjects of her language and the political agents in her narrative are women. Here we must recall that, like the resistance literature of many other oppressed peoples, Korean resistance literature traditionally has exploited women's bodies as metaphors, even when, or especially when, they were protesting against state cruelty or the invasion of foreign forces. Ever since Japan forcefully annexed Korea in 1910, the most popular metaphor in the Korean nationalistic literary discourse was the country being raped by a foreign force. Writers who discuss the army of Korean women that provided public prostitutes for Japanese soldiers as a symbol of national humiliation do not understand the issue in the context of imperialism *and* gender, imperialistic *and* sexual violence.[9] When Koreans discussed the neo-imperialist domination of Korea by the United States, again the most widely used metaphor was Korean prostitutes proliferating around the U.S. Army bases, but the discussion failed to recognize actual female bodies violated and destroyed.[10] Female bodies have indeed been metaphorized and exploited by nationalistic discourses.

Korean national literature has produced numerous politically conscious and oppositional writers, such as Hwang Sokyong, Kim Jiha, Ko Un, Song Kisuk, Cho Chongrae, Hyon Kiyong, and Pak Wanso. With the exception of Pak Wanso, they are all male writers, whose works centralize not only mass struggles but masculinized struggles; see, for example, *Chang Kilsan* by Hwang Sokyong, *Nokdujangkun* [General Nokdu] by Song Kisuk, and *Taebaeksanmaek* [The Taebaek mountains] by Cho Chongrae. Even when their narratives portray women, the female characters are represented as innocent victims and are conflated with the imagery of Korean nature and landscape. *Daesol nam* [The south, a grand narrative] by Kim Jiha and *Maninbo* [Poems on ten thousand people] by Ko Un also have the tendency to foreground male subjectivity as a politically mobile and healthy mass ideal. Hyon Kiyong's *Paramtanun som* [Island on wind] is exceptional in that it deals with women's struggles against the Japanese colonial regime and offers a potential paradigm for the representation of female revolutionary subjects. Pak Wanso's *Ommaui maltuk* [Mother's stake] is also valuable for narrating modern Korean history from a woman's viewpoint and for centralizing the domestic space.

On the other hand, the works of Pak Nohae, the worker poet, offer ambivalent views on the issue of gender. In his first publication, *Nodongui saebyok* [Labor's dawn], Pak's poems display remarkably radical views of domestic labor, "romantic" relationships, and the ideology of family. Yet a later collection, *Ch'amdoen sijak* [True beginning], participates in the tradition of rhetoric that identifies women with the domestic sphere and familial space, thus metaphorizing them. For example, his powerfully evocative and appealing poem "Omoni" [Mother] argues that revolutionaries need to defy their mothers' *oson doson pyongonhan kajongeui paraem* [wish for a cozy and comfortable home] until they achieve the goals set for class struggle. By conflating the figure of mother and the cozy domestic space, which, in turn, emblematizes the acceptance of the status quo, Pak not only metaphorizes women but preempts any possible discursive space for the discussion of domestic labor and the exploitation of women—in or beyond the domestic space.[11]

E. San Juan, describing the proliferation of the sex-tourism industry and the emergence of socialist feminism in the Philippines, stresses the importance of getting beyond the male-dominated nationalist discourse as follows:

So there's no doubt about it: a quantum leap has occurred, even though it is just the germinal or incipient stage of a thoroughgoing and profound reversal of the terms of discourse, of the univocal and deductive logic of identity invested by male reason which underlies the profit-centered status quo. No longer do Filipina activists accept unquestioningly the hegemonic representation of women, a mode and strategy based on representation based on biology ("anatomy is destiny") and on assorted cultural determinisms (nature/woman vs. culture/man). No longer is the dominant phallogocentrism—the logocentric discourse of male supremacy—left unchallenged in the Philippines to hierarchize gender and affirm the male as the transcendental subject of order, reason, and progress.[12]

In the discourse of nationalism as well as in the representation of the democratization movement in Korea and the Philippines, women have been either subsumed under the transcendental male subject or associated with mother nature/mother country, suffering from foreign invasion and brutality. What goes on more or less unnoticed is the material exploitation of and (sexual) violence against these women by Korean or Filipino men as well as by outside forces. Either invisible as political agents or assimilated into the natural scenery of the mother country, these women's bodies have been written out of existence in colonial/neocolonial discourses and nationalist/oppositional discourses alike.

In a similar context, Chabram-Dernersesian discusses the importance of recovering the Chicana identity in "Chicano literature," which has been subsumed "into a universal ethnic subject that speaks with the masculine instead of the feminine and embodies itself in a Chicano male."[13] Like the author of "The Flag," Chabram-Dernersesian seeks a way of creating women's discourse and reclaiming women's subjectivities in collective struggle:

> Like Cotera, Lopez avoids the grand narratives of his/her-stories which recount singular historic deeds of remarkable individuals. She reenacts a collective struggle of group survival, constructing her identity with a barrage of affirmations that variously link her to the "weary campesina" (female farm worker) who "stoops," "sweats," and "toils," and to the farm worker who has been denied the right to live like other human beings.[14]

Likewise in "The Flag," women workers begin to reclaim their bodies (which "stoop," "sweat," and "toil") in a way that does not exploit, use, or nullify their bodies under any circumstances. This does not mean that they start celebrating their bodies right away. As things are, they are violated, scarred, bleeding, sick bodies, literally and metaphorically. Yet they begin to recognize themselves as autonomous members of a working class and as citizens of a third world country struggling within the neo-imperialist global order, so that "they would start again."[15]

Through painful recognition of the significance of their beings and bodies in the public sphere, Hong's women workers not only remember the Kwangju Uprising but constantly relive it and carry it on. And through these newly born revolutionary subjectivities, the uprising obtains its meaning as a genuine Revolution. Rosa Luxemburg argues:

> The Revolution . . . is something other and something more than bloodshed. In contradiction to the police interpretation, which views the revolution exclusively from the standpoint of street disturbances and rioting, that is, from the standpoint of "disorder," the interpretation of scientific socialism sees in the revolution above all a thoroughgoing internal reversal of social class relations.[16]

In that sense, to focus solely on the barbarity of the state power and the bloody sign of terror deliberately constructed by the military state on the Kwangju streets might be to follow the lead of "the police interpretation." By restricting the significance of the event to the bloodshed, "the police interpretation" adjudicates the frame of interpretation that reads the revolution as primarily "street disturbances and rioting," rather than as a thoroughgoing reinterpretation and reevaluation of class relations, which *are* the state.[17] Only by insisting on the interpretation of revolution as "a thoroughgoing internal reversal of social class relations" can the revolution, especially if it is one which seems to have been suppressed by state power, become a motivating power that can help the survivors "start again."

If we are to understand revolutions as not just graphic bloodshed and scattered glorious moments (certainly part of any revolution) but rather as a full-scale restructuring of class relations and history-making processes, the significance of violence has to be reexamined. Since the 1963 publication of the English translation of the chapter entitled "Concerning Violence" in Frantz Fanon's *Wretched of Earth,* the topic of violence has been taken up in many quarters of the Western world.[18] Addressing the issue of violence in the colonial situation, Fanon posits a theory of inevitability as follows:

> The existence of an armed struggle shows that the people are decided to trust to violent methods only. He of whom *they* have never stopped saying that the only language he understands is that of force, decides to give utterance by force. In fact, as always, the settler has shown him the way he should take if he is to become free. The argument the native chooses has been furnished by the settler, and by an ironic turning of the tables it is the native who now af-

firms that the colonialist understands nothing but force. The colonial regime owes its legitimacy to force and at no time tries to hide this aspect of things.[19]

Even though Fanon is explicitly discussing Algeria under the French colonial regime, his reading of the dynamics of the Algerian people's struggle for emancipation in terms of their use of violence is still applicable to many postcolonial societies. This is all the more significant because, as Fanon himself points out in the chapter "The Pitfalls of National Consciousness," in certain postcolonial societies where emancipation from class and other forms of oppression did not occur after decolonization, colonial structures of domination based on brutal force remain intact. "The Flag" addresses the issue of violence as follows:

> Citizens were appropriating the legitimacy of violence. The special military troops' ruthless massacre shook their lives beyond the atmosphere of terror. Young people didn't even have places to hide in. Those youths who lived in communities close to the downtown were wandering in the suburbs to stay away from the house searches. Even there, the troops were everywhere. Ultimately it was life or death. Fundamental violence erupting from crushed human dignity exploded. (184)

As Paulo Freire said, "Never in history has violence been initiated by the oppressed."[20] When a system of oppression in a postcolonial society reveals its ultimate illegitimacy through its arbitrary use of violence, the masses come to a realization that the system they are dealing with is once again the colonial regime of brutality in nativist disguise, a regime that understands only "the language of force." Following this recognition, the available options present themselves in painful clarity: armed struggle or "crushed human dignity" and the loss of lives. After more than thirty years of "postcolonial" history, the immediacy of Fanon's reading of imperialism and anti-imperialist struggle takes us by surprise.

"The Flag," nevertheless, is more than just a reiteration of Fanon's thesis on decolonization. It also provokes questions about female subjects and gender roles in the context of struggle and violence, and again raises questions about the masculinist assumptions of Korean nationalist discourse. The narrative of the story says that, even during the revolution, people tend to adhere to the gendered division of labor. The men discuss strategies and carry the guns, while the women prepare food in the kitchen. Tellingly, when she confronts her own imminent death, Hyongja asked for a gun for herself.

"Can I get a gun?"
"Why?"
"I think I will need it after all."
"We have guns, but not enough bullets."

The member of the SWAT team hurried away. Hyongja looked into the division rooms and acquired an M1 which did not have bullets. It looked as if no one wanted such an antique. . . . Yet her mind became calm and assured. She embraced the gun with both hands. It was cold. Yet, as the warmth of her own cheek moved onto the body of the gun, she felt an affection for it as if she had been using it everyday. (203)

In this scene, both the discussion of femininity and the outcry against the violence are rendered irrelevant. Hyongja feels affection for the gun, as if it is part of her own body (when "the warmth of her cheek moves onto it") and her everyday life. At that point, the gun is empowerment, enabling her to assert the sanctity of her life. When you confront the military state, which violates human dignity in a most flagrant manner, acquiring a gun signifies that you will at least obtain a chance to act as an agent. As in Audre Lorde's description of the resistance of African American women against racism and sexism, Hyongja finds peace, "remembering / we were never meant to survive".[21]

Here, I am deliberately drawing a correlation between the Korean female workers' armed struggle against the military state and African American women's resistance against a racist, sexist society. It is my belief that, despite Fanon's apparent blindness to the issue of gender, his thesis that genuine decolonization is only possible when formal decolonization is followed by emancipation from other types of injustices can also prove applicable to gender oppression. I believe it is important for postcolonial critics and theorists to remember that there is shared suffering as well as "structural similarity" in third world women's plights and struggles. E. San Juan's description of the revolution in the Philippines stresses the significance of women's struggles within the patriarchal capitalist system on a global level: "Socialist feminism, one can suggest, exists in the Philippines today inscribed in spontaneous practices, unable as yet to fully theorize itself within the precincts of the economistic and class-reductionist inheritance of the traditional left, but yet visible as an insistent lacuna, a hiatus of the thought-process, the necessary key to the decisive undermining of the authoritarian-patriarchal discourse of global capitalism."[22] Women's emancipation in a neocolonial society is "the necessary key to the decisive undermining" of global capitalism because, as Maria Mies has argued, one of the characteristics of late-twentieth-century transnational capitalism is a heightened exploitation of women as the cheapest sources of labor—housewives, workers, and sexual commodities in the third world. Mies also argues that such exploitation of women's bodies and labor power is reinforced by violence directed against women by the patriarchal capitalist state, violence that paralleled the brutalizing of workers, male and female, in neocolonial society. Mies finds "a structural similarity between women's struggles and the struggle of third world countries against imperialism . . . as the revolt of all those who had been defined as being outside of capitalism."[23] Reality, in fact, is precisely the opposite, as Marx and Rosa Luxemburg argued in their theses on primitive accumulation. Those "defined as being outside of capitalism" because they presumably do not produce surplus value and because they are not integrated in the wage system and the Western market economy (women and workers in colonial and neocolonial social formations) are exactly the ones who provide the necessary basis on which the visible phenomenon of the accumulation of capital goes on in a seemingly self-sufficient way. That is why "capitalism cannot function without patriarchy," and why "the goal of this system, namely the never-ending process of capital accumulation, cannot be achieved unless patriarchal man-woman relations are maintained or newly created."[24] Thus, when a Korean female worker, Hyongja, picks up a gun and feels empowered and assured, she has committed an act of subversion that poses a serious threat not only to the military state of Korea but also to global capitalism based on patriarchy.

I am not suggesting violence as a panacea or even as an ideal solution to postcolonial/neocolonial situations. As San Juan says, "The central issue is not the use or non-use of violence as a tactical means of struggle—violence . . . is never 'an easy, attractive option' for socialists or Marxist-Leninists; the issue is whether the goal of liberation, equality and collective/communal development can be achieved without pursuing, in total consciousness and responsibility, the project of a national liberation struggle for independence, freedom, and justice."[25] If we focus exclusively on the bloodshed and the scene of terror in reading the Kwangju Uprising and follow the model of police interpretation, we will be negligent in our responsibility to attain "total consciousness" in regarding the uprising as part of an ongoing struggle. Rather, we should reconfigure class and gender relations in the global context, using historical knowledge produced during the praxis of revolutionary actions, and start mapping out new strategies of struggle, with the final goal of total emancipation. Thus placing too much emphasis on the issue of violence as if it were the main and only concern would be not only misleading but dangerous. What is needed here, I believe, is total commitment to the "project of a national liberation struggle for independence, freedom and justice" in a way that does not preclude the use of violence but that regards violence as neither the goal nor the solution.[26]

At the end of "The Flag," an intellectual male who failed to be faithful to the uprising asks the female workers the meaning of an artwork. Earlier the narrative voice has described the visual image as follows:

> On the wall right over the bookcase, there was an unframed woodcut print on yellowish paper. A worker had a bowl in one hand and a book entitled *The Standard Labor Law* in the other hand. It was not "Burning Tears" but "A Burning Body" with flames blazing up all over the picture. The worker was Jon Tae-il. (215)

To construe the significance of the picture, you need to be familiar with the history of workers' and students' movements in Korea in the 1980s. Jon Tae-il was a twenty-two-year-old youth who burned himself to death on 13 November 1970 to protest a barbarous working environment and labor exploitation. In the 1980s, after the Kwangju Uprising, many Korean workers and students burned themselves to death in public places. It was the ultimate assertion of their individual bodies in the public sphere, and it forced the state and society as a whole to acknowledge the political significance of private bodies being turned into mere numbers in the labor market. In the picture, the worker is holding a book entitled *The Standard Labor Law*. The Law is being represented as a force antithetical to the repressive government.

Significantly, the female workers who participated in and survived "the May Revolution" now reevaluate and resituate the picture's signification in a revolution that is still living on. They fully appreciate the symbolic meaning of that particular type of the struggle, yet they do not romanticize it. Labor standard law could be a way of obtaining basic rights for the workers. Yet to these female workers who witnessed the slaughter committed by the state and lost family members and friends to the military regime under the guise of law, the criteria of legality is irrelevant.

Lukács seems to address the issue in his article "Legality and Illegality": "If [the proletariat of Central and Western Europe] is to become conscious of its historical mission and of the legitimacy of its rule it must first grasp the fact that the problem of legality and illegality is purely tactical in nature. It must be able to slough off both the cretinism of legality and the romanticism of illegality."[27]

"Cretinism of legality." Maybe that is the passage I have been looking for ever since I came home from school to an empty house and learned that my grandfather who was fighting for Law had somehow been defined as an "illegal" being by the state. I also believe that it is what I have been looking for in my class, where I have tried to map out configurations of the oppression of women in the imperialist context. My students and I look at the way women have redefined and reimagined themselves, society, and history when social "order" has become destabilized and denaturalized. We also investigate the ways the (female) body is imagined as a series of political signifiers when strict orders of signification are disturbed. More than that, we try to explore the potential of resistance that the discourses of women's work and the body possess. Tracing the pattern of imperialist discourse that finds its way into "realistic" writings and investigating the strategies of women writers who have resisted such an imperialist discourse, we attempt to construe how imperialist discourse is encoded, subverted, and sometimes resisted in certain postcolonial texts.

Finally, decoding documents of Western civilization that are "at the same time document[s] of barbarism,"[28] I try to come up with a discursive strategy that will allow me to narrate the history of my grandmother, my mother, myself, and ultimately my daughter, a history that has been silenced and marginalized by "big men's" history. I believe that the only way to break out of "a chain of events" and "one single catastrophe which keeps piling wreckage upon wreckage and hurls it in front of his feet,"[29] which I name patriarchal imperialism, is to insist on recognizing the diverse catastrophes that remain unnarrated and on tracing the patterns running through these catastrophes. I believe we need to discuss the issues of race, class, and gender in terms of imperialism and to bring these issues together without obscuring the specificities of each. It goes without saying that this is an ongoing project, just as the Korean masses' struggle against imperialism and women's struggle against patriarchy are our living reality.

1 For my grandfather's life and writings, see *Simdang Yi Pyonglin pyonhosa munjip* [Writings of Yi Pyonglin the lawyer] (Seoul: Dure, 1991).

2 This paper was originally drafted for a conference in 1991, though I have re-worked it over the intervening years. Some historians argue that the Korean democratization movement, led by workers and women as well as by intellectuals and students, reached its climax in June 1987, and that the subsequent repression and the election of President Kim significantly reduced and dissipated the oppositional force. Though I agree that the revolutionary fervor of 1986–87 has gone underground for the most part, I argue that the impact of that struggle is still very much alive, and I believe my thesis concerning the radicalization of the Korean democratization movement after the Kwangju Uprising remains valid. For a discussion of the Korean democratization movement after 1987 see "90 nyondae jungbanui simin undongkwa minjung undong" [Civil movements and mass movements in the mid-nineties], *Ch'angjakkwa Pip'yong* 21, no. 3 (fall 1993): 8–89. For a discussion of more recent democratization movements in terms of culture and the significance of the Kwangju Uprising see Paik-Nakchung, "Jigusi dae-ui minjok munhak" [National literature in the global age] *Ch'angjakkwa Pip'yong* 21, no. 3 (fall 1993): 90–121.

3 Hong Huidam, "Kitpal" [The flag], *Ch'angjakkwa Pip'yong* 16, no. 1 (spring 1988): 187; my translation. Future references appear in the text. bell hooks discusses the politics of genres in the context of the writing praxis of women of color in *Talking Back: Thinking Feminist, Thinking Black* (Boston: South End, 1989) as follows: "One must write and one must have time to write. Having time to write, having time to wait through silences, time to go to the pen and paper or typewriter when the breakthrough finally comes, affects the type of work that is written" (145). Female workers in "The Flag" include in their booklet "poems, autobiographical pieces, letters home, and essays"—whatever form of writing they can materially afford. It is suggestive that the narrative itself was published in *Ch'angjakkwa Pip'yong*, the progressive journal committed to social change that attempts to integrate "high culture" and mass culture. The journal, a leading force in the Korean democratization movement, publishes short stories and reports from worker-writers as well as theoretical articles by academic intellectuals. Because of its uncompromisingly radical nature, the journal was forcibly closed by the Korean government, which canceled its registration in 1980. "The Flag" was published in the first issue of the journal after the government allowed it to be reregistered in 1988.

4 The way the uprising has been represented and discussed in the United States more than makes my case. There has been little attention given to the incident, and most "reports" have simply reiterated the U.S. government's official stance, in which the U.S. government absolves itself from all blame

and replicates the Korean government's representation of the uprising. *The Kwangju Uprising: Shadows over the Regime in South Korea*, ed. Donald N. Clark (Boulder, Colo.: Westview, 1988) is exceptional in that it attempts to approach the uprising from various points of view. Yet even for this collection of essays written by Korean specialists in the American academy, the objective seems to be that of easing Americans' consciences and protecting "national integrity." The focus of discussion is the reputation of "American public servants," not what happened (and might happen again, according to the author) to the "South Korean people" on whom any stray Korean military general can turn his guns with "tacit support" from the U.S. military commanders. Again, nobody can reproach American scholars for adopting "a point of view which is strictly" American. But we should also point out that holocausts, like torture, "as might well be expected," affect most profoundly the people who are injured, mutilated, and killed, and not those who, for whatever reasons, stand at the other end of the gun.

5  Georg Lukács, *History and Class Consciousness: Studies in Marxist Dialectics* (Cambridge: MIT Press, 1971), 152.

6  Lukács, *History and Class Consciousness*, 159.

7  For a discussion of the concepts of "freedom" and "necessity" see Antonio Gramsci, *Selections from the Prison Notebooks* (New York: International Publishers, 1971), 206–276, 317, 322–380.

8  The way we name the incident, I argue, profoundly affects our reading of it. The Korean government originally called it "a riot," whereas those people who participated in the uprising have always called it "a revolution." Women workers in "The Flag" call it "the May Revolution." In this paper, I mostly use the term *uprising* unless I am arguing for the possibility of the maturation of the uprising into revolution.

9  For a discussion of Korean women's struggles in the eighteenth and early nineteenth centuries see Kumari Jayawardena, *Feminism and Nationalism in the Third World* (London: Zed, 1986), 213–225. Although because of her lack of understanding of Japanese imperialism, Jayawardena fails to address crucial factors in Asian history during this period, the book provides historical background of Asian women's struggles. Chungmoo Choi argues for the need to address third world women's issues in the context of imperialism, patriarchy, and capitalism. She points out that the issue of "comfort women" should be addressed within the problematic of imperialism *and* patriarchy in her essay "Korean Women in a Culture of Inequality," in *Korea Briefing, 1992*, ed. Donald Clark (Boulder, Colo.: Westview, 1992). I also argue that the issue of sex tourism and the exploitation of Korean and other Asian women's bodies in the "advanced capitalistic world system," which is being reinforced and perpetuated by the patriarchal system inside their society, has to be interrogated in the problematic of imperialism, capitalism, and patriarchy. See Maria Mies, *Patriarchy and Accumulation on a World Scale: Women in the International Division of Labor* (London:

Zed, 1986), 75–106. See also Miranda Davies, ed., *Third World–Second Sex: Women's Struggles and National Liberation, Third World Women Speak Out* (London: Zed, 1983); and Yayori Matsui, *Women's Asia* (London: Zed, 1987).

10 For a feminist rewriting of the situation see Kim Pyola's short story "Kkut-naji anun norae" [The song that hasn't ended], *Ch'angjakkwa Pip'yong* 21, no. 3 (fall 1993): 222–240. For a discussion of the significance of the ideology of the female body in Korean national literature see You-me Park, "Decolonization and the Discourse of Body in Korean National Literature," in *In Pursuit of Contemporary East Asian Culture,* ed. Xiaobing Tang (Boulder, Colo.: Westview, 1995).

11 For a discussion of Pak Nohae's works within the larger context of Korean national literature see Paik Nak-chung, "Onului minjokmum-hakkwa minjokunding" [Today's national literature and national movement"], *Ch'angjakkwa Pip'yong* 16, no. 1 (spring 1988): 222–223. See also Im Ch'olgyu, "Pak Nohaeron" [Discussion on Pak Nohae], *Ch'angjakkwa Pip'yong* 21, no. 4 (winter 1993).

12 E. San Juan, *Crisis in the Philippines: The Making of a Revolution* (South Hadley: Bergin and Garvey, 1986), 174–175.

13 Angie Chabram-Dernersesian, "I Throw Punches for My Race, but I Don't Want to Be a Man: Writing Us—Chica-nos (Girl, Us)/Chicanas—into the Movement Script," in *Cultural Studies,* eds. Lawrence Grossberg, Cary Nelson, and Paula Treichler (New York: Routledge, 1992), 82.

14 Chabram-Dernersesian, "I Throw Punches," 84.

15 Even though "The Flag" addresses the issue of the representation of the body, it does not foreground the female body as a gender-specific body. I read such hesitancy on the part of the author as an act of negotiation of the discursive formation of Korean national literature, which tends to either biologize and sexualize female bodies or negate them altogether. Hong seems to probe a possibility of representing women's bodies without falling into either of these traps.

16 Rosa Luxemburg, "The Mass Strike, the Political Party, and the Trade Unions," *Rosa Luxemburg Speaks* (New York: Pathfinder, 1970), 186.

17 In *A Theory of Capitalist Regulation: The U.S. Experience* (London: NLB, 1979), 32, Michel Aglietta argues that twentieth century imperialism is based on the formation of a system of states that guarantees the circulation of capital on a global scale, and that, in that sense, the state *is* the wage system. The unique nature of the Korean state, which is a product of World War II and the Cold War, and its operation as a wage system in the context of global imperialism has to be thoroughly interrogated. For a discussion of "the form of state-capitalism" in Korea see Chungmoo Choi, "The Discourse of Decolonization and Popular Memory: South Korea," *positions* 1, no. 1 (spring 1993): 77–102. Contrary to the dearth of material in the United States and other first world intellectual communities, the discussion revolving around the division of labor and the wage system within the global

(dis)order in South Korea has been a heated and productive one. The central site of dialogue seems to have been and continues to be *Ch'angjakkwa Pip'yong*, in which "The Flag" was published in 1988. See also Paik Nak-Chung, "South Korea: Unification and the Democratic Challenge," *New Left Review* 197 (1993): 67–84.

18 It seems that this tendency will go on for some time for one reason or another. Homi K. Bhabha predicts that "[revolutionary psychoanalyst Frantz Fanon]'s moment in cultural studies has yet to come" ("Postcolonial Authority and Postmodern Guilt," in Grossberg et al., *Cultural Studies,* 64). The political implications of such interest in certain aspects of Fanon's work will be discussed later. For the discussion of the way Fanon's theory of decolonization has been (mis)represented and co-opted in certain forms of "postcolonial" discourse see Cedric Robinson, "The Appropriation of Frantz Fanon," *Race and Class* 35, no. 1 (1993): 79–89.

19 Frantz Fanon, *The Wretched of the Earth* (New York: Grove, 1963), 84.

20 Paulo Freire, *Pedagogy of the Oppressed* (New York: Continuum, 1990), 41.

21 Audre Lorde, "A Litany for Survival," in *Black Unicorn* (New York: Norton, 1978), 32.

22 San Juan, *Crisis in the Philippines,* 15.

23 Mies, *Patriarchy and Accumulation,* 27–32. On the topic of women's labor and capitalism see also Mariarosa Dalla Costa and Selma James, *The Power of Woman and the Subversion of the Community* (Bristol: Falling Wall, 1972).

24 Mies, *Patriarchy and Accumulation,* 38.

25 San Juan, *Crisis in the Philippines,* 40.

26 In this context, it is suggestive that most discussions of Fanon among Western academics revolve exclusively around two issues: psychoanalytical interpretation of colonial mentality, which Fanon discusses in *Black Skin, White Masks* (New York: Grove, 1967) but later transcends and fundamentally revises in *Wretched of the Earth,* and his discussion of violence. Without firmly contextualizing his major texts within the history of Algerian revolutionary struggles as well as Fanon's own evolution as a revolutionary intellectual, his theory on colonial mentality and violence can be (ab)used to reinforce sensationalism and bourgeois individualism, which Fanon argued is the foremost detrimental influence of colonialism and which the colonized must overcome to attain emancipation.

27 Lukács, *History and Class Consciousness,* 270.

28 Walter Benjamin, *Illuminations* (New York: Schocken, 1968), 256.

29 Ibid., 257.

# LA JEUNESSE

中國郵務局特准掛號認爲新聞紙類

青年雜誌

第一卷　第一号

卡內基

## Spring, Temporality, and History in Li Dazhao

■ At this moment of radical crisis for Marxism, the questions of how to approach the work of China's first Marxist, Li Dazhao, and why, are questions of the utmost seriousness. In regard to the first, the question of approach, one is governed by Li's status as a Marxist thinker, and that requires a present revaluation of his thought as political doctrine. In regard to the second but nonetheless significant problem of why Li Dazhao's record compels rereading, I would respond that by virtue of his innovations Li contributed to the bridge-building work of Marxists who have, over the course of this century, accorded a definitive singularity to modern Chinese thinking.[1]

In the wake of the definitive collapse of the socialist states and the current crisis of European parliamentary regimes, we now face our own emergent crisis. This is in part due to the consolidation of a rigid consensus that holds the "market economy" supreme. But the fault also lies partly with the dimming of the possibility of emancipatory politics globally, the same "revolutionary politics" that for two centuries now has provided progressives with a common beacon. Consequently, we find ourselves surrounded by a generalized belief in the brutality of profit taking as the sole condition of social life. And because these immediate realities—decline of emancipatory thinking and the abandonment of alternatives to marketization—shape modern political culture, approaching the thinking of Li Dazhao is made doubly difficult.

What I propose here is a way out of our present tangle, a way that stresses the singular subjective attitude of the intellectual Li Dazhao within China's very special political and social conditions. However, my analysis also reminds us that our own intellectual impasse may indeed have much in common with that which Chinese intellectuals encountered at the beginning of the first decade of this century. Though it would be misleading to say that we find ourselves in the exact same state as Li Dazhao, it is true that, different as our immediate circumstances may be, we share with him the general decay in the framework of cultural references that previously situated our politics: this is the malaise, if not despair, that we as progressive intellectuals experience, and that forges our kinship with the intellectuals of that other time. (Though they endured their own situations of loss in the same way that we must suffer ours, one must still always be careful with such analogies.)

How would this possibly dangerous analogy work? The ideological situation immediately following the collapse of the Chinese empire in 1911–12 was extraordinarily confused. Obvious failure was attending the establishment of a modern parliamentary system, and widespread hopes for the Chinese Republic were fading. These factors did nothing but aggravate the immediate, unprecedented political crisis. But—as we are coming to find with the political crisis at the end of the century—the crisis included the annihilation of all past traditional references. It did not seem at all self-evident to the men and women in Li Dazhao's time that "Western" political and cultural references were importable, or even that, in the event of their being imported, they would prove suitable to Chinese conditions.

It bears repeating that, while the ingredient codes of Chinese heritage were increasingly dispersed and fragmented, enlightened Chinese intellectuals around 1914 had no reason to consider the promises held out by Western Enlightenment heritage as anything but precarious. The failure of the republican enterprise in China, on the one hand, and the Great War in Europe, on the other, were the two main factors contributing to widespread disillusion among Chinese intellectuals. Though the young Li Dazhao spent these years writing about the "great grief" engendered by the cruel, bewildering postimperial order, another great intellectual of the previous generation, Yan Fu, was busy renouncing his earlier commitment to diffusing modern Western thought, and planning means, albeit in a pathetic mode, of returning to staunch Confucian values out of disgust for the ideological morass of World War I.[2] And yet, in the second half of the 1910s, there arose a new generation of intellectuals, formed in that context of radical cultural crisis, who pioneered what is arguably the most intellectually fertile period in Chinese thought over the course of this century—I am referring to the New Culture Movement. In the climate of the early May Fourth, Chinese art, politics, science, and language became subjects of intense examination in a moment of great inventiveness.

But this, of course, is the crucial difficulty: the very catastrophes experienced under Marxist state regimes, what Alain Badiou has recently called "obscure disaster," arose out of the same Marxist political culture that these creative and inventive enlightenment figures in China shaped at the historical moment of the May Fourth era under the very same extraordinary intellectual impulses.[3] Moreover, since at least the mid-1980s, references to the May Fourth have become exceedingly problematic among Chinese intellectuals (this is widely understood, and I am not subscribing to the official stand on the May Fourth). These factors contribute to the difficulty of evaluating the sequence of intellectual events that lead from Li Dazhao to the "obscure disaster" of the post-Liberation era. No doubt another order of difficulty has been added by the events of 1989 in Tiananmen Square and the fall of the Soviet empire. In any case, the intelligibility of the period of the "origins of Chinese Marxism" has, for all these reasons, reached a rather serious impasse among scholars inside China and elsewhere.

It is now time—indeed, it is indispensable to our own situation— that we rethink some very important elements of what has been, over the last decades, the progressive scholar's position on the May Fourth, and it is important in doing so to avoid any hint of a sort of smug repetition. Let me give an example of what I mean. Maurice Meisner's brilliant 1967 monograph *Li Ta-chao and the Origins of Chinese Marxism* continues to be a basic reference on Li Dazhao and an accurate study of the intellectual history of those crucial years leading Li toward an embrace of Marxism.[4] Meisner reconstructed the entire process of Li's thinking to 1927 and the founding of the Chinese communist movement. But, as a book, *Origins* is deeply marked by its author's subjective commitment to engaging the thinking of his subject, Li Dazhao. Meisner's very commitment must provoke us to ask where are the problematics today that would enable us to study a thinker like Li Dazhao in a similarly committed dialogue. Meisner published at the height of the Great Proletarian Cultural Revolution, after all—indeed, on the eve of May 1968, which was a moment of intensely felt Marxist enthusiasm all over the world. The question facing us is quite different: what should be done now to understand the origins of Chinese Marxism in light of the global disaster of Marxism today?

What I propose to do here is to reconsider Li Dazhao's thought in a slightly different light and as pivoting around a question about subjectivity in politics and the intelligibility of Time or temporality. I will argue that this axis of subjectivity and temporality enabled Li to elaborate the modernity of a nation's people and not vice versa. In this sense, Li Dazhao's conception of State differed remarkably from the dominant tradition in Chinese thought, and yet was far from being a mere copy of notions inherited from the European storehouse of political philosophy. Recalling once again that World War I was actually the point of no return as regards to the nineteenth-century notion of the nation-state, it is important to stress that in the years immediately following it, Li was preoccupied with analyzing how the war had affected political ideology and what changes it had wrought on state forms. In his writings he dealt primarily with concrete political situations and relatively less with notions of the ideal state. At that same time he established his constitutional political vision, though he did not share the illusions of many of his compatriots who were parliamentarians. What I want to stress here is the essentially modern appeal of Li Dazhao's vision of a state deeply rooted in a sphere of subjectivity and thinking. This modern vision, I would argue moreover, may conceivably offer us acutely interesting insights under our present pressing conditions.

## SPRING

Li Dazhao's ideas concerning the subjective wellsprings of states so deeply influenced Chen Duxiu that, in September 1915, Chen founded *Qingnian zazhi* [Review of youth], later *Xin qingnian* [New youth], the most influential review of the subsequent decade. As the famous "Jinggao qingnian" ["Call to youth"] in the inaugural issue made clear, Chen had transformed his early pessimistic outlook.[5] His call expressed a desire for fresh ethics which would be able to inspire new intellectual research aimed at a radical political and cultural renewal of the country. But *New Youth* was also an important testing ground for Li Dazhao. "Qingchun" ["Spring"], Li's long October 1916 prose poem, was a fundamental contribution and proved to be a constant source of inspiration for an entire generation of intellectuals, to say nothing of being one of the best literary texts produced in the 1910s. I state this because, although Li Dazhao made a great effort to write in elegant classical Chinese, one can also perceive that he is on the threshold of modern *baihua,* or colloquialized, written Chinese. But the problem of written expression is not secondary in texts where an author must cope with renegotiating new, founding categories and political terminologies. Li's complex "half-literary, half-modern" (*ban-wen, ban-bai*) style, brought over what was actually a double tension, in that it was not only a newly surfacing, colloquialized written medium but also one that sought to convey a new means of thinking.[6]

To develop this point through an example, one might remark that the title "Qingchun" means both "Spring" and "Youth." Li played the doubled meaning as a poet might, squeezing out the multiple possibilities latent in the joined words. But he also sought another, altogether different meaning for *qingchun*. A question underlies the poem: if *qingchun*'s mainstream combined meaning is "a season of life" or "a season of the year," (i.e., Spring and Youth), then isn't the sense of the word closely connected to time? This is what Li discovers in his poeticizing, and when he treats "Spring" as a category of thought he brings the question of temporality directly into the text:

Humanity in the universe is as tiny as a drop in the ocean.
To delight forever in the happiness of Spring, we must ask
    ourselves:
In the universe and in nature, is Spring endless?

.  .  .  .  .  .  .  .  .  .  .  .  .

Whether the universe is endless or not
depends on its having an end or a beginning.
Did the universe ever have a beginning? I say: The beginning was
    in nothingness.
Will the universe really have an end? I say: The end will be in
    nothingness.
In other words, there is no end and no beginning.
This lack of a beginning, of an end,
as far as space goes, is infinity;
as far as time, eternity.
In absolute terms, non-being is the essence of all this.
In relative terms, in the universe there is also evolution.
If there is evolution, involution is also necessary:
myriads of singular and different phenomena are generated.
As for these myriads of phenomena,
in totality there is singularity, in Life there are lives;
the whole of singularity, however large, has an end,
a life, however long, will come to pass.
Therefore, if there is life, there is death; if there is prosperity,
    there is decline,
if there is *yin*, there is *yang*; if there is *pi*, there is *tai*,

if there is *bo*, there is *fu*; if there is contraction, there is
    expansion,
if there is decrease, there is increase; if there is fullness, there is
    emptiness,
if there is fortune, there is misfortune;
if there is something auspicious, there is something
    inauspicious;
if there is Spring-youth, there is old age; if there is vigor, there is
    decrepitude.
The essence of all this is the there-being.[7]

From the primary polarity of *yin/yang*, through the long strand of
oppositions that Li lifts out of the *Yijing* (that enigmatic condensa-
tion of political knowledge and ancient wisdom literature), the major
references of the poem are, besides the *Yijing*, the *Lao Zi* and the
*Zhuangzi*.[8] The difference between this philosophical reflection and
myriad others on these same sources in previous eras lies in the fact
that Li Dazhao is not searching for equilibrium. He is attempting to
figure out ways of thinking about time. That is why each example he
brings forth demonstrates that what he is referring to is the essence
of Spring. Li's object in this demonstration is to cross over old clichés
of cyclicity, and locate a theoretical division of time that can allow us
to think of time in its singularity as well as in its relation to eternity.
Lying at the center of the text, then, is the main category of "spring
ego," or *qingchun zhi wo*. This notion, developed out of a really archaic
vision, extracted temporality from ideas of eternity while shedding the
notion of cyclicity in the process: it became a break in the line of Daoist thinking about temporality, the context Li specifically refers to in
the poem.

Li Dazhao's break with convention and search for a noncyclical eternity made his impulse remarkably different from the iconoclasm that
permeated Chen Duxiu's appeal in "Call to Youth." The difference
lay in Li's pioneering forms of logic, as well. Li proposed his category of Spring ego as essentially consisting of a double temporal discontinuity: to attain the eternity of Spring, the task of today's Spring
ego involves not only "killing" the yesterday's Spring ego (this was
the limit of Chen Duxiu's appeal) but also anticipating the conditions
under which tomorrow's old Spring ego will abdicate in the future.[9] Of
course, this second break is far more difficult to bring about, because
it requires the capacity to anticipate a future interruption of time. In
these openings, Li sees an anticipation of the novelties of temporality

and the guarantee that the present is not only a link within a cyclical chain but also a site for decisions and thinking, and thus a step forward toward making time intelligible.

> The conscience of youth consists
> in breaking the links of past history,
> in destroying the prison of old rotten doctrines.
> Young people should not only keep old skeletons
> from entangling the vitality of the present ego,
> but, with the present Spring,
> they must kill the Spring ego of the past
> and induce today's Spring ego
> to abdicate in favor of tomorrow's.
> They should get rid of artificial, inconsistent, and hypocritical
>   life,
> and stand fast with their independent ego,
> in a universe of perpetual change.
> Thus, bare and unhampered, in all their beauty and nobleness,
> they should not only kill today's old ego,
> but with today's old ego,
> prescribe the killing of tomorrow's old Spring ego.

What I see in Li Dazhao's notion of "prescribing the killing of tomorrow's old Spring ego," is something rather consonant with Heidegger's idea of the "anticipation of death." Now, the German philosopher considered that anticipation of death was the only authentically ontological position available with relation to time. That meant he excluded all possible means of thinking about temporality from any specific point of "visibility" in any particular "present."[10] Heidegger understood the "anticipation of death" to be ontological (i.e., intrinsically philosophical), and thus in direct contrast to the "ontic," or experiential nature of the "present."[11] But it seems to me that Li Dazhao's figure of "the killing of tomorrow's old Spring ego" may be considered somewhat more complexly—that is, as exceeding this (in relative terms) crude Heideggerian notion. "The killing of tomorrow's old Spring ego" is for Li Dazhao neither ontic nor ontological, nor, in the last analysis, strictly philosophical, inasmuch as the "present" is mainly the site of a decision (be it political, scientific, or artistic) concerning the anticipation of the future. The real time of the Spring ego is a "future perfect," and in this regard perhaps Alain Badiou has more closely approximated what Li is conveying in the poem. As Badiou puts it, "*The time of what is called totalitarianism is the past, its legitimacy is legendary or racial. Parliamentary time is the nullity of the present, the sum total of a bookkeeping process. Lastly, classical revolutionary time is the future. But real political time is a future perfect. It implies organization through its double dimension of anteriority and future."*[12]

There is a second way of grasping Li's vision of temporality and that is by attempting to discern the way he understood and used the term *zhong* (center or centering; e.g., in *Zhongguo* [China]).

When our country was founded it was given a fine name:
*Zhonghua*. What does *Zhonghua* mean?
*Zhong* is what lies at the center of an area;
but it is the duty of our generation's youth
to consider this *zhong* not just from the point of view of space,
as if China were at the center of the world,
but also from the point of view of time.
Let us look at the history of the world:
so many changes from antiquity to now!
We must stand in today's Spring
and mark out a point that acts as *zhong*.
Before this *zhong*, history restricted itself
to recording the birth and evolution of humanity, nations, and
    states,
just like evolutionary theory restricted itself to studying
the birth and evolution of the sun and earth, of plants and
    animals,
all the way up to humankind.
But after this *zhong*, history will consider all these things
the scope of ancient history,
and will attempt to register the rebirth
of the Springtime of humanity, nations, and states.
History before this *zhong*
is finished, burnt, and buried.
Whereas history after this *zhong*
is like a blank sheet of paper, yet intact,
waiting to be marvelously painted.
History before this *zhong*
is old, a history of the dead;
whereas after this *zhong*
it is a Springtime history, a history of young people in their
    vitality.
Young people! Let us assume with all possible determination

the responsibility of standing firm, as rocks in mid-stream;
In this year's Spring, let us at once consider today's *ksana*
as the starting point of this *zhong* of time.

What I find absolutely remarkable is that in attributing this new sense to *zhong*, Li Dazhao is at the same time operating directly on the signifier "China," since *zhong* is part of that nation's name. In this manner, he sidesteps the tendency to spatialize the notion and offers a temporal notation in its place. No longer is *Zhongguo* or *Zhonghua* used to denote a sort of self-congratulation, or better still in those tragic years, a narcissistic model of self-consolation; rather, Li argues, there has arisen an urgent need to periodize the very existence of China, beginning from its immediate, present disaster. More important still, by forcing the name "China" to pass through the realm of poetic invention and inserting it in a semantic play on *zhong* in its temporal sense, Li Dazhao marks the definitive introduction of the question of temporality, and of its unavoidable, noncyclical discontinuities, into Chinese intellectual space.[13] I would argue that, by relocating China's very name from a generally spatial to a time-oriented semantics, Li brought about Chinese thinking's entrance into modernity.

Thus, although Li's "Qingchun" seems to share some of the moral and ethical intonations of Chen Duxiu's "Call to Youth," the temporal factors he introduced effectively relocated the problem from the moral/ethical context to an historical/political plane. Moreover, by interjecting the notion of eternity, he raised the question of the subject's immortality. This, however, did not occur in a religious framework. For Li Dazhao, as for Badiou nearly a century later, only the independent subjectivity within the present *zhong* is ever eternal, and only this independence—that of the subject in an immediate, given, temporalized spatiality—can be considered in terms of true faithfulness to the inner essence of the Spring ego. We should not dismiss this question of eternity. Because it deals with the question of immortality and the infinite, the question of eternity expands the multiple possibilities inherent in a reality. This is what Badiou means in his 1993 volume *L'éthique*.

An immortal: such indeed is Man [*sic*], as is shown by the worst situations which can be inflicted on him, inasmuch as he attains singularity in the multiform and rapacious flux of life. This must be our starting point when thinking anything about Man. So that, if "Human rights" do exist, surely they are not the rights of life over death, nor the rights of survival over destitution and poverty. They are, rather, the self-asserting rights of the Immortal, or the rights of Infinity, exerting their sovereignty over the contingency of suffering and death. That in the end we will all die, and nothing will be left but dust, doesn't make one bit of difference, as far as the identity of Man as immortal is concerned, when he asserts what he is in opposition to the will-of-being-an-animal that circumstances expose him to. And, as everybody knows, each Man has the unexpected capacity for being this immortal, in the course of greater or lesser circumstances and for the sake of important or not so important truths. In all instances, subjectivation, which is immortal, is what actually makes Man. Beyond this, there is nothing but a biological species, a "featherless biped" whose charms are not all that obvious.[14]

The independent ego, according to Li Dazhao, is *the condition* for recognizing the singularity of the times. Chinese youth, he writes

should get rid of artificial, inconsistent, and hypocritical life,
and keep firm with an independent ego,
in a universe of perpetual change.

## TODAY

As Li Dazhao eventually made clear in a 1923 essay, his research on time had to be conducted independent of any field of knowledge, philosophy included, because none of the established disciplines were capable of correctly answering his simple question, "What is time?" Thus: "I have put forth this question to metaphysics, epistemology, psychology, mathematics, physics, astronomy, but I have received only partial explanations." Li remained unconvinced by the explanations favored by certain physicists regarding "ether" (a basic concept for the philosopher Tan Sitong, as well), but he also found much to be dissatisfied with in the responses he labeled "chronology" (i.e., quantitative measurement of time) and psychology (time as a state of mind). Li was even less convinced by the philosophical theories according to which time would have been "like a line in space that always leads further . . . made up of a succession of points comprehending the past, the present and the future." In Li's view, the main problem that these theories had left unanswered was precisely the place held by the present. "If the line that has already been drawn is the past," he argued, "and the one which has not yet been drawn is the future, then where does the present lie?" His own response or answer to the question, "What is time?" was that in the relation between past and future, in the "movement" between them, the present is implied, not as a simple natural passage from past to future but rather as a driving force. "The present," he wrote, "is life, force, action and creation. If a kṣaṇa were without action and movement, its present would return to nothingness and its life would be lost."[15]

Five years earlier, in April 1918, Li had published "Jin" ["Today"] in the pages of *New Youth* dedicated to the problems of the present. This followed "Spring" by two years, and in the course of that time, the nation's internal situation had become more complex, and the New Culture Movement had already developed a series of key debates on science, democracy, language, literature, and so on, but China's present was still quite gloomy. Indeed, under the disastrous oppression of the warlord conflicts and the uncertainty of what the end of World War I would bring for the nation, one could very easily imagine that China's present was hopeless. The only event running counter to the logic of war was the October Revolution, the real contents of which, however, were almost unknown in China, even among progressive intellectuals like those in *New Youth*. And yet, this was the eve of the May Fourth Movement, and Li had perceptively discerned that the general situation was showing signs of imminent change. The problem, as he saw it, was that the direction of change was still quite undetermined: would it entail further catastrophe, or the intellectual rejuvenation of the country? It was this specific question that pressured Li to broaden his investigation of time, as developed earlier in "Spring," by focusing on the nature of the present.

"Today" is dominated by an apparent contradiction. On the one hand, it appears to deal only with the relation between past and present, and advocates the primacy of the latter; on the other, the movement of Li's argumentation is underscored by an unvoiced question, the question of the future. This does not surface until the end of the text, and, as we will see, its main referent is once again Chen Duxiu. As for the central part of the essay, it begins with a discussion on the notion of "today" and quotes mainly the work of Emerson; here, however, the references to Bergson's thought are probably even more important, though not openly declared.

> The most precious thing in the world is "today," and "today" is also the easiest thing to lose. And it is precisely because it is so easy to lose that I think that it is the most precious. . . . Why is "today"

so easy to lose? Because the great transformations of the universe are unceasingly moving. Time, even if cherished and considered precious, cannot abide long among humans. Which *kṣaṇa,* among the infinite *kalpas,* is this "today" and this "present" I am talking about? I have just mentioned "today" and the "present," and immediately, quick as wind or lightning, they have already turned to 'past.' Wouldn't it be a pity to waste it in vain? (*LDZWJ* 1:532)

Here we encounter two kinds of questions. The first, and less complex one, involves the obvious references to contemporary Western philosophers like Emerson and Bergson. In my opinion, it would be best not to consider these references in terms of discrete philosophical systems; rather, they are side-glances supporting the contemporary intellectual relevance of the question of time in Li Dazhao. The emphasis here, in other words, is not so much to be seen in the intellectual transmission of a philosophy as in its relevance to the contemporary world and to the immediate pressures that brought Li Dazhao to consider the problem of time in the first place. The second issue is the whole question of the primacy of the present. In this latter regard, it is helpful to keep in mind Heidegger's remark against the simple "visibility" of the present as a means of access to the question of temporality. We might say that when the "primacy of the present" is in the foreground, time flows in a scattered, imperceptible fashion. One will recall, however, that in Li Dazhao's text there is a double discontinuity, since the basic category of his vision of temporality stems from his notion of "Spring ego." Thus for Li time is both "eternal change" and "persistence." Temporality is informed both by infinity and by singularity.

> An epoch's changes are not lost at all, but last into the next epoch, where they become infinitely diffused. In the world there is a perennial nature of reciprocal ties: the events of yesterday and those of today form complex events which, together with those of tomorrow, will form further complex events. Forces combine with other forces, questions imply other questions. The infinite "past" has the "present" to go back to, the infinite "future" has its origin in the "present." Between "past" and "future" there is always a link in the "present" which makes them eternal and turns them into the great reality, beginningless and endless. (*LDZWJ* 1:533)

In the passage above, Li Dazhao meditates on the means by which we can rethink relations of past, present, and future outside the notion

of spatial succession; thus he establishes that there are forms quali-
fying time other than those determined by ordinary common sense.
The ability to think in this novel way depends, Li argues, on a subjective attitude toward the present, and it is in this sense that the present
is "the most precious." What Li seeks to demonstrate here is precisely
the possibility of thinking of the "present" as a site for decisions regarding the future. The essay addresses two emerging attitudes toward
the "present": there are those who do not love "today" because they
find it disgusting, and there are those who are altogether too well satisfied with it. He distinguishes two further types among the disgusted
ones: those who romanticize the "past," hoping for a restoration of antiquity, and those who are dissatisfied with the present, but dream so
vividly of an imaginary future that they lose all contact with present
reality.

> They often shift into illusion, so that many of the undertakings
> which they dedicate their efforts to in the "present" are never real-
> ized, and they indulge only in the empty reign of the illusory. These
> two kinds of people not only cannot be of any help for progress, but
> are moreover a hindrance to it. Those that are content with "today"
> in general are people without aspirations and without conscious-
> ness, completely satisfied with the "present," people that within
> their own situation think that they can live a comfortable life and
> should not do anything to create something new. This sort of per-
> son loses what is good in "today" and blocks the progressive stream
> in a way not altogether different from that of those who find them-
> selves disgusted by "today." (*LDZWJ* 1:533)

Li counters this criticism by arguing that it is possible to assume
another attitude toward the "present" and to consider it as a subjective
division of time: to really think about the future, rather than simply
imagining it, one must take a calculated risk and decide about the
future from within the present.

> In this world it is not possible to be disgusted by "today" and turn to
> the "past" or the dream of the "future," thereby wasting the efforts
> of the "present." Nor is it possible to be pleased with "today" without
> making any effort in the "present" to look at the developments of
> the "future." Merits and guilt are created by "today" and can never
> be eliminated. The principal task of human life is to create virtue
> for posterity, to follow the process of reality in order that the eternal
> "ego" will be able to benefit from it, expand and diffuse itself into

infinity, because, quite definitely, "the universe is the ego and the ego is the universe."

In this quotation, Li Dazhao once again proposes the idea of "present" that he had developed earlier in "Spring." But here he interjects something more, the notion of virtue (*gongde*). It is in creating gongde that our main task lies when "creating the future." Nor is it relevant that gongde echoes the "*de*," or virtue, of both the Daoist and Confucian discourses, for the notion of gongde actually comes from the Buddhist tradition, where it means the merits accruing to good deeds. Li's notion of virtue is measured against the future: its testing ground is not the adequacy of religious belief but the absolutely precarious concept of unknown posterity. "To create virtue for posterity" is its impulse. In this sense, Li's gongde has a resoundingly political content. I am thinking here of the famous sentence uttered by Robespierre at the Convention of 5 February 1794, in his speech on the principle of public morals: "What is the principal foundation of democratic and popular government? Virtue. I hear that it is public virtue which accomplished such marvellous things in Greece and Rome and which has accomplished even more admirable things in Republican France; this virtue which is none other than the love of country and law." This leads me to recall Marx's own critique in *The Holy Family,* in which he said that this "illusion of Terror agents" stemmed from an ignorance of Ancient History. But even more interesting is the analysis of Robespierre's thought made by Sylvain Lazarus: "I will posit that liberty, virtue, justice are not an historical apparel, but rather are the terms of political thought. The Jacobins were not caught in an illusion."[16] In any case, for Li, as for Robespierre, virtue is resoundingly political.

"Virtue" became, thereby, a subjective prescription in Li Dazhao's thinking. Under the conditions of an unknown future, only "virtue" can make thinking the "present" possible as an unprecedented temporal experience. The "present" is made important because of the double decision that it implies: one must decide on the past, but on the future as well. The "Spring ego" is therefore today's risk in decision and it marks a discontinuity within the eternal flux of time; "Spring ego" establishes a new beginning that is not decided simply by the past and its pressures but rather by a decision that changes the perspectives of the future radically.

These were the temporal categories that Li Dazhao employed to think his way through the intricate doctrines of Marxism. It is thus not at all surprising that when he came to publish "My Vision of Marxism" in *New Youth*, the first serious introduction of Marxism to Chinese readers, he distinguished three parts in the new doctrine, corresponding to past, present, and future. "In Marx's theory of socialism," he argued, and it is clear that his threefold scheme is far more than a mere didactic device,

> it is possible to distinguish three main parts. The first concerns the past and is his theory of history, also called the theory of the evolution of social organization. The second concerns the present and is his economic theory, also known as the economic theory of capitalism. The third concerns the future and is his political theory, also known as the theory of socialist movements or social democracy. (*LDZWJ* 2: 50)

As Li accurately perceived, the crucial point of this temporal knot was precisely the "past" or the question of Marxism's historical vision. "It is simply impossible," he reasoned, "to take into consideration [Marx's] socialism apart from his peculiar conception of history. As a matter of fact, it is from his conception of history that Marx defines what the fundamental reasons for change in the social organization of life are" (*LDZWJ* 2: 50).

Leafing through Li's *Collected Works,* one comes to the obvious realization that his analysis of history and historiography gathered its greatest thrust from this distinctive approach to Marxism. About the time when "Spring" was drafted, he had finally become acquainted with historiography and had been studying Leopold von Ranke.[17] It is also likely that, as a student in Japan, Li Dazhao had come to read something of Hegel's conception of History; this is especially relevant when comparing Hegel's notion of "the present" to Li's.[18] But it was only when Li actually approached Marxism that the question of History became one of his central intellectual concerns.

The point at which Li Dazhao encountered most difficulties was that of distinguishing Marxism's political philosophy from its conception of History. It is remarkable that he attempted, relying for the most part on his own founding categories, to draw an accurate distinction between one temporality of Marxism, addressed to the *past* (i.e., the materialist conception of history), and another one, addressed to the *future* (i.e., political theory). As for placing "Marxist economic theory" in the "present," one should recall how completely Li's notion of the "present" was subjectively overdetermined. There is very little space in his scheme of things for any objectivism or economism. Rather, his interest in Marxian theory is not one of mere adherence to a given doctrine, but a means of access to an extraordinary field of research that allows him to put his own categories of consciousness, time, passions, and subjectivity to further test.[19]

The question of history, however, requires a specific critique because of its entanglement with politics in Marxist thinking and culture. The various objections that Li raised in his discussion of Marxist theory seem to be aimed at proving that politics are independent of history, while at the same time seeking to demonstrate the intellectual novelty and value, for historiography, of a "materialist conception of history." In this latter sense, the careful attention accorded to historiography after 1920 may be considered a further comparison with the philosophy of history. At Peking University, where Li taught the history of Western historiography, he systematically analyzed the thought of authors ranging from Jean Bodin, Louis Leroy, Montesquieu, Vico, and Comte, to Condorcet, Saint Simon, and Karl Marx.[20] Moreover, in his 1924 pamphlet *Shixue yaolun* [Elements of historiography] Li combined all his research and teaching materials with a tentative theory of historiography, to raise subtle distinctions between the categories of history, historiography, and philosophy of history (*LDZWJ* 2:713–765). The book abounds with outlines aimed at distinguishing the three fields of knowledge, as well as illustrating how many disciplines historians must take into consideration to do serious work. These ranged, in Li's view, from linguistics to anthropology, economics, aesthetics, archaeology, natural history, and so on. He mobilized myriad Western historians and thinkers, from Herodotus to Li's own contemporaries, as a means of stressing the distinction between historiography and documentation. In a subsidiary text, *Yanjiu lishide renwu* [The task of studying history], he even proposed concrete ways of carrying out the "analysis of sources," illustrating, for instance, how to evaluate early Chinese written texts that contain the word *bei*, or shell, either as a full character or as a radical, in view of a parallel contextual knowledge of early economic history, of a time when shells were used as a form of currency.

Each of these cases shows how important historiography proved to be for Li's intellectual work.[21] Moreover, I would add that he made this extraordinary effort precisely to maintain the distinction between history and politics. Take, for instance, the critique that Li leveled against the English historian Freeman, who promoted the view that "history is the politics of the past, politics the history of the present" (*LDZWJ* 2:716). Li Dazhao objected to this, saying that Freeman "considers politics and history to be the same thing and cannot distinguish one from the other. Interpreting history in this way is rather restrictive. History is lively, it is the life of the whole of humanity, which is not only political, but also economic, moral, religious, artistic, and so on. If, as Freeman says, history is politics, could it be said that all the rest, such as economy, religion, morality, art, and so on, does not belong to human life? Can all these things be left outside history?" (*LDZWJ* 2:716). Besides, the confusion of politics and history would have wreaked serious havoc on politics as well, by linking two different kinds of temporality—past and future—as well as making politics dependent on history. In other words, the intelligibility of the future would be held ransom by the burden of rendering the past intelligible. This was the essential tenet of historicism that Li firmly resisted, to the best of his capacity, while stubbornly maintaining, through a full deployment of his own categories, a distinct vision of political temporality that opened out onto a future time fully subjected to human inventiveness.

I will end on a last, and perhaps, in these times of disillusionment, most controversial (or, at least, most embarrassing to many a Chinese scholar), thesis forwarded by the Marxist Li Dazhao, namely, the notion of "mutual aid," or *huzhu*. Li used "mutual aid," in a contrastive sense along with "class struggle" even after the founding of the Chinese Communist Party. But, according to my way of thinking, the orthodox perspective that considers his continuing reliance on this notion merely an unresolved residue of his previous alleged populist or bourgeois democratic view is per se the result of dogmatic historicism. The explanation Li himself gave for pursuing that notion, that it formed the intersection between material and spiritual factors, cannot be taken altogether literally.

> Many people consider Marxism completely wrong because according to them this doctrine denies all ethical conceptions; they maintain that people will not accept the theory of class conflict. Marx, however, does not at all deny noble individual aspirations; he merely establishes the fact that a moral attitude, where reflecting the average ethical nature most common among individuals generally, can-

not influence conscious collective activity in the field of economic interests. We believe, on the contrary, that in this society, built on an economic base of class opposition, the ethical conception of socialism, as well as the ideas of mutual aid and brotherhood, are not in fact absent, though they are not allowed to implement themselves due to their daily destruction by the economic phenomena of class conflict. (*LDZWJ* 2:67)

In other words, Li Dazhao was not talking about a dialectic process between the ethical-spiritual and the economic-material; if we examine it carefully, the question he raises is rather one of the temporality of politics. By class conflict, he means history precisely in the Marxian sense of the history of class struggle. For Li, this pertains to the past. If we keep in mind the fact that, in Li's vision of Marxism, economy stands for "the present," we could translate his writing on "economic phenomena of class conflict" as meaning those phenomena through which the present is linked to the past.

Politics, in other words, cannot exactly reside on the side of class struggle. In fact, politics must emerge on another side altogether. That side is what Li Dazhao calls "mutual aid" and considers to be the unprecedented termination of class struggle. *Huzhu*, in this case, is actually an emblem of politics, and pertains properly to a future anticipated by the risk of decisions in the present, like those inherent in organizing communist politics in the years in which Li Dazhao was active. When Li advocated *huzhu*, he was actually extremely close to Marx's own most immediate political concern: close, that is, to Marx's remark that he was not the inventor of class or class struggle, but, rather, that he had *derived* it from reading closely all "bourgeois historians and economists," and that he was in fact interested in his own work only in demonstrating that class struggle would be resolved in a future which he called communism.

## NOTES

I wish to thank Tani E. Barlow for patience during her accurate reading and stylish editing of my Italo-English text and for her suggestions. Thanks also go to Sabrina Ardizzoni for all her help.

1 This should not divert our attention from Marxism's responsibility for certain orientalizing approaches in Chinese studies, but I would add that Marxist studies have been less culpable in this regard than other scholastic traditions.

2 "The Great Grief" [Da aipian] is the title of one of Li Dazhao's first articles,

published in April 1913. See *Li Dazhao wenji* (hereafter *LDZWJ*) [Collected works of Li Dazhao] (Beijing: Renmin chubanshe, 1984), 1:4–7.

3  I am employing the title and work of Alain Badiou's recent work dealing with the "death of communism" and its effects on our times. See Badiou, *D'un désastre obscure (Droit, État, Politique)* (Paris: Aube, 1991).

4  Maurice Meisner, *Li Ta-chao and the Origins of Chinese Marxism* (Cambridge: Harvard University Press, 1967).

5  I am referring here to the 1914–15 debate between Chen Duxiu and Li Dazhao. The first published an essay entitled "Yanshixin yu zijuexin" [Pessimism and consciousness], arguing that the question of the state could not be treated with a fatalistic attitude. Even in the worst conditions, the question of the state had to be considered, for Li, as the question of a subjectivity capable of thinking the existence of the State on a rational basis. In this sense, Li criticized the "pessimistic" attitude of Chen. See *Chen Duxiu wenzhang xuanbian* [Collected essays of Chenduxiu] (Beijing: Sanlian shudian, 1984), 1:67–72; *LDZWJ* 1:145–152.

6  The exhaustion of the older literary language was due to its inadequacy in expressing contemporary "modern" contents, according to a widely shared view. From the second half of the nineteenth century, particularly in the years of the 1898 Reform Movement, there had already been a vast number of *baihua* journals circulating among intellectuals, suggesting a deep-felt need for a means of expression accessible to all social strata rather than a literacy restricted to the bureaucratic-intellectual elite. The language that these journals pioneered proliferated into the mass literate arena only after Lu Xun's *Diary of a Madman* gave literary poignancy to *baihua*.

7  I have chosen to translate this difficult text in long lines of verse because the density of the original does not help us understand its meaning. Indeed, to translate it in discursive form would produce a flux of reading and a loss of the main ideas. I have tried by these means to avoid inattention and to provide guidance. This allows the reader to grasp the poetic contents of the essay, which is often rich in classical quotations that are not glossed by Li and are inserted into his text without comment in the Chinese literary style of the *sanwen*. I have employed this solution in my volume of edited translations of Li Dazhao entitled *Primavera* (Parma: Pratiche Editrice, 1994). For a full translation of the poetic essay into English see *positions* 3, no. 2 (1995): 306–328.

8  Li Dazhao's position on the Daoist tradition reminds me of an interesting observation that Isabelle Robinet made on the difficulty of defining boundaries between Daoism and Chinese popular religion on the one side, and Daoism and the thought of intellectual elites on the other. See Robinet, *Histoire du Taoisme des Origines aux XIV siecle* (Paris: Cerf, 1991).

9  The difficulty of finding a translation for *qingchun zhi wo* is now evident. I have chosen "Spring ego" to stress the fact that Li is here developing a category of the subjective. In this regard, I found of great interest Lydia H.

Liu's essay "Translingual Practice: The Discourse of Individualism be-tween China and the West" (*positions* 1 [spring 1993]: 160–193), in which she thoroughly examines the contemporary debate on individuals. Her essay confirms my opinion that the *wo* Li employs here is not the same as the one his contemporaries were developing. This convinces me that Li means a subjectivity rather than an individuality. With subtle political calibration, Li Dazhao displaced the level of the debate, in fact, to propose something different, which was neither individualism nor egoism, but sub-jectivity.

10 Martin Heidegger, introduction to *Being and Time*, in *Basic Writings* (New York: Harper and Row, 1977), 197.

11 In his recent volume, *Storiografia, cronologia e politica: Ipotesi sulla modernità delle questioni del tempo* (Napoli: Linguori Editore, 1992), Valerio Romitelli has objected to this scheme, arguing that the time of "anticipation of death" is still "ontic," because it concerns the physical "being" of man.

12 Alain Badiou, *Peut-on penser la politique?* (Paris: Seuil, 1985), 107.

13 Of course, he was not the first to introduce this problem. The question of thinking about temporality was a crucial intellectual concern at least since the "reformers" of the 1890s, such as Yan Fu, Tan Sitong, and Kang Youwei. But I propose to consider Li's position as a definitive break with the cyclical vision of time, typical of the "Chinese classical episteme" that was still in-ternal to the intellectual horizon of that previous generation. On this point see the important essay by Charlotte Furth, "Intellectual Change from the Reform Movement to the May Fourth Movement, 1895–1920," in *Cam-bridge History of China* (Cambridge: Cambridge University Press, 1982), 12:1, 321–405. The point of no return with this vision of time was, in my opinion, the category of "*qingchun zhi wo*," because of its double disconti-nuity toward the past and the future, which excluded any possible cyclicity.

14 Alain Badiou, *L'ethique* (Paris: Hatier, 1993), 14.

15 See *Shi* [Time], in *LDZWJ*, 2:665.

16 See Sylvain Lazarus, *La Categorie de revolution dans la Revolution Francaise*, "Les Conferences du Perroquet," no. 15 (Paris: Potemkine, 1988), 30.

17 Von Ranke is the German historian who formulated history's task as the study of the past "precisely as it has been." In today's thought, this cele-brated formula may be dismissed for its naive objectivism.

18 According to Hegel: "When comprehending world history, we are involved with history first of all in the aspect of why it presents itself as a past. But it is not less true that we are always involved with the present. What is true is eternal in itself and for itself; it is not yesterday, nor tomorrow, but it is certainly the present, it is 'now' in the sense of absolute presence. In the Ideal, what seems past is also preserved in eternity. The Idea is present, the spirit is immortal; there is no time in which it would not have existed or it would not exist; it is not past, nor future, but it is absolutely 'now.'" This statement seems to state an analogous position to the one that Li took

in "Spring" and "Today." However, it is crucial to point out that Li's "now" does not "link" each temporal configuration; it rather takes "now" as a site of temporal "untying" of the past and the future through—as I have pointed out—the decision, taken in advance, of achieving the "death of the Spring ego of tomorrow." I have quoted from the Italian translation of Hegel, *Lezioni sulla filosofia della storia* (Firenze: La Nuova Italia, 1941, 1981), 1:189.

19  See Romitelli, *Storiografia, Cronologia e Politica*, 84–85, for the brilliant distinction that he draws vis-à-vis "chrono-logic." He distinguishes the political and historiographic level as follows: "The thought of historiography as description of an infra-temporality between past and present . . . the political thought as prescription of a contemporaneity yet to come" (85). Romitelli's notion of "contemporaneity meaning the anticipation of a future of which the premises are not yet present" has been extremely helpful to me in my work on Li Dazhao.

20  See *Shixue sixiang shi jianyi* [Lessons of history of historiographic thought], in *LDZWJ*, 2:264–370.

21  In *Revolution and History: Origins of Marxist Historiography in China, 1919–1937* (Berkeley: University of California Press, 1978), Arif Dirlik stressed that modern historiographic research began in China after 1927. This is certainly true. Dirlik's periodization is also significant because it allows us to reflect on the origins of Chinese historiography after that important political event. But it is also too restrictive. That is to say, what subsequently became modern Chinese historiographical culture, from Gu Jiegang and Guo Moruo onward, could not have existed without Li Dazhao's original efforts in the early 1920s. Moreover, Li acted as a promoter of the cultural modernization of historiography and therefore had a double impact on what followed him. Dirlik considered Li Dazhao marginal, I suspect, because the 1984 edition of Li's *Collected Works* was not yet extant when he published *Revolution and History*; thus, Dirlik doubtless had no access to the important texts on the question of history that I am discussing in full here.

Spring


Spring days bring sun.
East wind melts frost.[1]
From these faraway Ying Islands[2] I turn to my country,
where overwhelming obscurity has become clear brightness,
and flowers blossom in an icy sky.
Each change of season rouses memories; but how can one recall
the many human beginnings, without being caught
by dejection, as a confined maiden,
or by anguish, as the poet of sorrow?
Now that Spring sprinkles the pear flowers with rain,
and heavy doors close on pain-racked poets,
alone, I lean against the railing of a tower,
and gaze at the budding greenness of thousands of willows all around
    me,
and at the colors of meadows reaching as far as the eye can see.
Maiden Spring[3] brings endless hopes and enthusiasms,
her tender beauty flies to youths, their futures long,
bearing the tacit promise of being there just for them.
My dear young students!
Wonderful maiden Spring makes us understand
the burden of responsibilities to come,
the need to grow in inward beauty.
Spring marks your efforts and loves your talent—
thus, every year, the face of maiden Spring
bestows encouragement and comfort on the Way.
Though each effort strives to achieve lofty ideals,
sacred missions, great tasks, arduous responsibilities,

we should take the time to smile at Spring,
to thank her for her love and beauty,
to value her sweetness and receive
her beneficial influence
so that Spring may be eternal.
The ego will thus change to a Spring ego, and ours to a family of Spring,
ours to a Spring State, ours to a Spring Nation.
Through its *nidāna*, this Spring ego shall deserve,
in the immensity of countless *kalpas*,[4]
to meet this loving Spring in one sole point
of space and time, to endless Spring belonging.


Humanity in the universe is as tiny as a drop in the ocean.[5]
To delight forever in the happiness of Spring, we must ask ourselves:
In the universe and in nature, is Spring endless?
If she were endless, even if our lives be long
as those of Peng Zu and Lao Dan, or quite eternal
as the universe, we could not
enjoy Spring forever.
But if she were endless,
if we but tried to rival the infinity of the universe,
couldn't we enjoy Spring forever?
Whether the universe is endless or not
depends on its having an end or a beginning.
Did the universe ever have a beginning? I say: The beginning was in
    nothingness.
Will the universe really have an end? I say: The end will be in noth-
    ingness.
In other words, there is no end and no beginning.
This lack of a beginning, of an end,
as far as space goes, is infinity;
as far as time, eternity.
In absolute terms, nonbeing is the essence of all this.
In relative terms, in the universe there is also evolution.
If there is evolution, involution is also necessary:
myriads of singular and different phenomena are generated.
As for these myriads of phenomena,
in totality there is singularity, in Life there are lives;
the whole of singularity, however large, has an end,
a life, however long, will come to pass.

Therefore, if there is life, there is death; if there is prosperity, there is
  decline,
if there is *yin,* there is *yang;* if there is *pi,* there is *tai,*
if there is *bo,* there is *fu;*[6] if there is contraction, there is expansion,
if there is decrease, there is increase; if there is fullness, there is emptiness,
if there is fortune, there is misfortune;
if there is something auspicious, there is something inauspicious;
if there is Spring-youth, there is old age; if there is vigor, there is decrepitude.
The essence of all this is the there-being.


In the *Zhuangzi* it is said: "A fungus, living only one morning,
does not know the waxing and waning of the moon;
the cicada, living one only season,
does not know the succession of springs and autumns."
Moreover, "a great knowledge is better than a small one,
a long life is better than a short one."[7]
Is there such a thing as months and seasons? And why is it that
fungi and insects do not know them, while other beings do?
Or is there no such thing? But why
are some beings aware of them, while fungi and insects are not?
The answer to these questions remains indefinite.
Since our knowledge as human beings
is lesser than the universe's own,
and our life is also much shorter,
if we want to define the there-being
or the non-there-being of the universe,
beyond which time and space cannot proceed,
we are just like fungi and cicadas as regards to months and seasons.
The universe has two poles: equality and difference,
*Kong* and *Se*[8] in Buddhist theory,
absolute and relative in philosophical theory,
the there-being or the non-there-being in mathematical theory,
*Zhou* and *Yi* in the *Book of Changes.*
This book is not called *Zhou Yi* in order to glorify the Zhou dynasty
as in Luo Pi's commentary *Lushi,*
but in the sense meant by Jin Shengtan in his *Preface to the Li Sao:*
"*Zhou* is substance, *Yi* is function.
In brief, *Zhou* means fixity, *Yi* means change.

*Zhou* is the sage's ability to grasp, *Yi* is change in the world.
The world in itself has no unique, unchanging existence,
but is transformed and retransformed each day.
Only a concerned sage can understand
that it is so always and everywhere, with no exception,
and also grasp that every space exists in time
and every time in space.
Then, when the world displays its changes,
the sage grasps its persistency.
This is why the book is called *Zhou Yi*."
Zhong Ni said: "If one considers difference,
liver and gall are as far from each other
as the States of Chu and of Yue.
But if one considers identity,
all things are one."
This is what discriminates identity from difference.
Su Dongpo said: "From the standpoint of change,
the world cannot exist for one single instant,
but from the standpoint of nonchange
I and things are endless."
This is the difference between change and nonchange.
Change is the process of Spring,
nonchange is endless Spring.
In the same way, difference and identity,
*Yi* and *Zhou*, there-being and non-there-being, relative and absolute,
*Kong* and *Se*, difference and equality,
are all aspects of Spring
in her process and in her eternal endlessness.
In like manner, life and death, prosperity and decline,
*yin* and *yang*, *pi* and *tai*, *bo* and *fu*, contraction and expansion,
decrease and increase, fullness and emptiness, fortune and misfor-
    tune,
auspiciousness and inauspiciousness, youth and old age, maturity and
    senility,
are nothing but the process of Spring.
Besides, endless Spring is the axis of this lack
of a beginning and an end, of limits and poles, of forms and figures.
Young progressives, who are always in the middle
of swirling and restless waves, should keep their spirit
as resolute as a river moving forward, as steady
as a mountain, firmly resisting every strong current.

One should answer change with nonchange,
deal with difference through identity,
grasp *Yi* with *Zhou*,
there-being with non-there-being,
one should command the relative through the absolute, lead *Se* with
    *Kong*,
regulate diversity with equality: only thus is it possible
to make the life and Spring of the universe one's own.
The endlessness of the universe is the endlessness of Spring,
which is the endlessness of the ego.
This is the spirit that conquers death and revives life,
this is the energy that moves mountains and builds the world.
Only those who really love Spring
know that in the universe there is an endless Spring
and only with that spirit and energy can they enjoy her forever.
The alternation of construction and destruction is the *Dao* of nature
the alternation of *yin* and *yang* is the *Dao* of change.
Thomson and Tait, two famous physicists,
argue that heaven and earth must have an end.
For cosmic movement depends on unbalance,
just as the flowing of water depends on a difference in level.
Today, the sun's warmth is constantly waning.
From variations in the orbit of comets we know
that ether produces braking effects in outer space,
with great loss of heat and waste of energy.
There is in the universe a tendency
for heat and energy to balance out,
and when this balance is finally reached
heaven and earth will be destroyed.
But when heaven and earth are destroyed
what will happen to everything in them?
"Heaven and earth" mean the earth's globe,
geologists have shown it to have a life of its own.
But today, is it in childhood, youth,
middle age, or old age?
There is no answer to this question yet.
If the earth is still in its childhood or youth
we could look upon a future of hope,
from which human life would exult and rejoice.
Even if the earth were in its middle age, it would be in full vigor,
and for this very reason we should go forward resolutely.

Only if the earth had already come to old age,
would the few remaining men, looking up every night
at an exhausted moon reflecting the last rays of sunlight,
consider this as the sad forewarning of the earth's own death.
How can one not be distressed at this thought?
Even if the earth is old, we are still young
and by virtue of our youth we slow down her aging.
One day of the earth's existence is for us humans;
one day's existence of Spring
one day of our Spring is
one day's existence of the earth's Spring.
We have the earth of the present *kṣaṇa*[9]
and the Spring of the present *kṣaṇa:*
thus, we are responsible for this *kṣaṇa* in the earth's regards.
We know that in a future *kṣaṇa* the earth will be destroyed,
but the Spring of the future *kṣaṇa* will not be destroyed.
In the future *kṣaṇa* the earth will not be the same as the present
    *kṣaṇa's*,
but the Spring of the future *kṣaṇa* will be the same as today's.
The ego of the future *kṣaṇa* will still be responsible
for the earth of the future *kṣaṇa.*
Why should we despair at the thought of the destruction
of the physical form of the earth?

Moreover, we can ask: is it young
or does it age day by day,
this humanity living on earth?
Will the moment of its destruction
occur naturally with the death of the earth itself?
Or, because of a change in climate,
will humanity die suddenly
together with animals and plants?
Or will this happen before these catastrophes,
as in the death of an individual or a nation?
It is difficult to answer these questions.
Biologists say that human life
runs against nature's.
Humanity, they say, acquired the upright position
when women ran away in fear, hugging their children;
because their breasts were naked, they had to cover themselves,
so humanity acquired clothing;

the food they carried on their frequent migrations spoiled easily,
so humanity acquired fire for cooking.
But with clothing humanity lost its fur, and with cooked food,
it lost the ability to digest what was raw.
As civilization progressed day by day,
people turned further and further away from what was natural.
With boats and cars, electricity and steam
people increasingly lost the use of their hands and feet;
with telescopes and telephones they lost the use of their eyes and ears.
Through the wide diffusion of books, newspapers, and cultural prod-
    ucts,
people lost their intellectual energy.
With the automatic 42 cm. cannon,
people's capacity for combat weakened.
The forms of labor organization in urban life
and the increase of places of leisure have brought new vices.
Biologists say that all this sends humanity toward its destruction:
can one escape disaster,
as if trying to stop the rushing river?
They have been going around and shouting this sad news,
hoping to stir people to some form of escape.
Believers differ here, and say that
the universe has been created by a deity,
who is in charge of its protection.
They believe that our people, being weak in wisdom,
have only the gods to rely upon to avoid evils and calamities.
Now, the believers say, biologists' theories
disparage the merits of the gods and induce humanity to pessimism:
for how could humanity do that
which the gods were unable to do?
So, deeply discouraged, humanity
will let itself fall into anguish.
In the face of current degeneration,
one cannot remain unconcerned.
So, our people should be more confident and believe
that God is all-knowing and almighty:
though sinful, they will atone with pious prayers.
As far as biologists are concerned, their theories
though easily conducive to pessimism, might
be able to urge humanity to correct a way of life
that has turned its back on nature.

This is their strong point.
As far as the believers are concerned, their ideas,
though making men's faith strong,
look forward to the soul's eternity in the Kingdom of Heaven,
and thus bring people to worship the power of God and belittle human
    abilities:
this contradicts scientific reality.
This is their weak point.
As for myself, I think that one should believe in the endless Spring of
    humanity,
in the same way that religious people believe in God;
more so, I think that one should tremble
in the face of biologists' warnings, and let one's self be roused,
though life may turn its back on nature, to seek a life
that follows nature by relying on the talent of mankind.
As for the old age of humanity,
even if we were in its utmost decrepitude,
we should surely be able, making use of our every effort,
to return to that endless Spring,
and save ourselves from death through a new life.

Each nation and country has its own life.
There are young nations and hoary ones,
there are young countries and hoary ones.
Our nation and country, are they young?
Or hoary?
If nation and country are hoary, we, the young,
should strive with conviction and determination
to retrieve their Spring.
But this requires a conscious attitude.
Abroad, China is often said to be
an ancient country and a dying nation.
From the dawn of history, countless nations and countries
have known prosperity and decline.
In Western history, Rome and Babylon,
though powerful and famous, turned to dust.
Today, Italy, France, Spain, Portugal,
Holland, Belgium, Denmark, Sweden, Norway, and
England are famous European nations
that in the course of their long life
have come to live through times of Spring

when each displayed in full a genius
of its own;
but now their days are gone,
their fame declining to an empty shell:
in the history of human civilization, they are already gone.
Among these recent nations,
in this war's bloody tide,
only Germany and Hungary, driven by their vital energy,
have recently exploded to display
their own national genius.
It follows from history that a nation in decline
will be defeated in its encounter with a rising nation.
When young vigorous life encounters dying life,
the latter meets with inevitable defeat;
when a people in their youth
encounter a people in hoary old age,
the latter meet with inevitable defeat.
From the time of the legendary Yellow Emperor,
for almost five thousand years,
China has been a mighty nation of East Asia,
with a very long history.
The Spring of the Chinese nation dates back to the distant Zhou dy-
    nasty
whose culture and institutions were in full splendor.
After that, a gradual decline began,
and only some of that splendor has remained today.
Is this our national glory, then?
If it is true that a man's life seldom exceeds a hundred years,
it is even rarer for a nation's life to last almost five thousand years.
India rose to give birth to Buddha,
but after the birth of Buddha, India died;
Judaea was created to give birth to Jesus,
but after the birth of Jesus, Judaea faded away;
China was established to give birth to Confucius,
but after the birth of Confucius, China declined.
That decline lasts to this very day,
nothing but skeletons, darkness everywhere:
the spirit of the nation is exhausted.
How can we hope to avoid destruction?
These words make us, young people, grow pale
with rage, with staring eyes,

for they are serious slander.
But there is nothing to be enraged at:
China has had such a long history,
that today it is encumbered by a heavy layer of dust,
which fetters our national life and brings about its decline.
This fact we cannot deny; but Chinese youth
instead of striving to show the world whether hoary China is alive or
    dead,
should strive to show that it is blazing a path
for the resurgence of a Springtime China.
Life is in fact a succession of death and resurgence.
Today the problem of humanity and of nations is not survival,
but a Spring-creating resurgence.
In Turkey, which was once considered as great an empire as ours,
young people have tried time and again to give birth to political move-
    ments.
Various Balkan countries have searched for their independence
through national movements, with wars and calamities
whose consequences in the world
are still obvious today.
Across the distant Himalayas one can see
the smoke from the fires of the Indian revolution:
it too is trying to revive its nation's Spring.
In China, with the *Xinghai* and the *Guichou* revolutions,
an unremitting and uproarious fight began
for the rebirth of our nation.[10]
When nations such as these begin to throw off the yoke of history,
clean up the filth of centuries, rebuild their life,
and bring back the nation's Spring,
they cannot but rely on youth.
When our country was founded it was given a fine name:
*Zhonghua*. What does *Zhonghua* mean?
*Zhong* is what lies at the center of an area;
but it is the duty of our generation's youth
to consider this *zhong* not just from the point of view of space,
as if China were at the center of the world,
but also from the point of view of time.
Let us look at the history of the world:
so many changes from antiquity to now!
We must stand in today's Spring
and mark out a point that acts as *zhong*.

Before this *zhong*, history restricted itself
to recording the birth and evolution of humanity, nations, and states,
just like evolutionary theory restricted itself to studying
the birth and evolution of the sun and earth, of plants and animals,
all the way up to humankind.
But after this *zhong*, history will consider all these things
the scope of ancient history,
and will attempt to register the rebirth
of the Springtime of humanity, nations, and states.
History before this *zhong*
is finished, burnt, and buried.
Whereas history after this *zhong*
is like a blank sheet of paper, yet intact,
waiting to be marvelously painted.
History before this *zhong*
is old, a history of the dead;
whereas after this *zhong*
it is a Springtime history, a history of young people in their vitality.
Young people! Let us assume with all possible determination
the responsibility of standing firm, as rocks in midstream;
In this year's Spring, let us at once consider today's *kṣaṇa*
as the starting point of this *zhong* of time;
let us deliver old history to the flames,
and develop only the *zhong* of this Springtime *Zhonghua*,
let us dedicate the beauty of our life to writing
the marvellous first page of this *zhong*'s history!
Let us not hesitate to undertake this task.
In *Zhonghua*, *hua* means the flowering of a civilization.
Flowers are followed by fruit, blossoming is followed by fading.
Old China is the flower from whose seed
Spring China is coming to birth,
Spring China is the flower from which old China is reborn.
Old China is a fading flower,
Spring China is a flower ready to bloom anew.
There is a fading China flower and a China flower in bloom.
Fading is the condition for blooming,
blooming is what follows fading.
Blooming and fading alternate infinitely.
There is an endless Spring in the universe,
there are always flowers in blossom.
We, the youth of Spring China

must nurture and water them, admire and love them.
Young people! Rather than longing for
flowers to remain fresh forever
in an everlasting Spring,
we should bring Spring back to China,
and even if Spring were absent and no flowers bloomed,
we should do our utmost to bring Spring back to China
and make it bloom again.
Chemists say that land, no matter how rich,
is soon exhausted and becomes barren
if forced to grow too many crops.
To improve it, one must grow certain plants
which can absorb nitrogen from the air
and put it back into the land, making it rich again.
Today, in the once-rich land of China,
we hear only the moaning of the autumn wind
and the rustle of the falling leaves.
Desolation has come to our ancient prosperity
because the land did not benefit from those fertilizing plants.
Young people are for society just what those plants are for the land:
if we give them enough room to strike deep roots,
within a few years Spring China will be
just like a tree, well-rooted in this world,
and once again our land will be rich and give bountiful harvests.
Our young people are sturdy, they are just like
Spring China on the point of blossoming again.

In life, people are unable to foresee
this universe's endless Spring,
because, from their first cry to their old age and death,
they feel time flowing even faster then a spark,
short-lasting, fleeting as a dream, ever so brief
as the life of fungi and cicadas.
And so Confucius sighed along the river:
"Time flows just as this water does";
and Qu Yuan sang along the river Xiang
of springs and autumns in their mutual sequence.
Some poets and writers never stop working, not even at night,
others try to avoid wasting one single instant.
Emperors and powerful men, approaching death,
when bidding their last farewell to the world,

cling to those earthly joys;
they do not want to leave,
and keep on sighing in regret.
However great, power and wealth
cannot prolong life one single instant.
Qin Shihuang, great conqueror of lands and seas,
during his last few years, for fear of dying
sent shamans to seek the elixir of life throughout the land
—but no one found it.
He died a sudden death, and the imperial chariot
departed in the night.
Han Wudi, great emperor who tamed
barbarians with the force of arms,
sang sighing in his last few years:
"In utmost happiness, what sorrow!
How short youth is, when old age comes!"
Recently, a very rich American,
who lived a life of contention and struggle,
was crowned "King of the Dollar"—
but, weak and sick, exclaimed upon his deathbed:
"I will give millions to whomever will
prolong my life one month."
How could this happen?
Human life is limited, desires have no limits;
but if we live a limited life
chasing unlimited desires,
the years will flow in vain, and then it will be hard
to find once more the flush of youth
upon one's face:
what is the use of complaining,
of losing hope
when our hair's turned to white?
Such are the thoughts that break us, make us desperate.
Thus, the wise too
lose all their benevolence and wits,
while the wicked indulge in vain pleasures:
the result will be nothing but a barren life.
How could young people draw their inspiration from this?
In this world the life of humankind
has not one single *kṣaṇa* which is not in Spring,
which is not part of endless Spring,

of the process of this endless Spring.
Some young people cannot enjoy Spring
since they live an artificial life
hankering for wealth and power. The proverb says:
"A hundred pieces of gold can buy a good horse,
a thousand pieces can buy a beautiful woman,
ten thousand pieces can buy even noble rank,
but where could one ever buy Spring?"
Not even all the wealth in the world
will buy Spring forever; indeed,
great wealth actually conceals the road to Spring.
The Roman Emperor Hadrian, at the height of his power and glory,
at the end of his life told his retinue that, in forty years,
only three of his days had been happy.
Neither power nor wealth were enough to make him happy.
And yet, is there anything more deplorable than having been happy
for only three days in forty years of Spring?
A young person should strive
to advance from the standpoint of a theory of the present.
Carlyle said that our life
is infinity held back by time.
This infinity displays itself in the ego,
which means in the present, not in the past or in the future.
To grasp the present is to grasp infinity.
Long ago, Jin Shengtan wrote in a poem:
"Whence and from whom this sound of jade flute?"
To the young Shi Kong who asked why
he had used the word "jade," Jin Shengtan answered:
"If someone had said: 'What I played was a metal flute,
so why do you write "jade flute"?,' I would have answered:
'What I wrote was "jade flute."
Why do you still play a metal flute?'
My talent is heaven-sent,
why should I enslave it to your metal flute?"
But why was Jin Shengtan so insistent
in not wanting to confuse jade with metal?
Because, while patiently fighting for the quality of that single word,
he was in fact fighting for the present of the ego.
To those who foretold him the tortures of hell
because of his loose and easygoing style of life,
Byron replied: "The Christian would like happiness in the next world

to come from suffering in this world.
He who is not a Christian will not avoid suffering in the next world
if he ignores his happiness in this world."
These statements, uttered by two poets,
are distant from each other in time, but not in meaning.
Byron's words are strong and full of irony.
As for myself, I think this world contains the pleasures of this world,
and the next world the pleasures of the next world,
just as this world contains this world's Spring,
and the next world contains the next world's Spring.
Thus, one shouldn't waste the pleasures and Spring of this world
out of a longing for pleasures and Spring in the next world,
and it is wrong that, through longing for the pleasures and Spring of
    this world
one should waste the pleasures and Spring of the next world.
Why should it not be right for mankind to seek pleasure,
and why is it necessarily wrong to distinguish between before and
    after,
between the present and the future? Emerson said:
"One who loves the past must make the best use of the present.
Yesterday is beyond recall and tomorrow is uncertain.
You can be certain only of the present day. Today is worth two tomor-
    rows."
Such words are well worth pondering,
for the present is the Springtime of our Spring.
If we return, with this Spring as our companion,
to the country of the Great Desert,
nothing will leave us unsatisfied.
And so, what could ever distress us?
Once freed from our anguish, what could we ever fear?
Epicurus said that one should not fear poverty, or exile, or prison;
what one should fear the most is fear itself.
The American statesman Roosevelt went hunting in the mountains,
after he had withdrawn from politics,
and with his iron hand he fought
against tigers, leopards, and bears.
One day, he tells in his autobiography,
he was attacked by a polar bear and almost devoured;
he said he was able to free himself from the bear's grip
only because he was not caught by terror
which would have lost him any chance of saving his life.

Fear cannot save a person in peril.
When some calamity is foreseen
no fear, however great, can make it less;
but the more we waste our energies today,
the less prepared we are
to face tomorrow's danger.
If difficulties loom ahead, we have nothing to count on
but the ego
and the present of the ego.
How could we ever indulge in hesitation and sigh:
"In front of me, I cannot see the person of the past
behind me, I cannot see the person of the future"?
To live, we should keep our heads high,
and be determined to advance by ourselves
without waiting for, or relying on, help from others.
What is the good of saying: "Watching the boundless sky and earth,
lonely and in bitterness I melt into tears"?
An artificial life wears out the present of the ego and the ego of the
    present
as much as the dusty layer of past history.
Those who spend their life seeking wealth and power,
are like ants grubbing for grease,
or moths fluttering round a flame.
Whoever spends half his life striving for wealth and power
and intends to go on doing it, how could he not be overwhelmed?
The greater their wealth and power,
the less are they able to retain their Spring.
The Bible says:
"It is easier for a camel to pass through the eye of a needle
than for a rich man to enter into the kingdom of Heaven."
In other words, Spring and thirst for wealth may not be reconciled.
The conscience of youth consists
in breaking the links of past history,
in destroying the prison of old rotten doctrines.
Young people should not only keep old skeletons
from entangling the vitality of the present ego,
but, with the present Spring,
they must kill the Spring ego of the past
and induce today's Spring ego
to abdicate in favor of tomorrow's.

They should get rid of artificial, inconsistent, and hypocritical life,
and stand fast with their independent ego,
in a universe of perpetual change.
Thus, bare and unhampered, in all their beauty and nobleness,
they should not only kill today's old ego,
but with today's old ego,
prescribe the killing of tomorrow's old Spring ego.
This should become the only aim of life,
the sole responsibility of youth.
Leopold von Ranke said:
"There is no greater happiness for mankind
than to retain Spring forever.
He who would receive much happiness should die young."
I should like our beloved youth
to live in Spring and die in Spring,
to live young and die young.
The German historian Mommsen criticized Julius Caesar:
"He drank the water of life from the cup of Spring,
swirled it in his mouth and spat it out."
I would like our beloved youth
to raise this cup, glittering in the light of the moon,
hold up the precious sweet liquor of human life
and drink it in one gulp.
Only thus can one remain untamed by things
and be unharmed by them.
Even if water were to rise to Heaven
he would not drown,
even if drought were to melt metals and burn mountains,
he would not be touched,
and his mortal remains could be forged
into a Yao and a Shun.[11]
How could the Spring of one's ego
change in accordance to changes in the outside world?
How could the lifeless ashes of history
choke the intelligence of youth?
Shinan Yiliao went to see the ruler of Lu
who was very sad in countenance.
Master Shinan told him then
how to abandon his toils and sorrows:
"My lord, leave your country, give up your habits

and wander around with the Dao as your aid."
The ruler answered:
"This Way is long and dangerous, there are rivers and mountains,
but I have neither boat, nor cart. What shall I do?"
Shinan answered:
"Relinquish your arrogance and palaces:
this will provide you with boat and cart."
The ruler said:
"This Way is remote, long, and lonely.
Who will be my companion? I have no rations
and shall be without food. How shall I be able to get there?"
Then Shinan said:
"Restrict your needs and reduce your desires
and you will get there even without rations.
You will cross the rivers and float on the open sea
where no shore is in sight.
The further you go, the less you will know where the sea ends.
Those who came to see you off will return from the shore,
then you will really be far away."
What here is called Dao is but the Way leading to Spring.
If our young people follow this Way,
and make it into their rationality,
if they strive to go toward the light,
and turn their back to darkness,
they will make their contribution to world civilization
and to humanity's happiness.
With their Spring ego, they will create Spring families,
Spring countries and nations,
a Spring humanity, Spring earth, and a Spring universe,
enriching an unlimited life with happiness.
Riding the wind and waves, they will travel far.
Why should they worry
about not being able to pursue the fleeting Spring?
This is the end of my essay, I hope I was not too long-winded.
In the last part, I have taken the liberty to quote
a few words from the Laquer Garden.

Thanks to help from many friends, my Italian translation is finally complete. I want to thank Geng Youzhaun, Barbara Hendrischke, Liu Guisheng, Zhao Xiuying, and Angela Zito. What appears here is the English translation of my Italian rendering of the poem. Deepest gratitude to Alessandro Passi for his help. [C. Pozzana, trans.]

This poem first appeared in *Xin Qingnian* [New Youth] 2, no. 1, on 1 October 1916. *Qingchun*, in *Li Dazhao Wenji* vol. 1 (Beijing: Renmin chubanshe 1984), 194–205. A partial translation (an arbitrary reduction of almost 60 percent of the text and complex parts simply summarized with no cuts signaled) by Gladys Yang and Yang Zianyi appears in *Chinese Literature* 8, no. 5 (1959): 11–18. A useful annotation of the entire text is available in Liu Guisheng, *Qingchun zhushiben* [Notes to *Spring*] (Beijing: History Museum of Beijing, c. 1984).

1 The first line is a quotation from *Shijing: Binfeng, Qiyue*. See *The Chinese Classics*, ed. J. Legge, vol. 4 (Hong Kong: Hong Kong University Press, 1960):228. Legge translates: "With the spring days the warmth begins." The second line is from *The Book of Rites* [*Liji*] *Yueling*. See Couvreur Séraphin, *Mémoires sur les bienséances et les cérémonies* [*Liji*] vol. 1 (Paris: Cathasia, 1950), 330–410.

2 "Ying Islands" is a very ancient expression used since Qin Shihuang in the second century B.C. to indicate the Japanese archipelago. See *Shiji*, ed. Ershiwushi (Hong Kong: Ershiwushi, 1959), 25.

3 The metaphor of Spring as a virgin, a maiden, is a cliché in the Western canon, but sounds strange in Chinese. In China, Spring is considered *yang* and not *yin*. By calling Spring a virgin, Li Dazhao seems to want to redetermine the signifier *Qingchun* and connect it to a female, virginal image, instead of a masculine one. That is why I employ the personal pronouns "she" and "her," instead of "it" or "he" in this rendition.

4 *Nidāna* (*yinyuan*) is a Buddhist term in Sanskrit: The twelve *nidāna*s define the causal links of existence, as brought about by *karman*. *Kalpa* (*jie*) is a Sanskrit term for a very long cosmic cycle of creation and dissolution of the universe.

5 *Zhuangzi buzhang* [Revision of Zhuangzi], ed. Liu Wendian (Kunming: Yunnan renmin chubanshe, 1980), 280.

6 *Yin-yang*, the dialectical principle of the Chinese cosmogony, indicates the couple female-male generating and constituting the multiple beings. *Pi*, the twelfth of the sixty-four exagrams of the *Book of Changes*, indicates stagnation, the moment when the opposites do not communicate. *Tai*, the eleventh of the sixty-four exagrams, indicates the harmonious moment when the opposites communicate. *Bo*, the twenty-third exagram, indicates the decay, the prevalence of the weakness on the strength. *Fu*, the twenty-fourth exagram, indicates the revival of strength. *A Concordance to*

*Yi Chang,* Harvard Yenching Index, no. 10 (Taipei: Chinese Materials and Research Aids Center, 1966): 15 n. 23.

7  Both quotations from *Zhuangzi buzhang,* 9.

8  *Kong* indicates emptiness and *Se* indicates the sensible world.

9  In Chinese *chana,* a phonetic transcription of the Sanskrit *kṣaṇa,* which is the Buddhist term for the smallest conceivable increment of time.

10  The 1911 and 1913 Revolutions.

11  First mythic emperor-culture heroes in the ancient canon.

The Probable Defeat: Preliminary Notes on the

Chinese Cultural Revolution

■ What makes it so difficult to discover any rational content in the Chinese Cultural Revolution? This is a question both for those who are still in search of a politics of equality and emancipation, and for those who have given up, not to mention those who have never been interested in it at all. The main difficulty, I would argue, is not the factual issue, nor our existential proximity to the matter. It cannot be, as Marc Bloch once suggested (and not without sarcasm), that not enough time has gone by to "spare Clio's chastity from the profanation of present controversy."[1] The real obstacle, I propose, is that it is hard for us to escape the perception, on our part, that this event, although so close to us in time, did, in fact, bring to an end an epoch, and that, when that epoch drew to a close, a certain familiar relationship between history and politics came to an end as well.

It is because of the Chinese Cultural Revolution (as well as many other worldwide political crises of the 1960s and 1970s) that some of the basic categories of modern knowledge concerned with the investigation of politics are now considered dubious. One can trace back to the 1960s and 1970s a growing uncertainty, not only about actual political value but also about the cultural substance of historicosocial categories such as class, class struggle, modes of production, the state, equality, political parties, and so forth. Furthermore, the conceptual field has since become more and more intellectually confused.

The question is not limited to Marxism; rather, it extends to the entire field of the historicosocial sciences, whose "archaeologic soil," to use a Foucauldian category,[2] has been essentially the same as that of Marxism. Moreover, in that thick network of political, historical, and social knowledge anchored in the modern *epistème*, Marxism was not only one component among others but also, paradoxically, an essential factor of cohesion. It certainly played a sourly critical and even threateningly apocalyptic role, but it was the ideological orientation that lent general coherence to that network of knowledge, even in terms of the state.

Socialist states professed to represent not only the revolutionary proletariat but also all of modern historicosocial rationality. No other kind of state has ever aimed to pursue such a wide cultural, philosophical, and scientific legitimation—albeit through a dialectical *Aufhebung*, as embodied in the doctrine of the extinction of the state. The definitive crisis of Marxism and of revolutionary political culture has been celebrated as the definitive victory of the maximum modern "political ideal"—liberal democracy—purified at last of its unwholesome tendencies.[3] But if one considers the role of cohesion Marxism has played within the field of modern historicopolitical knowledge, the consequences of its crisis cannot be so reassuring.

The fall of the European socialist states—the most inglorious fall one could possibly imagine—was the late-coming death certificate that concluded a crisis in socialism and Marxism, a crisis that had, in fact, reached a point of no return thirteen years before, with the close of the Chinese Great Proletarian Cultural Revolution. Philip Huang has addressed the issue of the "paradigmatic crisis in the study of modern Chinese economic and social history," which he considers "part and parcel of a worldwide crisis" involving visions both of history and of politics.[4] I would also suggest that a far more serious predicament be recognized specifically within the field of the political historiography of modern China, at one time one of the pillars of China studies. The epicenter of this predicament, I shall argue, is our present impasse in the "historical understanding" of the Cultural Revolution.

The Cultural Revolution dramatically marks the final stage of a long epoch during which one could account for *revolution* as a major working category both for political discourse and for historical discourse, inasmuch as it instituted a fundamental connection between the two and traced a network of shared paths and extensively articulated conceptual bridges. For the Cultural Revolution, as well as for other modern political phenomena, the problem for anybody who is interested in politics is one of rethinking these categories today, now that this network of connections, this circulation of common referents, has come undone. More generally, the problem is how to reflect on each political situation as singular and endowed with its own proper mode of political thinking, not simply as belonging to what we could call the modern political *epistème,* or to the space of modern political and historical knowledge.

## TEN YEARS DEDUCTED

Although it is true that each great political situation creates difficulties and controversies in historiography, in the case of the Cultural Revolution one deals with an almost total intellectual block. With respect to the Cultural Revolution, besides the general lack of controversy, one meets with a fundamental unanimity in discarding any hypotheses beyond the familiar "horrors of totalitarianism," leading ineluctably to catastrophe and disaster. For most of the few scholarly works written on the subject, both Chinese and Western, the Cultural Revolution was essentially the worst repetition of the worst that had already happened elsewhere.

I will limit myself here to recalling some of the most influential theses. For Gao Gao and Yan Jiaqi, for instance, the Cultural Revolution was the tragic result of the combination of a personality cult with the imperial tradition: the premise of their book, essentially in line with the official consensus of the Chinese government, is that Mao launched the Cultural Revolution to reestablish his own absolute supremacy, which he felt to be steadily eroding.[5] For Andrew Walder, the Cultural Revolution was essentially a series of "variations on a Stalinist theme," albeit more populist and perhaps more egalitarian. With its insistence on the danger of capitalist restoration, it was a Chinese version of the great purges; as in the 1930s in the Soviet Union, its ideological dogma was a conspiracy theory, that is, that of the danger of subversion from hidden enemies.[6] For Maurice Meisner, the Cultural Revolution was Mao's "last desperate attempt to revive a revolution that he believed was dying," involving the typical, irresponsible attitudes of the worst voluntaristic political traditions.[7] Others, to be sure, have taken the opportunity to equate Mao and Hitler, an equation that entails no historiographic thesis other than an image of "radical evil" or of politics as Evil.

To see the Cultural Revolution as deriving from a certain national cultural tradition is a familiar hedge, since everything is thereby reduced to the idea that "the Chinese have always acted in such and such a manner." More interesting, since more politically oriented, are the questions raised by Walder's comparison of the Cultural Revolution with the Stalinist vision and by Meisner's evaluation that Mao was convinced the revolution was dying. I will discuss some of the implications of both points of view.

Besides, one should not underestimate the fact that in China there has been a long-term official ban on independent research on the subject—the effects of which assume surreal proportions. A well-known short story of the 1980s—"Ten Years Deducted," by Shen Rong—considers what transpires when a rumor circulates that the Party is about to decree that every Chinese person deduct the ten years of the Cultural Revolution from his or her age.[8] The short story's rather amusing plot is less fanciful than might be thought. In fact, the Chinese government has decreed that decade totally unthinkable.

The ban placed on studies of the Cultural Revolution, supported by a near-total consensus of scholarly opinion in China, has sparked, both in China and abroad, an increasing uncertainty over the evaluation of the entire modern political era. That is to say, to decree that the Cultural Revolution should not be considered part of any modern political tradition has had the consequence of discrediting the most relevant political events of the century in China. This is precisely because the Cultural Revolution itself never ceased to refer to these events. Mao Zedong and his followers, the unmentionable Gang of Four, held themselves to be the spiritual heirs of the May Fourth movement, Sun Yatsen republicanism, the Chinese progressives of the nineteenth century who introduced into Chinese political culture Montesquieu and Darwin, the Taiping Heavenly Kingdom, and even some of the earlier Qing government's efforts at avoiding subalternization and colonization—not to mention the Maoists' own special sympathy for Han Feizi, the great political thinker of the third century B.C., and the two-thousand-year-old Legalist tradition.

And yet Mao Zedong stubbornly supported the Cultural Revolution up to the end. But the fact that, after 1976, the Cultural Revolution's political content was totally denied (*chedi fouding*) could not but discredit all the political events that Mao and his followers presented as their own historical forerunners. All the various efforts at limiting official repudiation to the errors committed by the "late Mao" have been patently fictitious, a crude compromise aimed at safeguarding continued state legitimacy rather than offering a tenable historiographic thesis. This compromise has unleashed destructive effects, amplifying and complicating the general crisis in Chinese culture. There presently reigns a condition of stolid embarrassment on how to conceive the whole of the modern political age. If the political content of the last event in China to call itself "revolution" is, in fact, null, then what are we to make of the entire Chinese revolution and its early synonym, modern China?

To cite only the most controversial example, can the May Fourth movement be thought of today as anything other than an exhausted, worn-out foundational myth? And if this event, heretofore positioned at the gateway of the contemporary age in China, as one of the intellectual mother lodes of the century, is now to be rethought, what events or entities cannot be made the subjects of equivocation? The opinion that has come about, even in such lively intellectual circles as those of artists in China today, is that perhaps May Fourth intellectuals should have refrained from political engagement completely.[9]

Here is the bewilderment we all share in today: the question of how to conceive of politics and history is by no means exclusively Chinese, but is, rather, part of an epochal epistemic impasse. In a sense, this impasse might be considered as an especially intricate example of what Marc Bloch has called "the virus of the present,"[10] those current assumptions and notions of which historians must rid their minds but which seem to have such an exceptionally violent hold on the questions relating to the Cultural Revolution.

## HISTORY UPSIDE DOWN

Let me give an anecdoctal example of the difficulty of how to conceive of politics and history. On the cover of the voluminous and influential "*Wenhua da geming" shi nian shi* [History of the ten years of the "Great Cultural Revolution"] by Gao Gao and Yan Jiaqi, one of the rare Chinese books on the topic worth reading, is an image: it consists of the word *lishi* (history), in large type against the outline of a map of China. At first glance, the image is more than a little confusing because *lishi* appears in alphabetic transcription and is printed upside down. The consequent icon is, however, graphically comprehensible, even trivial. It alludes to the universally familiar argument that the "tragedy of the Cultural Revolution," the "national catastrophe," the "ten lost years," and so on, "overturned history" in the space of a decade. The reversal conveyed by the complex graphics on the book's cover refers, however, to a very specific object: not to politics nor to humanity, categorically understood, nor even to justice, but instead to history and history alone. More precisely, to history in its privileged relationship to politics. "Here history is lost in thought,"[11] proclaims the cover of another widely disseminated collection of edifying anecdotes about the political leadership overthrown in 1966.

If we read the image as a symptom, this is a good clue to the situation in which we find ourselves, since the great obstacle to a historical understanding of the Cultural Revolution is that we are not able to identify any steady connection between political discourse and historical discourse in it, nor to invoke categories that previously allowed for a fully historical judgment on political situations. The categories circulating between history and politics, or "circulating categories" as Sylvain Lazarus calls them,[12] are those of class and class struggle, modes of production, the dialectics of objective and subjective factors (the material and the spiritual), and other related categories—all of which fostered the epochal conviction that politics and history were completely homogeneous.

In summary, these categories belonged to the historicopolitical conceptual apparatus of the Marxist tradition, but were, at the same time, held as a common heritage (albeit with variations) of modern political historiography. The categories being no longer recognizable in the Cultural Revolution, that political phenomenon can no longer be conceived of under the aegis of history. That is why, read against the backdrop of those unthinkable ten years in China, history itself appears to be turned upside down, perplexed.

Which class interests were at stake in the 1960s in China? Was there, at the base, an old mode of production wherein some new productive forces were in excess? Which were the objective factors influencing subjective behaviors? When one searches for answers to such questions, the results cannot but be vague and confused, since, in those very years in China, such historicopolitical categories were undergoing a cataclysmic and largely enigmatic process, in which any possible rational content was disputed up to the end.

Let us take as an example the notion of class, specifically that of the working class, clearly the crucial category in Marxist political culture. What is discoverable in the Cultural Revolution if one looks for classes in the Marxist sense, or even if, from a more Weberian perspective, one looks to see which status groups were fighting each other for a form of dominion more favorable to their material and spiritual interests? It is not that classes or interest groups did not exist; rather, it is not these categories that are able to identify the most politically relevant elements of the situation. More important, during those years in

China the category of the working class was at the center of an un-precedented turbulence at the subjective level.

The January storm of 1967 in Shanghai marked a breakdown within the existing conceptual framework of the notion of the working class, and of its complex connections both to the socialist state and to history. The main political clash was between an increasing number of workers' independent political organizations, on one side, and the cadres of the party-state, on the other, who did their best to mobilize in their defense legions of "model workers." The latter were "Scarlet Guards," while the rebel workers were more often Red Guards.[13] Did not this acute contradiction between shades of red reflect a subjective breakdown internal to the working class? In fact, the questions that divided the groups were intensely political, and they were often bravely argued and refuted: they concerned nothing less important than the political existence of workers. Was the worker, as a political figure, a part of a socialist state, linked to it for ascertainable historicopolitical, economic, and even philosophical reasons? Or could this very web of connections no longer guarantee any political relevance for the category of worker, other than in disciplinary terms, so that it became urgent to find a new path?

It is true that no new path was found, but here again the question cannot be seen as strictly Chinese. On the contrary, one can date back to those events the first point of no return in a prolonged worldwide crisis of the category of the working class — a crisis that deepened during the 1970s, and was marked by comparable situations of strong worker mobilization: from workers' struggles in Italy and France to the Polish Solidarity movement.[14] If today the worker is virtually invisible as a political figure, the archaeology of this absence should be researched in the workers' political movements of the 1960s and 1970s, rather than in the shifts of the capitalist mode of production.

One could cite other examples of historicopolitical categories that were disputed during those years. For example, that of the political party as representative of class interests in the state. If one looks at China in the decade beginning in the mid-1960s, one can identify one of the major stages in the crisis in the conceptual nexus connecting notions of class, political parties, and the state. As was true for the crisis of the working class, the crisis of the category *political party* would develop its worldwide character later, to be fully consummated in the 1980s, when the political role of parties in the state had become precarious in countries well beyond the sphere of the socialist states. The same might be said, too, for the conceptual exhaustion of the historicopolitical dialectics of the modes of production, whose first major crisis should likewise be traced back to the Cultural Revolution.

## THE PROBABLE DEFEAT

If, however, the categories at work during the Cultural Revolution were limited to those typical of a historicopolitical discourse undergoing a process of epistemic deregulation, the current unanimous evaluation of the Cultural Revolution as the worst repetition of the worst that had happened elsewhere would be accurate. Searching for the political singularity of the Cultural Revolution, on the contrary, implies that there must have been some politically operating, original ideas. There is, in fact, at least one political thesis, recurrent in Mao's statements of those years, and playing a key role in the situation, that cannot easily be integrated into the standard historicopolitical categories of revolutionary discourse; indeed, it introduces a peculiar dissonance: Mao launched, supported, and never repudiated the Cultural Revolution, saying it was to be carried on "up to the end"; but he was equally stubborn in declaring that it would probably be defeated.

How shall we understand this strange proposition?[15] The case of the Cultural Revolution is especially intricate, since it hewed so strictly to Marxist-Leninist doctrine, to the point that it was representable as the ultimate defense of the whole revolutionary *epistème* against the powerful, internally hidden enemy, revisionism. But where in the revolutionary *epistème*—especially in its Marxist-Leninist formulation —can the category of the "probable, imminent defeat of the revolution" be found? Actually, nowhere—since in that vision of politics, as basically guaranteed by a conception of history, only certainty of victory could exist. Moreover, probable defeat was not enunciated as a renunciatory or capitulationist proposition, but in fact as an appeal for political mobilization—definitely an unusual appeal in revolutionary tradition.

In mid-1967, Mao justified and clarified this position to a visiting Albanian military delegation (whom we can imagine were highly perplexed) when he said: "Most probably revisionism will win out, and we will be defeated. Through probable defeat, we will arouse everyone's attention" (*yong keneng shibai qu tixing dajia*).[16] With another Albanian delegation, he insisted, "There are two possibilities: That revisionism will overthrow us, or that we will overthrow revisionism. Why do I put defeat as the more probable outcome? [*Wo weishenma ba shibai fangzai di yi keneng ne?*] Because it helps us to see the problems more clearly."[17]

Conversely, "Victory is the mother of many illusions," as Mao told André Malraux in 1965, talking about the destiny of socialism in China and the Soviet Union.[18]

Probable defeat as a key political theme is recorded in many comments by Mao during those years. Another famous example is Mao's letter to Jiang Qing of June 1966, just at the beginning of the revolutionary "high tide," in which he predicts that the right will seize power after his death. But the probable defeat Mao predicted extended much further than the specific political project to which he was personally committed. When he said that revisionism would probably win and predicted "we will be defeated," that we was much more general. It involved, moreover, a subjective question concerning the fortunes of an entire epoch of political culture.

At least since the Khrushchev Report of 1956, Mao had experienced serious intellectual conflict about the possible destiny of Marxism, of revolutionary ideology, and of communist politics. One of his chief concerns was that all those conceptions—political, historical, philosophical, economic, and so forth—that constituted the basic reference points for political decisions within the revolutionary or socialist camp could no longer be seen on an ascertainable or steady cultural horizon, nor were they necessarily a guarantee in the search for new political possibilities.[19]

To reflect with less prejudice than may be possible when confronting current opinion, one can see this line of thinking starting from Mao's 1957 statement, from *On Contradictions Among the People:* the question of who will win "within the ideological sphere," whether socialism or capitalism, "has not been really solved yet" (*hai mei you zhenzheng jiejue*).[20] In fact in the last directives of 1975–1976, Mao surprisingly concluded his career by stating that socialism "is not so different" (*mei you duoshao chabie*) from capitalism, except for the "form of ownership."[21]

Mao's political statements in his last twenty years were increasingly oriented toward the question of whether the socialist state itself was or was not the singular horizon for a contemporary politics of collective emancipation, as well as toward the increasing suspicion that the very space of political culture embodied by the socialist state's apparatus approximated a major downfall. In this sense, Meisner is right in writing that Mao considered that the revolution was dying, though this does not mean that he thought he could simply bring it back to life. If in his attitude there is something still worth considering by us, it is not a nostalgia for the "good old revolutionary days," but an obscure obstinacy in wishing to treat the probability of defeat as a subjective theme, even as an appeal for political mobilization.

In fact, the idea of probable defeat, as put forward since the mid-1960s, not only was a radicalization of previous concerns[22] and a much more disenchanted description of the present situation, but also claimed to be an original political thesis, paradoxical indeed, but nonetheless aiming to be prescriptive. Revolution, the modern name for political experimentation in forms of equality, was to be taken up to the end, while bearing in mind the probability of its imminent defeat.

But if the problem was how to pursue political activity within a certain space of cultural referents while thinking about the likelihood of an epochal defeat and at the same time not capitulating to it, Mao's thesis was totally meaningless in the terms of the classic revolutionary *epistème,* above all because politics and history cannot be integrated within that proposition. Situating political militancy in conditions where defeat was a probable conclusion, and discarding certainty of victory as an illusion, undermined some of the key elements of the historicopolitical horizon—in particular, the formerly inextricable connection of politics to the state.

Inextricably attached to the thesis of the certainty of victory in Stalinism was the foundational status of the socialist state. As the logical political outcome of the history of class struggle, the socialist state allegedly provided a definitive and sedimented proof of the historical foundation of politics. Certainty of victory was, first of all, the certainty of history, which, embodied in a state, provided a scientific and even a philosophical guarantee for politics.

The probability of defeat could not give any comparable guarantee, but instead restored infinite precariousness to politics. For these reasons, the very idea of probable defeat was virtually unspeakable within the dominant Marxist-Leninist political culture. There, it was more often pronounced in the better-known form of the "danger of the restoration of capitalism," whose coherence with Stalinist political culture is easily argued.[23] This last proposition can be said to be a variation on a theme of historicopolitical music, more than simply on a Stalinist one, but the proper political *enjeu* of the situation was probably beyond the limits of that tonal system. Dropping the metaphor, I would suggest that one of the main issues at stake was how to create new conditions for politics in a situation in which an epochal vision of politics and history was much more precarious than it appeared to be, given the solidity of the state apparatus of the time.

Was there, in fact, a genuine search for these new conditions for politics? If so, under which forms and with what limits? Assuming that probable defeat was an operating political thesis, were there any original political forms under which it could be organized? Among the numerous issues these questions imply, I will limit myself here to a discussion of only one, the political role of the Red Guards.

First, I will opt for a short periodization of the Cultural Revolution, based on the fact that the decisive circumstances were concentrated in the first two years.[24] The extreme dates of the core sequence fall between late 1965 and mid-1968, a period marked by a complex coexistence of two different political processes, partly separated, but finally overlapping one another and leading to an impasse. I would describe them as a dismissal-process and a pluralization-process, respectively.

On the one hand was the clash internal to the party-state, the process of dismissal that exploded in the late autumn of 1965 and dominated the political scene until the following spring. On the other hand was a process of the creation of a wide plurality of political organizations, which began in June 1966. The two processes are distinguishable from one another only for the duration of a strictly limited period lasting until January 1967, after which the trend was that of an increasing amalgamation, whose major phenomenology was the factional struggle that dominated China by mid-1967. A year later, the impasse was openly acknowledged with the dissolution of rebel organizations that concluded the core sequence.[25] A closer analysis of the period of 1965–1968 reveals three separate subsequences, each of which I shall consider separately.

In the first one, as noted, the only process operating was strictly an intrastate one. This could be called a *process of dismissal,* not only, as might be assumed, in homage to the famous historical drama *Hai Rui Dismissed from Office,* which provided a pivotal theme for the prelude to the Cultural Revolution,[26] but also because it resulted in the dismissal of some important functions of the state apparatus, as well as the dismissal of some ministers and high officials. This process was personally promoted by Mao, whose increasingly stubborn attitude after the *Hai Rui* affair was essential to later developments.

The frontline of this clash was the politico-ideological authority of the state cultural apparatuses. Its very first targets were not the intellectuals but the highest bureaucratic posts in key "state ideological apparatuses," to use Louis Althusser's famous category,[27] which encompass institutions of culture, the press and propaganda, schools and universities, and so on. In fact, more than any individual powerholder, what was disavowed was the very ideological authority of those apparatuses. Why, exactly, those apparatuses? Why such a stubborn attack on cultural authorities, which were, we must remember, the most orthodox representatives of socialist culture in China? To understand this, we must take into consideration the fact that, in socialist states, the distinction between ideological and repressive apparatuses is actually quite indefinite. In China, the cultural and ideological apparatuses also carried out highly repressive functions, not only policing thought but also often directly cooperating with the police *tout court,* to deal with "dangerous ideological mistakes" or to treat "bad subjects."

Now, if the underlying question was one of probable defeat, if a public dispute about the uncertain political destinies of socialism and of revolution had to be opened up to arouse everyone's attention so they could see the problems more clearly, then Mao could not hope that this would happen within the regular functioning of the cultural apparatuses of the socialist state. Since the mid-1950s, he had repeatedly experienced those apparatuses as capable of intractable resistance to any questioning of the destinies of the very culture they embodied.[28] And with good reason: those cultural apparatuses, so essential to the functioning of the socialist state—a very cultural and historical state, indeed—had been established to propagandize the certainty of victory, the historical guarantee for politics, and not to enable a dispute over a probable defeat.

The attack on the cultural ministries could therefore be considered both as a precondition and, presumably, a premeditated move. If Mao wanted to open a mass dispute on such political questions, it was first necessary to seriously limit the authority of those apparatuses, whose power could make use of ideology and violence to prevent and repress "unhealthy tendencies."

In the first months of the Cultural Revolution Mao liked to quote one of his favorite classical novels, *Xiyouji* (Journey to the west), likening the effects of his own political moves to the chaos created by Sun Wukong, the fantastic Monkey who, with his magic thousand-pound stick, created havoc in the heavenly palaces. Like the novel's hero, Mao wanted to "overturn the palace of the king of hell and set the little devils free," as he put it.[29] The cluster of classical quotations, so typical of Mao's style, had, however, very specific referents: the palace of the king of hell was in fact the ministry of culture and propaganda, or the heart of the state ideological apparatuses, and the little devils were more or less all the "poor devils" living under the ideological-repressive domination of those apparatuses.

Initially distinct from this process of dismissal, the second, or *pluralization*, process began in June 1966. With the palace of the king of hell already in great disarray, the little devils began to manifest themselves.[30] After the "May 16 Decision" (a central committee document approving Mao's positions against the cultural apparatuses, namely, the attack initiated six months earlier with the criticism of Wu Han's drama) openly disavowed the ideological infallibility of the palace and dramatically limited its repressive *force de frappe*, some of the little devils actually came out; first among them were students (both university and middle-school), but after a few months these were joined by workers and others from a wide variety of walks of life. In the latter half of the year, a new situation arose, one in which an indefinite plurality of political organizations, created from nothing, claimed an unprecedented space of freedom for declaring their political propositions, writing *dazibaos*—the large-character posters that became the famous carriers of the disputes—and publishing and distributing papers.

During this period, though external to the party-state, these participants authorized their own existences as political organizations and repeatedly insisted that their statements with regard to the current political crisis should not be treated as counterrevolutionary by the party apparatus, which was doing its best to stifle their very existence. It is arguable that such a situation would hardly have been possible without the previous troubles in the palace of the king of hell; for under the normal functioning conditions of socialist culture, the question was easily resolved: Everything existing outside of the party-state was at best apolitical, and if it claimed to be political, it would automatically be considered counterrevolutionary.

Political controversies over the issue extended throughout the second half of 1966, fostering the birth of a variety of independent organizations that reached a climax in the January storm, with the largest and most problematic forms of worker activism Shanghai had ever experienced. Also in Shanghai, numerous independent political organizations authorized their own existences and confronted a local party apparatus totally incapable of treating them without hostility.

The fall of the Shanghai local authorities was a turning point, opening a new, extremely intricate situation at the national level; this situation should be seen as the third of the three subsequences to which I refer above. Its primary phenomenon was the factionalist struggles that developed within a few months and spread throughout the country until mid-1968—with such regularity they could be said to be special cases of the Durkheimian *fait social*. The result was a drastic limitation of the political effectiveness of these organizations as they were increasingly absorbed into a strict frame of conflicts between essentially two factions, everywhere exhausting each other in repeated brawls aimed at gaining a grotesque political supremacy, and often a military one as well. The tragic results of the situation have been reported in many autobiographical accounts, but the factionalism itself, with the related degeneration of Red Guard organizations, remains a puzzling political phenomenon.

How can one understand that an originally indeterminate plurality of political sites was finally reduced to the fixed number of two? Here, a decisive shift in the content of the organizations' political propositions must be stressed. During the factional struggles, the controversies no longer concerned the self-authorization of independent political organizations, but the dismissal of certain local and central party-state functionaries. In virtually every *danwei*, the basic unit of Chinese socialist organization, two factions were fighting over the dismissal of a certain group of leaders, which was supported by one faction against the opposition of another—and vice versa. Antagonistic alliances were formed, not to claim an independent capacity of political judgment but primarily to become the steel "nucleus," as they said, of a regenerated party-state, whose legitimacy was subordinated to the dismissal of a number of leaders, and eventually to the annihilation of the other faction. Thus we can see that the previously distinct processes—the dismissal of state-apparatus authority (and officials, as well) and the pluralization of independent and self-authorizing organizations—had by this stage of the Cultural Revolution become indistinguishable.

As is often remarked, the Red Guard factionalism was the worst possible copy of central factionalism. In fact, the reciprocal dismissal, more or less violent, of groups of leaders was a major form of political dynamics in socialist states and in revolutionary organizations as well. The terrorist features of the socialist state were reproduced and exacerbated in the factional struggle at the bottom: Thus, whereas the previous process was that of a wide pluralization of political forms, the prevailing dynamics of factionalism were instead increasingly concentrated into a uniform situation, which reduced the organizations involved into opposing paramilitary groups lacking any political distinctiveness.

This blurring of the two processes as the main circumstance of factionalism in the Cultural Revolution has been described by Lynn White in terms of "unintended consequences" of previous, typically socialist state policies ("labeling, monitoring, and campaigning") grafted onto the peculiar political dynamics that began in 1966.[31] While this perspective is useful in identifying some distinctive features of each process, it can benefit from a closer analysis of the political propositions that operated at different stages of the Cultural Revolution. I would, furthermore, propose that a major impasse should be located not only at the intersection between the two dynamics but also, more precisely, in the effects that the thesis of probable defeat had on this double process.

In fact, a double process of political dynamics—one essentially consonant with intrastate dynamics, the other disseminated in a plurality of political sites—was not a novelty in itself; indeed, it has been a recurrent feature in revolutionary situations. In modern political culture, a successful revolution can be considered as the outcome of a political process partly external to the state, but finally finding an inscription in intrastate dynamics. Marxism-Leninism reinforced this vision with strong historicopolitical arguments. From the perspective of probable defeat, however, it was difficult, if not impossible, to discover such a historicopolitical inscription.

SATURATION

A radical impasse was de facto acknowledged in July 1968 at the last meeting between the Maoist central group and the Beijing rebel leaders; it finally led to the dissolution of the Red Guard organizations at the end of the year. The decision stopped the most disruptive effects of the factional struggles but left something essential unresolved. This initiated the beginning of another, extremely tortuous stage, marked by various intraparty clashes, which continued until 1976. In the last analysis, the entire Chinese political scene during those years was perplexed by the dilemma of how to deal with the impasse without completely repudiating the Cultural Revolution.

More precisely, in the long final sequence of the Cultural Revolution, most of the efforts of Maoists were aimed at avoiding a repudiation of the mass activities of the central years of late 1965 to mid-1968 and at demonstrating that the impasse might be overcome if political tensions could find an appropriate outlet within experiments with institutional change. Some of these experiments were pursued quite seriously: In July 1968, for instance, when Mao bade farewell to the exhausted "little generals" who had degenerated into petty warlords, he also welcomed the "Shanghai Machine Tool Plant Worker University," which he considered a terrain of experiments for new visions of both the factory and the university and which became an important reference point in the following years.

During the core sequence of the Cultural Revolution, factories and universities had revealed themselves to be the weakest links of the institutional chain, as well as poor carriers of the ideological functions they embodied—a fact that explains why, after 1968, Maoist political experiments were concentrated in these two places. Both were key institutional forms with highly ideological foundations and, for reasons discussed above, were also particularly sensitive points within a political situation in which the cultural foundations of the state were placed under discussion.

As for the factories, it is self-evident that they localized a historico-political legitimacy, as well as a principle of institutional organization, connecting the working class, politics, and the party-state. In many respects, the working class can be understood as the lowest stratum of socialist officials, and the industrial *danwei* as the paradigm of the institutional unification of Chinese society.[32]

Nor should the primary importance of the university system be underestimated. A focal point for the cultural functions of the party-state, the university system was also a setting for the training of various kinds of officials, as well as a major source of socialist culture itself. As Jacques Lacan ironically reminded some of the most leftist Paris students sometime around 1968, the socialist state was the prime example of the preeminence of what he called the *discours de l'université*[33]—a kind of discourse, no doubt, coextensive with the historicopolitical variety. Even without invoking the historical tradition of scholar-officials, there were enough contemporary issues to make factories and universities key fields of controversy in Chinese politics over the course of the decade.

The worker universities, for example, proclaimed their intent to reforge a relation between the worker and the factory. It was to be based on a democratization of the existing division of labor and the related forms of command and would no longer depend on the disciplinary use of the historicopolitical reference to the working class, not to mention the more conventionally understood commodification of the labor force. But if the workers had to be trained in the worker university to become technicians—the critics of the experiment argued—why not simply acknowledge their personal ascent to a higher status on the chain of command in the socialist factory? Why, instead, insist on link-ing the results of those "universities" (no more than technical schools, the critics said) with the fundamental questioning of the relationships of authority in the factory (which is precisely what supporters of the experiments did)?

Political experiments in the more academic universities were more contradictory, but nonetheless addressed questions such as the rela-tion between social inequalities and teaching institutions and, more generally, state policies regarding the formation and transmission of knowledge. They implied, for instance, that the university system could be, in principle, separated from its typical socialist functions (both ideological and organizational) of reproducing the various ranks of state personnel. An idea, to be sure, that the critics considered totally absurd, viewing it from the perspective of the most consoli-dated patterns of modern educational policies, both in socialist and nonsocialist states. In fact, these issues involved not only the alloca-tion of the outputs of the school system but also the very relation of the modern state to the general field of knowledge.

In the post-1976 verdict, these experiments were definitely asso-ciated with the plots of the Gang of Four for usurping power. They were, it is true, limited to situations in which the core sequence of the Cultural Revolution was most intense and the Maoists were more active, as in Shanghai, and they also involved intraparty factional splits, although not in the tragic forms of 1967–1968. But the experiments and the alternatives they tested were, in fact, politically relevant and not reducible to simple devices for the purposes of usurping power, a point very well recorded in contemporary disputes.

But it is also evident that such political contrasts were made more and more opaque by the use of the common system of references in which all the participants articulated their propositions. "The working class must lead in everything" (*gongren jieji yao lingdao yiqie*), the Mao-ists had repeated in defense of certain spaces of political experimenta-tion since 1968, but the working class was the same historicopolitical category to which their adversaries also referred, with the aggravating factor that the Maoists were committed to defending political dynam-ics rooted in turbulent, mass-scale indecision on what working class really meant as a political category.

Mao himself declared that "both among the proletariat [*wuchanjieji zhong*] and among the officials of the state apparatus [*jiguan gongzuo renyuan zhong*]" a "new bourgeoisie" could be formed.[34] How could the identification of new categories allow one to face—without capitulating—this historicopolitical aporia? And how could social and institutional experimentation help in the search for new paths? Mao's adversaries, it must be remembered, replied that his were only empty words and that the true meaning of working class lay essentially in its established connections within the ideology and organization of the party-state.

During their 1975–1976 clash with the Gang of Four, the strictness of Deng Xiaoping and his allies' defense of the most orthodox Marxist-Leninist arguments is significant. This orthodoxy was calculated to dismiss as slander any questioning of the incorruptible substance of the socialist state and its personnel, including the working class. For Deng and his allies, all the experiments the Maoists supported in their search for new visions of the issue were totally meaningless, as well as a source of disorder to be rectified as quickly as possible. And since those experiments could be pursued only on the condition of not repudiating the Cultural Revolution, the confrontation was definitely antagonistic.

The period of 1968–1976, and in particular its last two or three years, was dominated by a peculiar atmosphere, which might be defined by a complete saturation of the cultural referents of revolutionary politics in China. The more the Maoists insisted on defending their political experiments—or the "newborn *things*" (*xinsheng shiwu*) as they said with a remarkably abstract expression—the more the standard system of historicopolitical *words* was brought to a saturation point. Claiming that those things were compatible with the socialist state and its culture, they had to lean on the same revolutionary *épistème* that, however, the subjective perspective of probable defeat made highly uncertain. Their adversaries were able to make use of the very same system of words, but to denigrate the same things that the Maoists defended. And unhampered by the assumption of probable defeat, they could do so much more easily. The political stalemate became unsolvable, and a modest coup d'état was sufficient to close off everything.

Buried as it was under the fall of the Gang of Four, this sequence, characterized by saturation, remains even less explored by historiographic research than the core sequence of the Cultural Revolution. It is my hope that the arguments offered in this essay can, at the very least, lead to reducing the violence of a certain "virus of the present" that is conditioning attitudes toward a political situation in which the greatest part of the contemporary intellectual difficulties over the relationship between history and politics is obscurely rooted.

A first version of this essay was drafted in 1994. The key arguments were presented in two talks, one given at the conference on "Mao Zedong, the Poetry and the Reality," held at the Civica Scuola di Lingue e Culture Orientali di Milano, 3–6 April 1995, and another at the seminar on "The French Revolution and the Birth of Modern Politics" organized by the Dipartimento di Discipline Storiche, University of Bologna, 22 May 1997. I wish to thank Tani E. Barlow for her invitation to submit this text, and for her help and that of Nancy Kool in editing the English version. I had the pleasure of discussing the content with Marilyn Young during her professorship at the University of Bologna in the spring of 1997. Thanks also to Claudia Pozzana for her long-term criticism and suggestions, and to Alex Passi for his linguistic advice.

1   Marc Bloch, *The Historian's Craft* (Manchester, England: Manchester University Press, 1954), 37.

2   Michel Foucault, *Les mots et les choses* (Paris: Gallimard, 1966); Foucault, *L'archéologie du savoir* (Paris: Gallimard, 1971).

3   This is the basic assumption of Francis Fukuyama, *The End of History and the Last Man* (New York: Free Press, 1992).

4   Philip C. C. Huang, "The Paradigmatic Crisis in Chinese Studies: Paradoxes in Social and Economic History," *Modern China* 17, no. 3 (July 1991): 299–341.

5   Gao Gao and Yan Jiaqi, *"Wenhua da geming" shi nian shi* [History of ten years of the "Great Cultural Revolution"] (Tianjin: Renmin Chubanshe, 1986). The book has been translated into English and edited by D. Kwok under the title *Turbulent Decade: A History of the Cultural Revolution* (Honolulu: University of Hawaii Press, 1996).

6   Andrew Walder, "Cultural Revolution Radicalism: Variations on a Stalinist Theme," in W. Joseph, C. Wong, and D. Zweig, eds., *New Perspectives on the Cultural Revolution*, Harvard Contemporary China Series, no. 8 (Cambridge: Harvard University Press, 1991), 41–61.

7   Maurice Meisner, *Mao's China and After: A History of the People's Republic* (New York: Free Press, 1977), 309.

8   Shen Rong, "Jianqu shi sui," *Renmin wenxue* 2 (1986). English translation, "Ten Years Deducted," trans. Gladys Yang, in Shen Rong, *At Middle Age* (Beijing: Panda Books, 1987), 342–364.

9   See Wang Xiaoming, "Yifen zazhi he yige 'shetuan': Lun 'wu si' wenxue chuantong" [A journal and an "association": on the literary tradition of "May fourth"], *Jintian* [Today] 3–4 (1991): 94–114. The journal and association being spoken of is none other than *Xin Qingnian* [New youth], which influenced the May Fourth movement more than any other journal. *Jintian,* founded in Beijing in 1978 to herald a turning point in contemporary

poetry, is, in turn, the most important journal of vanguard Chinese literature. It is presently being published in exile.

10 Bloch, *The Historian's Craft*, 37.

11 Zhou Ming, ed., *Lishi zai zheli chensi* [Here history is lost in thought] (Beijing: Huaxia Chubanshe), 1986.

12 Sylvain Lazarus, *Anthropologie du nom* (Paris: Seuil, 1996). My research
was greatly stimulated by Lazarus's distinction between "circulating categories" and "properly political categories," argued in this book, as well as by
Valerio Romitelli in his important study concerning the category of revolution in modern political culture: *Sulle origini e la fine della Rivoluzione:
Storia di una categoria politica e culturale* (Bologna: Clueb, 1996). Above all,
the distinction crosses the category of revolution itself. As Lazarus subtly
argues (in *Anthropologie du nom*, 203–232), revolution operated as a properly political category only in a very short sequence of the French Revolution between 1792 and 1794. After the Thermidor coup d'état, however,
revolution ceased to be a strictly political category, i.e., proper to a peculiar political situation. In the following century, and until a few decades
ago, the immense fortune *revolution* acquired was, in fact, that of another
category—it no longer pertained to any specific political event but rather
became a key signifier in various fields of modern knowledge, mainly the
historical and social ones. It became an essential linking point that allowed
a conceptual "circulation" between visions of history and politics, especially in Marxist theory. Romitelli's book (*Sulle origini*, 99–133) explores
in detail how the relations between revolution as a political category and
revolution as a circulating or cultural category rest on the complex relations between the French Revolution and German classical philosophy. It
was mainly through Hegel's philosophy of history that the French Revolution acquired its intellectual relevance in modern culture. Another clear
example of a category circulating between the regimes of history and politics, as well as other fields of modern knowledge, is that of class. As Marx
himself acknowledged, he did not discover class or class struggle, but he
derived them from the "bourgeois" economists and historians. He added,
for his part, a political theory of the end of classes.

13 As has been well documented by Elizabeth J. Perry and Li Xun, available
statistics on class background and other demographic characteristics of the
rebel leaders do not reveal any significant distinctions between them and
their conservative rivals, or between them and the workforce as a whole.
The split, the authors argue, was purely subjective. See *Proletarian Power:
Shanghai in the Cultural Revolution* (Boulder, Colo.: Westview Press, 1997),
39–41. More than twenty years after the events, while conducting a survey
in two factories, I had the chance to interview workers from both the East
Wind and Red Flag factions in Guangzhou, which witnessed a split similar
to that in Shanghai. Asked for the reasons for their involvment in the Cultural Revolution, one answered, "in defense of the results of socialism," but

another said, "for fighting against all the injustice." I have analyzed some of the aspects of this survey in "Ouvrier et danwei: Note de recherche sur une enquête d'anthropologie ouvrière menée dans deux usines de Guangzhou en avril–mai 1989," *Cahiers du CIASOC* 1 (1990): 9–38.

14 Sylvain Lazarus has presented this view, tracing a sequence from Shanghai to Gdansk, in another report on the above-mentioned survey made in Guangzhou, *Chercher ailleurs et autrement: Sur la doctrine des lieux, l'économie, l'effondrement du socialisme* (Paris: Les Conférences du Perroquet, No. 35, Mai 1992). The research group in Guanzhou, besides Lazarus and myself, included Claudia Pozzana and Valerio Romitelli.

15 If we were able to dismiss the conviction that any politics is essentially derivable from a certain culture or a space of knowledge or a kind of discourse (that is the current scholarly alternative to the vision of politics as an effect of history) and tried to conceive of politics as a mode of thinking, an index of its very existence should be searched for in its displacement from a given discourse. In fact, no proper category of thinking can exist without creating a certain degree of discontinuity, of dissonance, albeit minimal, in a discourse or knowledge or cultural space, however much it appears integrated to it.

16 *Mao Zedong sixiang wansui* [Long live Mao Zedong thought] (n.p., 1969), 673. This well-known collection of previously unpublished texts by Mao was edited by the Red Guards. At least a dozen volumes of Mao's texts not included in the *Collected Works of Mao Zedong* were published under the same title, but this collection is probably the best source for post-1949 texts.

17 Ibid., 663.

18 André Malraux, *Antimémoires* (Paris, 1967). I quote from the Italian translation: *Antimemorie* (Milano: Bompiani, 1967), 494. A somewhat different version of this conversation appears in *Mao Zedong sixiang wansui* (ed. 1969), 673–679.

19 Mao engaged also in a personal research into the key issues of Marxist-Leninist revolutionary knowledge. His most systematic effort is the "Reading notes" of 1960 on the Soviet *Textbook of Political Economy*. See "Du 'Zhengzhi jingjixue jiaokeshu' (shehuizhuyi bufen)," in *Mao Zedong sixiang wansui* (ed. 1967), 167–247.

20 *Mao Zedong xuanji*, vol. 5 (Beijing: Renmin Chubanshe, 1977), 389. This specific passage appeared in the revised edition. For the original speech, equally concerned with the issue, see "On the Correct Handling of Contradictions among the People (Speaking Notes)," in *The Secret Speeches of Chairman Mao*, Harvard Contemporary China Series, no. 6, ed. R. MacFarquhar, T. Cheek, and E. Wu (Cambridge: Harvard University Press, 1989), 130–189.

21 Quoted in *Renmin ribao*, 22 February 1975.

22 Mao often quoted a speech from 1962 as the first occasion on which he

openly addressed this question. See *Mao Zedong sixiang wansui* (1969), 399–423. Translation, "Talk at an Enlarged Central Work Conference (30 January 1962)," in S. Schram, ed., *Mao Tse-tung Unrehearsed: Talks and Letters 1956–71* (Middlesex, England: Penguin Books, 1974), 158–187.

23 Looking more carefully, however, the theme of the restoration of capitalism was not always discussed in a conventional Stalinist mode. See Joseph W. Esherick, "On the 'Restoration of Capitalism': Mao and the Marxist Theory," *Modern China* 5, no. 1 (January 1979): 41–78.

24 The government version of the decade refers only to the state decision (a coup d'état, actually) that declared the process closed.

25 Those organizations had been in open crisis for many months, but their political end was actually declared in the famous last meeting of July 1968 of Mao, the central group, and the leaders of Red Guards in the capital. See "Zhaojian shoudu hongdaihui fuzeren de tanhua [Talks with the leaders of Beijing Red Guard Congress] (July 28, 1968)," in *Mao Zedong sixiang wansui* (1969), 687–716. The importance of this meeting in the periodization of the Cultural Revolution is stressed by Hong Yung Lee, *The Politics of the Cultural Revolution: A Case Study* (Berkeley: University of California Press, 1978), 1.

26 The drama, written in the late 1950s by Wu Han, at the time one of the most influential historians in China as well as a high political and cultural authority, was at the center of the opening dispute of the Cultural Revolution. In the late autumn of 1965, the drama was criticized by an article inspired by Mao and signed by Yao Wenyuan published in the Shanghai newspaper *Wenhui Bao*.

27 Louis Althusser, "Idéologie et appareils idéologique d'Etat," *La Pensée* 151 (June 1970). Reprinted in Althusser, *Positions* (Paris: Editions Sociales, 1976), 79–137.

28 For some very interesting examples, see the talks translated in MacFarquhar et al., *Secret Speeches*.

29 *Mao Zedong sixiang wansui* (1969), 641.

30 This summary necessarily neglects many details; however, it is essentially accurate.

31 Lynn T. White, *Policies of Chaos: Organizational Causes of Violence in China's Cultural Revolution* (Princeton, N.J.: Princeton University Press, 1989); White, "The Cultural Revolution as Unintended Results of Administrative Policies," in W. Joseph, C. Wong, and D. Zweig, eds., *New Perspectives on the Cultural Revolution, 83–104*.

32 I discuss this point in Russo, "Ouvrier et danwei," 39–49.

33 Jacques Lacan, *L'envers de la psychanalyse* (*Le Séminaire, Livre XVII*) (Paris: Seuil, 1991), 237.

34 Quoted in *Renmin ribao*, 22 February 1975.

SANJAY SETH

Interpreting Revolutionary Excess: The Naxalite

Movement in India, 1967–1971

■ Marxism and liberalism are not only products of the modern age but also champions of it. They share concerns and make assumptions about human society and reason which mark them unmistakably as progeny of the Enlightenment, and they see in the modern that which is both inevitable and desirable.

How this modern future is imagined serves, of course, to sharply distinguish Marxism from liberalism, as do their conceptions of the mechanisms of the transition to this future. For Marxists, since the development of a theory of "imperialism," and with it the abandonment of the notion that bourgeois societies would "carry" capitalism to nonbourgeois countries in an uncomplicated way, it has been an article of faith that development and modernization are incompatible with the existing pattern of power relations in "backward" countries. The question of progress toward the modern has thus been framed in the context of "revolution." This is a line of thought with many variations—Guevarist, Maoist, and so on—but what all these have in common is the assumption that structures of domination and exploitation (domestic, as between ruling classes and ruled; and international, as between imperialist and colonial countries) are also impediments to development, and therefore that the struggle of the oppressed for emancipation will also be the catalyst for modernization.

Marxist theory and communist politics were in this way made relevant to countries such as China and India, where feudal and semi-feudal relations still predominated in much of the countryside. The claim in these latter cases was usually that feudal relations in the countryside were so much tied up with bourgeois relations in the city, and with the interests of imperialism, that the peasants' struggle was by its very nature also a struggle against the fetters which limited the country's independence and hampered the development of its productive forces. This reformulation of Marxism, one where it was no longer held necessary to await the development of capitalism in backward countries for the socialist project to become feasible, but rather where development was itself seen as contingent on revolution, was a plausible one, given certain assumptions. It was also elegant, for it is an amended version of Marx's immensely powerful and elegant schema/prophecy of socialist revolution.

In the first and preliminary part of this essay, I argue that the structural similarities between these two "models" obscured a crucial difference. I suggest that the schema of revolution in an agrarian society entailed the "forgetting" or misreading of aspects of peasant experience and consciousness. The remainder of this essay seeks to show that the Naxalite-led peasant struggles in India were an instance of "un-forgetting"; one of those rare moments in the history of the Indian communist movement where communists did not just use and seek to direct peasant rebellion, but where Marxist categories came to be penetrated and shaped by the categories informing peasant insurgency.

## REVOLUTION AND MODERNITY

In Marx's schema of socialist revolution, as is well known, the development and the supersession of capitalism are part of one and the same movement. The processes which mark the development of bourgeois society serve, at the same time, to bring closer the moment of its revolutionary overthrow. This is so, on the one hand, because of structural contradictions at the very heart of capitalist production. Most notable among these is that between the socialized nature of production and the private appropriation of its fruits, a contradiction which manifests itself in the form of economic crises of increasing magnitude and frequency. The "socialized nature of production" is also a description of the maturation of the structural conditions which make resistance possible and, indeed, inevitable; as Marx and Engels put it in the *Manifesto of the Communist Party*, "not only has the bourgeoisie forged the weapons that bring death to itself; it has also called into existence the men who are to wield those weapons—the modern working class."[1] For the processes of capitalist development and expansion are the very processes which bring workers together in large cities and factories, which standardize the conditions of their work and life, and which make it possible and necessary for them to fight against their exploitation. All of this facilitates what Marx once characterized as the proletariats' transition from a "class against capital" to a "class for itself."[2]

There is a harmony between the maturation of the structural conditions for the overthrow of bourgeois society on the one hand, and the revolutionary consciousness which guides the agents of that overthrow on the other. The development of capitalism—and its structural contradictions—proceeds *pari passu* not only with a growth in the size of the proletariat but also with the development of working class organization and consciousness. The earliest phases of capitalism produce the Luddite, who does not properly understand what it is that is destroying his way of life, and who lashes out blindly at machines. The further development of capitalism, including the bringing together of workers in the production process and in large cities, produces the trade unionist, aware of his class interests and class solidarities. He in turn eventually becomes the working-class revolutionary, a member of a revolutionary party, seeking the overthrow of bourgeois society rather than the representation of working-class interests within it.

At this point, the homology between this and the Marxist "model" of revolution in a backward country breaks down. In Marx's sketch, as argued above, there is a "fit" between the structure of exploitation and class rule and the oppositional consciousness which it generates. However, in the Marxist model(s) of revolution in backward countries, the agents of change no longer need be fully conscious of the transformation they are to effect. Self-emancipation, so powerful and appealing an aspect of Marx's model, undergoes a curious twist; in seeking primarily to emancipate themselves from feudal exploitation, peasants simultaneously and more or less unwittingly also emancipate themselves from imperialism and "backwardness."[3]

This is so because in this argument "structure" is made to bear more weight than "consciousness"; or to put it another way, a gap is opened up between structure and consciousness. Let me illustrate this point by means of an example: Communist Party of India analyses and programmatic documents of the 1950s and 1960s frequently claimed that feudal exploitation had come to be linked to a capitalist market, and the landlord class were symbiotically tied to the urban bourgeoisie—which is why the peasants' struggle against the landlord and moneylender dovetailed with the workers' struggle against the bourgeoisie, and why both culminated in a radical-democratic, or socialist modern. But the peasant, even if exposed to the vagaries of the market in addition to the weight of feudal exploitation, was still a peasant, not an urban worker. And inasmuch as his immediate superior and exploiter was the landlord and not the distant bourgeois or neocolonialist, the consciousness which informed his resistance and struggle was largely antifeudal and premodern or nonmodern, even if the "effect" of his rebellion (in this Marxist reading) also undermined neocolonialism and the bourgeoisie.

In the history of the communist movement, this gap has usually been dealt with in one of two ways. It has sometimes been denied or "forgotten" and, implicitly or explicitly, a subjectivity or consciousness has been attributed to the peasant that is not, and could not be, his own. If the *effect* of peasant struggles is to undermine not only feudalism but also thereby the bourgeois-feudal-neocolonial nexus, cannot one then assume that this is the *intention* of the subjects engaged in these struggles?[4] That is, an argument about the effects of peasant struggles is illegitimately read backward into the consciousness that informs these struggles. Never completely so, for any communist party seriously engaged in working among the peasantry could not regard the peasantry as a class which dreams of a transparent, secular society rendered subject to human control. But even with this qualification, the point remains: whereas in the case of the working class, its conditions of existence are assumed to conduce to the development of the right sort of revolutionary politics, in the case of the peasantry, the localism, territoriality, religiosity, and so on, which are characteristic of peasant life and peasant rebellion—and which have certainly been characteristic of peasant rebellion in South Asia—are downplayed and/or derided, and treated as "limitations," which, while they may be unavoidable, and which can and should be used, must also be overcome.

Or else, it is simply accepted that there is a gap or mismatch between intention and outcome and the task of the vanguard party is precisely to ensure that the peasant, mired in localism and medieval obscurantism, wages a struggle which has beneficial outcomes, even if they are of a type he or she could scarcely imagine, let alone consciously fight for.[5] For instance: the peasant will be mobilized around the fight for land, bread, and peace, and the party will ensure that the potential implications of this—soviets, five-year plans, international solidarity, and futurist art—unrealized by the peasant (and sometimes unwanted), will in fact be fulfilled.

In either case, and this is the central point, the consciousness which *in fact* informs peasant revolt is not registered. The more "backward" the country—and from here on in my remarks shall be specific to India—that is, the more the consciousness which informs peasant struggle is formed by feudal relations and is one which dreams of turning the world upside down rather than rendering it transparent, the more it is organized around religion and kinship rather than secular ideology and class, as has been the case with peasant insurgencies in India—the more necessary it becomes to read it as something other than what it is, and/or to depreciate it (as prepolitical, unorganized, and so on) at the same time that it is utilized in a more or less instrumental fashion. What I am suggesting is that Marxism in a "backward" country such as India *has been a political project which relies on a rebellious consciousness which it denies/misreads, and/or seeks to utilize instrumentally while "quarantining" it lest it infect Marxist categories.*

In what follows, I investigate an exception to the argument advanced above. The Naxalite movement in India in the years from about 1969–1971, I shall argue in the remainder of this essay, was one in which an insurgent peasant consciousness was neither misread nor simply utilized in an instrumentalist fashion, but rather left its imprint not only on communist practice but also on communist theoretical categories.

I begin by providing a brief account of the Naxalite revolt in India during its most active years, from 1967–1971, focusing in particular on the Naxalite efforts to mobilize the peasantry. That the Naxalites sought to engage with the peasantry and lead peasant struggles is not in itself remarkable. While the communist movement in India had for most of its history been orthodox in assigning centrality in the revolutionary struggle to the working class, it had not neglected peasant work, and had led major peasant movements in Bengal in 1946–1948 and in what is now the state of Andhra Pradesh in 1946–1951.[6]

What was unusual and significant about the Naxalites was that their Maoist-influenced theory not only urged involvement in peasant struggles but was in turn affected and even shaped by the consciousness which informed these struggles. For aspects of their ideology and practice—the centrality it accorded to peasant rebellion, its emphasis on the antifeudal character of peasant struggles, and the injunction that communists had to "learn from the peasant masses"—resulted in a certain "openness" or receptivity in Naxalite theory, making it possible for this consciousness to impact on and influence that theory. Specifically, this impact can be seen, I shall suggest, in certain features of Naxalite politics which have commonly been characterized (and criticized) as exemplars of the "ultraleftist" and "adventurist" nature of this movement. This "adventurism," I argue, is open to an alternative reading: what otherwise appear as the "excesses" of the Naxalite movement are possessed of a clear logic once one looks for that logic not simply in the categories of Marxism but in the categories of antifeudal peasant insurgency.

This essay offers a reading of the meaning and significance of certain episodes in the Naxalite movement which is not consonant with the Naxalites' self-understanding of what they were engaged in and what it meant. This alternative reading presupposes some conception of the categories informing peasant insurgency and working-class militancy in India. For this, I draw on Ranajit Guha's work on peasant insurgency in nineteenth-century India and on Dipesh Chakrabarty's work on the Calcutta working class in colonial India. The writings of these historians of the subaltern studies group have helped me frame and develop my own argument. It is ironic, but fitting, that the subaltern studies project itself arose out of an intellectual milieu in which the legacy of Naxalbari loomed large.

What counts as "evidence" in any interpretive exercise of this type varies from the norm prevailing in empirical historiography—something greatly exacerbated in this case, where our claims regarding the character of an "insurgent peasant consciousness" are themselves readings, rather than firsthand testimony from those engaged in insurgency. As a result, what is offered as evidence in this essay are correspondences rather than causality, and plausibility and intelligibility rather than empirical "proof."

## THE NAXALITES

The split in the communist movement which eventually gave birth to the Communist Party of India (Marxist-Leninist) followed close on the heels of an earlier split. In 1964, a significant number of Communist Party of India (CPI) members left to form the Communist Party of India–Marxist (CPI-M). Those who left were, generally speaking, more sympathetic to the Chinese party than to the Soviet party and more radical on domestic issues and strategies than those who stayed in the CPI.

Many within the newly formed CPI-M hoped that the split heralded an unreserved embrace of the Chinese communists' position on all international issues, and a break with the moderate and parliamentarist path followed by the CPI since the 1950s. They were soon disillusioned. The outbreak of the Indo-Pakistan war in September 1965 saw the CPI-M supporting India's stand, while the CPC aligned itself with Pakistan; and while sympathetic to the CPC in its polemics against the Soviet party, the CPI-M proved unwilling to go all the way with the CPC in its condemnations of the Soviet "revisionists." On domestic issues, while locating itself to the left of the CPI, the CPI-M proved itself no less eager to engage in parliamentary politics, and indeed proved successful in this endeavor. Elections in February 1967 saw coalition governments take power in the states of West Bengal and Kerala, governments in which the CPI-M—to the distress of its more radically inclined cadre—was an important constituent.[7]

A discernible shift to the left in this period, of which the electoral successes of the CPI-M were a symptom, also brought conflicts within that party to a head. In Naxalbari, in the Darjeeling district of the state of West Bengal, the newly elected United Front government of West Bengal faced a peasant revolt led by radical CPI-M cadre. After initial efforts to find some compromise, the CPI-M leadership made clear that confronted with a choice, it would opt to suppress the movement rather than face continuing embarrassment in office. Disaffection over the path being taken by the CPI-M saw dissident CPI-M cadre forming Maoist groups also in Andhra Pradesh and elsewhere. The Naxalite insurgency was in the meantime hailed by China as the beginning of a Maoist wave that would sweep India.[8] With this additional encouragement, the dissidents in the CPI-M formed an All-India Coordination Committee of Communist Revolutionaries (AIC-CCR) in November 1967 to coordinate the activities of the various Maoist groups in the country. In 1969 this loose structure was formalized into the CPI-ML, though at a cost, for a number of Maoist groups—most notably the Maoist Communist Centre in West Bengal and the Nagi Reddy group in Andhra Pradesh—declined to join a party which they felt was being prematurely foisted on them, and with which they had some unresolved tactical differences.

The main points of difference between the Naxalites and the two non-Maoist communist parties were over international questions (especially the degree of loyalty to the Chinese Communist Party), and over characterizations of the class configuration in India, and the character and strategy appropriate to the Indian revolution. The Naxalites hailed the CPC as the leader of the international communist movement, followed its lead on all important issues, and created a veritable cult around Chairman Mao.

On the nature of the Indian social formation, the Naxalites held that India, on the attaining of "formal" independence in 1947, became a "neo-colony of several imperialist powers, chief among which were the United States and the Soviet Union."[9] India was "a semi-colonial and semi-feudal country," and the Indian state was a "state of the big land-lords and comprador-bureaucrat capitalists."[10] Dependence on and subjugation by foreign interests, exploitation of the workers, and feudal backwardness and oppression were all parts of a seamless whole; the Indian ruling classes and Indian state did not even defend the interests of Indian capitalism because they were so hopelessly subservient to imperialism.

Such a characterization had important political and strategic consequences. The insistence on the totally and irremediably comprador and reactionary character of all the dominant classes and institutions of the Indian state implied a much more radical strategy than would otherwise have been the case. These formulations, unlike those of the CPI and the CPI-M, allowed no scope for playing off one section of the dominant classes against another, nor for "using" institutions like parliament to advance revolutionary interests. They led instead to denunciations of the "illusion" that revolutionary transformation could follow on the building up of mass organizations, and to a vehement rejection of peaceful and parliamentary struggle. One of the early resolutions adopted by the AIC-CCR (in May 1968) declared that "bourgeois parliamentary institutions, already historically obsolete, have become a positive impediment to the advance of revolutions in general and to revolutions in semifeudal, semicolonial countries like India, in particular,"[11] and called on the people to boycott the forthcoming elections. Against the "revisionist" parliamentary path of the other two communist parties, the Naxalites counterposed the method of armed struggle, which alone, they declared, could accomplish the Indian revolution.

The emphasis on the agrarian and semifeudal nature of Indian society meant that the armed struggle would be primarily an agrarian struggle, a guerrilla war. India, the AICCCR repeatedly declared, would follow China's path: "Under the leadership of the working class, the peasantry, the main force of the revolution, must set up revolutionary base areas in the countryside, wage a protracted armed struggle, encircle the cities from the countryside and finally seize them and win ultimate nation-wide victory."[12]

This resolution paid lip service to the leadership of the working class, but not all documents were to do so, and in fact Naxalite efforts were overwhelmingly to do with peasants rather than workers. Mazumdar made this clear—"We must build our party basically among the peasant masses."[13] This was because at the heart of the Indian revolution was the struggle against feudalism, and this antifeudal revolution would be led by the peasantry; though the peasant struggle against feudalism would also, because of the structural links between all these, undermine imperialism and bureaucratic capitalism.[14]

The Naxalites movement was not, as mentioned earlier, the first time communists in India had attached importance to the peasantry and sought to lead peasant struggles. But the preponderant emphasis on peasant insurrection was relatively new, and certainly significant. The claim now was not simply that peasant struggles were part of the revolution but rather, that they were its very heart. Moreover, in another act with important practical ramifications, these were declared to be struggles against feudalism, and the struggle against feudalism was declared the key to the Indian revolution. As one author writes: "The strategic implication of calling India a semi-feudal and semi-colonial country was . . . the identification of feudalism as the principal contradiction, and the *jotedars* [large landowners] as the main enemy of the people."[15] The Naxalites identified the enemy in unambiguous terms as the feudal oppressor, and their emphasis was clearly on transforming power relations in the countryside. Moreover, the declaration that the Indian state was wholly and unambiguously an instrument of the ruling classes meant that these struggles were not and could not become attempts to compel the state to act (to increase the share of sharecroppers under law, to effect land reform, and so on); they were, instead, a struggle between the peasant and his oppressor, and they were struggles to the finish.

Had the differences between the Naxalites and the other communist parties been confined to such matters, the split of 1967 would have remained an event of local significance, yet another episode in the Indian communist movement's long history of doctrinal and strategic disputes. However, while Naxalite polemics employed a Maoist variation of the same deadening prose as the rest of the communist movement in India, and while their political and strategic formulations made something of a display of their derivative character, the adoption of Maoist strategy and slogans had the important effect of placing an overwhelming emphasis on the peasantry and peasant struggles, and in highlighting the antifeudal character of such struggles. Partly as a result of this, this became a dispute with a difference, for "unlike earlier inner-party struggles, this struggle was accompanied by revolutionary practice."[16]

It was this engagement with revolutionary struggles which made the Naxalite movement something more than just another Party split. The catalyst for the formation of independent Maoist groups, as well the occasion which gave the movement a name, was the peasant uprising in northern Bengal. Within days of the formation of the United Front government, peasant conferences were organized by local CPI-M leaders intent on launching a peasant agitation under the new and more favorable political conditions. The local CPI-M leaders were almost all on the left of the party. Charu Mazumdar, who was soon to become the preeminent leader of the Naxalites, had been active in his youth in the Tebhaga peasant struggle of 1946–1948. He was the (unsuccessful) communist candidate in a by-election for a seat in the state parliament in 1963, and when the party split in 1964, he joined the CPI-M. Mazumdar became a critic of the direction the new party was taking, and authored a number of articles elaborating a Maoist model for revolution in India. Other important figures in the area included Kanu Sanyal, a local leader of middle-class origins who had been living and working among the peasantry of the area for several years, and Jangal Santhal, a peasant leader. Under the leadership of the latter two men, and with Charu Mazumdar providing some general theoretical and strategic guidance, the peasants were organized in peasants' committees and mobilized around militant demands. The peasants set up parallel administrations in many villiages, canceled debts, reclaimed *benami* lands, and burnt land records. The ensuing clashes with landlords and rural notables saw the struggle take an increasingly violent turn, until it became apparent that a mini-insurgency was taking place. At this point, in July 1967, the United Front government authorized a major police operation against the rebels, which by the latter part of the year had quelled the movement and captured most of its leaders.[17]

The differences between the Naxalites and other Indian communists continued to be argued out with reference to, and in the course of involvement in, peasant movements. From late 1968, the Srikakulam District Coordination Committee launched a peasant guerrilla struggle against the dominant rural classes. Guerrilla bands forcibly harvested the crops of rich landlords, seized property, canceled peasant debt, killed "notorious" landlords and moneylenders, and terrorized others into submission. Charu Mazumdar, who visited the area in March 1969—he was embraced by the revolutionaries as their leader, which cemented his position as the leading figure in the Naxalite movement—predicted that it would become India's Yenan. This was a struggle waged on a larger scale and with greater intensity than the earlier Naxalbari struggle, and one which established Maoist control of at least a few areas in this northern part of the province of Andhra Pradesh, before massive police repression subdued it in the latter part of 1969 and 1970.

In the second half of 1969, a simmering revolt of peasants in the Midnapur district of West Bengal was given new direction by CPI-ML cadres. In Debra and Gopiballavpur CPI-ML groups killed a number of landlords and caused many others to flee, creating a power vacuum which was temporarily filled by the party and peasant organizations. Crops on the lands of big landlords were seized, all peasant debts to moneylenders canceled, and wages for agricultural workers were fixed. The peasant revolt was not crushed until the United Front government called in the Eastern Frontier Rifles to subdue it, a task which was achieved in 1970. Toward the end of the same year a struggle was launched in Birbhum in West Bengal, near the Bihar border. Again, land seizure, burning of debt records, the installation of peasant committees and people's courts, and the execution of some landlords saw a collapse of state authority for a period, and only the intervention of the army restored it. Similar struggles, albeit on a smaller scale, occurred in Bihar, Punjab, and Uttar Pradesh.

Thus, while the adoption of Maoism meant the substitution of a new jargon for old, and of one unquestioned authority (the CPC) for another (the CPSU), it nonetheless also facilitated a communist championing of and involvement in the sort of peasant struggles described above. Below I shall suggest that the engagement with peasants' struggles against their oppressors became an engagement with another world of politics, an engagement which left its mark on certain of the Naxalites' categories and strategies, taking them, in a sense, "beyond" Maoism.

INTERPRETING "EXCESS"

Naxalite strategy and ideology changed in the course of involvement in such struggles. In particular, there was a significant change from about 1969. The reduced importance attached to organizational forms such as trade unions, peasant organizations, and student unions; the increasing centrality accorded to the "annihilation of class enemies"; and the emphasis on the symbolic and existential dimensions of violence appear to be interrelated developments. Our aim in discussing them will be to explore what they collectively signified.

From their beginnings, the Naxalites had expressed a certain suspicion of the communist preoccupation with trade unions and peasant organizations, regarding such a preoccupation as symptomatic of that "economism" which underlay the comfortable and reformist politics of the two communist parties. As Charu Mazumdar wrote in 1965, "The first [principle] among revisionist thought is to regard *Krishak Sabha* (peasants' organizations) and trade unions as the only Party activity."[18] However, at this point, what was being criticized was an exclusive focus on such organizations, not the organizations as such. Thus in the document quoted above, Mazumdar immediately went on to write, "It should be remembered that the trade union and peasants' organizations are one of the many weapons for serving our purpose."[19]

From about 1969, there was a perceptible shift in emphasis. In April of that year, the "Resolution on Party Organization" adopted by the AICCCR laid down that "the Party should concentrate, in the main, on developing guerrilla forms of armed struggle and not waste time and its energies in holding open mass meetings and forming *kisan sabhas* in the old style."[20] Later in the same year Mazumdar concluded that "the revolutionary peasantry has demonstrated through its struggle that neither mass movement nor mass organization is indispensable for waging guerrilla warfare."[21]

As the above statements indicate, the depreciation of "open, mass" struggles through trade unions and the like was intimately connected with the elevation of guerrilla struggle, which the Party Program adopted at the first Congress in 1970 had declared "is and will remain the basic form of struggle through the entire period of our democratic revolution."[22] However, and this was the second and indeed most significant change, guerrilla struggle itself was increasingly reduced to and equated with the policy of *khatam,* or "annihilation." By 1969 revolutionaries in Srikakulam were busy implementing it. The "annihilation" or killing of a local landlord or moneylender by a guerrilla squad at least partly composed of poor and landless peasants was a "higher form of class struggle," according to Mazumdar.[23] It was a crucial weapon in the guerrilla struggle to destroy the domination of the feudal classes and replace it with "the political power of peasants in the countryside."[24]

As to why annihilation was so central, a number of reasons were advanced. It was held to be tactically and strategically efficacious, for the annihilation of a few especially oppressive individuals would lead, it was claimed, to many other landlords fleeing the village, while those remaining were more likely to submit to the dictates of the peasant rebels. Conversely, such a demonstration of strength would rally doubting and uncertain elements to the revolutionary cause. In any case, annihilation was declared to be central. Sometimes presented as a trigger for or an important aspect of guerrilla struggle, at other times it came to be equated with guerrilla war. The importance of annihilation came to be more and more stressed, and at the Party's first Congress Mazumdar made support of the annihilation policy the dividing line between true revolutionaries and compromising elements inside and outside the Party. Mazumdar declared, "Comrades, anyone who opposes this battle of annihilation cannot remain with us. We will not allow him to remain inside our Party."[25]

Elevated to importance along with the need to eliminate class enemies was the manner in which they were eliminated. In the early stages of the struggle at least, annihilations were to be accomplished wherever possible by the traditional weapons of the peasants, such as knives, spears, and sickles, rather than firearms. According to Mazumdar, peasants had to be encouraged to believe that their revolutionary struggle did not have to wait on the acquisition of sufficient numbers of firearms. Moreover, killing with weapons that were an extension of one's hands entailed greater physicality than firing a gun; it emboldened the peasant, and it released his initiative and daring, whereas firearms tended to stifle it.[26]

Connected with this was an emphasis on the symbolic dimensions of violence — on violence in excess of that necessary for the achievement of tactical ends. Naxalite rhetoric displayed a tendency toward the bloodthirsty, and the movement itself was violent in ways that were not required to achieve the goal toward which violence was ostensibly the means. *Liberation* would regularly and approvingly report on how peasants' "class hatred" led to such "excess":

> The people's hatred and anger found expression when they painted slogans with his blood and hung his head from the roof of his house.
> The wrath and class hatred of the guerrillas were so intense that they beheaded him and kicked his severed head out of the house.[27]

Mazumdar was to make such "excess" part of the very definition of revolutionary action and politics. In a statement that was later to be quoted against him by many of his critics, he declared, "A time will come when the battlecry will be, 'He who has not dipped his hands in the blood of class enemies can hardly be called a communist.'"[28]

It is these policies, aspects of what appears to have been a "radicalization" of Naxalite politics, which were to become the object of severe criticism from those who otherwise were sympathetic to the Naxalites. In 1969 Promode Sengupta, who had early been involved in the AICCCR but who left the movement precisely over policies such as these, wrote a comprehensive indictment of Naxalite politics. Annihilation, wrote Sengupta, "is not at all the theory of Maoist guerrilla warfare or peoples' war, it is merely an anarchist-terrorist theory";[29] the neglect of mass organizations similarly was nothing less than "petit-bourgeois anarchism."[30] "Charubabu," concluded the indictment, "is spreading Guevara's politics in the name of the Chairman."[31] Soon the debate was occurring inside the Party, as stalwarts like Sushital Roy Chowdhury began to question the Party line. In 1970 Roy Chowdhury circulated an inner-party document which denounced as serious mistakes the neglect of mass movements, the excessive recourse to secrecy, the indiscriminate application of the annihilation policy, mistaken policies in urban areas, and authoritarianism in the Party. Together these errors added up to an "ultra-adventurism" which Roy Chowdhury called on his comrades to guard against and combat.[32] Sourin Bose, a Central Committee member, ascribed this "ultra-leftism" to a wishful and subjective reading of the objective situation, declaring, "We are suffering from a petty-bourgeois impatience."[33] Before Charu Mazumdar's death in 1972 an "Open Letter" circulated by six leading party members confessed to "Left adventurist deviations," while laying the bulk of the blame for this squarely at Charu Mazumdar's feet.[34]

The criticisms soon built up into a crescendo. From inside the Party and from without, various aspects of Naxalite policy and practice were declared to be seriously and damagingly mistaken. Almost all critics agreed that the tendency to downgrade mass organizations was a mistake; most agreed that the annihilation policy was also, either in conception or else in execution. In most cases the various mistakes were explained/characterized as symptomatic of "adventurism," "ultra-leftism," "petit bourgeois subjectivism," militarism, and so on and so forth. By the mid-1970s, with the Naxalites defeated and now split into a number of sects, it was almost a commonplace among those "to the left of the CPI-M" that the Naxalite experience, while heroic and correct in its general orientation, had suffered from debilitating mistakes. The indictment ran something like this: The Naxalites had quite rightly accused the CPI-M of not being militant enough; but as their own movement progressed they erred in the opposite direction, mistaking wish for reality and projecting their revolutionary desires onto the objective situation. Instead of tailoring their strategy to the need for a long and protracted struggle, they sought shortcuts in "annihilation"; instead of engaging in the patient work of arousing and organizing the masses, they increasingly acted on their behalf; and as the movement faltered and met with severe repression, dramatic "gestures" replaced the less dramatic but more important work of organizing and promoting revolutionary consciousness and activity.

Implicit in such a critique is the belief that the issues raised by the Naxalite movement can be discussed within a single conceptual language (Marxism), and its positions plotted along the one grid (of militancy). Indeed, part of the aim of the exercise is to find the *via media,* the exactly right place on the grid, somewhere between right and left deviationism. I do not wish to challenge or displace this reading, for I find it persuasive, as far as it goes. But I do wish to add something to it, which I think helps make better sense of the Naxalite "excesses."

## POWER AND INSURGENCY

Asit Sen, who had been presiding over the May Day rally in 1969 where the formation of the CPI-ML had been announced, but who soon came to differ sharply with the strategy adopted by the new party, wrote years later that when a proper Marxist understanding "is replaced by a theory of physical extermination of individuals, philosophically that amounts to an idealist conception of class, that is, [that] a landlord is created by some supernatural power and if he can be removed physically from the earth, the feudal system will automatically be done away with." Against this he reiterated his understanding of the correct Marxist conceptions of class and of power: "A person belongs to a class by virtue of his position in relation to the productive system. That is, a landlord ceases to be so, if he can be deprived of his vested position which is protected by the power of the state."[35]

If this were a statement about the bourgeoisie, it would be largely true. The power of the capitalist, which is largely derived from his ownership of the means of production, may well disappear when he is deprived of that ownership. It is a feature of bourgeois society that surplus appropriation is effected through noncoercive means (through the capital-wage labor contract), and thus that exploitation is perfectly compatible with the political and juridical equality of all citizens. But in the semifeudal world of the Indian peasantry, the insignia of domination and subordination were everywhere inscribed—in the naked use of force, in dress, in language and body language, as well, of course, as in economic exploitation. There existed an elaborate semiotics of power, and because domination was exercised in and through many sites, rebellion against it could never be simply a matter of "expropriating the expropriator." It was not enough to deprive the landlord of land.

That is precisely why, when the peasantry did rise in rebellion, that rebellion was usually marked by an effort to "turn the world upside down"—to reverse the insignia of subordination by defying and overturning the hierarchical codes of language and dress as well as by attempting to seize land, destroy debt records, and so on. This struggle was nothing if not "political," but it was not political in a way easily recognizable as such through categories which take the structures of bourgeois society as their model. As Ranajit Guha puts it in his study of peasant insurgency in colonial India, "The fact that this [revolt] was designed primarily to destroy the authority of the superordinate elite and carried no elaborate blueprint for its replacement, does not put it outside the realm of politics. On the contrary, insurgency affirmed its political character precisely by its negative and inversive procedure."[36]

Once we recognize this, an alternative or supplementary understanding of the annihilation of landlords and moneylenders becomes possible, one where it appears possessed of an other than purely "tactical" logic. Feudal authority could not be destroyed simply by depriving landlords of their land; but killing a landlord did eliminate one of the nodal points at which many manifestations of feudal power intersected and through which they were exercised. Killing did not simply remove an individual and serve to scare and subdue others; it also undermined and reversed the feudal code of power in one of the most dramatic ways possible. The "logic" of annihilation can be interpreted, then, as a logic directly derived from the structures of feudal domination.

How, then, should we read the annihilation campaign: as an excess of militancy, and/or (since the two readings do not necessarily exclude each other) as an inversion of the feudal code of power? We cannot resolve this question by appealing directly to the peasants' consciousness of what they were doing, for the evidence on this is scant and already reaches us filtered through Maoist categories. We must instead ask what explains annihilation, what "makes sense" of it. That annihilation was born of an excess of revolutionary zeal is perfectly plausible, for the Naxalites themselves explained and justified it largely in Marxist categories, and thus in the language of "militancy," "tactics," and so on. However, also present in their rhetoric at times were strains of a different understanding, one less concerned with how radical such actions were than with their connection to specifically feudal structures of domination and rule. This is evident, for instance, in Naxalite propaganda linking annihilation to the weakening of the prestige and authority of the feudal class, and in Charu Mazumdar's remark that annihilation "does not only mean liquidating an individual, but also means liquidating the political, economic and social authority of the class enemy."[37] We can see it also in the noninstrumental character of Naxalite violence, discussed below. This interpretation becomes all the more persuasive because we can then connect it to the peasants who were the subjects of insurgency; that is, we need not interpret a peasant-based strategy only with reference to the ideology and intentions of its (largely nonpeasant) leadership. For even if we cannot directly "know" what annihilation meant for the peasantry, we can and have offered an explanation of what it might plausibly have meant, an explanation grounded in an understanding of the structures and conditions of peasant existence and peasant rebellion.

If then, as we suggest, annihilation was a dramatic way of challenging the power and prestige of feudal elites, it could also be important to the peasant creating a new sense of self. In this semi-feudal society the peasant's identity was negatively constituted: "His identity amounted to the sum of his subalternity. In other words, he learnt to recognize himself not by the properties and attributes of his own social being but by a diminution, if not negation, of those of his superiors."[38] In killing his oppressor he at one stroke effaced his subordination *and* created, or created the space for, a new identity for himself. Again, there is no "proof" of this. However, it helps make sense, I think, of something inexplicable in purely instrumentalist terms, namely, the Naxalite emphasis on how annihilations were done, by what weapons, and with what degree of bloodshed. In a zero-sum game, where the landlord's authority and prestige were his precisely by virtue of the distance between him and the peasant, killing his enemy could help the peasant define himself anew, and the greater the violence and display with which he did it, the greater the distance he put between himself and his previous identity as a subordinate. In Mazumdar's words—words which, if read only along a grid of "militancy" would indeed appear "excessive" if not bizarre—only "by waging class struggle—the battle of annihilation—[will] the new man . . . be created," a man who, by contrast with the deferential, fearful, and calculating peasant he replaces, "will defy death and will be free from all thoughts of self-interest."[39]

What, finally, of the Naxalite mistrust and even rejection of certain organizations, even those, like trade unions and *kisan sabhas,* normally considered central to communist practice? This rejection was clearly connected with a widespread perception in Naxalite ranks that immersion in such organizational forms could lead to corruption and a loss of revolutionary élan, as had happened with the CPI-M. Here, too, I do not wish to challenge the dominant explanation of Naxalite neglect and mistrust of these organization forms—namely, that it was borne of a misplaced militancy itself rooted in "impatience." I do, however, wish to add to it, by drawing on Dipesh Chakrabarty's work on the Calcutta working class to connect the question of organization with that of culture.

Organizations such as trade unions, Chakrabarty points out, have certain cultural presumptions built into their functioning. A trade union, while aiming at building solidaristic ties, assumes "voluntary" membership, contractual relations, "representation,"and so on and so forth. It presumes, in short, the existence of a certain level of bourgeois culture. Chakrabarty quotes Gramsci: "These are organizations born on the terrain of bourgeois democracy and political liberty, as an affirmation and development of political freedom. . . . They do not supersede the bourgeois state."[40]

The absence of the bourgeois culture presumed by trade unions is part of the explanation for why it proved so difficult to organize the Calcutta workers into unions, and why so many of those unions created did not flourish or even survive. But it is not simply a case of the absence of a particular culture, but of the presence of another; for it is not as if there was no working-class resistance and working-class politics in Bengal. On the contrary: the "paradox" of working-class politics in colonial Bengal was that of "so much militancy, yet so little organization."[41] That is, working class struggles often reflected modes of organization, authority, and power other than the bourgeois sort. Even where unions were organized, they were often, according to Chakrabarty, "run as though they were the leaders' *zamindaris* [feudal estates]."[42] Such organizations were sometimes very militant, but they were inherently unstable. Again, alternative principles of organization and mobilization shaped these unions, not as the democratic, stable organizations they were meant to be, but rather as personal fiefdoms based on the loyalty a leader could command from workers.

What was true of the Calcutta working class applies even more so to the peasantry, relatively less uprooted from its "traditional" ways. Still possessed of an alternative language of public life and political mobilization, this peasantry, when it rebelled, frequently did so in a fashion—around religious themes, on the basis of ethnic and kinship ties, and so on—which has sometimes condescendingly and inaccurately been described as "unorganized" and "prepolitical" by contemporary historians. In fact, such rebellions always included forms of organization and mobilization, often precapitalist in character[43]—even where they developed into class revolts under communist leadership. This was the case with many Naxalite-led struggles. For example, for the tribal Santal peasantry of West Bengal, ethnically and culturally distinct from their feudal exploiters, solidaristic ties and organizational forms drew heavily on kinship structures and sentiments. In his study of Naxalite mobilization among the Santals of West Bengal, Duyker observes that "the grass roots organizational structure of CPI(M-L) in Midnapore and Birbhum often owed more to indigenous cultural factors than to its April 1969 resolution on political organization . . . many Naxalite cells and action squads had hierarchies, lines of communication and logistic support which were rooted in the local kinship system." As whole families of Santals joined the Naxalite-led struggle, "kinship organization began to parallel guerrilla organization," and "on a number of occasions, the natural authority of the elders i.e., fathers, uncles and husbands, appears to have become a political and military authority over sons, nephews and wives who also joined the movement."[44] What I wish to additionally suggest is that the Naxalite movement "made a space" for this idiom of peasant politics not only in its practice but also in its theory. The Naxalite's emphasis on the importance of small-group actions and local initiative meant they were more likely to encounter and accommodate localized forms of peasant organization, and the Maoist stress on "learning from the peasant masses" meant they were more receptive to what they encountered. I am suggesting that the Naxalite distrust of those organizational forms which presupposed a certain measure of bourgeois culture was in part borne of, and was a reflection of, their immersion in forms of mobilization and organization rooted in a different culture and consciousness. What was most puzzling and distressing to sympathetic critics of the Naxalites—the fact that they did not merely neglect trade unions and *kisan sabhas,* but seemed to be almost actively hostile to them—can be read, then, not just as an infantile disorder, but as an attempt to formulate, in Marxist categories and vocabulary, an incipient critique of these organizational forms and the culture they presupposed.

Modernity first came to India as a "gift" of colonialism; that is, it did not develop autochthonously but arrived at the point of a bayonet. Ironically, it was to become a staple remonstration of almost all nationalist discourse that the British had failed to complete the job they had, wittingly or unwittingly, begun. Already by the nineteenth century, voices were being heard complaining that the colonial ruler had been remiss in promoting the policies and institutions conducive to progress toward a modern India. By the turn of the century a more militant nationalism was declaring that there was a structural incompatibility between British rule on the one hand, and economic and social modernization on the other. Colonialism, most nationalist arguments in the twentieth century were to declare, had retarded the transition to the modern:[45] therefore, modernization required as its precondition the severance of the colonial relationship.

Part of the agenda of those who took the helm of the newly independent Indian nation-state in 1947 was to complete the transition begun, but also then thwarted, by colonialism. The official discourse of the Indian state further proclaimed—first under Nehru, and then in the early years of Indira Gandhi's rule—that the goal of modernization and the ideal of social justice were necessarily intertwined. Measures to address and alleviate poverty would also promote development, just as development was the sine qua non of social justice. This faith was widely shared—certainly, was shared by the left in India— even if *which* measures conduced to it were the subject of bitter contestation.

In this, as in so many other matters, the emergency imposed by Indira Gandhi in 1975 marked a turning point. Unable to deliver on the populist slogan of *garibi hatao* (abolish poverty), which had helped Congress win the 1971 elections, with the declaration of emergency the Indian state and the dominant classes in India decided that if poverty could not be abolished, the poor must be. They were forcibly moved off the pavements and out of their ramshackle dwellings in a (failed) effort to ensure that the urban middle classes would not have to constantly witness these living eyesores, testimony to the "incompleteness" of India's modernity. Simultaneously, the state-sponsored campaign of forced sterilization aimed at ensuring that there would be fewer poor in the future.

From about 1975, it has been clear, at least to the privileged classes in India, that the peculiarities and "distortions" of Indian development are a function not of some "incompleteness" about to be overcome but rather structural features of a modernity which has already "arrived." And so, with an almost audible sigh of relief, these classes have decided to embrace and celebrate this discovery; they have accepted that it is in the very nature of this Indian modernity that the latest consumer goods coexist with extreme poverty, and that the information superhighway celebrated in their magazines runs parallel to dirt tracks.

It has been a feature of this Indian modernity that modern institutions and ideologies, for the larger part, have presumed and spoken a political "language" different from that of many of the people whom they have sought to represent and—until recently—mobilize and transform. In shorthand form, one could characterize the differences as follows: "One is the language characteristic of the project of nation-building and involves the rituals of the state, political representation, citizenship, citizen's rights, etc. . . . The other [nonmodern] language derives its grammar from relationships of power, authority and hierarchy."[46] These two domains or idioms of politics, one primarily the preserve of elites and the other of the lower orders, have coexisted since the colonial period. They have of course changed, and the gap between them has been bridged somewhat, but the vision of a "completed" and undistorted modernity, where the gap would be effaced, has not been realized.

Instead, these two domains have frequently overlapped and interlaced, in which case each has influenced the other. Unequally so, however, for while peasants have often learned to speak and dream of rights, democracy, and even socialism, elite discourses have taken recourse to the language of the lower orders not out of conviction but usually for pragmatic reasons—and this has generally been done shamefacedly and secretively. To continue the linguistic metaphor: elites have occasionally become bilingual for pragmatic purposes, but they have sought to ensure that one language remains dominant and that there is no "interference" from the other. In the case of Marxism, I argued at the beginning of this essay, a "forgetting" or misreading, or else an instrumentalist approach to peasant consciousness and politics, was written into the very idea of revolution in a semifeudal country.

The Naxalite-led struggles were one of those rare occasions in the history of Marxism in India when the grammar of this subaltern political language left its imprint not only on communist practice but also on Marxist theoretical formulations and categories, via the medium of an insurgent peasant consciousness. What has commonly been read as the "ultra-leftism" of Naxalite politics was, in part at least, this essay has argued, born of an interlacing of an elite, modern discourse with a subaltern, prebourgeois one, in which the former, because engaged with the peasantry in an "open-ended" and noninstrumentalist way, came to incorporate and express elements of the latter.

This helps explain, I think, why the Naxalite movement was significant. That it was in fact an important moment in the contemporary history of India is a judgment in which many, including many of its critics, would concur. Yet why that is so is not apparent at first glance. Certainly, it was not because of Naxalite political successes, which were limited in number and short-lived, nor because of their Marxist theory and their strategy, which were naive and derivative. The significance of the Naxalite movement lay, I suggest by way of conclusion, in the fact that it became the site where, for a period, two idioms of Indian politics came together, and came together in a way where one was not simply the instrument of the other. In this relatively brief moment, those committed to making revolution had a glimpse of another world, a glimpse which revealed, to those willing to see, how much still remained to be done before the language in which revolution was conceived could become adequate to its task.

## NOTES

Thanks to the School of Social Sciences at La Trobe University for awarding me a travel grant to conduct research for this article in India; Sumanta Banerjee, with whom I had an enjoyable and illuminating discussion; Dipesh Chakrabarty, for his comments on an earlier version; and Ranajit Guha, to whose work on peasant insurgency this article is deeply indebted.

1 Karl Marx and Frederich Engels, *Manifesto of the Communist Party* (Peking: Foreign Languages Press, 1968), 39.

2 Karl Marx, *The Poverty of Philosophy* (Moscow: Progress Publishers, 1975), 160.

3 Thus, for example, Mao in his Hunan report defends, indeed extols, the "excesses" of the peasants—their smashing of the sedan chairs of the gentry, lolling in the ivory-inlaid beds of their young ladies, and so on. He characterizes these as defensible aspects of an attempt to "smash the political prestige and power of the landlord class," that is, as actions which derive their logic and significance as responses to a specifically *feudal* oppression. It is part of Mao's importance that he recognized this—that he did not, to use the terms of my argument, "misread" or deny the consciousness which

informed this revolt. But even so, Mao also—because he was a communist—inserts this revolt of the Hunan peasantry into a narrative which is ultimately to culminate in a strong, united, and socialist (and in all these ways modern) nation-state.

4 There is a parallel here with how the question of colonial nationalism was treated within Marxism. The fact that from the Second Congress of the Comintern, colonial nationalism was adjudged to be anti-imperialist easily led to the (frequently unwarranted) conclusion that colonial nationalism was inherently "progressive," that is, that it was the bearer of historical progress within the nation and not just by virtue of its destabilizing effects for the imperialist system. For a discussion of this, and of the characteristic conflation in Marxist theorizing of "politically desirable" with "historically progressive," see my *Marxist Theory and Nationalist Politics: The Case of Colonial India* (New Delhi: Sage, 1995), chap. 1 and conclusion.

5 The issue here is much more than the thorny question of vanguardism, for in this case the party is not simply in advance of the class, urging and pulling it along, but rather has achieved a consciousness the class *cannot* achieve, because of the (precapitalist) conditions under which it works and lives. The transformation of peasants into citizens who dream socialist dreams becomes a task for the postrevolutionary state.

6 The latter, Telengana movement became a full-fledged insurrection, and the local communist leadership was more than a little influenced by the strategy being followed in China. The Naxalites were to regard the Telengana struggle, in particular, as a sort of spiritual precursor to their own movement, and for good reason: at least some of the arguments advanced here regarding the Naxalites would also hold true, I think, for the Telengana struggle.

7 Such United Front governments were to be in office in Kerala until October 1969, and in West Bengal until November 1967 and then again from early 1969 until early 1970.

8 Chinese radio broadcasts in June 1967, and subsequently a *People's Daily* editorial entitled "Spring Thunder Breaks over India," hailed the actions of the dissident CPI-M cadre in Naxalbari and condemned the non-Congress United Front government in West Bengal.

9 "Declaration of the All-India Coordination Committee of Communist Revolutionaries" (May 1968), rpt. in J. C. Johari, *Naxalite Politics in India* (New Delhi: Research Publication, 1972), 147.

10 "Political Resolution of the Communist Party of India (Marxist-Leninist)," in *The Historic Turning Point: A Liberation Anthology,* ed. Suniti Kumar Gosh (Calcutta, 1992), 46.

11 "Resolution on Elections," in Ghosh, *Liberation Anthology,* 33.

12 "Declaration of AICCCR," in Johari, *Naxalite Politics,* 148.

13 Charu Mazumdar, "Undertake the Work of Building a Revolutionary Party," in Ghosh, *Liberation Anthology,* 102.

14  "By liberating themselves from the yoke of feudalism, the Indian people will liberate themselves also from the yoke of imperialism and comprador-bureaucrat capital, because the struggle against feudalism is also a struggle against the other two enemies" ("Political Resolution of the CPI-ML," in ibid., 47).

15  Rabindra Ray, *The Naxalites and their Ideology* (New Delhi: Oxford University Press, 1988), 182.

16  "Declaration of the Revolutionaries in the Communist Party of India (Marxist)" (November 1967), in Ghosh, Liberation Anthology, 28.

17  For an account of the movement in this region see the report by one of its leaders, modeled closely upon Mao's Hunan Report—Kanu Sanyal, "Report on the Peasant Movement in the Terai Region" (October 1968), in Ghosh, *Liberation Anthology*, 345–363. For a detailed study of the movements in Naxalbari, Debra-Gopiballavpur, and Birbhum, see Amiya K. Samanta, *Left Extremist Movement in West Bengal* (Calcutta: Firma KLM, 1984). Among the numerous histories of the Naxalites, see especially Sumanta Banerjee, *India's Simmering Revolution* (London: Zed, 1984), and Ray, *Naxalites and Their Ideology*.

18  Charu Mazumdar, "Our Tasks in the Present Situation." Rpt. in Marius Dumas, *Approaching Naxalbari* (Calcutta: Radical Impression, 1991), 244.

19  Ibid., 245.

20  In Ghosh, *Liberation Anthology*, 395.

21  Charu Mazumdar, "March Forward by Summing Up the Experience of the Peasant Revolutionary Struggle of India," *Liberation* 3, no. 2 (December 1969): 10.

22  In Samar Sen, Debabrata Panda, and Ashish Lahiri, *Naxalbari and After: A Frontier Anthology* (Calcutta: Kathashilpa, 1978), 2:282.

23  Charu Mazumdar, "Peasant Revolutionary Struggle of India," *Liberation* 3, no. 2 (December 1969): 13.

24  Ibid.

25  In Sen, Panda, and Lahir, *Naxalbari and After*, 2:295.

26  See, for instance, ibid., 294; see also Charu Mazumdar, "A Few Words about Guerrilla Actions," *Liberation* 3, no. 4 (February 1970).

27  These and other similar examples from *Liberation* are quoted in Biplab Dasgupta, *The Naxalite Movement* (Bombay: Allied Publishers, 1975), 46.

28  Mazumdar, "A Few Words about Guerrilla Actions," 21.

29  Promode Sengupta, *Naxalbari and Indian Revolution* (Calcutta: Research India Publications, 1983), 95. Though published in 1983, this work was written in 1969.

30  Ibid., 26.

31  Ibid., 56.

32  "Problems and Crises of Indian Revolution," in Sen, Pauda, and Lahiri, *Naxalbari and After*, 2:296–313.

33  Quoted in Correspondent, "CPI(ML): The Twilight Hour," in ibid., 117.

34  See "Open Letter," in ibid., 322–326.

35  Asit Sen, *An Approach to Naxalbari* (Calcutta: Institute of Scientific Thoughts, 1980), 123.

36  Ranajit Guha, *Elementary Aspects of Peasant Insurgency in Colonial India* (New Delhi: Oxford University Press, 1983), 9.

37  Mazumdar, "Peasant Revolutionary Struggle" 13.

38  Guha, *Elementary Aspects,* 18.

39  "On the Political-Organisational Report," in Sen, Panda, and Lahiri, *Naxalbari and After,* 2:293.

40  Dipesh Chakrabarty, *Rethinking Working Class History: Bengal, 1890–1940* (Princeton, N.J.: Princeton University Press, 1987), 133.

41  Ibid., 123.

42  Ibid., 141.

43  For numerous nineteenth-century examples, see Guha, *Elementary Aspects.*

44  Edward Duyker, *Tribal Guerrillas: The Santals of West Bengal and the Naxalite Movement* (New Delhi: Oxford University Press, 1987), 103.

45  The following passage from Nehru is representative: "The British became dominant in India . . . because they were the heralds of the new big-machine industrial civilization. They represented a new historic force which was going to change the world . . . and yet they deliberately tried to prevent change [in India]. . . . Their outlook and objectives were reactionary . . . chiefly because of a deliberate desire to check changes in a progressive direction, as these might strengthen the Indian people and thus ultimately weaken the British hold on India" (Jawaharlal Nehru, *The Discovery of India* [Calcutta: Signet, 1956], 330).

46  Dipesh Chakrabarty, "Invitation to a Dialogue," in *Subaltern Studies 4,* ed. Ranajit Guha (Delhi: Oxford University Press, 1985), 374.

# Marxism, Anti-Americanism, and Democracy in South Korea: An Examination of Nationalist Intellectual Discourse

> Our movements of transformation aim to obtain a national liberation people's democracy. Attainment of a national liberation people's democracy through anti-American and anti-fascist struggles is the logical development toward liberty, justice, and human liberation in Korean history, and will bring genuine democracy to the Korean people.
>
> —Chamint'u, "Haebang sŏnŏn 2" [Liberation declaration 2]

■ The nationalist emphasis in this leaflet written by a radical student group called Chamint'u vividly indicates the dramatic political departure of Korean democratization movements in the 1980s from earlier movements that had focused for the most part on securing civil rights and a democratic government.[1] The call seeks more than the democratization of Korean society and politics; it links democratization to national liberation from foreign dominance, believing the former to be unobtainable without the latter. It also makes the United States a main protest target because of its historical support for highly repressive and authoritarian regimes in postwar Korea. Since 1982 all four main U.S. Information Centers in Korea have been torched, invaded, or both, and anti-American banners and slogans filled the streets during the 1980s democratization movements.

The rise of Korean anti-Americanism is not a phenomenon confined to student activists or the intellectual left but has spread widely throughout Korea. A 1990 national survey of "civil consciousness" conducted by the Institute of Population and Development of Seoul National University showed that more than one-third of respondents supported anti-American movements; over two-thirds considered anti-American sentiment to be quite serious; and more than half felt American military forces should withdraw from Korea. Although popular anti-Americanism is not new or unique to Korea and is not exactly an echo of the radical rhetoric quoted above, no one can deny that Korea witnessed a strong, anti-American, nationalist surge in the 1980s.

While the growth of Korean anti-Americanism has been taken up in scholarly and policy-related works, most of these have attributed it to structural causes, such as the alleged U.S. involvement in the 1980 Kwangju uprisings, continued U.S. support for the Korean military dictatorship, recent economic pressure to open the Korean market, including the agricultural sector, and a massive distortion of U.S. policy positions by the government-controlled Korean media and the U.S. failure to correct it.[2] Earlier scholarship has left largely unexplored the ideological underpinnings of anti-Americanism, dismissing anti-Americanism as a passing, emotional phenomenon, and overlooking differences between popular and intellectual expressions. While popular anti-Americanism decries American political and economic domination and reflects a growing self-confidence on the part of the Koreans (and thus is hardly ideological),[3] at the intellectual level anti-Americanism is in fact an ideological struggle over how to define and redefine the U.S. role in Korea. Grasping the historical process of the intellectual articulation of anti-Americanism as a counterhegemony to the dominant state anticommunism is central to comprehending the nature of the 1980s prodemocracy movements.

This article examines the articulation of intellectual anti-Americanism by looking in detail at the "social formation debates" [sahoe kusŏngch'e nonjaeng] that took place among Korean Marxist scholars, student activists, and chaeya (literally, "being in the field") activists in the 1980s.[4] Believing earlier democratic movements had failed primarily because they lacked adequate analysis of the nature and structure of Korea's social formation, the debates sought a more "scientific" analysis of the Korean economy and society. The intellectual discourse articulated the goals, meanings, targets, tactics, and strategies of the 1980s anti-American, nationalist democratic movements in a fashion reminiscent of the kōzaha-rōnōha debates among Japanese Marxists in the 1920s and 1930s and the 1930s debates on Chinese capitalism. Like their counterparts in Japan and China, Korean Marxists and dissident intellectuals believed a proper specification of the nature of Korean economic and political development was necessary to guide their movements. I focus on what I argue are the two major ideological sources of anti-Americanism in Korea and the third world generally, Marxism and nationalism. An evaluation of why, despite early successes, Korean dissidents failed to sustain popular support after the late 1980s and a brief discussion of the issues and problems they face today concludes this article.

## AMERICAN HEGEMONY IN POSTWAR KOREA

The United States had little interest in Korea until at least the early 1940s, when the United States was drawn into the Pacific War against Japan. In fact, the secret Taft-Katsura Agreement of July 1905 endorsed Japan's takeover of Korea in return for Japan's recognition of U.S. rule in the Philippines. But as soon as Japan surrendered to the Allies in 1945, Korea was immediately incorporated into the postwar American hegemony. Furthermore, as the cold war conflict intensified, Korea's strategic importance to the United States increased. Not only did the United States mobilize troops under the United Nations flag to fight communists in the Korean War (1950–1953), it pumped massive economic and military aid into South Korea. Most observers also agree that the U.S. market was critical to Korea's export-based economic success, especially after the 1960s. Bruce Cumings has pointed out that to understand the success of Korean economic development it is necessary to recognize the role played by American hegemony in the northeast Asian political economy.[5] Korea clearly represents the success of the American postwar "containment" policy in Asia; what failed in Vietnam, and perhaps in the Philippines, evidently succeeded in Korea.

American "success" in Korea, however, exacted a heavy price because it required that the United States back a series of authoritarian regimes. When occupational forces landed in Korea in September 1945, they sided with former Japanese collaborators, rather than heeding the Korean people's cry for reform. This reactionary policy, as American military government officer Grant Meade acutely observed, provoked among the populace the belief that "the only real difference between the former overlord and the present was in skin pigmentation."[6] Discontent culminated in uprisings that started in Taegu on 1 October 1946 and spread into other areas in the South, eventually becoming the most serious outbreak of its kind since the 1894 Tonghak peasant wars.[7] Immediately characterized as Russian or North Korean communist agitation, the uprisings were denounced and brutally suppressed by the national police backed by the American military government. The repression instilled chilling memories, and since then, accusations of communist agitation have been used to justify government suppression of all prodemocratic movements in South Korea.

The 1950–1953 Korean War not only militarized Korean society but legitimated authoritarian governments through the doctrine of "anticommunism." Government charged that prodemocratic forces or antigovernment movements (often identical) were procommunist, and memories of communist aggression and cold war ideology made government legitimization tactics highly effective, creating a "red complex" among the populace. The Korean War also resulted in the 1954[8] treaty giving the United States operational control over Korean armed forces under the structure of the American-Korean Combined Forces Command. The United States is often alleged to have insinuated itself into Korean politics through the command, and thereby to have explicitly or implicitly supported authoritarian and military regimes.

Yet until the 1980s, most Koreans did not subscribe to anti-Americanism and still regarded the United States very favorably. As Gregory Henderson, a well-known Korean observer, points out, "we [Americans] were more than a friend to Seoul, we were *the* friend . . . ; until the late May 1980 Kwangju uprising . . . anti-Americanism was about as common in South Korea as fish in trees" (emphasis in original).[8] Shorrock explains this favorable attitude as "the legacy of anticommunism and memories of the Korean War, [which produced] . . . a strong fear of the Soviet Union and North Korea and a feeling of genuine warmth towards the United States for supporting South Korea with the sacrifice of thousands of young men and millions of dollars in aid."[9] Even most Korean dissidents viewed the United States as a friendly power, supportive of their democratization movements. In fact, anti-Japanism outweighed any form of anti-Americanism. Prevailing sentiments, however, were shattered when the American commitment to human rights and democracy came to a test, particularly in the 1980 Kwangju uprisings.

On 18 May 1980 approximately five hundred students demonstrated in Kwangju, a southwestern city, demanding an end to martial law, which had been declared on 17 May, and the resignation of General Chun Doo Hwan. The general had seized power after the assassination of President Park Chung Hee on 26 October 1979 by Korean Central Intelligence Agency (KCIA) director Kim Chaegyu. Martial law troops reinforced by "Black Beret" paratroopers surrounded demonstrators and spectators and indiscriminately beat and bayoneted them, killing several dozen. The next day, shocked citizens joined student demonstrations in over thirty locations. Main streets overflowed with tens of thousands of people. By 21 May, the number of demonstrators swelled to about two hundred thousand. Obtaining arms from police stations and army stockpiles, they took over the city until martial law troops invaded on 27 May. An estimated one thousand or more were killed by the military during the uprising, the most tragic event to occur in the region since the 1946 uprisings.[10]

Kwangju fundamentally altered Koreans' view of the United States. Many demonstrators had vainly expected that the United States would or should intervene to stop the confrontation. Anthropologist Linda Lewis recalls that her field notes jotted down during the uprisings, "and even for months afterwards make reference to conversations with both friends and strangers about their initial expectations of American support and, later, their surprise and distress at its absence."[11] Instead, the United States allegedly consented through the structure of the command to the use of Korean troops to suppress the uprising. Although the United States denied its involvement by referring to an unpublished 1978 agreement that removed American operational control from those South Korean forces "not directly concerned on a daily basis with the nation's forward defense," most Koreans continued to suspect an American role.[12] The U.S. invitation of then President Chun for a first state visit to President Reagan's White House in early 1981 further confirmed Korean popular suspicion.[13] As Henderson points out, many Koreans began to "perceive the United States as the midwife of the Chun regime's 1979–80 takeover of power and as the continued backer of this 'puppet' of our [American] 'imperialism'."[14] While the United States complained that the Korean government-controlled media was painting a distorted picture of the U.S. role in the violence, most Koreans came to share the view of their fellows in many third world countries that the United States has a double standard, one (democratic) for U.S. domestic affairs, the other (imperialist) for foreign countries.[15]

The alleged U.S. involvement in the uprising and the subsequent establishment of the authoritarian Fifth Republic first fostered despair and a sense of betrayal among many Koreans; later, they provided raw material for radical groups to exploit in democratization movements. As the December 1986 issue of *The Way to Democratization* [*Minjuhwa ŭi kil*], a dissident journal, explains:

> Even in the 1970s there were some activists who recognized the imperialist nature of the U.S. presence in Korea. Yet the public perceived the United States to be a liberator of Korea from Japanese colonialism, a country that helped restore Korea's war-devastated economy, a supporter of democracy that helped overthrow the autocratic Rhee regime. . . . The May Kwangju uprisings, the most massive popular struggle in decades, . . . offered a critical turning point to overcome this obstacle. . . . The U.S. role in the uprising and subsequent U.S. policy increased the Korean public's awareness of the imperialist nature of the American presence in Korea.[16]

Criticizing the previous strategy that had sought American support in establishing a civil and democratic government, many Korean activists became convinced that without national liberation from foreign power (primarily U.S.), democracy in Korea would not take root. The alleged U.S. complicity in quelling the uprising and support for the Chun regime thus transformed "once a Western-oriented movement based largely on middle-class resentment of Park Chung Hee's military dictatorship" into "a nationalist struggle for independence from foreign intervention, and eventual unification."[17]

Further, growing American protectionism and economic pressure to liberalize Korean import markets offered more concrete examples of self-interested American policy. Korea, which had chronically suffered a negative trade balance with the United States until the early 1980s, began to show a surplus.[18] In the mid–1980s, it fell under heavy U.S. pressure to open its market to American products, including agricultural crops and capital goods. No longer considered simply a recipient of American aid and protection, Korea was asked to redress its trade surplus with the United States, often under threat of the retaliatory use of the Super 301. Such economic pressure drove even otherwise-conservative and pro-American farmers to protest. For instance, in 1985 several hundred farmers marched on the U.S. embassy in Seoul to decry U.S. pressure to liberalize beef and grain imports; farmers' protests spread into the countryside, erupting in about twenty counties in late 1985. Pressure to open the rice market especially evoked nationalist resentment as it was considered an attack on Korea's pride and survival. Activists wasted no time in cultivating the consequent popular anti-American sentiments for use in democratization movements.

The late-1984 and early-1985 discussion of the nature of democratic movements is known as the "CNP debate," with CNP representing the initial letters of the three major ideological camps involved: the Civil Democratic Revolution (CDR), the National Democratic Revolution (NDR), and the People's Democratic Revolution (PDR).[19] According to members of the *Minch'ŏngnyŏn* (Youth association for democratization movements), a major protest-movement organization in the mid-1980s, the basic problem was "who should lead transformation movements, and what kind of relations with the middle class and opposition politicians."[20] The effort to articulate a class basis for the movement had not occupied the earlier *minjung* ("people" or "masses") movement, the Korean version of the populism current in Latin America in the early decades of this century. As Hagen Koo points out, Korean populist ideology emerged in the early 1970s as a political reaction to the installation of the bureaucratic-authoritarian *Yushin* (Revitalization) regime, and to widening economic disparities.[21] Populism juxtaposed the masses with the ruling class, the oppressed with the oppressors. Perhaps because of the prevailing anticommunist sentiments of society, the early *minjung* ideology eschewed Marxist class terminologies and presented a crude image of a polarized society where the workers, peasants, and shopkeepers suffered from oppression by the "ruling class," which was composed of the state elite, conglomerate capital, and foreign power.[22] The CNP debate was thus a first major effort to articulate more finely the earlier movement's class basis and to rethink previous strategies that had focused on moral critiques of economic inequality and conscientious critiques of oppressive political power made by students, intellectuals, and the progressive underclass.

The CDR group stressed the overthrow of the military regime and expected U.S. support in reinstating civilian government. Thus their main target was not imperialist power, but the military dictatorship. This group believed that since the Korean proletariat was still weak, the movement should be led by the middle class, including intellectuals, students, and conscientious politicians. Their position basically echoes the earlier *minjung* ideology.[23] On the other hand, both the NDR and PDR considered the overthrow of the imperialist powers essential to real democracy in Korea. They held imperialist rule primarily responsible for the failure of the people's efforts to introduce democracy by way of the Kwangju uprisings. They therefore deemed national liberation and democracy inseparable, though the NDR stressed the former and the PDR the latter. Also, they differed over who should lead the movement. The NDR argued that while workers, peasants, and the urban poor should lead the movement or revolution, they must ally with the middle class. In contrast, the PDR dismissed the importance of such an alliance; its stress on the working class as the main agent of democratic movements clearly departed from the earlier *minjung* strategy. In Henry Em's words, "the social category of *minjung* was made synonymous with the revolutionary subject," and the movement should be directed in terms of "class-based politics."[24] The NDR appeared to enjoy the widest support among intellectuals: the CDR was criticized as "opportunistic" and the PDR as "radical leftism."[25] This early debate among Korean radicals evolved into the first major social formation debate, which revolved around whether Korea was a state-monopoly capitalist or a peripheral capitalist society.

### MARXISM, NATIONALISM, AND ANTI-AMERICANISM

Comparative studies identify Marxism and nationalism as the two major ideological sources for third world anti-Americanism (in Muslim countries Islamic fundamentalism is another). Nationalism is most widespread and easily merges with Marxism (as well as fundamentalism). Marxism offers a more coherent intellectual version than nationalism, but derives much of its political force from its critique of imperialism, a nationalist theme.[26] As Eric Hobsbawm points out, "Since Lenin, Marxists have recognized and analyzed its [nationalism's] revolutionary historic significance, and have stressed its political force . . . [in] the liberation movements of colonial and semi-colonial peoples, and the struggle of the European nations against Fascism."[27] Korea evinces this linkage. In particular, (neo)Marxism (in the form of dependency/world-system theory that sees the democratization movements of the third world as inherently linked to national liberation from imperialism) and nationalism (especially the North Korean *chuch'e* (self-reliance) ideology that emphasizes the people's struggle for national liberation from imperialist forces) greatly influenced radical intellectuals' thought in the 1980s and provided a frame of reference that organized their anti-American discourse.

## Marxism and the Concept of "Social Formation"

The history of Marxism in Korea goes back to the colonial period. When the March First Nationalist Movement of 1919, inspired by the Wilsonian idealism of self-determination, failed to obtain its goal of independence from Japanese colonialism, Korean progressive intellectuals turned to Marxism as an alternative ideology of national liberation. It is no surprise that Marxism dominated nationalist discourse in 1920s and 1930s Korea, especially in radical intellectuals' critique of cultural nationalism, although they faced great difficulty in applying orthodox Marxism to an agrarian colonial society like Korea. Liberation from Japanese rule did not end but rather deepened the ideological schisms between Korean intellectuals, eventually leading to the division of the nation.[28] While nationalist Marxism became the ideological basis of the northern regime, in the south Marxism was severely suppressed under the anticommunist cold war hegemony backed by the National Security Law. Consequently, most South Korean intellectuals, except a few underground activists, took up a non-Marxist populism, such as the *minjung* ideology. Nonetheless, throughout the 1960s and 1970s, Marxist thought spread gradually through underground circles and reading groups on and off campuses.[29] By the 1980s the basic tenets of Marxism and Marxism-Leninism had been sufficiently absorbed in Korean intellectual circles to become a major source for formulating a counterhegemony to the dominant cold war, anticommunist ideology. Increasingly, Marxist influences were giving the earlier, populist *minjung* movement a more class-based profile.

Understandably, debates among Korean radicals centered on the Marxist concept of social formation.[30] Critics focused on the question of which Marxist-Leninist interpretation of historical development best characterized the Korean society, economy, and politics. Radicals felt that earlier democratic movements had failed largely because of an inadequate analysis of Korean social and political development and the inability to provide a coherent oppositional hegemony. These new radical theorists subscribed to Frank's claim that "colonial and class structures generate ideological counterparts to justify themselves. . . . the real responsibility of . . . intellectuals [is to] complement revolutionary practice with the necessary revolutionary theory."[31] As Schwartz points out about Chinese Marxists who engaged in the 1930s debates on Chinese capitalism, "Theory here does not mean simply a well-thought out political strategy. It means nothing more nor less than a thorough sociological analysis of the society in which the revolution is to take place."[32] Keeping this totalizing impulse in mind, it is clear why the Korean debates concerned not just one aspect of Korea — social, economic, political, or ideological — but rather encompassed all of these under the rubric of "social formation."

According to Hindess and Hirst, social formation is "a Marxist concept which may loosely be said to correspond to the ideological notion of 'society.'" While for Marx, the economy is the determining factor for a particular mode of production, certain social, ideological, or political conditions are necessary for the existence of that mode of production. Although the mode of production prescribes "the limits of variation" in the forms of social formation, the latter is "not deducible" from the former.[33] In Alavi's words, the mode of production is "an analytical concept" to define "the *structure* of social relations of production," whereas social formation is a "descriptive term."[34] Accordingly, different societies with the same capitalist mode of production may have various social formations such as peripheral capitalism or monopoly state capitalism.

Further, the particular structure of economic, political, and ideological conditions in the social formation greatly influences forms, strategies, and outcomes of attendant class struggles. Conversely, social formation is "secured, modified, or transformed as the outcome of specific class struggles."[35] The two rounds during the 1980s of Korean debate on social formation were thus attempts to analyze Korean society in its economic, political, social, and ideological aspects, so as to guide democratization and nationalist movements in Korea. In this effort, the first largely sought to be faithful to orthodox Marxism, whereas the second, with the rise of the national liberation thesis, pursued an indigenous application of Marxism to a particular Korean situation.

*Peripheral Capitalism or State Monopoly Capitalism?*

In the first round of the Korean social formation debate, Marxist influence was notable. Neo-Marxism in the form of dependency or world-system theories strongly impressed academics and activists in the 1980s. Dependency theory, developed by Latin American scholars to explain prolonged underdevelopment in the region, was hailed as an alternative to modernization theory, then popular in Korea. Korean intellectuals read widely in the works of Paul Baran, Andre Gunder Frank, Samir Amin, and Immanuel Wallerstein. Relying on Lenin's theory of imperialism, these dependency/world-system theorists argue that third world underdevelopment (not undevelopment) is primarily the consequence of exploitation by core powers through unequal exchange, investment, and loans. While direct colonial rule has been the exception in most third world countries since World War II, they point out that neocolonialism is far from ended. Since underdevelopment in these countries comes from their peripheralization or exploitation by core interests, social revolution implies national liberation from imperialism.

Dependency theory also rejects the notion of universal development and stresses the particular features of peripheral capitalism. As Amin argues, "The formations of the periphery are fundamentally different from those of the center," so the same capitalist mode of production in core and periphery entail different social formations. Amin alleges that the forms peripheral societies assume depend on "the nature of the precapitalist formations that were there previously . . . [and on] the forms and epochs in which they were integrated into the world system."[36] The main task for Korean radicals who adopted this view was to specify the nature of Korean peripheral social formation.

The initial debate began with an exchange of articles between Yi Taegŭn and Pak Hyŏnch'ae published in the fall 1985 issue of *Ch'angjakkwa pip'yŏng* [Creation and critique], a leading progressive journal. Yi analyzed Korean social formation from a dependency perspective, characterizing it as "peripheral capitalist." Since Korea was forcefully incorporated into the world capitalist system by Japanese colonialism, he argued, its social formation cannot be properly understood using a framework developed to analyze Western capitalism. According to Yi, Korean peripheral social formation has three distinctive features: first, Korea was peripheralized in the very late stage of monopoly capitalism; second, a semiperipheral country, Japan, established Korean peripheralization; and third, even during Japanese colonial rule, Korea achieved some degree of industrialization. However, he pointed out, despite these features, colonial Korea never reached the state of peripheral capitalism, since the basic economic structure was maintained by "colonial landlordism."[37] Korea entered the stage of peripheral capitalism in the 1950s after accumulating "commercial capital" through land reform and American aid. Notwithstanding some economic success in the 1960s and 1970s, the imperialist powers (primarily U.S. and Japanese) had skewed Korean development. In short, Korea followed the peripheral capitalist course of most other third world countries, and thus, imperialism should be a primary target of democratization movements.

Pak criticized Yi's interpretation as overemphasizing particular historical situations in Korea.[38] Pak forwarded the state-monopoly-capitalist view, originally developed by neo-Marxists such as Paul Sweezy and Maurice Dobb to explain why Marx's prediction of the demise of Western capitalism had not occurred. Dobb, for instance, had argued that the state's alliance with monopoly capitalists postponed socialist revolution in advanced capitalist societies.[39] On his part, Pak suggested that although particular features of a given social formation should not be overlooked, they must be examined in the context of a general theory of the political economy of capitalism. In his view, the Korean social formation was more similar to what had occurred earlier in the West than to what had occurred in other regions of the third world in the postwar era.[40]

According to Pak, Korea had followed the same stages of capitalist development as Western nations: (1) primitive accumulation (1905–1918), (2) industrial capitalism (1919–1929), (3) financial capitalism (1930–1945), and (4) state monopoly capitalism since 1961. In other words, though under colonial domination, Korea had already entered the capitalist stage by the 1920s. State monopoly capitalism had spawned monopoly capitalists and a working class, and, in his view, this latter entity should lead democratic movements against the primary targets of the military regime and the domestic monopoly capitalists since national liberation was less crucial than proletarian revolution. Probably because of the strong labor movements of the mid-1980s, the state-monopoly-capitalist view, emphasizing class struggle over national struggle, ended up triumphing over the peripheral-capitalist view in the first round of the social formation debate.[41] A major concern of Korean radicals in the first debate was how to be "faithful to orthodox Marxism," and the state-monopoly-capitalist view was held to be more consistent with a fundamentalist Marxist theory of capitalism.

Yet some issues persisted. Most pressing was the question of the continued imperialist presence and its influence in the Korean economy and politics. Some intellectuals began to argue that *both* "national contradiction" stressed by the peripheral-capitalist view *and* "class contradiction" emphasized by the state-monopoly-capitalist view were operating in Korea. When efforts began to reevaluate the significance of the Kwangju uprising and the alleged American role in the massacre, the imperialist issue reemerged. In the second, subsequent round of debate, the focus on imperialism increased Korean radical intellectuals' awareness that Marxism had to be adjusted to the particulars of the Korean situation. First, however, I must lay out the background of the second round of the debate.

*Emergence of the National Liberation Thesis*

Although imperialism was already present in CNP debate in the early 1980s, it was not primary, because the first debate focused on how best to apply Marxist historical teleology to Korea. As Namhee Lee indicates, "The prevalent sentiment was then that it was premature to bring up the question of foreign dominance. It was thought that 'ordinary people' were not yet ready to tackle that issue. . . . Anti-Americanism . . . remained at the level of individual acts and pamphlets calling for restraint and 'repent' [sic] on the part of the United States."[42] Around 1985 the question of imperialism, particularly U.S. imperialism in Korea, emerged as a primary issue. Students and radical activists began reevaluating earlier anti-American political initiatives such as the 1982 seizure of the U.S. Cultural Center in Pusan, which was criticized at the time as an act of "radical leftism." Similar actions ensued. From 23 to 25 May 1985, seventy-three students occupied the U.S. Information Service building in downtown Seoul, demanding a formal U.S. apology "for its role in the Kwangju massacre"; on 12 August, five students unsuccessfully attempted to invade the U.S. embassy in Seoul; and on 4 November, fourteen students occupied the U.S. Chamber of Commerce office in Seoul, protesting reported U.S. pressure to increase agricultural imports into Korea.[43] The formation of a united front among different student groups, *sammint'u* [Struggle committee for *minjung*, democracy, and national liberation], was instrumental.[44] The three *min* line, namely *minjok* (nation), *minju* (democracy), and *minjung* (people), symbolized the strategy and social analysis taken by the united front. As Dong indicates, "Only a very small fraction of the 1980 student activists shared anti-American sentiments; but by 1985 it was apparent that most student activists subscribed to the view that the United States was primarily responsible for the very existence of the military-authoritarian regime."[45]

A growing awareness of imperialist and nationalist issues suggested the need to reexamine the people's struggles against foreign powers throughout Korean history, starting with the 1894 Tonghak peasant wars, and continuing through the March First Movement, the peasant and labor movements during colonial rule, and the post-war political movements which were increasingly felt to represent ongoing national liberation efforts.[46] One radical reading circle studying "national liberation movements" explained the necessity for re-thinking colonial-period popular movements as follows: "The colonial period is not simply an era of the past but constitutes a critical part of the present. A proper understanding of the colonial period struggles against foreign power is essential to analyzing the nature and historical implication of transformation movements since 1945."[47]

What is at stake, as Lee indicates, is the power to "reinterpret historical events hidden from the knowledge of the people and long co-opted and distorted by the powers-that-be."[48] In Choi's words, re-interpretation was an effort to "decolonize" people's consciousness or reconstruct "popular memory" of the resistance from the people's per-spective, and therefore to trace the legitimacy of contemporary movements back into the pre-1945 period.[49] Dissident intellectuals took one further step when they attempted to popularize their new reading of Korean history. The Korean People's History [Han'guk minjungsa] (1986) and A History of People's Movements in Modern Korea [Kŭndae han'guk minjung undongsa] (1989) are prime examples of works written for the "intelligent public." Rather than use the nationalist and/or communist frameworks that conventional scholarship proposes, these volumes analyze the worker and peasant movements in the colonial era as social and political movements in the national liberation struggle.

Some South Korean activists also began pressing the issue of Korean reunification and reading North Korean writings. Through one particular student group called Chamint'u [Committee for the anti-U.S. struggle for independence and the antifascist struggle for democ-racy], formed on 11 April 1986, North Korean "self-reliance" or chuch'e sasang ideology began influencing some dissident activists. Chuch'e defines the substance of history as "the struggle for people's self-reliance" and thus assigns modern Korea's beginnings to "the rise and development of anti-imperial and anti-feudal national movements," from the Tonghak peasant wars through colonial resistance (especially armed struggle in Manchuria), the postwar struggles, and the civil war. Kim Il Sung's North achieved national liberation from feudal-ism and imperialism, according to this argument, while the South remained a semifeudal colonial society in the thrall of American im-perialism.[50] American military power had supported (and continued to support) antinationalist authoritarian regimes.

A few illegal, underground revolutionary organizations in the

South during the 1960s and 1970s had adopted North Korean *chuch'e* ideology. For instance, *T'ongil hyŏngmyŏngdang* (the Unification Revolutionary Party or URP) declared in 1969 that "the Korean revolution is rooted in Kim Il Sung-led armed struggles and its way is clearly described in the *chuch'e* ideology of revolutionary truth and the light of history,"[51] and attempted to "raise anti-government and anti-American consciousness," primarily through its publication *Ch'ŏngmaek* and efforts to organize "liberal intellectuals." Many URP leaders had experience in the South Korean Worker's Party, the People's Committee, and the guerrilla struggles before the civil war. Such activists, however, made few inroads even among liberal and critical intellectuals.

By the mid-1980s, however, the situation had changed. Reevaluating the American role at Kwangju and tackling the imperialism issue in the summer of 1985 led student activists and dissident intellectuals to raise questions about the role of North Korea and its *chuch'e* ideology in Korean revolution and reunification. They soon concluded that revolutionary movement in the South could not be understood in the context of the South alone but needed to be seen within the overall Korean revolution, and that reunification was integral to that revolution. North Korean works expressing *chuch'e* ideology such as *Chosŏn chŏnsa* [The complete history of Korea], *Kŭndae Chosŏn rŏyksa* [Modern Korean history], and *Hyŏndae Chosŏn rŏyksa* [Contemporary Korean history], were reprinted or published as edited volumes and circulated among activists and the intellectual left.

It was the *Chamint'u*, the dominant radical student organization, that adopted *chuch'e* ideology outright when it proclaimed the need for a National Liberation People's Democratic Revolution (NLPDR).[52] Defining modern Korean history as one of "imperial aggression and the people's resistance against it" and contemporary history as one of "struggle between American imperialism and the Korean people," the *Chamint'u* specified five areas of struggle necessary for national liberation: (1) struggle against American imperialism, (2) efforts to remove nuclear weapons from Korea, (3) moves toward peaceful reunification of the motherland, (4) struggle for the people's rights in the workplace, and (5) resistance to American economic imperialism.[53] Obviously, the *Chamint'u* emphasized reunification and national liberation from American imperialism. Supporters considered North Korea "a beacon because of its long practice of independence and self-reliance" and felt that only the North could claim revolutionary legitimacy for the nation of Korea. Since South Korea is subordinated to the same American imperial power that supported its repressive regimes, national liberation and democratization are inextricable. They argue further-more that democratization without national liberation and reunifica-tion would mean accepting a cold war or *pundan* [division] ideology. *Chamint'u*'s ideology of NLPDR dominated mid-1980s student activ-ism.[54] The national liberation thesis and its strong influence on stu-dent activism paved the way for the second round of the social forma-tion debate which unfolded in the late 1980s.

### Semifeudal Colonialism or Neocolonial State Monopoly Capitalism?

Strongly nationalistic, the second-round debate undertook to explain the imperialist nature of Korean social formation. All attempts to be "faithful to orthodox Marxism-Leninism" were abandoned in the effort to create an "indigenous application" of Marxism to a national context characterized by an imperial presence and a division of the nation. Questions of semifeudal colonialism and neocolonial state-monopoly-capitalism dominated the debates. The former was particu-larly strongly influenced by North Korean *chuch'e* scholarship, which limns modern Korea from 1876 to 1945 as a "semi-feudal colonial society . . . [a] product of imperialism and a specific type of capital-ism."[55]

Those who adopted the thesis of the semifeudal colonial group con-tended that Korean society's most fundamental character was rule by colonial power and thus that a national liberation revolution (NLR) was required. They sought to focus debate on "how to explain the colonial and semi-feudal character of Korean society."[56] In contrast to the state-monopoly-capitalism view, this tendency stressed the incorporation into the postwar South of American hegemony through occupation and a war that established a reactionary government. The presence in Korea of the U.S. military, embassy, and CIA as well as reaction-ary bureaucrats and a military dictatorship, they argued, are prime emblems of American colonial rule. Survival of American imperial rule rested on the exploitation of the Korean people and a distortion of the national economic structure, illustrated by the existence of a rural landlord class, an indicator of the semifeudal character of Korean society.

Semifeudal colonialists advocated an unabashedly nationalistic per-spective to explain Korean society, since the "ideology of division" was unacceptable to them and the only unit of social-formation analysis left was united Korea. In fact, they argued, South Korea's semifeudal character stood out more clearly in this perspective because "insofar as the national division is fixed, a unified nation is denied, and the basis of the national economy is destroyed, mere development of capitalism does not remove a semi-feudal character."[57] Accordingly, political movements should aim at eliminating American imperialist rule and all reactionary forces including bureaucrats, landlords, and the military.

The stress on imperialism and the nationalistic perspective caused many involved, even those not necessarily subscribing to the *chuch'e* ideology, to rethink their previous views and movement strategy generally. People who had argued the position of state-monopoly-capitalism in the first round now took the position of "neocolonial state-monopoly-capitalism," in which postwar American policy was thought to have placed Korea in a neocolonial position. Thus, the analysis went, U.S. efforts to contain the spread of communism in Asia consolidated former bureaucrats who had served under Japanese rule, comprador bourgeoisie, and landlords, while suppressing national liberation forces.

Proponents of the neocolonial state-monopoly model, however, objected to characterizing Korean society as semifeudal and colonial. Specifically, this side severely criticized its opponent on the following grounds: (1) failure to differentiate colonial from neocolonial rule, (2) an arbitrary definition of "semi-feudalism," and (3) uncritical acceptance and application of the North Korean *chuch'e* ideology. Although postwar Korea entered the sphere of American hegemony, they conceded, it did not remain semi-feudal but achieved monopoly-capitalist status by the late 1950s by virtue of massive American aid. This view did not deny the significance of liberation from American neocolonial rule, but it placed greater emphasis on "class revolution" led by the working class, and it rejected dogmatic application of the North Korean *chuch'e* ideology.[58] While some analysts taking the position of the semifeudal colonialists have responded to criticism by speaking of "colonial capitalism," "neo-colonial capitalism," or "colonial semi-capitalism,"[59] it is clear that the neocolonial state-monopoly-capitalist model has had a wider audience on the Korean left during the debate.

## THE LIMITS AND FUTURE OF KOREAN RADICALISM

Examining social-formation debates as intellectual discourse shows very clearly that anti-Americanism has deep ideological and political underpinnings. To be sure, alleged American involvement in the Kwangju massacre, continued support for an authoritarian regime, economic pressure to liberalize the market, and Korean media distortion of American positions have all contributed, in one way or the other, to the rise and development of anti-Americanism in Korea. Yet more significantly, the critique is a product of a long symbolic struggle over how to define and redefine the U.S. role in South Korea. The social-formation debates examined here exemplify an effort to articulate anti-Americanism using the "raw" materials listed above. As in most third world countries, Korean intellectuals relied on Marxism and nationalism, especially dependency/world-system theory and North Korean *chuch'e* ideology. The articulation of anti-Americanism was therefore an essential part of a "war of position" in the Gramscian sense, or a "politics of signification" to use Hall's term, undertaken in a highly unfavorable political condition under an anticommunist, repressive regime.[60] Debates had to be disseminated to the public by intellectual circles through grassroots publications such as underground newspapers, leaflets, posters, and pamphlets, as well as dissident academic journals.

Anti-Americanism has also been used effectively to organize and mobilize Korean democratization movements and has gained much ground beyond the campuses, filling the streets with anti-American slogans. Horowitz's explanation for the effective use of anti-Americanism in Latin American political movements well captures the Korean situation:

> Problems arise at "tactical" rather than "principled" levels. It becomes far simpler to organize cadres around the evils of U.S. capitalism than to forge a positive doctrine of socialism or communism that can elicit broad popular support. . . . Ultimately, it is less the contents of anti-Americanism as a negative ideology than the function of the concept itself that has acquired a compelling force.[61]

Tactically, it made more sense in Korea to criticize American domination than to praise a communist system. The media's continued depiction of U.S. patronage and the Reagan administration's "quiet diplomacy" helped spark the flame of anti-Americanism, and Korean radicals achieved some modest success in linking anti-American sentiments to democratization issues. By the late 1980s, "anti-American themes, slogans and messages, which were initially contained in activist leaflets and pamphlets, gradually but steadily . . . permeated into various genres of popular culture, such as films, various visual art works, cartoons, popular songs, novels, and even poetry, thereby con-tributing to formulating an irreversible intellectual undercurrent, even in the mainstream South Korean society."[62] Needless to say, dur-ing the 1980s Korean prodemocracy movements, as in German peace movements or third world political movements, anti-Americanism be-came a key ideological resource, belying Huntington's claim that "in the 1980s . . . supporters for democracy carried the American flag."[63] That Korean intellectuals provoked anti-Americanism in democratiza-tion movements also attests to their identification with the third world rather than the West.

While the Korean intellectual left successfully challenged the anticommunist authoritarian state with its articulation of anti-Americanism as a counterhegemony, they have been much less effec-tive in dealing with developments in domestic and international poli-tics since the late 1980s. Anti-American rhetoric had great difficulty explaining the American role in the 1987 Korean transition to democ-racy and the 1989 collapse of European communism. Furthermore, its radicalization with the rise of national liberation thesis, especially with *Chamint'u*'s adoption of *chuch'e* ideology, came increasingly to close rich public discourse and alienate the public who shared anti-American sentiments. As a result, by the early 1990s many of the ar-guments that made up anti-Americanism were challenged, forfeiting support from even the most politically vocal and active group, college students. For instance, a 1990 survey of civil consciousness by the In-stitute of Population and Development of Seoul National University found that only 12.1 percent of the public agreed with the North Korean claim that "the Korean war was one of national liberation": even among those who supported anti-American movements, only 14.6 percent concurred with the statement.[64] A 1991 college survey of student con-sciousness by the Korea Institute of Social Studies reported a slightly higher figure (19 percent), but the overwhelming majority (66 per-cent) disagree.[65] Clearly anti-Americanism these days is still evident at the popular level, but Korean public opinion does not appear to have embraced radical national liberation rhetoric.

Marxist revolutionary logic does not seem to have much public sup-port, either, as the college survey suggests. More than half of college students surveyed agree that "Marxism-Leninism has lost its ideo-logical power." The figure is much higher for the "new middle class," a major ally during the 1980s democratic movements, of whom 72 percent of the people sampled responded affirmatively.[66] While many view anticommunism as an ideology that fosters a permanent division

of the nation and ascribe responsibility for the political authoritarianism, human rights violations, economic dependency, and division of
the nation to the United States, they do not for that reason subscribe
to revolutionary Marxism or *chuch'e* ideology.[67] Anti-American rhetoric that nurtures popular issues such as the alleged American role in
Kwangju and American economic pressure on Korea has become too
abstract and distant from the everyday lives of most people.

The new historical context has engendered a crisis among radical intellectuals, who have attempted to revise their ideological and
political positions to better explain current conditions and to devise
new strategies for mobilizing popular support. Many have abandoned
orthodox Marxism-Leninism for Social Democracy or post-Marxism.
Some have become active in less radical, more pragmatic organizations like the Citizen's Coalition for Economic Justice (*Kyŏngje chŏngŭi
shilch'ŏn simin yŏnhap*) or the recently formed Solidarity for Participation and Human Rights (*Ch'amyŏ wa inkwŏn ŭl uihan simin yŏndae*).
Some have even entered the ruling party. It would appear that only a
fraction have remained faithful to Marxism-Leninism, or at the very
least to the view that the collapse of communism does not vindicate
capitalism but is instead the consequence of dogmatic applications
of Marxism such as Stalinism.[68] It would appear too that by the early
1990s, Marxist nationalist discourse had lost its earlier dominance
among Korean intellectuals, and had lost ground to other less radical
forms of social analysis like the discourse on civil society.[69]

To conclude, the Korean intellectual left undoubtedly shaped anti-
American rhetoric and was effective at mobilizing it and using it as an
ideological resource during 1980s democratization the movements.
The anti-American nationalism that characterized the movements of
the 1980s will no doubt leave its mark on Korean intellectual and
political history. Yet continued dogmatic reliance on dated, nonviable
explanatory models like dependency theory and *chuch'e* ideology has
impeded the left's ability to enrich public discourse, sustain popular
support, and effectively confront the changing domestic and international environment. Progressive democratization and the collapse of
communism pose a direct challenge to leftist politics in Korea in the
1990s.

NOTES

I am very grateful to Bruce Cumings, Michael Robinson, Henry Park,
and two anonymous reviewers for *positions* for their valuable comments.

A grant from the National Endowment for the Humanities (FA-32712–94) aided me in completing research for and writing this article.

1  Chamint'u, "Haebang sŏnŏn 2" [Liberation declaration 2], rpt. in *Haksaeng undong nonjaengsa* [History of debate on student movements], ed. Ilsonjŏng (Seoul: Ilsongjŏng, 1988), 117.

2  See Jinwung Kim, "Recent Anti-Americanism in South Korea: The Causes," *Asian Survey* 29, no. 8 (1989), and *Han'gugin ŭi panmi kamjŏng* [Anti-American sentiments of Koreans] (Seoul: Iljogak, 1992); Tim Shorrock, "The Struggle for Democracy in South Korea in the 1980s and the Rise of Anti-Americanism," *Third World Quarterly* 8, no. 4 (1986): 1195–1218; Selig Harrison, *The South Korean Political Crisis and American Policy Options* (Washington, D.C.: Washington Institute, 1987); Jae-Kyoung Lee, "Anti-Americanism in South Korea: The Media and the Politics of Signification" (Ph.D. dissertation, University of Iowa, 1993).

3  Gi-Wook Shin, "Korean Anti-Americanism in Comparative Perspective," paper delivered at the conference on "Transformation in the Korean Peninsula toward the Twenty-First Century," East Lansing, Mich., July 1993.

4  It should be noted that church leaders (both Protestant and Catholic) have also played a significant role in nationalist democratic movements. However, this article focuses on Marxist discourse. For church involvement, see George Ogle, *South Korea: Dissent within the Miracle* (London: Zed, 1990).

5  See Bruce Cumings, "The Origins and Development of the Northeast Asian Political Economy," *International Organization* 38 (Winter 1984): 1–40.

6  Grant Meade, *American Military Government in Korea* (New York: King's Crown, 1951), 62.

7  See Gi-Wook Shin, "The Historical Making of Collective Action: The Korean Peasant Uprisings of 1946," *American Journal of Sociology* 99 (1994): 1596–1624.

8  Gregory Henderson, "Why Koreans Turn against Us," *Washington Post*, 1 July 1986.

9  Shorrock, "Struggle for Democracy," 1198–1199.

10  The exact death figures remain unknown. The Korean government claims no more than two hundred died, but opposition forces say between two thousand and three thousand died. For a concise examination of the uprising, see Donald Clark, ed., *The Kwangju Uprising: Shadows over the Regime in South Korea* (Boulder, Colo.: Westview, 1988).

11  Linda Lewis, "The Kwangju Incident Observed: An Anthropological Perspective on Civil Uprisings," in Clark, *Kwangju Uprising*, 23.

12  William H. Gleysteen Jr., the U.S. ambassador to Korea at the time, admits that the 20th Infantry Division, under a U.S. commander, moved to Kwangju from Seoul with American consent. See William Gleysteen Jr., "Korea: A Special Target of American Concern," in *The Diplomacy of Human Rights*, ed. David Newsom (Lanham, Md.: University Press of America, 1986), 85–99.

13  Gleysteen explains the invitation of Chun to the United States was a deal to release opposition leader Kim Daejung, who had been sentenced to death by the military court. See Gleysteen, "A Special Target," 97–98.

14  Henderson, "Why Koreans Turn against Us."

15  According to Jae-Kyoung Lee's analysis of the Korean news media, the regime effectively forced the media to convey two themes to South Koreans: (1) "U.S. support for and approval of the actions taken by the military," and (2) the "U.S. commitment to South Korea's security." Consequently, "the media were forced to completely ignore all U.S. reactions that publicly expressed its disapproval and displeasure," especially by the Carter administration. Lee concludes: "Any reader who just followed Korean media coverage had to reach the conclusion that the United States was in close consultation with the military rulers and that major common concern was North Korean aggression." A 1989 "U.S. government statement on the events in Kwangju, Republic of Korea in May 1980" written in response to questions submitted by the Korean National Assembly's Special Committee on the Kwangju Incident also contends: "The U.S. policy of aloofness and public displeasure with the Chun takeover was known to the world, but not to the Korean people. The Chun regime used its control over the media under total martial law to distort the U.S. position, portraying it not as condemnation but as support" (see Lee, "Anti-Americanism," 101).

16  Quoted and translated from Pak Hyŏnch'ae and Cho Hŭiyŏn, *Han'guk sahoe kusŏngch'e nonjaeng* [Debates on the social formation of Korea—Debates], vol. 1. (Seoul: Chuksan, 1989), 50–51.

17  Shorrock, "Struggle for Democracy," 1205.

18  Korea's trade surplus with the United States grew from $4.3 billion in 1985 to $9.6 billion in 1987 and $8.7 billion in 1988.

19  Even before the CNP debate, student activists held numerous debates on movement tactics, such as the ones between *murim* and *hangnim* in 1980, and *yahak pip'an* and *chŏnmang* in 1982. See Cho Kije, *Taehaksaengtŭl ŭi chyakyŏnghwa kwajŏng e kwanhan yŏn'gu* [A study of the radicalization process of college students] (Seoul: Hyŏndae sahoe yŏn'guso, 1987). However, these debates yielded no comprehensive analysis of Korean society, politics, and the economy as in the social formation debates discussed below. For a CNP debate summary, see Ilsongjŏng, *History of Debate*, 57–65.

20  Cho Hŭiyŏn, "80 nyŏndae sahoe undong kwa sahoe kusŏngch'e nonjaeng [Social movements and social formation debates in 1980s Korea]," in Pak and Cho, *Debates*, 1:15.

21  Hagen Koo, "Middle Classes, Democratization, and Class Formation," *Theory and Society* 20 (1991): 485–509.

22  See Han'guk sinhak yŏn'guso, *Han'guk minjungnon* (Seoul: Han'guk sinhak yon'guso, 1984). In the 1920s, Korean intellectuals, finding orthodox Marxist theory difficult to apply to colonial agrarian Korea, also used general and

vague categories such as "propertied" (*yusanja*) and "propertyless" (*musanja*) instead of bourgeoisie and proletariat. As Michael Robinson shows, this formula pitted "the small minority of the rich, comprised of capitalists, landlords, and elements of an urban leisure class, against the overwhelming majority of poor Korean peasants and laborers," regardless of many other criteria for class distinction (see Robinson, *Cultural Nationalism in Colonial Korea, 1920–1925* [Seattle: University of Washington Press, 1988], 121).

23  Although most views expressed in the CNP and later social formation debates reflect *minjung* thought in a broad sense, I separate the earlier (before the 1970s) *minjung* ideology from later views to highlight the development of Marxist nationalist discourse in the 1980s as shown below.

24  Henry H. Em, " 'Overcoming' Korea's Division: Narrative Strategies in Recent South Korean Historiography," *positions* 1 (fall 1993): 469.

25  See Ilsongjŏng, *History of Debate*.

26  See Alvin Rubinstein and Donald Smith, eds., *Anti-Americanism in the Third World* (New York: Praeger, 1985).

27  Eric Hobsbawm, "Some Reflections on Nationalism," in *Imagination and Precision in the Social Sciences: Essays in Memory of Peter Nettl*, ed. T. J. Nossiterpp, A. H. Hanson, and Stein Rokkan (London, 1972), 386.

28  See Bruce Cumings, *The Origins of the Korean War*, vol. 1 (Princeton, N.J.: Princeton University Press, 1981).

29  See Cho Hŭiyŏn, *Hyŏndae han'guk sahoe undong kwa chojik* [Social movements and organizations in contemporary Korea] (Seoul: Han'ul, 1993).

30  Scholars use different terms to define the 1980s debates among dissident intellectuals and Marxist scholars. Some label them "debates on Korean capitalism," others, "debates on modern and contemporary Korean history," and still others, "debates on the character of Korean society." I choose "social formation debates," a broader term that better suggests Marxist influence.

31  Andre G. Frank, *Latin America: Underdevelopment or Revolution* (New York: Monthly Review, 1969), 402–408.

32  Benjamin Schwartz, "A Marxist Controversy on China," *Far Eastern Quarterly* 13, no. 2 (1954): 144.

33  Barry Hindess and Paul Q. Hirst, *Pre-Capitalist Modes of Production* (London: Routledge and Kegan Paul, 1975), 15.

34  Hamza Alavi, "The Structure of Peripheral Capitalism," in *Introduction to the Sociology of Developing Societies*, ed. Hamza Alavi and Theodore Shanin (New York: Monthly Review, 1982).

35  Hindess and Hirst, *Pre-Capitalist, Modes of Production* 15.

36  Samir Amin, *Accumulation on a World Scale* (New York: Monthly Review, 1974), 393.

37  See Yi Taegŭn, "Han'guk chabonjuŭi sŏnggyŏk e taehayŏ" [On the charac-

ter of Korean capitalism], *Ch'angjakkwa pip'yŏng* 1 (1985): 346–373, rpt. in Pak and Cho, *Debates*, 252–253.

38  See Pak Hyŏnch'ae, "Hyŏndae han'guk sahoe ŭi sŏnggyŏk kwa paljŏn tangye e kwanhan yŏn'gu" [A study of the character and developmental stage of contemporary Korean society], *Ch'angjakkwa pip'yŏng*, 1, (1985): 310–345; rpt. in Pak and Cho, *Debates*, 197–229.

39  See Maurice Dobb, *Studies in the Development of Capitalism* (London: Routledge and Kegan Paul, 1946).

40  In similar fashion, sociologists also have debated the character of Korean class formation—that is, whether it resembles the proletarianization of the West or the semiproletarianization of the third world. See Hagen Koo, "From Farm to Factory: Proletarianization in Korea," *American Sociological Review* 55 (1990): 669–681.

41  See Chŏng Sŏngjin, "80 nyŏndae han'guk sahoe kusŏngch'e nonjaeng kwa chubyŏnbu chabonjuŭiron" [Debate on the social formation of Korea and peripheral capitalism], *Han'guk sahoe yŏn'gu* 5 (1987): 7–33; rpt. in Pak and Cho, *Debates*, 627–651.

42  Namhee Lee, "The South Korean Student Movements, 1980–1987," in *Chicago Occasional Papers on Korea*, ed. Bruce Cumings (Chicago: The Center for East Asian Studies/University of Chicago, 1991), 225.

43  See Shim Jae Hoon, "Echoes of Kwangju," *Far Eastern Economic Review*, 6 June 1985, 24.

44  Although *sammint'u* was officially an organ of *chŏnhangnyŏn* (the National Student Association), in actual function the former was a vanguard independent organization. See Cho, *Radicalization Process of College Students*.

45  Wonmo Dong, "University Students in South Korean Politics: Patterns of Radicalization in the 1980s," *Journal of International Affairs* 40 (1987): 246.

46  Bruce Cumings' revisionist view of the Korean War was highly influential among Korean student activists and dissident intellectuals in provoking such nationalist historiography. His "American Policy and Korean Liberation" in *Without Parallel* (New York: Pantheon, 1973) and vol. 1 of his well-known *The Origins of the Korean War* (1981) were translated into Korean in 1983 and 1986, respectively. See Em, "Overcoming Korea's Division," for a discussion of Cumings' influence on Korean intellectuals.

47  Yŏksa munje yŏn'guso minjok haebang undongsa yŏn'guban [A study group on national liberation movements of the Center for Historical Studies], *Minjok haebang undongsa—chaengjŏm kwa kwaje* [History of national liberation movements—issues and tasks] (Seoul: Yŏksa pip'yŏngsa, 1990), 12–13.

48  Lee, "South Korean Student Movements," 210.

49  See Chungmoo Choi, "The Discourse of Decolonization and Popular Memory: South Korea," *positions* 1, no. 1 (spring 1993), 77–102.

50  See Yŏng-Ho Ch'oe, "Reinterpreting Traditional History in North Korea,"

*Journal of Asian Studies* 40 (1981): 503–523, and Jin-Soon Doe, "The Periodization of Modern and Contemporary History in North Korea Academic Circles," *Korea Journal* 31, no. 2 (1991): 41–55.

51 Pak T'aesun and Kim Tongch'un, 1960 *nyŏndae ŭi sahoe undong* [Social movements in the 1960s] (Seoul: Kkach'i, 1991), 238–239.

52 Yun Sŏggin, "1986 nyŏn sangban'gi haksaeng undong naebu nonjaeng kaegwan" [Internal debates in student movements in the first half of 1986], in Pak and Cho, *Debates*, 338–352. A relatively moderate student group, *minmint'u* (Struggle Committee Against Imperialism, the Military and Fascism and for the Nation and Democracy), organized on 21 March 1986, emphasizes an antifascist, antigovernment struggle and seeks to raise the consciousness of workers, farmers, and the urban poor. Ideologically it is committed to "national democratic revolution" (see also Cho, *Radicalization Processes of College Students*).

53 Ilsongjŏng, *History of Debate*, 118.

54 See Yun, "Internal Debates," 338–352

55 Doe, "Periodization of History," 49.

56 Chŏng Min, "Han'guk chabonchuŭi ŭi sŏnggyŏk kyujŏng," rpt. in Pak and Cho, *Debates*, 354.

57 Cho, "Social Movements," 27.

58 See Pak and Cho, *Debates*, 421–461.

59 See Chŏng, "Debate on Social Formation," 7–33.

60 Antonio Gramsci, *Selections from the Prison Notebooks*, ed. and trans. Quinten Hoare and Geoffrey N. Smith (London: Lawrence and Wishart, 1971); and Stuart Hall, "The Rediscovery of Ideology: Return of the Repressed in Media Studies," in *Culture, Society, and the Media* ed. M. Gurevitch, T. Bennett, J. Curran, and J. Woolacott (Beverly Hills, Calif.: Sage, 1982), 56–90.

61 Horowitz, "Latin America," 51, 63.

62 Lee, "Anti-Americanism in South Korea," 212.

63 Samuel Huntington, *The Third Wave: Democratization in the Late Twentieth Century* (Norman: University of Oklahoma Press, 1991), 286.

64 Sŏul taehakkyo ingu mit paljŏn munje yŏn'guso, "Kwangbok 45 chunyŏn han'guk sahoe wa kungmin ŭisik chosa yŏn'gu" [A survey of Korean society and civil consciousness after 45 years of liberation] (Seoul: Sŏul taehakkyo ingu mit paljŏn munje yŏn'guso, 1990).

65 Hyŏndae sahoe yŏn'guso, "Taehaksaeng ŭisik chosa yŏn'gu" [A survey of college student consciousness] (Seoul: Hyŏndae sahoe yŏn'guso, 1991).

66 Hyŏndae sahoe yŏn'guso, "Sin chungsanch'ŭng ŭi silt'ae wa sahoe paljŏn e kwanhan yŏn'gu" [A survey of reality of the Korean new middle class and social development] (Seoul: Hyŏndae sahoe yŏn'guso, 1992).

67 See Shin, "Korean Anti-Americanism."

68 See Pak Hyŏnch'ae and Cho Hŭiyŏn, *Han'gute sahoe kusŏngch'e nonjaeng*

[Debates on the social formation of Korea—debates], vol. 4 (Seoul: Chue-san, 1992).

69 See Han'guk sahoe hakhoe and Han'guk chŏngch'i hakhoe, eds. *Han'guk ŭi kukkawa simin sahoe* [State and Civil Society in Korea], (Seoul: Hanul, 1992).

"Who Am I?"—Questions of Voluntarism in the

Paradigm of Socialist Alienation

■ Any significant chronicle of post-Mao intellectual history would have to start with the emergence of the problematic of humanism in the early 1980s. No matter how contemptuously Chinese avant-garde writers and critics now regard those earliest specimens of exposé literature that promoted the "value and dignity of human beings" in crude confessional realism, it is precisely the literature's complicitous relationship with the postrevolutionary politics of humanism that accounted for its quick popularity both at home, albeit for a short while, and abroad for a decade and beyond. Historical amnesia may be a malady that plagues the Chinese populace in the age of boom economics, but back in the late 1970s and early 1980s, remembrance was an exercise in which intellectuals and writers were engaged with unrelieved piety. For just under half a decade, confessions and self-introspection not only pervaded literary discourse, they emerged as a dominant trope in political discourse as well.

Certain unorthodox acknowledgments that Chinese Marxism was conscious of its own self-alienation characterizes the soul-searching mood no less poignantly and theatrically than the creative writers' sentimental homage to the problem expressed in literary texts like the popular novel *Ah, Human Beings! Human Beings! (Ren, a ren)*.[1] What was being remembered were not only personal wounds inflicted on each individual by the Revolution and the Gang of Four—a clichéd formula that had outlived its appeal by the mid-1980s—but also the repressed memory of the early history of Marxism, specifically, the humanist epistemology of the young Marx epitomized in his *Economic and Philosophic Manuscripts of 1844.* In the immediate wake of the defeat of ultraleftism, what needed rehabilitation was certainly not just so-called individual victims of Revolution, but Marx himself. The historical philosopher, Marx, who had cried out against alienation,[2] now provided disillusioned Party intellectuals with a new chance at reinventing Chinese Marxism.

The stakes were exceedingly high at the beginning of the 1980s. Future historians will commend the enormous moral courage and personal risk Wang Ruoshui and Zhou Yang took in pioneering the theoretical notion of "socialist alienation" and the theoretical critique of the Cultural Revolution. In the absence of the alienation school, Chinese humanism would never have occupied such a prominent place in the national agenda, and the liberatory vision could not have been so deeply engraved on the intellectual history of the 1980s. New terrains of inquiry opened up in later years precisely because alienation theorists proved that transgression into forbidden ideological domains made self-introspection viable.

What Wang Ruoshui, Zhou Yang, and their collaborators set out to achieve in the early 1980s was less a condemnation of dogmatic Marxism than the seizure of a historical opportunity for reconstructing a genuine ethical humanism within the ideological confines of Chinese Marxism. So, more often than not, in its introduction and critique of Sartre and existentialist humanism, the alienation school took pains to dispel suspicion that it might be Sartre and not the young Marx who served as the theoretical point of departure for a "Marxist humanism." And yet, Chinese discourse on Sartre remained intriguingly double-edged, a point that has not attracted much attention from scholars abroad. Precisely because indigenous scholars cannot afford to probe into it without inviting official intervention, I suggest that we take a closer look at some theorists' strategic approaches to Sartre vis-à-vis the young Marx during the debate. Eventually, the problem I wish to address is this: certain theoretical limitations inhering in the notion of "socialist alienation" and also related to Chinese intellectuals' attitude toward the voluntarist aspect of Sartre's humanism (i.e., the "greater valorization of subjective forces"[3]) underlay and animated the emotive content of the thesis of "socialist alienation." My question: what characterizes that relation between subjectivity and the critical or theoretical question of de-alienation and can we recognize the urgency of the problem of "socialist alienation" while at the same time criticizing the terms in which it was framed?[4]

Most theorists of the Chinese alienation school were slow to acknowledge Georg Lukács's contribution to the exegesis of the Marxist theory of alienation. There seemed to be a conscious and concerted effort among alienation theorists to not remind powerful opponents that it was Lukács, "the idealist," who had brought Marxism's theme of alienation into the limelight in his 1923 *Geschichte und Klassenbeweusstsein*. It is certainly intriguing that while many Chinese theorists insisted on distinguishing the Hegelian notion of "objectification" (*duixiang hua; Vergegenstandlichung*) from that of alienation,[5] they seem to involuntarily gloss over the issue of the conceptual affiliation or distinction between "reification" (*wuhua; Verdinglichung*) and "alienation."[6] The interchangeability of these two terms in post-Mao China serves as a meaningful comment on the Chinese theorists' silent acknowledgment of the "rational elements in Lukács' thought."[7]

While the term *alienation* has been a cliché since the mid-1940s in the Europeanized West, its resurfacing in post-Mao China rang fresh. Wang Ruoshui, the deputy editor of the *People's Daily*, was already raising in 1980 the proposition of "socialist alienation" and had even delineated its three major manifestations in China,[8] a viewpoint reiterated almost verbatim by Zhou Yang in his speech commemorating Marx's centennial in 1983. While identifying these as "the alienation of thought attributed to the cult of Mao Zedong," "political alienation," and "economic alienation," Wang clearly foregrounded "political alienation" instead of "economic alienation," as the origin and culmination of socialist alienation in China.

Moreover, it was not Soviet but Polish, Hungarian, Czech, and Yugoslav communists who emerged into prominence for the Chinese alienation school. The works of Adam Schaff, a member of the Central Committee of the Polish Communist Party, and those by the Yugoslav Gajo Petrovic appeared in great abundance in *Zhexue yicong* [Translations of philosophical texts] between 1979 and 1982. Stringent critiques of socialism made around 1965 by Eastern European communists sounded no doubt like bombshells when they were first translated into Chinese in 1979. Schaff's assertion that "in all forms of socialist society different forms of alienation occur,"[9] and Petrovic's declaration that the "de-alienation of economic life also requires the abolition of state property,"[10] had indeed found continual repercussions in Wang Ruoshui's and his colleagues' inquiries into the problematic of socialist alienation in Mao's China. Adam Schaff's perspective was particularly crucial to the development of Wang Ruoshui's theoretical framework. The major question Schaff addressed—"Is it true that private property is at the basis of all alienation? And consequently, does the end of capitalism mean the end of all alienation?"[11] — were transported verbatim into the agenda of Chinese theorists. Wang Ruoshui was selective, of course. While deploring the continued existence of the coercive state machinery, Schaff had recognized that the state "will not wither away" as a bureaucracy and that labor on "an assembly line is inherently the same regardless of government."[12] This view, which asserts that labor should not have been identified as a category of alienation in the first place, is a point of contestation that Wang Ruoshui chose not to pursue, for it subverted his effort at revalorizing the alienation paradigm proposed by the young Marx. In the early 1980s, what intrigued Wang Ruoshui was Schaff's open censure of communism. Wang found particularly inspiring Schaff's discussion of the relationship between the "cult of personality" and the communist state as an alienating force. Defending humanism, the Chinese theorist echoed the position of the Polish communist regarding the controversy over the young versus the mature Marx, namely, the emphasis on unity in the development of Marxism, and consequently, the possibility of integrating the "scientific motivation of Marxism with an ethical, humanist one."[13]

Underlying both communist critiques of socialism was the ominous accusation that while capitalist alienation is economic, and therefore partial, communist alienation is political and total. Hu Qiaomu and elements hostile to this line of thinking within the Chinese Communist Party proper were aware of the problem. If, as Wang Ruoshui proclaimed, alienation, now in the guise of political estrangement of the people from the Party, had not disappeared with the implementation of public ownership of productive materials,[14] then implied heavily was the suggestion that the old Marxist category of "private property" as the root cause of alienation had to give way to a new category of "power." And what did Wang Ruoshui involuntarily propagate here, according to his Party critics, if not the total elimination of bureaucratic power?[15]

Though the charge that the alienation school tendered an anarchist tendency was carried out within the fragile illusion of academic exchange, more underhanded recrimination was deployed against Wang Ruoshui and took an unmistakably political course. At issue was Wang's alleged "relapse" into the ideology of "permanent revolution" advocated by the ultraleftists during Mao's era. Those familiar with the subtle strategies of criticism and countercriticism at which Chinese (politicians and commoners alike) have become adept throughout their history would know how to decipher this treacherous device of counterattack. Not in the least would they take the Party's indictment of Wang Ruoshui's alleged "leftism" at face value. Those speaking for the Party knew only too well that Wang's subscription to Mao's popular thesis of "permanent revolution" amounted to nothing more than a defensive gesture adopted for the purpose of camouflaging his own theoretical premise about "continuous alienation" under socialism, his reasoning being that if Mao Zedong could talk about an endless series of social contractions and struggles, then surely Wang Ruoshui's vision of a socialist society suffering from continual reification could not be immediately judged heretical. What Wang Ruoshui the strategist did not expect was that his own conceptual position might backfire. Quoting Mao as the theoretical underpinning for his own proposition of everlasting alienation ("Human history is a history of the continual development from the realm of necessity to the realm of freedom. This history will never come to an end"), Wang Ruoshui was so preoccupied with his preemptive strike against imagined critics that he momentarily forgot that the Party could beat him at his own game at any time by simply accusing him of making a renewed alliance with the now stigmatized word *leftism*. The subtle mechanism underlying this psychological warfare undoubtedly obscured the initial hidden agenda of both the accused and the accuser. Yet given the fact that both Wang Ruoshui and his attackers (Deng Liqun among them)[16] were bad-faith players in a roundabout rhetoric, the quick conclusions of some Western observers about the close resemblance between the alienation school and leftists of the Cultural Revolution should be carefully reexamined.[17]

Despite the highly rhetorical charges and countercharges, the intense collision between the alienation school and its opponents on the three specific forms of socialist alienation laid bare only too clearly the subtext of the debate as none other than a critique of the Cultural Revolution, and by extension, of the Great Helmsman himself. Now officially the Party had been generous in its criticism of Mao (Hu Qiaomu, veteran Party historian, saved harsh words for the chairman) but it still insisted that an all-out critique of the Revolution could only culminate in a categorical condemnation of the socialist system in general. Thus despite Zhou Yang's assurances that the causes of alienation did not lie in the socialist system itself, and his position that the Third Plenum of the Eleventh Central Committee had already taken measures to overcome each of the three forms of alienation,[18] Hu Qiaomu adamantly charged that further discussion of "socialist alienation" was ideologically suspect. Everything, he raged, including the prestige of

Mao Zedong and the historical standing of the Revolution, might be compromised except the sacred aura of socialism itself. Wang Ruoshui and Zhou Yang, Hu's indictment charged, had wittingly stepped into forbidden territory by merely suggesting that alienation, a category integral only to capitalism, existed in socialism, too. For what had the two theorists breached if not faith in the utopian capacity of socialism to eliminate all forms of alienation? In one speculative move, Hu Qiaomu succeeded in equating a simple proposition of alienation with the incriminating heresy that "socialism might be negated by dynamics internal to itself."[19] All of a sudden, Party ideological apparachiks unleashed relentlessly the same accusation—alienation theory "would necessarily lead to the assertion that socialism itself is the root cause of 'socialist alienation.'"[20]

Such an irrevocable indictment could only lead to one possible outcome. Hu's talk, published in January 1984, not only ended the debate in an official manner but initiated another political campaign. Wang Ruoshui was dismissed from his editorial post at the *People's Daily;* Zhou Yang was forced to compromise his views; Deng Liqun, who had spoken like an enlightened Party official in April 1983 against the political persecution of humanist advocates in the name of "adhering to the 'Two Hundreds' policy,"[21] now quickly reversed his position and joined the burgeoning major campaign against the alienation school; Deng Xiaoping himself raised the slogan of anti–"spiritual pollution" at the Second Plenum of the Twelfth Central Committee in October 1983. A full-fledged campaign, the so-called Anti–Spiritual Pollution movement targeting pornography and early Marxism, strange bedfellows indeed, was unleashed at last.

Whether or not Hu Qiaomu and his collaborators overestimated the subversive potential of the alienation school remains to be investigated. I should perhaps rephrase the issue as follows: had the alienation critique actually identified anything more than a formulaic root-cause of ultraleftism to explain the petrification of socialist praxis? Did any of the advocates of the alienation school ever say, in the same daring fashion as Albrecht Wellmer, "We must start from the assumption that . . . if not the nucleus then at least a theoretical correlative for the decline in [socialist] practice must be available in the theory itself"?[22] Did Wang Ruoshui and Zhou Yang, and indeed, any of the intellectuals who claimed to be victims of the system, ever genuinely contemplate the possibility that domination and alienation might have been reproduced with the complicitous cooperation of the oppressed themselves?

A closer look would reveal the school's limited understanding of oppression and of the necessary means of alleviating alienation. Whether expounding the meaning of the "fetishism of politics" (*zhengzhi baiwu jiao*)[23] or engaging in a speculation of the various factors that triggered "economic alienation," none of the theorists succeeded in breaking away from the epistemological constraint that dictates a clear-cut dichotomy of oppressor and oppressed. Nor did anyone contest China's postrevolutionary wisdom that the origin of oppression is located externally. Whether the critic in question fingered for blame the repressive bureaucratic party-state, identified with Lin Biao and Jiang Qing, or Mao Zedong's voluntarism, or even residual feudalism, critics all viewed alienation as an alien machinery, imposed on one, and therefore an aberration that could only be eliminated from the outside.

The theoretical possibility of "internalized oppression"—after all, why had the whole country fanatically attempted the Great Leap Forward—never troubled the theorists' discussion of "economic alienation." Although Wang Ruoshui attributed China's economic backwardness to "voluntarism," he stopped short of exploring the intriguing issue of collusion and internalized tyranny; indeed, he halted in the face of the entire dimension of subjectivity to which the term *voluntarism* refers. Instead, he opted for scapegoating exterior machineries like "bureaucratism," the "institutional structure (*tizhi*), and the Party's failure to understand the "objective law of economics."

Theoretically, Wang Ruoshui's proposition of "economic alienation" under socialism is far more subversive than that of "political alienation." While the latter addresses a specific case of socialist praxis gone astray, the former touches the theoretical core of Marxism's fundamental tenets. This could be the point of entry for a vigorous critique of Marx. Yet what could Wang Ruoshui do in the intense ideological climate but utter an uncommitted and shorthand commentary: "Didn't [they] say," he commented laconically, "that once the system of public property is established, all problems will be resolved? According to Marx and Engels' original conception, it seems that all forms of alienation originate from private property. It seems as long as and as soon as society gains control over productive materials, alienation will be exterminated."[24] This remark, inconclusive as it may sound, probably constitutes Wang Ruoshui's most radical statement during the debate in terms of its potential to undermine the political economy of Marxism itself.

Silence on the issue of the relationship between public ownership and economic exploitation under socialism, however, opened further gaps in Wang Ruoshui's discourse on "socialist alienation." It seems predictable that his critique of the Great Leap Forward would fail to open up a critical space for a comparative study of functional capitalist exploitation vis-à-vis the authoritarian socialist system of *institutionalized* exploitation. No seasoned politician would make the mistake of undertaking such a task. And the closest Wang Ruoshui ever came to such a dangerous comparison was his veiled complaint that in the realm of productive relations in socialist China, primacy was given to production rates and development indices, and that bureaucratic economic planning objectives were pursued at the systematic expense of human labor.[25] What remained to be pursued, of course, was the burning issue of the exclusive state ownership of the means of production and how such a mode of ownership had given rise to exploitation which may be qualitatively, but not quantitatively, different from the mode of exploitation that resulted from private ownership. Needless to say, in the early 1980s, the political climate for such a discussion had not yet matured. It was not until 1987 that the emergence of the term *guandao* (governmental corruption) succeeded in sharpening the people's consciousness that the Party had been the sole entrepreneur under state socialism which possessed the exclusive right of control over the materials and process of production. In Wang Ruoshui's time, it would have been too impious to suggest that the Party entrepreneurs were nothing other than the socialist counterparts of capitalists.

Wang Ruoshui's criticisms of *tizhi* (polity or institutional structure), of course, also conjures up other forms of "systematized" alienation that he could not address in the open. One such form arises with the institutionalization of a new revolutionary class structure that the humanists swore to dismantle with their impassioned slogan, "human nature is not equal to class nature." Just as in the Soviet Union, social inequalities were institutionalized through the oligarchical system of *nomenklatura*,[26] Mao's China was divided into the revolutionary hierarchy of *hong wulei* (five red categories), *hei wulei* (five black categories), and *niu gui she shen* (monsters and demons). Why this particular form of alienation was bypassed by Wang Ruoshui and Zhou Yang hardly needs any explanation. The concept of class struggle and the privileged position of the proletariat were givens of Maoism-Marxism that left no room for contestation in the early 1980s.

Yet class stigma, like many other devices of economic and political alienation enumerated by Wang and Zhou, were after all tools of oppression utilized by an outside agent. So far, the alienation school's emphasis on the external origin of political and economic alienation under state socialism seems convincing enough for them to argue that de-alienation could be achieved simply by resorting to the *objective* emancipatory means delivered and implemented by a revitalized socialist system and an enlightened Party leadership, a historical turning point already materialized at the Second Plenum of the Twelfth Central Committee. It seems that the Party alone held the keys to the removal of estrangement defined in political, economic, or class terms. This is precisely the eulogy that Zhou Yang paid to the Party for its full capacity to initiate and accomplish de-alienation, an article of faith that both the critics and spokesmen of the Party had embraced wholeheartedly. But, I argue, it is precisely because of the alienation school's failure to critique "alienation" from within—the subjective practice of the oppressed on the one hand, and a critique of Marxist theory on the other—and above all, its obliviousness to the entire issue of internalized oppression that Zhou Yang's proposal for securing external means for eliminating "socialist alienation" suffered such serious theoretical limitations.

## "INTERNALIZED OPPRESSION"

Indeed, we find evaded the whole question of the subjective dimension of domination and oppression, or in Irving Fetscher's terms, the issue of "structural guilt and sin which may be immanent [*sic*] in certain social orders,"[27] a particular constitution of "national character" that allowed someone like Stalin or Mao Zedong to remain in power for so many decades. If the critique of "socialist alienation" were to have any practical value for future emancipatory praxes, Wang Ruoshui and his colleagues would have had to have dwelt less on Mao Zedong's tyrannical rule than on the recognition that struggles for de-alienation are "often eroded and defeated 'from within' by the effects of internalized oppression."[28] One might condone (though not forget) the complicity of the oppressor and the oppressed during the revolutionary years, for the entire country's deification of Mao Zedong as a cult figure, a phenomenon that Wang Ruoshui and Zhou Yang designated as the "alienation of thought," was an irreversible trend of revolutionary romanticism or even fanaticism. But has postrevolutionary China outgrown the vicious cycle of the semi-autonomous mechanism of internalized oppression?

The events following the Party's call for the Anti–Spiritual Pollution campaign in the winter of 1983 "prove beyond the shadow of a doubt," for Stuart Schram, that, "despite the categorical statement, in early

1979, that 'campaigns' or 'movements' would no longer be launched in China, the Chinese people are still so deeply marked by the reflexes created previously that, as soon as a target is designated, they all feel that their loyalty and activism are being tested in a campaign, and respond very much as they did to the calls of the past."[29] Although directives issued from the headquarters of the Central Command quickly held in check the intensification of the campaign, it was the leftist repercussions at the grassroots—local witch-hunting activities—that reinforced more than ever the haunting spectacle of the perpetuation of oppression by the oppressed themselves.

What the alienation school failed to theorize and bring to consciousness, then, is the problematic of subjectivity as a means of emancipation. That is to say, theorists fell far short of demonstrating that de-alienation is not a quasi-automatic result of the end of the external conditions of oppression, nor does it necessarily follow the dissolution of alienated labor. De-alienation, in other words, does not inevitably and miraculously descend on the earth with the coming of communism. The case of both China and the former Soviet Union serves as a compelling rebuttal against Marx's classical "production paradigm"[30] with its derivative dialectics of alienation and de-alienation. Oppression cannot be adjudicated simply by a monological search for resources available from the outside.

While the alienation school implicitly questioned the dogmatic presupposition that emancipation is an unproblematic outcome of revolution, they risked repeating the same dogmatic political practice by staking the entire program of de-alienation on means completely extraneous to the individual's subjective consciousness. Until the alienation paradigm addresses the problematic of emancipatory subjectivity, it cannot pose itself as a genuine oppositional movement against a reified, ossified, deracinated Party Marxism.

Perhaps because of this very conceptual constraint, the breakthrough of the controversy over "socialist alienation" never occurred. The issue of subjectivity did not emerge until the latter half of the 1980s. But even then, Chinese cultural theorists were too obsessed with the problematic of China's cultural subjectivity in the the face of neocolonial discursive hegemony to pay much attention to the emancipatory possibilities of the subjective practice of the individual. These two issues, alienation and subjectivity, have remained disconnected to the present day. De-alienation continued to be conceptualized in terms of the malfunction of the public sphere, which a benevolent political order, more specifically, the Party's Four Modernizations

Program, was considered sufficient to redress. The awareness of de-alienation as a subjective practice that only takes place in the private space of every oppressed individual has yet to find its way into the crowded cultural agenda of the nation. Despite their urgent call for liberation, Chinese critics are slow to recognize that their most intractable nemesis is neither Mao Zedong nor Marxism but the faceless oppressor internalized within each individual.

To criticize the absence of the problematic of subjectivity in the alienation paradigm, however, is not to underestimate the difficulties of addressing such a thesis at the turn of the 1980s. For one thing, it was humanity not subjectivity that captured the epochal imagination at that particular historical juncture. A few theorists did speak of the "initiating capacity of the subject" (ren de zhudong xing)[31] and of human beings as the "subject of praxis" (shijian zhuti) and the "subject of history" (lishi zhuti).[32] But the persistent repudiation of Mao's voluntarism that came from both the official and unofficial fronts continued to cast a shadow over any significant attempt at reinventing the issue of subjectivity. Both Wang Ruoshui and Zhou Yang criticized Mao for his overemphasis on "the subjective and motivating force of human beings" (zhuguan nengdong xing).[33] The revalorization of subjective forces, if misunderstood, could easily conjure up memories of the Great Leap Forward and would almost guarantee attacks by the newly converted antileftist ideologues. This was exactly the scenario that confronted Wang Ruoshui which Yang Xianzhen accused him of being a "voluntarist" for advocating a modest proposal for Marxian humanism.

Perhaps the most formidable barrier that precluded the alienation school from probing into the issue of subjectivity could be attributed to the difficulty that all Marxists in socialist countries encountered in the reassessment of the Party's vanguard position. It should surprise no one that the Chinese Communist Party reacted with such vigilance against the proposition of the alienation school. For Hu Qiaomu and Deng Xiaoping knew only too well that the subtext that loomed large in the debate over "socialist alienation" was none other than whether the Party itself could be made into the sole legitimate subject of history.

Chinese Marxists were familiar with the perennial battle waged between revisionists and Leninists in their interpretation of the proletariat's role in the movement of liberation. While the former viewed the proletariat as a repository of self-consciousness and a spontaneous vehicle of self-emancipation, the Leninists, to cite one of their typical spokesmen, E. M. Sitnikov, dismissed such a proposition as a mere reincarnation of the Hegelian thesis of the Absolute Spirit.[34] The progressive consciousness of the proletarian subject, they insisted, could not possibly arise without the guidance of the Party. If the proletariat, or more specifically, the oppressed as a whole, were capable of becoming conscious of their reified condition and thus could trigger a spontaneous process of de-alienation on their own initiative, then the raison d'être of the Leninist elite party would evaporate.

The subtext here challenged the legitimacy of the Party as the self-ordained subject of history. Conceivably, Wang Ruoshui and the alienation school kept a profound silence on the issue. No attempt was made to rehearse the terms of debate between the Leninists and anti-Leninists. As a matter of fact, not only were they restrained from criticizing Leninist politics, Zhou Yang, as I mentioned earlier, had attempted just the opposite tactic: that is, to forestall the Party's reaction, he had reaffirmed its vanguard role in leading the oppressed out of the dilemma of "socialist alienation." Complete avoidance—should the Party serve as aid or authoritative leader of the people in de-alienation?—led eventually to the eclipse of the issue of the subjectivity of the oppressed.

Inasmuch as the Marxist-Leninist Party had been conceived as the sole engineer of emancipation, and so long as the concept of liberation was reduced to being a historically determined collective movement, the oppressed once again emerged as an inert mass whose self-consciousness remained as oblique as their individuality. Under such a theoretical premise, the issue of the emancipatory potential of the human subject could only appear irrelevant, or superfluous at best. The Party question and the issue of the self-consciousness of the oppressed cannot but be deeply interlocked—the cancellation of one issue automatically leads to the abortion of the other. It would be easy for us to exonerate Wang Ruoshui and his colleagues' disregard of the issue of subjectivity by simply attributing theoretical oversight to their acute awareness of the familiar impasse—that is, the stakes were too high. I am, however, dubious about their ability to even comprehend fully how far the subtext of the Party question would have led them into the issue of the subjective domain of de-alienation. I doubt that they were ever aware that the Party question and the subjectivity question make up two sides of the same coin. That Wang Ruoshui was aware of the specter that the first question evoked hardly guaranteed his recognition of the second issue, that of subjectivity. Ironically, it was probably Hu Qiaomu rather than Wang Ruoshui who had correctly appraised the subversive potential that underlay the submerged question regarding the Party and the undeclared agenda of subjectivity.

## COUNTERPROPOSALS

Yet most Western specialists commenting on the controversy over "socialist alienation" were generally more critical of the Party's position while endorsing Wang Ruoshui and Zhou Yang's thesis without qualification. Such an anti-Party stance seems a default position which was ultimately meaningless in the absence of a genuine engagement in some of the counterproposals Hu Qiaomu's camp forwarded that called for a serious inquiry rather than instantaneous dismissal. First of all, some of Wang and Zhou's critics were opposed to the two theorists' adoption of the term *yihua* as a vague catchall for all the inhuman "residue" that can be found in a new society.[35] Although underlying this proposal is the ideological position that "alienation" is meaningful only if it remains a conceptual category confined within the historical context of capitalist society, yet seen from a different ideological standpoint, the notion of imposing a moratorium on the use of the term may not be totally irrational. The ideological standpoint I am referring to comes very close to Hu Qiaomu's famous critique of the circular logic of the alienation paradigm. In emphasizing the dialectics of the negation of the negation (i.e., unalienated human nature—alienated human nature—de-alienated human nature), the humanists, Hu argued, were merely reiterating the worn-out theological formula of "paradise—paradise lost—paradise regained."[36] The succession of communism to capitalism," he continued, "signifies the great progress humankind made on their productive forces and social relations, but not at all a return of some abstract and determinate human nature."[37]

Ironically, this is a viewpoint to which many Western Marxists also subscribed. Commenting on Habermas's critique of Marx's production paradigm,[38] Ludwig Nagl concluded that the "alienation/de-alienation scheme" embedded in Marxian paradigm is "an expression of a 'monological philosophy of consciousness.'"[39] Habermas regards the Marxian faith in the programmed "homecoming" of alienated human nature as an embodiment of the "philosophy of reflection" which valorizes the notions of autonomy and self-formative process (i.e., the autonomous completion of the dialectics of alienation)[40] at the expense of "the philosophy of praxis." The structure of modern society, in other words, can hardly be analyzed adequately in terms of the romantic concept of "return to an origin" which "in Habermas's view infests all classical versions of the alienation/de-alienation theory."[41] As both Chinese and Western critics of the alienation paradigm argued, human history is far too complicated to be contained within the single metaphysical configuration of the downfall and return of a human nature originating in primeval plenitude. The dialectic structure of alienation which dictates that a loss must be reconquered and a lack refilled also presupposes, as Lukács took for granted, that once a subject is reified into a commodity, the situation of reification "would at once become primed for consciousness."[42] What Lukács envisioned is thus nothing short of an idealist myth that the oppressed, simply because of their entrenchment in oppression, are not only automatically endowed with an emancipatory consciousness but are also capable of concocting their own therapy and reversing the situation. The Hegelian overtones of dialectic—the self-propelling impetus of the negation of the negation—thus turns the alienation paradigm from its potential of being grounded in a social theory of praxis into a pure "speculative philosophy" (*sibian zhexue*). Truly, as Huan Nansen challenged alienation theorists, "Why cannot alienation lead to more alienation rather than a return to the origin?"[43] The inquiry boils down to an even more specific question, "What is the driving force that motivates this process [of return]?"[44] It is now obvious that attributing this force to the mere working of the dialectics of the negation of the negation is just too simple to be of any explanatory value. It is also highly questionable whether human beings' return to the original nature is necessarily self-conscious as both Marx and Lukács assumed. And, furthermore, to presuppose that such a return can only be a complete return only reveals the utopian mode of contemplative thought. Modern Chinese history—specifically, Mao's revolution—has shown us time and again that no emancipatory subjective practice can escape its own reification and its tragic complicity with domination. The belief, even on the most theoretical level, in the "*completion*" of a liberatory cycle—that is, in the existence of a hypothetical finale—risks nourishing a self-deceptive mode of thinking that Chinese revolutionaries have practiced diligently for more than a decade. The Revolution, they have learned in retrospect, is not the acme, but the biggest delusion of all. In a strange, ironical twist, the concept of Mao Zedong's "permanent revolution" looms large once more as a parable for human beings' continual struggle against reification.

This critique of the young Marx's alienation theory should serve to illustrate that the theoretical value of the semi-autonomous process of de-alienation has to be sought elsewhere than in its validity as a social theory. Brugger was incisive in his speculations on the potential contribution that the alienation school could have made to the emancipatory task confronting the Party at the beginning of the 1980s, had the controversy not been terminated so abruptly. Such a contribution was specified as the possible working out of "a socialist telos which takes unalienated human nature as its goal."[45] The beginning of any emancipatory practice should indeed start with the setting up of the term of emancipatory goals by which the objective technological possibilities (i.e., modernization) could then be evaluated. But Deng Xiaoping and the orthodox circle of Marxists adamantly believed that they could proceed in the task without such a goal. What they had aspired to—turning the means into an end in itself—has indeed materialized, at an escalating speed, in the 1990s. Modernization for modernization's sake rather than for humanity's sake has given birth to a monster named Development which will in no time witness the reenactment of alienation in the post-Mao era in different ideological terms. The "brave new world" that seems to be emerging may yet turn out to be one in which even the authentic version of Marx's alienation à la capitalism may finally have a future in China.

Perhaps if Deng Xiaoping and his inner circle had foreseen the ideological disintegration of Marxism that followed the slow winding down of the campaign against spiritual pollution, the Party would have resisted less vigorously the idea of incorporating "socialist alienation" into the official interpretive compass of Marxism, thus opening up a space for the discussion of a genuine socialist humanism.

## MARXIST HUMANISM AND THE QUESTION OF "VOLUNTARISM"

The official refutation of the thesis of "socialist alienation," however, could not but foreclose on "humanism" as well. Presented in a single ideological package, "alienation" and "humanism" go hand in hand. Inasmuch as the overcoming of alienation entails the return of humanity, the young Marx reemerged, for the Chinese alienation theorists, a humanist at large. The battle between the school and its opponents was too predictable to be worthy of a thorough treatment here. The Party's stance was clear: the young Marx treated humans (*ren*) as an abstract and universal category—an idealist standpoint under the heavy influence of Kantian-Hegelian-humanist anthropology—while the mature Marx understood *ren* correctly in terms of social relationships. It also insisted on the total absence of any historical continuity between the two Marxes. As a result, the myth of two Marxisms, namely, Humanist Marxism and Materialist Marxism, is simply a theoretical fallacy to be dismissed.[46] To combat such an uncompromising perspective, the alienation school even sought ideological backup from Soviet, Polish, and Yugoslav philosophers[47] who argued in the same impassioned tone that the two Marxisms by no means form an antagonistic relationship. Citing Lenin, Adam Schaff, and other socialist comrades, Chinese theorists proclaimed that there is no epistemological break between the young and mature Marx,[48] that the biological nature of human beings is fundamentally immutable while their social attributes are historically determined, that Marxism and humanism are complementary to each other,[49] and that even some Soviet philosophers propounded the existence of an abstract human nature that "never disappears regardless of any circumstances, and which just 'underwent transformation in different historical ages.'"[50]

It was Wang Ruoshui again who initiated the controversy over Marxist humanism by attempting the reintegration of the value of the individual into Marxism. His two seminal essays, "Ren shi Makesi zhuyi de chufa dian" [Human beings are the starting point of Marxism] and "Wei renda zhuyi bianhu" [In defense of humanism] made a daring declaration that human nature is not equal to class nature, a statement that challenged Maoist-Marxist-Leninist orthodoxy and which anticipated severe criticism from the ideological police. First of all, Wang reminded his readers of the historical contribution that humanism had made to anti-bourgeois ideology in Western societies. Yet he cautiously insisted that a theoretical emphasis on the value of the individual by no means amounts to an endorsement of individualism. On the contrary, such a view could only help remedy the socialist philosophy of class nature, which, according to Wang, reduces a human being to a creature no less abstract than that to be found in bourgeois ideology. We made a mistake during the Cultural Revolution, Wang Ruoshui said, in setting up an antithetical relationship between "revolution" and "humanism,"[51] a mistake that led to antihumanism.

In the end, the two essays did not address anything that the Chinese people had not already experienced firsthand, and they certainly appeared to be a cliché to most modern Western readers, no matter how violently they electrified the Chinese nation at the time. And yet even reading Wang's essays today still serves to evoke historical memory of a resistance cast in a powerful rhetorical move: "Humanism is opposed to two things, the deification of the leader (*shendao zhuyi* or, literally, "god-ism") and the degradation of human beings into animals (*shoudao zhuyi* or, literally, 'animalism')."[52]

Such earnest resistance was certainly not lost on Hu Qiaomu, whose rebuttal could not help incorporating a partial concession to such an impassioned call for humanism defined in staunchly Marxist terms. It was a relief to Wang Ruoshui that, in his critique, Hu actually affirmed the general currency of Wang's two core terms, namely, *socialist humanism* and *revolutionary humanism*—two old Maoist catchphrases.[53] But Hu insisted that socialist humanism should only function as an ethical principle, not a worldview that could account for the evolution of human history and society,[54] a mistake that Hu ascribed to Wang Ruoshui's idealist approach.

By February 1984, in response to Hu Qiaomu's charges, Wang Ruoshui had already started formulating a counterargument published as an internally circulated essay titled "My Views on the Question of Humanism" [Wo dui rendao zhuyi wenti de kanfa]. In this rebuttal, Wang's defensive gesture forced him into the self-defeating position of having continually to redraw the ideological boundaries of humanism. To cite one typical example of his hemming and hawing: "Humanism certainly needs an ideological foundation. But that foundation can either be idealism or materialism. It can either be a historical view based on the concept of abstract human nature, or a historical view based on materialism and science."[55] By highlighting the concept of "sublation" (*pipan de jicheng*), Wang argued that there existed between Marxism and various historical ideologies of bourgeois humanism in the past a dialectical rather than an oppositional relationship. In addition to fundamental moral and ethical principles, he enumerated the content of such shared heritage with historical humanism as "human freedom," "human liberation," and the totalized evolution of "homo universal."[56] But just as his rhetoric edged dangerously close to a proposition of bourgeois humanism, Wang Ruoshui steered clear of troubled waters by retreating into an equivocal "neither-nor" rhetorical strategy. In every twist and turn of his argument, he never forgot to remain uncommitted so that he would avoid pinning himself down to a single position. It is no small wonder, then, that Wang Ruoshui's endorsement of the voluntarist aspect of humanism suffered continual qualifications as he maintained that "the fundamental principle of humanism does not have any binding relationship with idealism, nor does it necessarily enter into any conflict with materialism."[57] This is tantamount to advocating the eclectic position to which theorists defending the thesis of the two Marxes usually subscribe, namely, the potential reconciliation of voluntarism and determinism, freedom and necessity. The propagation of this kind of dialectics appears to be more a sophist mode of persuasion than a genuine engagement in the issues. One cannot, however, blame those who got stuck in this abortive debate. Hu Qiaomu's insinuation of the ideological incorrectness of the humanists' views almost already guaranteed their need to adopt slippery, malleable terms of debate.

Nothing more can be said about the predictable dialogues between the humanists and their rivals without reproducing ideological clichés that would hardly deepen our understanding of the controversy in question. What I wish to pursue now is an issue I posed at the beginning of this paper, namely, the strategic position of Sartre's existential humanism within this entire brouhaha.

To speak of Sartre, of course, is to return to the issue of voluntarism. In their encounter with existentialism, Chinese theorists of humanism found themselves caught in a double bind: they were spellbound by the Sartrean appeal to free will, but to introduce existentialism into the Chinese intellectual domain, they had, simultaneously, to defeat it rhetorically, using a Chinese Marxist determinist critique. It was actually difficult to tell sometimes whether such a seemingly perfunctory critique was simply an ideological reflex or a disingenuous measure consciously adopted to desensitize the system of censorship. In any case, the treatises and books on Sartre that flowed into production did not mystify a savvy Chinese reading public who very well knew the formula of "introduction plus critique" and could follow it, in the case of the seasoned reader, as a menu for helping oneself to the real meat while relegating rhetoric to the scrap heap.

Such was the scenario that a Chinese reader encountered when he or she was exposed to a critical introduction to Sartrean existentialism. They learned that Sartre had designated his existentialism "human philosophy" (renxue), that this science propagated self-transcendence and self-realization, that the starting point of Sartrean humanism is the individual, that human essence is self-determined rather than historically determined, and that this philosophy, because of its emphasis on subjectivity, provided the "missing link" in Marxism. Such explications of Sartre, usually saturated with ideological ambiguities, were almost always followed immediately by a counteractive critique that dwelled on the incompatibility of Marxism and existentialism.[58] Everything endorsed by Sartrean humanism was under fire and amended: human beings are always the product of the sum total of social relations, not of subjective will; the individual is never absolutely free to make his or her own choice since every choice is made under a historically specific circumstance, and so on. To complete this doubled-edged, existentialist promotion package, a dogmatic conclusion that Sartre was ideologically suspect had to be inserted subsequently— no matter how half-hearted and ambiguous this condemnation might sound. Also, included in the rhetorical castigation was the routine critique that Sartre had mistakenly pitted a naive voluntarism against mechanical determinism, that his humanist philosophy amounted to nothing other than a petite-bourgeoisie's resistance to domination, and that his optimism had no concrete social reality.[59]

That Sartre would surface, however fleetingly, in the Chinese controversy over humanism raises the inevitable question: to whom was the citation of existentialism beneficial or detrimental? It almost goes without saying that in the realm of state ideology, the young Marx had emerged as the debate's center of gravity. Sartre, however, enjoyed an independent prestige in post-Mao China once existentialism began sweeping college campuses and converting many disillusioned young students. It was strategically suicidal for the alienation school to respond to the beckoning allure of existentialism, for they were well aware that the core of Sartre's philosophy had always been petit-bourgeois subjectivity. Both Wang Ruoshui and Zhou Yang were cautious not to overstep the ideological boundary of Marxism whenever their discussion of humanism brought them close to an encounter with Sartre. In fact, in defining socialist humanism, Wang Ruoshui was careful not to conjure up the haunting presence of existentialist humanism even though he stressed "issues of human value, human dignity, human liberation, and human freedom" in conjunction with his discussion of proletarian revolution and communism.[60] Zhou Yang, a more seasoned politician, well versed in making preemptive strikes, went a step further by expressing concerns over the negative impact on young Chinese students of "certain [humanist] schools of modern Western philosophy." Undoubtedly, it was existentialism that he was alluding to here. In either case, Zhou and Wang had withstood far too many hostile attacks in their defense of the young Marx to court more danger. The best they could do was either evade the entire issue of existentialism or publicly reject any affiliation with Sartre.[61]

Yet, while the two leading theoreticians of the alienation school were thus theoretically constrained within the Marxist framework in their approach to the issue of humanism, some of their supporters displayed fewer scruples about playing the Sartrean card. The occasion of Sartre's death in April 1980 provided a convenient opportunity for the publication of many academic essays on Sartre. In the name of critiquing the philosopher, Chinese theorists did not hesitate to elaborate on the major tenets of existentialism, and more importantly, to foreground those aspects of his philosophy that promised a cross-fertilization with a critically defined Marxism, namely, the thrust of existentialism to unite philosophy and praxis, the identification of freedom with revolution, and no less significantly, the simultaneous anti-Stalinist and anticapitalist articulation of the philosopher. Speaking in Sartre's voice, such essays reiterated and succeeded in reinforcing what the alienation school had already propagated time and again: Marxism has undergone an ossification and transformed itself into "anti-humanism."[62] Perhaps the most deadly ammunition that the explication of Sartre provided for Chinese alienation theorists was Sartre's pungent criticism of the Soviet Union and his forceful condemnation of the phenomenon of "socialist alienation," which, in the philosopher's view, took the particular form of "expansionism, bureaucratism, authoritarianism, and doctrinairism."[63] No Chinese readers confronting those pages could mistake such innuendoes against the CCP for an innocuous analysis of Sartrean philosophy. Oddly enough, however, the veiled criticism of "socialist alienation" Chinese theorists made via Sartre attracted far less attention than did Sartre's endorsement of voluntarism.

In the end, the debate of "socialist alienation" and Marxist humanism failed to rescue itself from the moot issue of voluntarism versus determinism. No alternative paradigm—whether it be Sartre or the young Marx—could emerge in that kind of political climate without being compromised, or more precisely, being proved incorrect before it was reassimilated, predictably, into the iron hold of historical determinism and cited as yet another statistical triumph of the perpetual logic of the dialectics of bipolarity. The legitimate comparison, or contrast, of Sartre and Marx, of voluntarism and determinism, and between the two Marxisms—opposite terms soon to be recast into mere variations of the same principle of dialectical opposition—only serves in the end to demonstrate nothing but "the structural differentiations of a single originally undifferentiated Marxism."[64] Hegelian dialects has the last laugh. Marx succeeds in co-opting Sartre. And in the process of merging the latter into the former, Marxism brings the final closure to its potentially infinite contestation with its rival philosophy.

And in doing that, it ends up disarming the self-motivating potency of existentialism.

What was being taken for granted is the view that an emancipatory practice motivated "from without"—the Party's mandate to end Mao's era—would ensure the liberation of the subject. The real lessons of Sartrean philosophy—that genuine emancipation is contingent and can only be self-motivated, and that the emancipatory character of subjectivity is not to be predetermined as the result of an inexorable progress guaranteed by reason and history—continued to elude Wang Ruoshui and his fellow travelers. Although Wang spelled out clearly in his preface to *In Defense of Humanism* that the "purpose of raising the problematic of humanism and alienation is precisely to awaken the subjective consciousness of humankind,"[65] he remained an obstinate believer in the benevolent laws of historical development and mistook the mere awakening of the subject for the attainment of subjective consciousness. The assumption that such a consciousness, long mystified under domination, will emerge by itself with the dawning of the new era only confirms the vicious cycle of dogmatic determinism. Perhaps Wang Ruoshui and his comrades have not jumped out of the ideological enclosure of materialist doctrine after all. For if he believed that the creation of an enlightened regime alone would lead to "the rupture with the continuum of domination,"[66] he proved to be deeply entrenched in the mode of thinking characteristic of historical determinism. What Chinese intellectuals can no longer afford to evade is the issue of the transformation of subjectivity whose eventual appearance is not guaranteed by the transformation of society alone. In this context, the rejuvenation of the problematic of voluntarism appears to be more urgent than ever. It needs to be uprooted from its conventional role as nothing more than an ideological foil for determinism. How to reinvent voluntarism to serve the cause of de-alienation has undoubtedly posed an unanswered challenge to the alienation school and Chinese humanist advocates. But unless one looks into the collusive relationship between subjectivity and the reproduction of domination, and until Chinese citizens are courageous enough to accept the moral responsibility for the failure of Maoist or revolution, the nation will never outgrow its habit of scapegoating the lesser evil. Perhaps it is high time for us to ask whether it was the voluntarism of one single person or the voluntary collusion of the entire nation that paved the way for "socialist alienation" and "anti-humanism" in China.

Finally, there is no better way of concluding this part of my discussion of subjective emancipatory consciousness than by citing Wei Jingsheng's most recent proclamation after his release from prison: "We cannot look to a savior or some 'righteous minister' to free us and save us, and we must not pin all our hopes in other places. Only when we are determined to rescue ourselves will others be willing or able to help us. There is a sense in which [the] cowardliness and vulnerability of a populace can be seen as a cause of a tyrant's violence."[67]

## WHO AM I? THE PROBLEMATIC SELF AND ALIENATION

Though foreclosed on in the realm of ideology, the discussion of "alienation" was by no means over. Not surprisingly, it was literature and not the intellectuals' ideological critique that undertook the mission of de-alienation and that championed the cause of humanism for several years to come. And though Chinese authors were by no means less immune to censorship than ideologists, and despite the expected infiltration of the official discourse into the realm of arts and literature, many writers who had mastered the knack of dodging frontal collisions accomplished a historical breakthrough despite the strict surveillance of the Party. The prohibition long imposed on the issues of "humanism," "human touch" (*renqing wei*), and a commonly defined "aesthetic appeal"—all ideological taboos in bygone days—witnessed its own dramatic thaw as veteran aesthetician Zhu Guangqian had fervently hoped.[68] All of a sudden, the theoretical possibility of the autonomous and infinitely open self gripped the imagination of writers and readers. For nearly five years, the celebration of the creative self, newly emancipated from ideological enclosures, made its imprint on every literary product, from Liu Xinwu's provocative statement, "I am I, myself,"[69] to Dai Houying's epochal novella *Ah, Human Beings! Human Beings!*

Still the liberatory rhetoric did not end in an all-encompassing eulogy to the omnipotence of the creative self. Crisscrossing the discourse of creative subjectivity in these years was also an awareness that the dissemination of the enclosed self made it necessarily problematic and paradoxical. For once set free to express itself, the self could not but register the dramatic changes and contradictions that took place in cultural, economic, and sociopolitical sectors.[70] Though some eclectic critics still insisted that the prevalent "contradictions" in socialist China were not necessarily the same as "alienation,"[71] still, a "Kafka tidal wave" (designated by one critic as nothing other than a "heat wave of alienation"[72]) swept over the field of literature well into the mid-1980s, apparently resonating with the emergence of the thematic of the problematic self.

It seems obvious that China's post-revolutionary writers would be most susceptible to Kafka and the literature of the absurd. Rampant political movements had not only alienated human beings from each other, they had also shattered the very foundation of self-identity, as the politics of survival and victimization turned every individual into an eyewitness of the psychic split between public (i.e., political) and private selves. This conception of "socialist alienation" was most vividly delineated by philosopher Gao Ertai as the inevitable outcome of the "absolutization of class struggle," by which he meant the political process that transformed every individual into his or her own enemy by mandating "self-exposure" and "self-critique."[73] Schizophrenia became the norm. Under such conditions, Kafka's dramatic parable of "metamorphosis" drove home to alienated Chinese intellectuals the insanity of revolutionary surreality. The "children of revolution," it would appear, felt like cornered beasts in their unexpected encounter with an anonymous alien power that subjugated them with their own cooperation. Not only were their daily lives marked by the contradiction between what they believed and what they professed to believe, they experienced yet another form of contradiction, namely, their dual identity as victims and victimizers at the same time. Herein lies the real absurdity of the revolutionary subject.

Genuine inquiry into alienated subjectivity did not come into being until the mid-1980s, when the "root-searching" (xungen) school and the young experimentalists heralded in a much more sophisticated cultural (or perhaps, in the latter case, an anticultural) aesthetic agenda. Still, in the various genres born in quick succession in the early 1980s, the "wounded literature" (shanghen wenxue), the "literature of self-reflection" (fansi wenxue), and mainstream humanist literature, what greeted readers remained a homogeneous configuration of self that was no less formulaic than that portrayed earlier in socialist realism. Only the formula was different. Now the individual rather than the collective hero and heroine appeared on the pedestal. But because postrevolutionary writers in the early 1980s immediately felt the moral compulsion to reinvent a fictional subjectivity that was diametrically opposed to the closed, passive, and apathetic persona of the revolutionary subject, no other alternative was prescribed except a complete categorical reversal of negative characteristics.

What was born then on urgent demand was a fictional persona "made of flesh and blood, love and hatred, a being full of emotions and desires with a capacity for contemplation"[74]—in other words, an open, dynamic, compassionate, and upbeat self that was larger than life itself. And yet the seamless consistency underlying such an optimistic portrait eventually afforded little opportunity for more somber reflection. It seemed to preclude the rifts and contradictions lurking in a wholesomeness so complete that its belief in the redemptive power of human love was ultimately not qualitatively different form the faith of the revolutionary hero—his former incarnation—in the regenerative potency of class love.

There were exceptions. Lu Yao's *Life* [*Rensheng*][75] and Li Ping's "When the Sunset Clouds Disappeared" [Wanxia xiaoshi de shihou],[76] touched, however superficially, on issues of the problematic self.[77] The public's fetishization of the saintly figure of Lu Wenting in Shen Rong's famous novel *At Middle Age* [Ren dao zhongnian][78] only reinforces the impression that China's postrevolutionary understanding of "socialist humanism" was still premised on an aesthetics of totality that could not but deliver a transparently poised human subject, again. Contradiction and psychic schism remained an untrodden territory. And it was in this context that Zong Pu's story "Who Am I" [Wo shi shei] brings forward an ambivalent epochal question as yet unarticulated and unaddressed. Whether the question got posed awkwardly or was aborted in the end should not defer us from rescuing the story from relative obscurity. It is not just another formulaic example of humanist literature. Any study of the modern history of the Chinese problematic self should begin with this unostentatious story because it captures in a nutshell precisely Gao Ertai's definition of what alienation is—"self-estrangement," "personality split," and "self-negation."[79]

"Who Am I" tells the story of a schizophrenic vision of a persecuted victim, Shu Mi, who lost her sanity after her lover committed suicide during the Cultural Revolution. Told in the first person, through deranged consciousness, the narration, albeit rhetorically unreliable like Lu Xun's famous "The Diary of a Mad Man," contains scathing commentary on the negative transformative power of the Revolution. Importantly, while in her hallucinatory fever, Shu Mi witnesses her own transformation from demon to snow-white flower, and then, in a moment of irony, into the horrible form of a huge worm. Here Kafka's parable fit remarkably into the new Chinese context, for what better metaphor is there of a nightmarish vision of species alienation and self-fragmentation than the metamorphosis of human nature into the nature of a beast?

Each transformation triggers in Shu Mi a moment of self-recognition that coincides with the troubled moment of self-inquiry and culminates in her increasingly weakened rhetorical question, "Who am I?" Caught in an alternating spiral movement of self-bewilderment and self-detachment, Shu Mi is ultimately unable to answer the question. "Am I therefore a poisonous worm? No! But who am I after all?"[80] And yet, absurdity is not a trademark of Chinese writers who trace their descent through revolutionary romanticism. The allure of a dramatic "return to the origin" proved too strong in the end for Zong Pu to resist. Predictably, Shu Mi's quest for reintegrated humanity must end positively. That moment arrives when the heroine sees, etched into the sky by a line of wild geese, the ideogram *ren,* or human being (an inverted "V"), while she jumps into the cold water of the lake to her suicidal death. In the theatrical encounter of the two epochal themes, alienation and humanism, it was the latter that gained the symbolic upper hand here.

Zong Pu's story, like many other sentimental morality tales chronicled in the early 1980s, voiced an extravagent faith in the resolution of an open-ended series of alienation through the simple answer of humanism. De-alienation, like the aerial sign of *ren,* occurred instantaneously in the dramatic form of deus ex machina. With the effortless recovery of Shu Mi's split self, the theme of the problematic self was launched in vain. The ironic inquiry of the protagonist, her self-image hovering ambivalently on the sign of the demonic and the beastly, is dissolved in a hollow congratulatory homage to a figurative humanism.

"Who am I?"—am I a victim or a victimizer, a self totalized or problematic, a human being or a demon? Without engaging, beyond the mere rhetorical level, with those post-Mao epochal questions, Wang Ruoshui and Zhou Yang's project of emancipation via humanism eventually remained as nominal as Zong Pu's. Is an emancipatory theory and practice ever possible without the exploration of the self-motivating process of de-alienation from within?

NOTES

1  Dai Houying *Ren, a ren* (Hong Kong: Xiangjiang, 1985).
2  In the *Manuscripts,* Marx speaks of three kinds of alienation. Human beings are alienated from their work, from their own products, and from other

human beings. Attributing alienation to the birth of private property in capitalist society, Marx believed that the total liberation of human beings could only take place on the complete elimination of private property. See *Karl Marx: Early Writings*, trans. Rodney Livingstone and Gregor Benton (New York: Vintage, 1975), 279–400.

3  Stuart Schram, *Ideology and Policy in China since the Third Plenum*, 1978–84 (London: University of London Press, 1984), 55.

4  See Schram, *Ideology and Policy*, 42–56. Also see Bill Brugger and David Kelly, *Chinese Marxism in the Post-Mao Era* (Stanford, Calif.: Stanford University Press, 1990), 139–170. Also see Kelly, "The Emergence of Humanism: Wang Ruoshui and the Critique of Socialist Alienation," in *China's Intellectuals and the State: In Search of a New Relationship*, ed. Merle Goldman et al. (Cambridge: Council on East Asian Studies/Harvard University Press, 1987), 159–182.

5  Chinese theorists emphasized that Marx dissociates himself from Hegel's belief that every objectification is necessarily an instance of alienation. Articles and books published in post-Mao China on the distinction between *duixianghua* and *yihua* were abundant.

6  Lukács himself admitted in 1967 that the term *reification* is "neither socially nor conceptually identical to alienation." For Lefèbvre and others, reification is only one of the manifestations of alienation, albeit the most radical one.

7  Zhou Guoping and Jia Zelin, "Sulian zhexue zhong de ren he rendao zhuyi wenti" [The question of (hu)man and humanism in Soviet philosophy], in *Ren shi Makesi zhuyi de chufa dian* [Human beings are the starting point of Marxism], ed. The Editorial Board of Renmin Chubanshe (Beijing: Renmin chubanshe, 1981), 242.

8  Wang Ruoshui, "Tan yihua wenti" [On the problem of alienation], in *Xinwen zhanxian* [The battle front of news] (8 August 1980), reprinted in *Wei rendao zhuyi bianhu* [In defense of humanism] (Beijing: Sanlian shudian, 1986), 186–199.

9  Adam Schaff, *Marxismus und das menschliche Individuum* (Vienna: Europa-Verlag, 1965), 168–169, 178, 180, 254.

10  Gajo Petrovic, "The Philosophical and Sociological Relevance of Marx's Concept of Alienation," in *Marx and the Western World*, ed. Nicholas Lobkowicz (Notre Dame, Ind.: University of Notre Dame Press, 1967), 152.

11  Schaff, *Marxism and the Human Individual*, ed. Robert S. Cohen, based on a translation by Olgierd Wojtasiewicz (New York: McGraw-Hill, 1970), 108.

12  Ibid., 131, 135.

13  Ibid., 15.

14  Wang Ruoshui, "Tan yihua wenti," 195.

15  Hu Qiaomu, "Guanyu rendao zhuyi he yihua wenti" [With regard to questions of humanism and alienation] in *Rendao zhuyi he yihua sanshi ti* [Thirty questions on humanism and alienation]), ed. The Research Institute of Phi-

losophy at the Shanghai Academy of the Social Sciences (Shanghai: Shanghai renmin chubanshe, 1984), 184.

16 Schram reported a conversation with Deng Liqun (director of the Propaganda Department of the Party's Central Committee) in 1984. During that conversation, Deng accused Wang of "reasserting the theory of continuous revolution under the dictatorship of the proletariat." Deng went even further by proclaiming that Wang suggested that "a new Cultural Revolution was necessary to overturn the privileged caste of Party officials" (see Schram, *Ideology and Policy*, 56).

17 Brugger and Kelly, *Chinese Marxism*, 145.

18 Zhou Yang, "Guanyu Makesi zhuyi de jige lilun wenti de tantao," *Renmin ribao*, 16 March 1983, 4.

19 Brugger and Kelly, *Chinese Marxism*, 153.

20 Shanghai Academy of Social Sciences, *Sanshi ti*, 185–186.

21 See " 'Makesi zhuyi yu ren' xueshu taolun hui chuanda Deng Liqun jianghua: Taolun rendao zhuyi renxing lun henyou haochu (1978.12–1983.4)" [Deng Liqun's talk at the symposium on "Marxism and Human Beings": The advantages of discussing humanism and the theory of humanity], originally published in *Renmin ribao*, 12 April 1983, 1; also in *Rendao zhuyi renxing lun yihua wenti yanjiu zhuanji (December* 1978 *–April* 1984) [Studies on humanism, theories of human nature, and the problem of alienation: A special collection of essays], ed. Center of Newspaper and Research Materials at People's University (Beijing: Renmin daxue, 1983), 5.

22 Albrecht Wellmer, *Critical Theory of Society*, trans. John Cumming (New York: Herder and Herder, 1971), 54.

23 Gao Ertai, "Yihua xianxiang jinguan" [A recent observation of the phenomenon of alienation], in Renmin Chubanshe, *Ren shi Makesi zhuyi de chufa dian*, 83. Gao elaborated on the definition of the "fetishism of politics" and identified it with "the fetishism of power." His definition of "political alienation" is by far the most innovative one. He identified all the obsequious and humiliating measures of securing one's political well-being during the revolutionary years as a kind of political "labor" that kept churning out political commodities—one's own soul, relatives, and friends—commodities that one sold for the exchange of political profits. During the 1950s and 1960s, Gao argued, it was power, not money, that served as the equivalent of Marx's exchange value (88).

24 Wang, "Tan yihua wenti," 195.

25 Ibid., 197.

26 F. Fehér and A. Heller, "Are There Prospects for Change in the U.S.S.R. and Eastern Europe?" *Praxis International* 5 (1985): 323–332.

27 Irving Fetscher, "Hegel, the Young Marx, and Soviet Philosophy: A Reply to E. M. Sitnikov," in "Appendix: Soviet Society and the Problem of Alienation" in Irving Fetscher, *Marx and Marxism* (New York: Herder and Herder, 1971), 342.

28  Erica Sherover-Marcuse, *Emancipation and Consciousness: Dogmatic and Dialectical Perspectives in the Early Marx* (Oxford: Basil Blackwell, 1986), 122.

29  Schram, *Ideology and Policy*, 49.

30  Many important issues related to the contemporary critique of the classical "production paradigm" cannot be fully explored here. One of the most well-known cases is Jean Baudrillard's questioning of the adaptability of the Marxian concepts of labor and production to postindustrial society, in *The Mirror of Production*, trans. Mark Poster (St. Louis, Mo.: Telos, 1975).

31  Wang Ruoshui, "Wo dui rendao zhuyi wenti de kanfa" [My views on the issue of humanism], *Wei rendao zhuyi bianhu*, 273.

32  Zhou and Jia, "Ren he rendao zhui; wenti," 242, 261.

33  Wang Ruoshui, "Ren shi Makesi zhuyi de chufa dian," *Wei rendao zhuyi bianhu*, 201. Also see Zhou Yang, "Jige lilun wenti de tantao," 8.

34  E. M. Sitnikov, "A Soviet Critique of 'Western' Interpretations of Marx," in "Appendix: Soviet Society and the Problem of Alienation," in Fetscher, *Marx and Marxism*, 320–321.

35  Shanghai Academy of Social Sciences, *Sanshi ti*, 186.

36  Hu, "Rendao zhuyi he yihua wenti" 60.

37  Ibid.

38  Jürgen Habermas, "On the Obsolescence of the Production Paradigm," in *The Philosophical Discourse of Modernity*, trans. Frederick Lawrence (Cambridge: MIT Press, 1987), 75–82.

39  Ludwig Nagl, "Obsolescence of the Production Paradigm?" in *Alienation, Society, and the Individual: Continuity and Change in Theory and Research*, ed. Felix Geyer and Walter R. Heinz (London: Transaction Publishers, 1992), 17.

40  Habermas, "On the Obsolescence of the Production Paradigm," 81.

41  Nagl, "Obsolescence of the Production Paradigm?"19.

42  Georg Lukács, *Geschichte und Klassenbewusstsein: Studien uber Marxistische dialektik* (Berlin: Der Malik-Verlag, 1923), 184.

43  Huang Nansen, "Guanyu ren de ruogan lilun wenti" [On several theoretical questions regarding human beings], *Makesi zhuyi yu ren* [Marxism and human beings], 16.

44  Ibid., 15.

45  Brugger, "Alienation Revisited," *Australian Journal of Chinese Affairs* 12 (1984): 150.

46  I want to point out that both the revisionist and orthodox Marxists made the exclusive claim that there is only one single authentic Marx. For the former, what the young Marx propagated is the only true Marxism; for the latter, it is the scientific Marxism advocated by the mature Marx. The thesis of an integral Marxism was supported by those theorists who proposed the paradigm of "socialist alienation."

47  See Zhao Fengqi, "Nansilafu zhexuejie guanyu ren he yihua wenti de yan-

jiu" [Studies on the problem of human beings and alienation in Yugoslav philosophy], *Zhexue yanjiu* 1(1981): 76–78. See also Zhou and Jia, "Ren he rendao zhuyi wenti," 241–289.

48  For instance, Ru Xin, director of the Philosophy Research Institute of the Chinese Academy of the Social Sciences, defended the historical continuity between the two Marxisms in his "Rendao zhuyi jiushi xiuzheng zhuyi ma?—Dui rendao zhuyi de zai renshi" [Is humanism revisionism? —Reacquainting with humanism], in *Renxing, rendao zhuyi wenti taolun ji* [Collection of essays on the discussion of the issues of human nature and humanism], ed. The Research Institute of Philosophy at the Chinese Academy of the Social Sciences (Beijing: Renmin chubanshe, 1983), 25. But Ru Xin was forced to retract many of his earlier views after the campaign was launched against the humanists. His later antihumanist views were found in "Pipan zichan jieji rendao zhuyi, xuanchuan shehui zhuyi rendao zhuyi" [Criticize bourgeois humanism, promote socialist humanism] *Renmin ribao,* 9 January 1984, 5.

49  Zhao Fengzi, "Nansilafu zhexue jie guanyu ren he yihua wenti de yanjiu," 76–78.

50  Zhou and Jia, "Ren he rendao zhuyi wenti," 266–267.

51  Wang Ruoshui, "Wei rendao zhuyi bianhu" [In defense of humanism], in *Wei rendao zhuyi bianhu,* 222.

52  Wang, "Ren shi Makesi zhuyi de chufa dian," 200.

53  In his essay on "Guanyu 'geming rendao zhuyi'" [Regarding "revolutionary humanism"], in *Wei rendao zhuyi bianhu,* Wang Ruoshui congratulated China on the popular currency of the two slogans, "Marxist humanism" and "socialist humanism" (236). In "Wo dui rendao zhuyi wenti de kanfa," Wang hailed the emergence of the slogan "socialist humanism" as "the most important achievement" produced by the debate (263). There was, however, really no good reason for Wang Ruoshui to be overjoyed at this. For Hu Qiaomu never gave up the thesis that "revolutionary humanism is the precursor of socialist humanism." Since the former term was concocted by Mao, he stripped the proposition of "socialist humanism" of any modern connotations of humanism.

54  Hu, "Rendao zhuyi he yihua wenti," 64.

55  Wang, "Wo dui rendao zhuyi de kanfa," 255.

56  Ibid., 250.

57  Ibid., 245.

58  Huang Songjie, Wu Xiaoming, and An Yanming, *Sate qi ren ji qi renxue* [Sartre the man and his humanist philosophy] (Shanghai: Fudan daxue, 1986), 269–270.

59  Wang Shouchang, "Sate de cunzai zhuyi rendao zhuyi tantao" [An inquiry into Sartrean existentialist humanism], in Renmin Chubanshe, *Ren shi Makesi zhuyi de chufa dian,* 223–234.

60  Wang, "Wei rendao zhuyi bianhu," 231.

61 Brugger and Kelly cite a source from the *Summary of World Broadcasts* to the effect that Wang Ruoshui criticized Sartre's anti-essentialist stance (see *Chinese Marxism in the Post-Mao Era*, 140).

62 Wang Shouchang, "Sate de cunzai zhuyi randao zhuyi," 239.

63 Ibid.

64 Alvin Gouldner, *The Two Marxisms* (New York: Oxford University Press, 1980), 34.

65 Wang, preface, *Wei rendao zhuyi bianhu*, 1.

66 Herbert Marcuse, "Re-Examination of the Concept of Revolution," in Marcuse, *Karl Marx and Contemporary Scientific Thought* (The Hague: Mouton, 1969), 481.

67 Wei Jingsheng, "Who Should Take the Responsibility?" *China Focus: A Publication of the Princeton China Initiative* 1, no. 10 (November 1993): 1. The abridged essay is taken from the first article that Wei published after his release. It originally appeared in *Open Magazine* 11 (1993), published in Hong Kong.

68 Zhu Guangqian, "Guanyu renxing, rendao zhuyi, renqingwei he gongtongmei wenti" [On the issues of human nature, humanism, human touch, and shared aesthetics], in Chinese Academy of Social Sciences, *Renxing rendao zhuyi wenti taolun ji*, 182.

69 *Renmin ribao* (overseas ed.), 24 January 1986.

70 Critic Lei Da dwelled on the definition of the "paradoxical self" in his "Zhuti yishi de qianghua: dui jinnian xiaoshuo fazhan de sikao" [The intensification of subjective consciousness: thoughts on the recent development of narrative fiction], *Wenxue pinglun* 1 (1986): 121–125. See also Lei Da's "Lun chuangzuo zhuti de duoyang hua qushi" [On the tendency of creative subjectivity toward diversity], *Wenxue pinglun* 1 (1986): 63–70.

71 The Association of Chinese Writers and the Chinese Federation of Writers held a joint symposium in April 1993 to discuss the issues of humanism and alienation in conjunction with the publication of Hu Qiaomu's seminal essay "Guanyu rendao zhuyi he yihua wenti." In the symposium, some writers suggested, in the spirit of reconciling the official line with their stance of critical realism (in opposition to revolutionary socialist realism), that "writing about contradictions is not tantamount to writing about alienation." See "Wenyi chuangzuo zhong yao genghao fanying shehui zhuyi rendao zhuyi" [Literary and artistic works should reflect socialist humanism better], *Renmin ribao*, 18 April 1984, 3.

72 Ye Lang, "Kafuka: yihua lun lishiguan de tujiezhe" [Kafka: The interpreter of the historical view of the theory of alienation], in *Rendao zhuyi he yihua wenti yanjiu*, ed. Philosophy Department of Beijing University (Beijing: Beida chubanshe, 1985), 186.

73 Gao Ertai, "Yihua xianxiang jinguan," 76.

74 Dai Houying, *Ren a ren*, 349.

75 Lu Yao, *Rensheng* (Beijing: Zhongguo qingnian chubanshe, 1982).

76  Li Ping, "Wanxia xiaoshi de shihou" [When the sunset clouds disappeared],
    *Shiyue* [October] 1 (1981): 77–134.

77  See Bai Hua's analysis of "When the Sunset Clouds Disappeared" in his
    "Dangqian wenyi chuangzuo zhong de renxing rendao zhuyi wenti" [The
    question of human nature and humanism in recent literary works], *Wenyi
    lilun* 1 (1984): 88–89. The article was originally published in *Wenyi lilun
    yanjiu* 3 (1983): 27–38.

78  The Chinese reading public was moved by the moral integrity and human-
    ist spirit that Lu Wenting displayed in her capacity as an altruistic doc-
    tor. The image of the suffering middle-aged intellectual also touched all
    her counterparts in real life. Portrayed as flawless and completely selfless,
    Lu's appeal to Chinese readers consists in the unambiguous totality of her
    noble character. For a typical analysis of Lu Wenting, see Tan Zhi, "Wenxue
    zhong de renxing yu rendao zhuyi wenti: Du Hu Qiaomu tongzhi 'Guanyu
    rendao zhuyi he yihua wenti' biji" [The question of human nature and
    humanism in literature: Notes on my reading of comrade Hu Qiaomu's
    "On humanism and the question of alienation"], *Wenyi lilun* 4 (1984): 35.

79  Gao Ertai, "Yihua jiqi lishi kaocha" [Alienation and its historical inquiry],
    in Renmin chubanshe, *Ren shi Makesi zhuyi de chufa dian*, 163.

80  Zong Pu, "Wo shi shei?" in *Zong Pu duanpian xiaoshuo xuan* [Selections of
    Zong Pu's short stories] (Beijing: Renmin wenxue chubanshe, 1991), 39.

*Tani E. Barlow* is the founder and senior editor of the journal *positions: east asia cultures critique* and teaches Chinese women's history at the University of Washington. She is the editor of *Formations of Colonial Modernity in East Asia* (1997) and *Gender Politics in Modern China: Writing and Feminism* (1993), both published by Duke University Press, and author of *The Question of Women in Chinese Feminism,* also forthcoming from Duke University Press.

*Dai Jinhua* is Professor at the Institute of Comparative Literature and Culture of Peking University.

*Michael Dutton* is Associate Professor of Political Science at the University of Melbourne, Australia.

*D. R. Howland* is Associate Professor of History at DePaul University.

*Marshall Johnson* is Associate Professor of History, Politics, and Sociology at the University of Wisconsin-Superior.

*Liu Kang* is Associate Professor of Comparative Literature and Chinese at Pennsylvania State University.

*You-me Park* is Assistant Professorial Lecturer in English at George Washington University.

*William Pietz* is a political activist in Los Angeles. He also writes essays on the history of law, religion, and social theory.

*Claudia Pozzana* is a researcher of Chinese Language and Literature in the Department of Linguistic and Oriental Studies at Bologna University.

*Alessandro Russo* is Professor in the Department of Linguistic and Oriental Studies at Bologna University.

*Sanjay Seth* is Senior Lecturer in the Department of Politics at LaTrobe University.

*Gi-Wook Shin* is Associate Professor of Sociology at the University of California, Los Angeles.

*Sugiyama Mitsunobu* is Professor at the University of Tokyo in the Division of Socio-Cultural Studies.

*Jing Wang* is S. C. Fang Professor of Chinese Language and Culture at the Massachusetts Institute of Technology and Director of the Luce Project on Contemporary Chinese Popular Culture.

THESE ESSAYS ORIGINALLY WERE PUBLISHED in the following issues of *positions:* Michael Dutton, "Dreaming of Better Times: 'Repetition with a Difference' and Community Policing in China," 3:2 (fall 1995); D. R. Howland, "Constructing Perry's 'Chinaman' in the Context of Adorno and Benjamin," 3:2 (fall 1995); Dai Jinhua, "Redemption and Consumption: Depicting Culture in the 1990s," 4:1 (spring 1996); Marshall Johnson, "Making Time: Historic Preservation and the Space of Nationality," 2:2 (fall 1994); Liu Kang, "Aesthetics and Chinese Marxism," 3:2 (fall 1995); Sugiyama Mitsunobu, "The World Conception of Japanese Social Science: The *Kōza* Faction, the Ōtsuka School, and the Uno School of Economics," 6:1 (spring 1998); You-me Park, "'And They Would Again': Women and Struggle in Korean Nationalist Literature," 3:2 (fall 1995); Claudia Pozzana, "Spring, Temporality, and History in Li Dazhao," 3:2 (fall 1995); Alessandro Russo, "The Probable Defeat: Preliminary Notes on the Chinese Cultural Revolution," 6:1 (spring 1998); Sanjay Seth, "Interpreting Revolutionary Excess: The Naxalite Movement in India, 1967–1971," 3:2 (fall 1995); Gi-Wook Shin, "Marxism, Anti-Americanism, and Democracy in South Korea: An Examination of Nationalist Intellectual Discourse," 3:2 (fall 1995); and Jing Wang, "'Who Am I?': Questions of Voluntarism in the Paradigm of 'Socialist Alienation,'" 3:2 (fall 1995).

LIBRARY OF CONGRESS CATALOGING-IN-PUBLICATION DATA

New Asian Marxisms / edited by Tani E. Barlow.

p. cm. — (A *positions* book)

Includes index.

ISBN 0-8223-2858-5 (cloth : alk. paper)

ISBN 0-8223-2873-9 (pbk. : alk. paper)

1. Communism—Asia. 2. Socialism—Asia. 3. Communism and society. 4. Socialism and society. I. Barlow, Tani E. II. Series.

HX376.A6 N48 2002

335.4'098—dc21    2001051137